Discovering that you don't have everything you thought you wanted is a surprise. Getting a promotion, finding new friends, learning you are attracted to women....

Nia Toyomoto has worked hard all her life to prove she was the best; she graduated early from high school, college, and got the dream job in Manhattan. Becoming a partner at the tender age of thirty she thought she had it all until the law firm made demands about her personal appearance and a few other things that made her change her life for the promotion. Then she realizes having everything isn't all that it is cracked up to be without someone to share it with...

A successful lawyer in the big city, choices have to made, sacrifices and surprises await this beautiful and talented woman....does she make the right ones though?

A K'Anne Meinel Novel

Also by K'Anne Meinel:

In Paperback:

SHIPS *CompanionSHIP,*
FriendSHIP, RelationSHIP
Long Distance Romance
Children of Another Mother
Erotica
The Claim
Bikini's Are Dangerous
The Complete Series
Germanic
Malice Masterpieces

The First Five Books
Represented
Timed Romance
Malice Masterpieces II
Books Six through Ten
The Journey Home
Out at the Inn
Shorts
Anthology Volume 1

Pocket Paperbacks:
Mysterious Malice (Book 1)

In E-Book Format:
Short Stories

Fantasy
Wet & Wet Again
Family Night
Quickie ~ Against
the Car
Quickie ~ Against
the Wall
Quickie ~ Over the
Couch

Mile High Club
Quickie ~ Under
the Pier
Heel or Heal
Kiss
Family Night 2
Beach Dreams
Internet Dreamers
Snoggered

The Rockhound
Stolen
Agitated
Quickie in an
Elevator, GOING
DOWN?
Into the Garden
Menage a WHAT?

Novellas

Bikini's are Dangerous
Kept
Ghostly Love
Bikini's are Dangerous 2
On the Parkway
Stable Affair
Sapphic Surfer

Bikini's are Dangerous 3
Bikini's are Dangerous 4
Bikini's are Dangerous 5
Mysterious Malice (Book 1)
Meticulous Malice (Book 2)
Mistaken Malice (Book 3)
Malicious Malice (Book 4)

Novellas Continued

Masterful Malice (Book 5)
Matrimonial Malice (Book 6)
Mourning Malice (Book 7)
Murderous Malice (Book 8)
Sapphic Cowgirl
Sapphic Cowboi
Mental Malice (Book 9)
Menacing Malice (Book 10)
Charming Thief

~Snake Island~
Charming Thief
*~Diamonds are a Girls Best
Friend~*
Minor Malice (Book 11)
Morally Malice (Book 12)
Morose Malice (Book 13)
Melancholy Malice (Book 14)

Novels

SHIPS *CompanionSHIP,*
FriendSHIP, RelationSHIP
Erotica Volume 1
Long Distance Romance
Bikini's Are Dangerous
The Complete Series
Malice Masterpieces
The First Five Books
To Love a Shooting Star
Children of Another Mother

Germanic
The Claim
Represented
Timed Romance
Malice Masterpieces II
Books Six through Ten
The Journey Home
Out at the Inn
Anthology Volume 1

Video

Biography of Books
Ships
Sapphic Surfer
Ghostly Love
Long Distance Romance
Germanic
Sensual Sapphic

Sapphic Cowgirl
Couples
Lie Next To Me
Sapphic Cowboi
Timed Romance
Readings (SHIPS)

K'ANNE MEINEL

LAWYERED

ISBN-13: 978-1499797107
ISBN-10: 1499797109

K'Anne Meinel is available for comments at KAnneMeinel@aim.com as well as on Facebook, Google +, or her blog @ http://kannemeinel.wordpress.com/ or on Twitter @ kannemeinelaim.com, or on her website @ www.kannemeinel.com if you would like to follow her to find out about stories and book's releases.

Beta Read by Lori S. Ray & Anonymous (you know who you are), many thanks for your efforts and time.

www.shadoepublishing.com

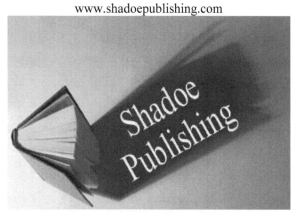

ShadoePublishing@gmail.com

PUBLISHER'S NOTE

❧ CHAPTER ONE ❧

The view from her window wasn't that impressive as she looked at the dismal aged and gray buildings outside on an equally dismal and gray day in New York, but at least she had a window and a view. Not all associates had a window, most were in inner offices but she was a senior associate, a lawyer of council if you will, and it was part of her perks. She looked out her window a long time, lost in thought even though she knew she should be getting to the pile of briefs on her desk. Instead she daydreamed about the incredible offer she had just received. She had known it was coming, she knew she deserved it, but at the moment wasn't sure if she should be insulted.

Nia Toyomoto worked for one of the most prestigious law firms in Manhattan. It wasn't a small thing to be an associate at Chase-Dunham. It wasn't a small thing to be a lawyer of council either. To be offered a partnership though was something that Nia had worked towards for years. Everyone knew she was on the fast track, everyone knew that she deserved it, but at this moment, she wasn't sure. When Stewart Dunham had scheduled this morning's meeting she had assumed it was for a personal update on certain cases that she was handling for him, for others, and with others. Although she had eventually expected the offer, the stipulations had surprised her. She didn't realize her personal life would be part of the offer. Not that she had anything to hide but being a partner at Chase-Dunham required a certain panache that Nia simply didn't have at this time. Stewart had kindly pointed out that they needed her to 'spruce' herself up, to become a bit more social. It was not a matter of her talents as a world class attorney, no, that was *why* they wanted her to be a partner. It was a matter of smoozing with the right people, having parties, attending the elite of the elite. Her reputation was such that she fit in but her appearance left a little to be desired. She was all business. They wanted her as a partner but they also wanted her to use every means at her disposal to get them new clients. Not that she hadn't drawn them in the past with her incredible expertise but being a partner meant that she would represent the firm on levels that she hadn't thus far. Her talents alone wouldn't sell the firm.

Nia sighed. She wasn't one to get ahead on her looks. She was overly tall for the average woman at 5'10" and this for someone of Asian descent was almost unheard of. Not that you could tell she was Asian except for the certain narrowing of her eyes that gave her a feline like appearance. Her father was pure Asian, a former executive from Japan, he had fallen in love with a German-American woman who Nia had inherited most of her

looks from. The clunky black glasses she wore hid the slightly exotic Asian tilt of her eyes. Her smooth round face v'd becomingly, but with her straight dark brown nearly black hair with occasional reddish tints that she held severely back in a bun, she gave herself a no nonsense appearance. She had never cared for her looks. She wasn't like other women. Her nails were cut short, purely functional; no polish had ever graced them. Her long legs were encased in nylons and this only because she was fairly pale in appearance and the style was to have a semblance of tan. She had business suits but these too were merely functional. She owned six or seven that she interchanged to provide variety but these were of lessor quality and again, she just hadn't cared. Now they were making her care, in fact making it a condition of her partnership.

The suggestion and not too subtly that her partnership hinged on her doing a makeover, buying better clothes, and a better place to live was ludicrous. But Nia knew that the good ole boy network could find other reasons to deny her this plum chance. She also knew at thirty that she would be one of the youngest partners in Manhattan. She also knew she deserved it. She had worked hard all her life for this very thing.

She had graduated high school in three and a half years and would have graduated in three but for the moron that was the principal at the time thought her too young at sixteen to graduate her junior year. She had to wait until she was seventeen and graduated halfway through her senior year. It wasn't that her grades hadn't warranted an early graduation, no, she had always been effortlessly at the top of her class but this was an age where he felt her social abilities would be hindered by not graduating with her peers. Nia didn't have a lot of friends and those who really knew her knew she was destined for great things. Graduating early would only expedite those goals she had set for herself. Once she graduated from high school she had gone straight to college. Attending Wellesley College, she had sailed through in three years before enrolling in Harvard Law School for her graduate work. If she could have done it in one year she would have but had done it in the normal three years before graduating at the top of her class. An offer from Wall Street and Chase-Dunham had been the culmination of her dream. She'd had other offers of course, many from those she had worked for in summer internships, but Wall Street and Chase-Dunham's reputation was such she knew that was where she wanted to be. For her to be an associate there had guaranteed her future, something she didn't really think about in the broad spectrum of life, instead she wanted very specific things in life and now this partnership was part of that dream.

To hold it up because she wasn't properly garbed or social or looked right for the part angered her but when she thought about it practically she understood. She was perfect for the job and she knew she would

eventually capitulate but it didn't set well with her that it was mandated by the men in this firm. Then she thought of how few partners over the years had been women, especially on Wall Street much less in Manhattan.

She thought for a long time about what other goals she had set for herself and realized that at thirty she had achieved most of them. She had gotten into Wellesley on a scholarship and paid for extras through the little her mother sent her after Papa's death. Papa had died after he knew his only child had graduated from high school and his life insurance had paid off their home but left very little for frivolous living, her mother had pinched every penny. Going to an Ivy League School had never been in doubt but paying for it had been. It was expensive to be so highly educated. Nia had taken that seriously. Never had she thought about any other school after Wellesley but Harvard. It had not been a dream but a serious plan that had only been in doubt due to a lack of funds. Nia had graduated in due time with debts so high that they boggled the mind. The job that she had expected from her high grades, internships, and moral standards had come through and she had begun to pay off those debts through her frugalness.

She lived in a studio apartment that was so small she couldn't swing a cat for hitting everything. Her mother had passed away and Nia had sold everything of value including the house that they owned except for nine boxes of 'trinkets,' paying off her student loans and using the little left to buy stocks to help fund her IRA and for security later in life. Her salary was such that she could move to a larger apartment and in fact she had enough now to buy a very nice place but she had no one she wanted to show her postage stamp apartment to, no one really saw it other than one or two close friends, she didn't need a larger one, until now. Her frugal living though would pay off now. She had the funds to do what they wanted and with style but her innate sense of fair play almost balked at the idea of changing her lifestyle, her appearance, her everything for a promotion. It was sexist and discriminatory and they would get away with it unless she refused to play, did she want to give up everything she had worked for to stand on the moral high ground? She could sue, theoretically. What they were asking *was* illegal but did she really want to be known as the lawyer who sued their own firm over her looks? That would certainly create waves in the legal community and also insure that she wouldn't get another job with any other firm in New York, much less Manhattan, *ever*.

A knock on her door had her spinning around in her leather chair and looking up surprised as Stewart Dunham stuck his head in the door. "You busy?" he inquired with a smile. Stewart Dunham was a spare man of fifty five who had inherited the firm of Chase-Dunham through the expedient manner of marrying Elliott Chase's daughter. They had worked together

through some lean years and had expanded it exponentially from their partnership. When Elliott Chase had passed away, Stewart Dunham had been one of the first on Wall Street to hire women and bring in clientele that had appreciated his foresight. The people he hired were excellent; he had an eye for talent and had picked Nia Toyomoto himself. She had worked a summer internship up in Boston for a friends firm and he had raved over her insight, her brilliance, and her enthusiasm. He had watched and learned as she participated in the debate team up at Harvard. An Alumni himself, he had availed himself of her records and been suitably impressed. He had romanced her into coming to work with his firm right out of college and had never regretted it. Her work was consistently superior and she deserved every promotion they had ever given her. His other partners had been worried that they were giving the youngster too much too soon but he knew she could handle it. She had been only twenty three when she graduated Harvard but had within one year won them an impossible case. The lawyer of record had to drop out at the last minute for cause and she had picked up the slack despite her lack of experience and with very little supervision had won and the senior partners had been suitably impressed. Her record since then had been equally impressive. If she just didn't look so…frumpy. From her horn rimmed square glasses to her unattractive and severe bun of hair she screamed 'old maid' and he knew some of the clients wouldn't want to work with a partner that made them feel like she was their grandmother. He had often wondered if she were a dyke but she gave no appearance of that either. She didn't date men, she didn't date women, she didn't date that he knew of. She was kind of uni-sex and that didn't set well with the partners. Many insisted that if she represented the firm she needed to take advantage of her feminity and had complained about her lack thereof for years, now they insisted on this change or no, they didn't want her as a partner.

She smiled kindly and this changed her austere appearance, without really answering the CEO of Chase-Dunham she asked instead, "What can I do for you Mr. Dunham?"

"Would you come with me for a moment?" he gestured outside her office.

Nia rose up and walked immediately over to her small office door. Stewart held the door for her and she walked out before him. He indicated the elevator and she assumed they were going up to the Senior Partner's level to the private offices of the CEO which were on a floor above the associates and counselor levels. They stood as equals as they waited for the elevator. Nia's own height was only an inch or two below Stewarts. He thought she would be even more impressive once she realized her full potential, it had to be her decision though, and she could still turn them down, although they both knew she would be foolish to do so. Stewart

was risking, big time, that she wouldn't take offense to what they had shoved down her throat in their offer. Instead he hoped, and gambled, that she would grasp it with both hands and prove the nay-sayers wrong, very wrong. He had always seen the potential of this woman from her days at Harvard, he still saw potential, if his daughters had shown any inkling of the talent of this young woman he would like to think they would be as good as she. His son had gone in a totally different direction and become an accountant. He had been very disappointed but survived the blow to his ego.

Stewart led, not to the CEO offices but to a corner office at the opposite end of the building. Nia hadn't really been to these offices since she had very little business with some of these partners and almost none with the senior partners except when they needed a consult on a case they were handling. They walked into a nice little office that would suit any executive secretary or assistant as people now called them. Through this empty and rather plain office they walked into an immense corner office that had not one but two banks of floor to ceiling windows. The room was absolutely bare of furniture. Stewart led her to the windows and they stood looking out at the impressive Manhattan skyline as Nia wondered why she had been brought here. They hadn't spoken the entire ride up in the elevator or really since they had left her office.

"I thought perhaps you might need a little something to make the offer even more worthwhile," Stewart began.

"Mr. Dunham, I assure you..." Nia began but stopped when he held up his hand.

"Please, if you accept this position you will have to begin calling me Stewart. This isn't a standard partner agreement we have offered you, Nia. This office is just one of the perks. You will have to choose a car that we will pay for. You will have to choose an apartment that we will make sure your mortgage is handled through our banking contacts and the payments reasonable. You will have six weeks paid vacation. The perks you might pass up from refusing are more than you realize."

Nia looked at him incredulously. They hadn't even discussed the perks of her partnership agreement. This office? It was incredible. She glanced around and for some reason the sun began to shine through the impressive windows. She could already picture the office with deep cherry wood furniture making it a warm and professional one. She could even put in an electric fireplace she thought barely controlling the grin that threatened at her thought. A car? What was wrong with her little Fiat? She realized though that she would be a fool to pass it up but she had played her cards too well for too long to show them to this master player. She nodded coldly as she considered her options which she really knew were few. She could quit but that would be self-defeating, besides she loved her job. She

could refuse and remain an associate but it would never be the same, they would treat her as though she had insulted them. She could sue but then she would never again work in Manhattan and who wanted to hang out their own shingle with *that* on their resume? She could accept and have a make-over. She needed to think about it but she had already told this man and his partner's that very thing when they made their initial offer.

"Here is one more thing for you to think about," Stewart finished with. Nia looked at him expectantly. "We are waiving your buy in, your bonus' will be deferred for the first three years but you do not have to come up with the normal buy in amount. Based on your performance and what we anticipate you bringing into the firm in the future we have decided that this will be enough for your buy in."

Nia was incredulous, this offer, this incredible deal was worth possibly a million dollars or more!

❖ CHAPTER TWO ❖

That night as she let herself into her apartment she thought about what a new apartment would mean. While material things didn't mean much to her she knew they did to some people. She liked nice things but you wouldn't know that for what she had in this minimalistic apartment. She didn't cook much and the stove was a joke, only two of the burners actually worked but she couldn't remember a time when she had needed all four. The only thing the oven ever got used for was to heat up pizza. She didn't even own a microwave, something her friends couldn't comprehend. She changed from her suit skirt to a pair of slacks that still managed to give her a professional appearance but a more relaxed one before going out to meet some women she had been socializing with for years.

There was group of ten of them from various walks of life who met every Thursday and caught up on each other's life. Some were closer than others, some didn't come every week but overall they had been friends for years. Tonight there were six of them who met at the same table in the same restaurant/bar and ordered the same drinks as they socialized.

"I heard you were up for partner." Tiffany toasted Nia with her wine.

Nia looked at her disbelievingly from behind her horn rimmed glasses. "How did you hear about that?" she asked.

"I have my sources." Tiffany grinned slyly.

Nia was sure she did. She slept with everyone so she was the center of many little webs that she wove. Tiffany ran an import/export business and sometimes some of her products were a little brow raising. Nia had helped her out of few tricky situations over the years with customs and others.

"Are you going to accept?" Eleanor asked astutely. Eleanor was the senior woman of their bunch of thirty something's and her mothering had annoyed and delighted all of them from time to time. She worked for a prestigious real estate firm and sold high end product.

Nia shrugged. "I'm not quite sure," she began.

"What are you waiting for?" Nadia asked outraged. "It would mean you're the youngest woman on Wall Street!"

Nia smiled at the blonde. "I don't actually work on Wall Street Nadia, it's a law firm that handles Wall Street firms as well as many other diverse clientele," she explained not sure if Nadia really understood.

"Whatever," the blonde retorted sounding about sixteen. "It would mean a lot of money." To Nadia, who had worked her way up from the streets and didn't realize that an education meant she would go farther, money was god.

They discussed Nia's options which really were few. When they heard the conditions they all jumped on board with opinions of their own and suggestions. Nia refrained from telling them about the buy in being waived, which was unheard of!

"You have got to get rid of those horrible glasses first thing," Millie dictated. Millie was in fashion and looking at her always demoralized Nia if she thought she could ever compete with that type.

"What's wrong with my glasses?" Nia goaded her; she knew already but thought it would be fun to hear the breathtakingly beautiful Millie go on about what she thought was wrong with Nia.

She took the bait and proceeded to outline exactly what Nia should do to 'improve' herself. That the others agreed for the most part was a surprise and an eye opener for Nia. She had thought she was fine as she was but apparently it was the consensus that she needed a makeover, and not just to land the promotion.

That night she lay in bed thinking over the offer. She did an excellent job didn't she? She knew the money she would make for the firm would be returned to her eventually in the dividends she would receive as a partner and eventually the bonuses. Why did she need to change her appearance to be even more successful? As she turned on her side to go to sleep she realized the answer to the last question, because she wanted *this*, it was the culmination of many of her dreams, a dream partnership...

That week she felt she had no time to really worry about it. She had been given a week to make up her mind and sign the papers to her partnership. It would go into effect two weeks later when she returned from her vacation. Since she was leaving shortly it meant she had to clear up everything on her desk before she left. If she accepted the position, she would return from vacation a partner in the firm of Chase-Dunham. The thought was exciting. By the end of the second day though she knew she wouldn't wait. Not a procrastinator by inclination or design, something the law community was good at and judges appreciated that she didn't play at; she went up to the CEO's office late that afternoon hoping to catch him before he left for the day.

"Is Mr. Dunham in?" she asked Sally his executive assistant or secretary as he still referred to her.

"Yes, but he is about to leave," Sally told her warmly. She liked Ms. Toyomoto. She was a kind and generous woman despite her reputation as a lethal litigator. Despite the Japanese name she looked nothing like a Japanese woman should. It always surprised new clients who had expected a small demure Asian woman and instead got this Saxon woman with the feline like eyes if they could see them at all under the heavy rims. Ms. Toyomoto had always been pleasant and kind to those under her and always remembered secretary's day and not just for her own secretary.

Any of the partners or associates she had worked with over the years and their assistants she made sure the secretaries received a bouquet of flowers for this day and at Christmas a box of those delicious and expensive Wrothman Chocolates. Those who hadn't worked with her understood but were envious of the few who got their presents from this woman. Her own secretary got extra perks and Colleen was the envy of those whose bosses weren't as kind or as thoughtful.

"Can I go in for minute?" Nia asked cautiously. It never paid to offend an assistant, they had more power than people realized. They made life easier for them all to do their jobs and do them well. God knew that Nia depended on Colleen for a lot. She made sure she was compensated accordingly as well as given perks.

"Yes, go right in," Sally smiled; she knew that Mr. Dunham wouldn't mind, he wasn't in conference, or on a phone call, and was just packing up to leave.

"Mr. Dunham?" Nia asked as she stuck her head around the open doorway into the luxurious and immense office.

Stewart looked up with genuine pleasure. "Nia! What a surprise! I was just getting ready to leave," he indicated the open briefcase he was placing papers in.

"I won't keep you then." She smiled. "I've decided to accept your offer."

He smiled very pleased, she hadn't kept them waiting and he found this to be the best sign yet. "And the stipulations?" he asked hesitantly, knowing they had been out of line, way out of line. He couldn't help himself as he looked at the horrible black horn rimmed glasses on her face.

She shook her head and rolled her eyes as she grinned at him. "Okay, I'll take care of them immediately."

He smiled and rubbed his hands together. "Good, good, I'll have the contracts drawn up for tomorrow. No reason to wait eh?"

She nodded once and said, "Have a good evening Mr. Dunham."

"Stewart," he corrected her and they shared a grin of mutual understanding.

Nia left work and went to a place called Head Hunters, one of the 'girls' had suggested it and probably it was Millie who knew everyone in fashion and who to go to. She had called ahead to get an appointment and been surprised to even get in. When she got there though she found Millie had called ahead and warned them that she 'might' be calling which was why they had an appointment available for her. She laughed, it was all about who you knew or what you knew about whom and she accepted that. She discussed with a 'consultant' about what she wanted. She didn't want

a total makeover where she wouldn't recognize herself but she knew she needed her hair done up professionally and attractively. Head Hunters was only the start. Because her hair was so dark and so straight they wanted to cut it short and in a pixie cut but she refused. She hated that look. It led to an argument with her 'consultant' and finally the manager intervened.

"What is going on here?" she asked in her false European accent. Nia spotted the fake tones immediately. She didn't want to insult the woman though and while she knew Millie had helped get this appointment she didn't want them chopping up her hair.

Nia explained politely that she was looking for a new 'do' and didn't want the pixie cut that the 'consultant' had suggested.

"Oh no, no, nooo, we won't do a pixie cut for you," the manager said taking over immediately. She turned Nia's head each way, spun her back and forth in the chair as she squinted at her and examined her from every angle. "I think for you we will do an 'angle' cut."

Before Nia could ask what an 'angle' cut was the manager reached out to a line of books on a shelf beside their station. She rapidly opened a book and looked for a diagram that she showed to Nia which explained what they would be doing. There were all sorts of 'angle' cuts but she suggested a one hundred eighty degree cut for Nia which would give her many layers that all were the same length if she stood on her head but once right side up would be many different lengths all over her head. "It will give you bounce, it will give you flair, people will rave over your beautiful hair," she picked at Nia's hair running her fingers through the long thick length as she eyed the Eurasian woman speculatively. "It will take a lot of weight off but give you I think some of the curls that are dying to come out from under that weight."

Nia looked at her doubtfully. This was why she hadn't wanted the 'pixie' cut. Her hair curled horribly when it was too short. She had done it once in high school and the resulting perm like results had been embarrassing. She had kept her hair long ever since. The woman had seen something though and she sounded more professional than the other 'consultant' and Nia trusted her as she nodded and agreed to the one hundred eighty degree cut.

Nia left the salon feeling wonderful. The woman had been right about the weight. Her head and neck felt weird without the mass of hair that had been up in a bun all these years. It still had the length halfway down her back but the riot of curls that came at the ends looked incredible. The woman had suggested she streak it too but Nia had balked since she needed professionalism in her career and the curls were enough of an effeminate look. She didn't need to go punk or something to play with her hair further. She found herself looking in shop windows as she walked down the street heading for another appointment she had.

Dr. Nelson had been her eye doctor since she had moved to Manhattan. She didn't go except for her once a year appointments and this suited them both fine. It had only been three months since her last appointment so he was concerned that she wanted to see him and so quickly. She had asked for an appointment the same day she called and but for a cancellation they would not have been able to accommodate her.

"What seems to be the problem Ms. Toyomoto?" he asked concerned when she was in his office.

"I need to get Lasik's surgery as soon as possible and contacts until then," she told him.

He was surprised. She had always seemed a plain and sensible woman to him. Not concerned about her appearance which was apparent by the ugly horn rimmed glasses that she always wore. He pulled her file up on the computer and was happy to see that her prescription was something they could accommodate easily. He was also relieved to find she had no stigmatism that might negate the ability to get her Lasik's surgery. "You understand we are going to have to destroy some of your eyesight for the Lasik to work and you might have to have this done more than once in your lifetime for it to continually work?" he explained. After a quick exam to determine that her sight had not changed he showed her how to put in the contact lenses. After a few tries and some watering eyes she got the hang of poking herself in the eye. Leaving the contact in was another lesson learned much less taking it out to try again. It didn't make her happy but she was determined. She left with a small supply of disposable contact lenses, her horn rimmed glasses in her purse, and an appointment for Lasik's surgery scheduled six weeks from now.

She was tired from her haircut and eye appointments and stopped for dinner at one of the numerous little restaurants that abounded in Manhattan. It was chilly this fine spring evening and she was grateful to eat alone as she watched the world walk by the windows of the cafe. She was surprised as she noted several men and women looking at her. She thought it was her imagination but she realized she looked totally different with her glasses gone and her new hair style. She was relieved to finish dinner and head for Macy's and Bloomingdales. She bought some higher end business suits and accessories from both but still didn't find what she was really looking for. She knew that she needed to go to some finer stores for the look she was trying to achieve. She couldn't do it all in one day but she wished she could, she wished it was that easy, she wished she was already *done*. She picked up some things for her vacation that she was leaving on the next week; she had needed some new swimsuits anyway.

She was pleased that a 'beauty' consultant was still working at Macy's and she found herself several hundred dollars poorer after the woman

taught her and explained the make-up she would need. She returned more than half of it the following day realizing she didn't and wouldn't need it all. Her skin was fine thanks to good genetics. A light base covered any freckles or imperfections from acne scars or any other age related blotches. The rainbow of colors for eye shadow and lipstick weren't necessary and she was fairly conservative. She didn't need every single one that the woman said she did. Nia was grateful though for her knowledge and expertise though as she learned from her. She practiced with the makeup all weekend long and found a look she could live with.

On Saturday she called Eleanor and asked her to help her find a new apartment, not to rent but to *buy*. That magic word 'buy' had Eleanor excited, especially when Nia told her the addresses she would consider.

"Can you afford that?" Eleanor nearly gasped knowing what apartments and co-ops cost in that area.

Nia smiled into the phone. "Oh absolutely," she answered confidently. She knew with the firm's help of a low interest mortgage that she could. She had lived frugally all her life and despite high rent in Manhattan had managed to sock a majority of her paychecks away for the last few years. She had a pretty good down payment and the loan she would get through the firm would be to her advantage. Her credit was excellent since she had never lived beyond her means and she knew what she could afford.

Eleanor was thrilled and asked if she wanted to start looking that very afternoon. Nia agreed meeting her outside of Macy's after she returned the excess makeup. Eleanor almost didn't recognize her friend. The new hairstyle looked great, the curls had come out in a riot after its washing, it was an easy style to brush out, and it look incredible on her, the light makeup and the casual clothes she was wearing turned many heads. "What happened to you?" she asked as Nia got in her Mercedes.

Nia smiled at her friend. "I accepted the position, effective immediately." She knew she looked pretty good and her smile reflected that. In fact for one of the first times in her life she felt pretty. She had never thought about it before. It was already giving her a confidence, a spring in her step that hadn't been there before.

"Wow, wait until the gals get a look at you!" Eleanor smiled in return. "You'll knock some of those bitches on their ends." She grinned evilly in anticipation and they both laughed.

Eleanor had two properties to show her that afternoon, it was all she could get on such short notice. The market in Manhattan was very competitive. But with the price range that Nia had given her and the addresses it narrowed down what was available considerably. Eleanor was pleased that Nia obviously knew what she wanted and that was quality, it made her life a whole lot easier than if she had said she just wanted a place

in New York. She had clients like that and it always boded for a bad situation when she couldn't satisfy their vague requests.

The first one was a fourth floor apartment in a building that had just gone co-op. The owners were out so they could look at the furnished apartment to their hearts content. Nia wasn't impressed, "This is what my money will buy?" she asked disappointed. It was small, it was cramped, the floors creaked, and it was stuffed wall to wall with their possessions, not giving a favorable appearance. It had a small living room, a separate kitchen, and a separate bedroom. It was a step up from her postage stamp but if she was going to own it, this wouldn't be it.

"We've only just started looking. I'm sure if you were serious about this place they would come down. Personally I think it's overpriced."

The second place was a little better but Nia hated the building on sight. It was built in the seventies and had a 'modern' look to it with metal in various colors interspersed with the windows. Personally she would have preferred all windows but the place was not properly set up and it was apparent that they had cut what had been a good sized apartment into two or possibly three apartments that now made everything way too small. Nia was already discouraged.

"Don't feel bad darling, we've only just begun to look. I've got several places in mind for you now that I know more of what you're looking for. No one gets it on the first try," Eleanor tried to console her.

Sunday wasn't much better. They went out in the morning and looked at a couple of places as well. Nia liked it better sometimes if the places were empty of furniture. It was even better when the homeowners weren't at home as they felt it was a personal attack on them if she dared to criticize the size of the place or something else.

Sunday afternoon she went and shopped and found a few more items to add to her wardrobe. She didn't want to go overboard yet but what she had bought already would allow her to get rid of a few of her 'bargain basement' suits as she was coming to realize they looked. Still it was giving her an immediate education and she looked forward to Monday's meeting with the few partners who would be there when she signed her agreement. They would be pleasantly surprised that she put their plan in action so soon, or at least she hoped they would. She liked what she saw already.

"Ms. Toyomoto?" Colleen said in surprise as Nia walked into their offices on Monday morning, her new red briefcase hanging from her shoulder.

Nia grinned. She knew she looked a lot different than she had on Friday and it felt good. It felt really good. For the first time in her life she felt desirable and attractive. Getting rid of the glasses had been a huge

adjustment but having her hair down had softened her otherwise severe features. "Yep, it's me," she smiled to her assistant.

"You look great!" Colleen enthused.

"Thank you," Nia said quietly appreciating the compliment. She handed Colleen several file folders and said, "These are for three of the cases that Burt gave me," before she proceeded into her cubicle of an office. Sitting on her desk was a thick book of office decor with a stick on ribbon on the cover. She laughed; it could have only come from Stewart who knew she would have to decorate her office. She spent about fifteen minutes paging through the book enjoying the decor she saw before she put it aside and got to work.

At ten in the morning she walked up the flight of steps to the Executive level instead of waiting for the elevator. It helped to keep her in shape taking the steps but also she avoided the delay the elevator could take or the potential for someone to button hole her in the elevator and she never discussed cases outside of the office. She was prompt as she presented herself into the boardroom. The partners and Stewart all stared in astonishment at the change in her. She held back her grin knowing it was drastic already and she had only begun to enact the changes they had requested. She signed her new contract with a flourish and received their congratulations and handshakes with aplomb. A few of the partners had resented the deal that Nia was offered but seeing her now and knowing the financials and her potential they realized it was a good investment. They welcomed her as though nothing had happened and she was grateful for the compliments she received.

"Well girlie, you did it," Stewart said with a grin after the others had left.

She nodded not sure what to say.

"Now, we are going to see you soar," he promised. "You sure surprised a few people today," his thumb indicated the partners who had witnessed her contract and left.

She grinned, "I live up to my agreements."

He examined her as he noted the makeup, the lack of glasses, and the new hair style. She really was an attractive woman. It had all been hidden before. He was really pleased with the surprising result. "Yes you do," he agreed. "Have you picked out a car yet?"

She shook her head laughing, she had only had the weekend to *think* about things much less *do* them, "I think I will have enough to do finding a new place to live," she said wryly.

"Where are you looking?" he fretted. It was important to have the right address for many reasons, safety, equity, prestige.

She told him the addresses she was considering and he nodded relieved knowing she was showing good sense. "Do you have a realtor?"

"Yes, I have Eleanor James handling it for me," she answered.

"Eleanor James?" his eyebrows rose in surprise. "I'm impressed. How did you get her to take you on as a client?"

She smiled, she knew Eleanor had a reputation as an exclusive but she was a friend. "I called her, she's a friend of mine, and she took me out over the weekend."

He was impressed. If she knew people like Eleanor James she had even more potential than they had thought. He was pleased she had risen so quickly to the challenge they had given her. "She won't steer you wrong."

K'ANNE MEINEL

❦ CHAPTER THREE ❧

All that week after work Nia and Eleanor looked at various properties. Nia was already sick of the process and Eleanor told her sometimes it took months to find the right place. It was *just* an apartment Nia thought for Christ's sake but Eleanor assured her it wasn't 'just' an apartment. It would be home, it would be a place she could have dinner parties, it was necessary to her new career as a partner at Chase-Dunham. Already people were talking about it in certain circles. Ms. Nia Toyomoto was the 'it' girl of the moment. She was one of the youngest women to hold such a lofty title as partner in a prestigious firm such as Chase-Dunham. Although a *junior* partner, she was none the less a *partner!*

Nia was leaving on Friday night for her vacation and wasn't thrilled that she hadn't found something already. She was already tired of looking, going through stranger's apartments, seeing their clutter or empty rooms; she had already become unhappy with the whole project. On Wednesday Eleanor had shown her a fairly new apartment in a building that had been newly converted. It had just become available. The building itself was very old but the owner, a middle aged woman was converting the former warehouse into beautiful apartments. They were of good size and open aired concepts or even lofts. This apartment had only become available because the previous owner was moving overseas unexpectedly for a job promotion. It was on the tenth floor and overlooked the city and a rooftop garden on the fifth floor. The view from the balcony that ran alongside the kitchen area was an open parking lot between the two adjacent buildings. Above the apartment was another rooftop garden that the owner had put in and Nia liked the feel of the place. It had hardwood floors that the building owner had newly sanded, the walls were natural brick except where the insulation had been re-installed around the huge windows. A loft upstairs meant she had two bedrooms and a second bath. The fixtures were all high end. The living space was enormous and there was a room under the loft for a den and the second bathroom. The kitchen was modern and high tech and the current owner was willing to sell their appliances but not their furniture with the apartment. They went back on Thursday for her to look at it once more and she again felt that if 'felt right.' She knew if she didn't snap it up that someone else would and Eleanor agreed.

After the second look she turned to Eleanor and said, "Do you think they would go down 10% on the price?"

Eleanor grinned, it was an incredible find. She knew that it wouldn't stay long on the market at the price it was but she knew the owner was

motivated to sell and couldn't wait to move to Europe. She could only ask.

"Ms. Toyomoto's office," Colleen answered the phone as she usually did a hundred or so times a day.

"Eleanor James for Nia Toyomoto please," a cool voice came over the line.

Colleen recognized the name that Nia had given her and answered, "One moment Ms. James." She called through to Nia who answered the phone distractedly. She was trying to clear her desk before noon so she could cut out of work early for her vacation. She was packed; she had traveler's checks and her passport and plenty of cash and credit cards, she was anxious to get going.

"Nia, Ms. James on line one for you," Colleen said in her very effeminate soprano.

"Thank you," she said as she looked up to press the button and adjust her headset so Eleanor could hear her. She usually used a headset to keep her hands free for notes, computer typing, or to gesture as she talked expressively on the phone. "Eleanor how *are* you?"

"I'm good Nia, I have great news. The owner is willing to accept your offer but only if you sign immediately," she enthused.

"Sign immediately? I'm leaving for the Yucatan tonight!" she informed her alarmed as she sat up straighter in her chair.

"I can have the papers drawn up and ready for you to sign within an hour. Can you write a check for the down payment and get the bank on the loan? That will take at least two weeks to go through anyway."

Nia thought for a moment, she had thought she was going to take care of the apartment when she got back. She realized though that a good apartment didn't wait for vacations, especially in Manhattan. She couldn't get a refund on her tickets and she didn't want to but she didn't want to lose this apartment either. Nodding she said, "Yes, I can. Do you want to meet me?"

"I'll come by with the papers in say an hour maybe an hour and a half. I have to stop and get some from the building owner too since you will have to be approved. I don't see any difficulty with that but you never know. Call your HR office and get started on that end," she advised as she knew about the incredible perk that Nia had gotten with her promotion.

"Okay, I'll see you in an hour or so," Nia agreed annoyed. She hadn't realized the building owner would be involved but then it did make sense that they didn't let just anyone in even if they could afford the high prices. In just the few years since this building had been converted the owner had bought up a couple other 'warehouses' and begun converting those as well.

Nia had been impressed to find out it was a woman and seeing the quality of the apartment knew why the paperwork would be so complicated. She herself didn't handle landlord tenant properties or contracts and was grateful. Those were a nightmare that she didn't want to get into. Although she would own her apartment she would still pay an amount in 'rent' for maintenance on the building. She didn't like it but it was a fact of life in New York. This undiscovered building had not realized its full potential until this woman had bought it and she deserved to capitalize on other's oversight. Nia wanted to live there now that she had seen it twice. She would jump through the necessary hoops to live there. She liked that the woman had put in the rooftop gardens. It made a difference. She liked the balcony that spanned the length of the apartment she had chosen and she could sit out at night and enjoy it. She loved that it was one of only two apartments on this floor instead of the four each that were on the other five levels of this section of the building. The privacy was something she was willing and able to pay for.

She called HR and Priscilla was happy to help her with the paperwork. Stewart had warned her that Nia was going to be buying a property and she had a file already for the partner, she hadn't expected to hear from her quite this soon but everyone knew Nia Toyomoto was efficient. Even though she wasn't starting as a partner until she returned from vacation, everyone wanted the new partner to be happy and would accommodate her. Priscilla walked over from Human Resources and entered Nia's office after a short knock. Looking around at the postage sized office she smiled. "You're really going to be coming up in the world," she commented as Nia looked up.

Nia grinned. References to her new office she knew caused envy. Even a couple of the partners had joked with her for having one of the best offices. It wasn't really but there were only so many corner offices to go around. Nia reached for the file folder and Priscilla waited while she perused and signed the papers. Speed reading was a gift and she had learned it as a child, it served her well when she had contracts to read over. The loan they were giving her was many times what she needed and she pointed this out to Priscilla.

"That's a contingency in case the apartment or co-op was more than what you found. Just have your realtor send in the X-nine-fourteen form and we will adjust no penalty, no additional interest. The payments will all be deducted automatically from your salary. Insurance, taxes, and maintenance fees will be included in those payments for your convenience," she explained pointing out the more relevant lines of Nia's payment contract and where Nia needed to initial her agreement and then sign.

Their business was soon concluded and Priscilla left her a card to give to Eleanor so they could conclude the transaction while Nia was away. Once Eleanor had Nia's signature on the rest of the papers they wouldn't need her for weeks anyway. She had already signed the letter of intent and Eleanor had presented the offer. Their acceptance was contingent on the building owner's acceptance and Nia's financial abilities.

"Ms. Toyomoto?" Colleen said sweetly as she knocked once on the door and escorted Eleanor inside. "Ms. James," she announced as she closed the door behind the realtor.

"Eleanor!" Nia smiled a welcome. She had just finished the last of her case files and put them aside on her desk.

"Nia, here is what you have to sign," she answered wasting no time as she presented the folder with a flourish. She had neatly put post it arrow stickers where Nia needed to sign but she knew the lawyer in Nia wouldn't just sign blindly despite their friendship. She was right as Nia began to peruse the paperwork. Eleanor was glad at how quickly Nia read the documents in front of her as she sat down and admired the small office. Word on the street was that Nia had gotten a huge office on the Executive level and the fact that they had helped her with the mortgage sweetened the deal. She looked around at the small office as she let Nia read and wondered how much larger the other office was.

Nia was soon signing the documents having found no errors or objections to the wording. It was pretty standard and straight forward but the little she knew of real estate law she was glad she wasn't an attorney that handled it. She had heard nightmares from a couple of the associates who had handled cases. "There you go," she smiled as she handed the packet back to Eleanor a good while later.

Eleanor double checked that all her stickers had a signature next to them before she put the folder in her briefcase. "We are going to have to celebrate when you get back from Mexico," she enthused as she looked at Nia in congratulations.

"I just hope nothing comes up while I'm gone," she indicated the packet she had just signed.

"I don't foresee any problem with this, I know it was kind of quick but that's the way it goes sometimes," Eleanor answered. "We could have dragged it out for months."

Nia nodded. It went that way in law too. An attorney could procrastinate or delay things until you were pulling out your hair but then the client suddenly wanted to settle for some reason and it often happened that way.

Eleanor got up to leave and reached across Nia's desk to shake her hand "I'm so happy you found something," she said quietly as she looked deeply into the feline like eyes. It was almost as though she was saying something or looking for something more as she squeezed Nia's hand meaningfully, but then Nia put it away as her imagination.

"I'm just grateful for your help," Nia answered as she too rose and shook Eleanor's outstretched hand.

As Eleanor made her way past the secretarial pool that were separated by cubicle partition boards she smiled at Colleen and looked at her speculatively. She had just made it to the elevator when she heard, "Why it's Eleanor James I do believe," and turned with a 'client' smile to see Stewart Dunham himself coming towards her with an arm outstretched.

"Stewart!" she smiled for real in response.

"Are you here for Nia Toyomoto?" he asked astutely.

She nodded and held up her suitcase slightly. "Yes, just some paperwork to be signed."

"Ah, she found a place already did she?" he rubbed his hands together excitedly in that way he had about him.

She nodded. "Yes, a real find and a good deal. I wanted to get this going before she left."

He frowned and asked, "Left?"

"On vacation?" she asked puzzled as she heard the elevator arriving.

He nodded as she reminded him, "Oh yes, I had almost forgotten."

"Well, I have to be going, nice seeing you Stewart!" She nodded and waved as she got on the waiting elevator.

Nia got home in enough time to shower and change into slacks and a nice blouse. This casual attire was a type of uniform for her. Her mother had drilled into her from little on that you always wore clean underwear, nice clothes for traveling, and showered once a day for good hygiene. Those lessons were never forgotten. She grabbed her carry on which contained a couple of changes of clothing and her new cosmetics as well as her shampoos and stuff. Her larger bag that she would check in carried the rest of her clothing and shoes. She got to the airport with plenty of time to spare, she tipped the cab driver and checked in at the International counter. Her new passport was checked. She was so excited about this trip. She hadn't taken a vacation in a lot of years, and she had never been outside the United States. Annie had insisted though, all work and no play makes Nia a dull girl. Nia had laughed and agreed. She had a lot of time accumulated. A day off here and there over the years didn't take up the weeks she had coming to her. This was the first real break she had ever given herself and she was going to enjoy it.

She was sitting in the lounge when she heard a familiar squeal and turned to take a very enthusiastic brunette into her welcoming arms. "Nia!" she heard as she was hugged ardently.

Nia smiled down at her friend. "Hey Annie, you made it!"

"Damn straight I made it. I wasn't going to miss this for the world." The brunette smiled up at her taller friend. Five inches shorter than the above average Nia she couldn't help but admire the new and improved bean pole. Her own luscious figure attracted people of both genders. Amply proportioned she smiled up at Nia and said, "That hair is awesome bean pole!"

"Look shorty; let's not start with name calling." Nia grinned down at her friend.

They both sat as they waited for their flight to be announced. "I can't wait to be sipping margaritas," Annie enthused.

"I'm sure you've started already," Nia said dryly with a hint of a grin.

"Well, I *am* on vacation," Annie said primly.

"When did that ever stop you?" Nia asked.

"You got rid of your glasses too, 'bout time four eyes," Annie teased.

"Yeah well it was part of the terms of agreement," Nia smiled at her friend's good natured teasing.

"Terms of agreement?" Annie asked puzzled.

Nia explained about the terms of her promotion and the broad hint that she had to 'improve' herself. She told about the new apartment and the new office. "When I get back I'm going to have to lease a new car at the company's expense," she grinned.

"Damn girl, you fell into it this time," Annie said enviously but proudly for her friend's success.

Nia nodded. They talked about what kind of car that she might get and then her cell phone rang. "Damn," she said as she saw the caller I.D.

"Can't escape work?" Annie said astutely as she watched Nia answer it.

She nodded as she answered the phone, "Hello?"

"Oh Nia, one last thing, I was cleaning up the office and I got those files off to Mr. Blake's office. I saw that you had several notes in that catalog for furniture. Did you want me to order any of it for the new office?" Colleen asked in her breathy soprano.

"Oh shit, I almost forgot. Some of that is going to take a lot of time too. Yes, could you order it for me?" she asked her assistant gratefully.

"Sure, which set up did you want? I see you tagged several pages."

Nia described what she wanted and from several different pages as she thought about exactly what she had seen in the catalog. She also authorized Colleen to set up the outer office with whatever she wanted.

"I'm moving too?" Colleen asked, genuinely puzzled.

Nia frowned. "Of course you are, I will need my assistant when we move upstairs. In fact, while I'm gone, if the furniture arrives in time, start moving us up there," she instructed her. "Didn't I tell you that you were moving with me?" she asked surprised, she had been sure she had.

Colleen was shaking her head and answered, "No, you didn't but I'll be glad to take care of that for you before I take my vacation," she gently reminded Nia that she was leaving too for only a week though. Assistants didn't have the perks associates did.

"Why are you still at work?" Nia asked looking at her watch in surprise.

Just then the announcement for their flight came over the loudspeaker and Annie rose with an expectant look at her friend. "Come on," she breathed in her excitement.

"I was just cleaning up for the week I am going to be gone," Colleen told her. It wasn't quite that late and she didn't want to leave until everything was done, she was efficient that way. She didn't want to go home anyway, the next week was going to be hell with nothing to do except be at home with her unemployed husband even if she did get paid for it.

"Well, go home and enjoy your vacation," Nia told her. She knew Colleen wasn't looking forward to her vacation as Nia was. Her husband Cletus was an absolute shit and Nia had offered several times to help Colleen with a divorce but she had stubbornly refused.

Colleen smiled. "I will, I will, I'll take care of this and then go." She was a highly effectual assistant and loved working for Nia Toyomoto. She had been lucky to get this job and knew it after a four year hiatus from working. Nia had asked her about it when she interviewed her after HR got done with their own strenuous questioning. Colleen's reply that she had married and her husband hadn't wanted her to work had been met with an incomprehensible look. Nia hadn't understood that kind of marriage. Her own parents had both worked hard and her mother had only stopped working once she had a child. Her father and his work ethics had been deeply ingrained in Nia's own psyche.

After hanging up with Nia, Colleen went over her notes carefully of what her boss wanted and typed on the computer a purchase order that she faxed to each company for the supplies and furniture that her boss and she wanted. She couldn't believe that Nia had given her basically carte blanche to decorate her own office. She was excited about the move into the larger and infinitely preferable offices upstairs on the Executive level. Being a partner in a firm as prestigious as Chase-Dunham was a real coup and being her Executive Assistant would garner Colleen her own prestige. Going from the secretarial pool to her own office would be a luxury. She

should have known that Nia wouldn't forget her when she went up the corporate ladder; she hadn't wanted to presume though.

Nia walked off the plane in the Yucatan at Soro Del Grande and breathed a sigh of pure bliss. The car from the resort met her and Annie and sped them through a rather dilapidated town before rapidly leaving it and going out into the countryside. Jungle soon enclosed the road and Nia began to get nervous in the strange locale before the gates of the resort and another town welcomed them to the Yucatan Peninsula and the infamous resort of Del Sudante. Nia was looking forward to this well-deserved vacation. She hadn't wanted to come originally when Annie had suggested it at Christmas but she was glad her friend had badgered her into it. They were ushered to a typical hotel desk before being shown to their bungalow. They had separate bedrooms with a huge living space that looked out over a large yard with a swimming pool and a view of the ocean.

Annie called, "Will you look at this," as she swung her arms wide and twirled.

Nia had to admit that this was luxurious and she enjoyed it immensely as she looked around at their accommodations.

One of the views from their windows showed the various bungalows on different levels all leading down to the main hotel that they had just come from.

"Come on, let's get naked!" Annie said as she rushed to change her clothes.

"Ah, I don't think so," Nia laughed as she went to one of the bedrooms with her bags. The rooms were nearly identical so it didn't matter who got which room.

They both changed into bikinis, Nia's was one of the new ones she had just purchased and she realized the bottom needed adjusting. Looking in the mirror she was surprised how it looked on her tall body. She was dismayed to see she needed more than the bikini wax she had given herself last night. Her pubic hair was peeking out and more than she wanted showing. It disgusted her and she quickly grabbed her nail scissors and began trimming. She trimmed both sides until it was well hidden behind the tiny scrap of material. Then she used her favorite gel to lather and using a razor she shaved the offending area's close until it was smooth as a baby's bottom. Rinsing it off she applied a lotion that would inhibit growth, smooth the irritated skin, and keep her from itching. She looked in the mirror and was pleased to see how sexy the bikini looked on her.

"Come on Nia!" Annie called from the door as she pounded on it.

Nia wrapped a sarong around her waist and adjusted it as she slipped on her sandals. She grabbed an open style purse that carried minimal identification, cash, and sunscreen in a waterproofed casing. She fluffed

her hair and was ready to go to dinner. The sun had set on their tropical paradise and eating in a bikini was an interesting sensation but she knew it was appreciated from their fellow vacationers as she and Annie tried various things on the menu. Eating Mexican food in America was vastly different than eating it in Mexico. They enjoyed their meal and then walked it off on the beach before heading back to their bungalow. They were both exhausted and wanted to be well rested for the morning's activities.

Nia carefully smoothed a heavy sunscreen on the white white skin of her buttocks that were exposed by the indecent bikini that she wore. The rest of her body that she could reach she put a sun tanning oil on asking Annie to finish where she couldn't contort on her long back.

"Damn girl this isn't fair," Annie complained as she rubbed down her back.

"What isn't?" Nia asked confused.

"You're going to get all tan and beautiful and I'm going to freckle!" Annie laughed.

"Tan maybe, beautiful, I don't think so!" Nia laughed with her friend.

"Don't you see it?" Annie asked.

"See what?" she was confused.

"That hair, those contacts, they brought it out of you girlfriend, you're a hottie now."

Nia looked at her friend as though she were nuts. She hadn't put make up on today because they were going into the ocean to learn to scuba dive and she knew it would wash off right away anyway. She hadn't been sure she should even wear her contacts but knew she needed them in one of her eyes at least to see clearly. She glanced at the mirror and tried to see what Annie saw and she had to admit she looked better these days. The austere and prissy looking Nia Toyomoto was gone and in its place was a more relaxed and pretty woman. Beautiful though? The jury was still out.

Nia loved learning about how to scuba dive. They had both signed up for lessons for beginners and the instructors were from all over the globe. The Australian, British, and American accents were funny to hear with all the tourists from all over as well. Annie quickly made friends with one of the scuba instructors and they made plans to meet later for dinner and drinks. Nia shook her head, Annie was incurable. If she couldn't find Ms. or Mr. Right, she would take Mr. or Ms. Right Now. A die-hard bi-sexual she felt that feeling good was the ultimate goal and didn't care that it left her with a few dead end relationships.

As Nia took a turn at floating and showing what she had learned she saw one of the scuba-instructors eyeing her up. She considered having a holiday fling but knew that these unsatisfying relationships were not for her. She had been with exactly two men in her life, one in her early

college years at Wellesley and one in her early days at Chase-Dunham with a fellow associate. Both had left her wanting something she couldn't describe. The sex had been interesting but nothing like she had hoped to find, nothing like the romance novels she had read as a teenager and pined her hopes on. No one had wanted Nia Toyomoto though with her horn rimmed glasses and serious bent on life. That had been fine with Nia, her studies and goals had been more important then. As she looked around at thirty though she wondered what she might be missing. The scuba instructor was good looking and had a fine healthy body but she admired him as she would any well-built or finely defined sculpture. He himself didn't really do anything for her and she wondered where that 'spark' was or if she were frigid like she suspected. The thought wasn't new, her boyfriend at the beginning of her career had planted the seed and she had come to terms with the idea. She just knew something had been missing with both of the men she had been with. She never felt that 'spark' or whatever the romance novels spoke about. They had enjoyed her body and managed to have orgasms, she learned how to give them to the men but her body never really came alive. Just when she thought it would they were usually finished. Maybe she had just met the wrong man. She just didn't know.

The view under the waves was incredible and Nia was in awe of the beauty that was presented to her as she took her first dive. Her regulator kept her breathing and she showed that she could clear her goggles when someone in their group accidentally knocked hers off. She didn't panic as it wasn't in her nature and she soon cleared the salt water from the lenses and her nose as well as her regulator and was giving the okay sign to her instructor. He seemed to take an inordinate amount of time to make sure she was okay as he also took the liberty of touching her repeatedly. Nia was wise to his ways and kept her grin to herself. She supposed these guys all liked the endless variety of tourists who came through so they could enjoy them. It was vacation and guests expected to be accommodated. Nia liked his touch but still only admired the work of art that was his sculpted and toned body.

That night at dinner which she ate alone since Annie and her friend had gone off together, she watched out of the corner of her eye as people paired off or were with their spouses or friends. There seemed to be an inordinate amount of gay couples which aroused her suspicions. Annie had booked this trip for her and it made her wonder if she had done it on purpose. Was this a gay resort?

"May I sit with you?" a voice asked politely and she looked up into the laughing blue eyes of the scuba instructor.

She didn't know if it was the relief that a male was asking after the realization of what Annie might have done to her here or was it genuine

attraction but she nodded and said, "Please do," as she indicated a chair next to her.

"We didn't really get properly introduced," he said kindly as he put his full plate down in the spot next to her and sat. "I'm Kyle Richards," he held out his hand to her.

"Nia Toyomoto," she answered automatically as she firmly shook his hand.

"Toyomoto? You don't look Asian," he grinned.

She smiled, it was a common misconception and she had run into it all her life. Her father's genes hadn't been predominate when he and her mother had decided to have a child. Her German Saxon genes had taken over. She looked European except for the slight angle of her eyes that gave them that feline like slant that now that she was wearing contacts showed off the velvety brown of her eyes beautifully instead of hidden behind those ugly black rimmed glasses she had been wearing. Her height too had always been a problem in finding clothing for her fine boned frame, another of the few things she had inherited from her father's side. "My father was Japanese, mother was German," she explained.

"What a combination," he grinned in a typically American way.

"What about you?" she asked trying to show some interest. He was good to look at. He obviously stayed fit and his work kept him in the water a lot.

"I'm a Cincinnati boy," he bragged with his boyish grin. "But I don't know anything about my background, I was adopted. I think I was part Atlantian which would explain why I love scuba diving so much."

"Wow, I've never met an Atlantian," Nia smiled as she teased him.

"Well, the hometown may be gone but we live on," he continued as though they were having a serious conversation.

Nia enjoyed his joke and they had a wonderful conversation as they both ate a delicious meal from the buffet. Each of them went back several times to try different foods that were laid out for the guests. After dinner they took a walk as they walked off the excellent food. Kyle invited her to the disco that night and she accepted knowing that she might see Annie and her friend there as well. She was on vacation and while not an avid dancer she thought she should do everything she didn't do in real life while she had the opportunity.

The next day Annie and Nia took a trip into the jungle where they had a cable that they could propel from across the tops and for a long way down a canyon. Zip lining was the new thing to try. The swoop made Nia's stomach ache and she probably wouldn't do it again as they were quite far up, it was worse than a carnival ride and she lost her stomach somewhere in the tree tops but she was glad she tried it once at least. They were having a marvelous time and her body was becoming quite dark from the

tropical sun beating down on it. She kept it well-oiled or sun blocked depending on the location. After a few days she didn't need the sunblock as Kyle rubbed in the oil all over her body where she let him. She decided by the end of the first week she would sleep with him, she was on vacation after all. He had asked after the third day and been polite about it. Both of them knew the score, they would take precautions and just enjoy themselves. Neither was asking for a commitment and they were both consenting adults. What could it harm?

Nia was left with the same empty feeling she had felt before. There was no 'spark' there was no 'flame.' Kyle enjoyed himself and she assured him that she had too but she lied. As ethical as she was as an attorney she knew the art of the technicality. She had enjoyed some of it but it did almost nothing for her. She knew she had been aroused, she knew the fluids from her body made it easier for him, but it did nothing for her as he thrust in and out of her. She wondered if it was because there was no emotional connection. She enjoyed the feel of him on top of her, she enjoyed the foreplay, the kissing, but the actual sex did nothing for her and she wondered, what was wrong with her?

The last week of her vacation she spent a lot of time with Kyle enjoying him. They went on boat rides and she got to pet the dolphins. She dove off reefs that some of the tourists would never see. She enjoyed herself immensely but no matter how often they had sex or 'made love' as Kyle put it, she felt nothing at the crucial moment. She wondered if Kyle even knew she faked the enjoyment.

Annie and her scuba friend had joined them for some of their excursions and Nia never felt uncomfortable with the fact that Annie was having a lesbian relationship. Nia shrugged it off as one of the unexplainable facts of life. Annie and her Ms. Right Now were none of her business but she could be friendly to the woman and found her to be fun. She could see why Annie would be friends with her but didn't understand the sexual side of their relationship at all.

Kyle and Annie's friend Mattie saw them both off as the hotel car drove them to the airport. For a holiday fling it had been a nice time but Nia was glad to be going back. Two weeks of sun and fun were enough for her. Annie looked a little down since she had enjoyed Mattie so much but she would bounce back shortly.

The five hour flight seemed endless as they sat and shared thoughts about the trip and what they had to come back to.

"You have to let me help you," Annie said as they discussed furnishing Nia's new apartment.

Nia laughed, she hadn't worried about it the whole while she was gone. She had checked in every two days at the office and nothing she couldn't handle by phone had come up. Furniture had started to arrive for her

office by the second week and Colleen was handling it. She couldn't imagine furnishing her apartment too. They discussed it for hours as they flew slowly north towards New York City. They took a cab to Nia's small apartment and shared her queen sized bed.

The next morning they were both up and laughing since they had nothing to wear but shorts and bikini's and these needed washing. Nia had two more days before she had to be back at work and they pulled on slacks and blouses to shop in some of the finer stores. Nia only wanted to window shop for her new furniture, she didn't want to buy anything until it could be delivered to her new apartment. Annie was fun and had her laughing at some of the more outrageous suggestions like the elephant planters or the giraffe statues she just *had* to have. Nia vaguely knew what she wanted and she made notes at what stores had what so she could come back and buy it when she was ready. She took salesmen's cards whenever she felt they were helpful and especially if they were on commission, she wanted them to get the credit if she did buy. She always felt working on commission was the biggest rip off.

Annie and she had a blast driving her Fiat out to the various luxury car lots to look at cars. Annie kept trying to steer her to Mercedes, BMW's, or even Porsche's but Nia saw nothing that really interested her and she was fine with her little Fiat. She didn't really see the point of getting another car, this was New York and cabs and the subway were available to a true New Yorker. She knew though that the other partner's wouldn't appreciate her eccentricity too long when she continued to park her Fiat at work. Her new parking spot would stick out like a sore thumb when she pulled in on Monday with her little old Fiat. They had a lot of fun 'trying' out the latest and greatest.

"So do I get to see this new apartment?" Annie asked as they sat on the edge of her bed watching television on her ancient small screened black and white TV from college and eating popcorn.

Nia looked around and commented dryly, "God this place is a dump," as they both collapsed into laughter and then tears over the small apartment.

They had discussed her buying some of the furniture they had been looking at and she couldn't imagine where she would store it until she could move into her new apartment. There was absolutely no room in this small apartment and she actually looked forward to moving out now that she had come to grips with the whole idea over the last three weeks.

Nia called Eleanor and found out that the apartment was already vacant and she would be able to move in approximately two weeks when all the paperwork had gone through. She was thrilled and surprised to hear that and made arrangements with Eleanor to see it again so that Annie could get a view of it.

"Oh my gawd, I'm going to have to get a partnership in a Manhattan law firm so I can have a place like this," she breathed in awe as she looked around admiring. Eleanor and Nia exchanged a look of amusement between them.

The place looked even bigger without the previous owner's furniture in it. The twenty foot walls were incredible and the place with its large windows just gave it a huge open appearance. The second floor was delightful with its warm wooden railings and 'loft' appearance. Nia was eager to move in and wondered if she could before the final paperwork had gone through but Eleanor told her no because what if something collapsed at the last minute and she was stuck in between the two places. It wouldn't be a ideal situation and Nia could see her point. Looking at the place though she realized the furniture she had already decided on would take up only a small fraction of the whole place. It was a place that you couldn't clutter up and since she didn't own a lot she wouldn't have a problem with that. As she looked in the kitchen she was grateful she didn't have to buy appliances and she had no idea what she would have put in the place of the high end ones that were left.

"You'd have to go to law school," Nia drawled in amusement at Annie's enthusiasm over her new home.

"Oh yeah, just one tiny hiccup," Annie dismissed with a wave of her hand.

They giggled in amusement and Eleanor was surprised to see this side of Nia Toyomoto. She had known her for many years and never known her to giggle. A lot had changed though about Nia. Before she had been nothing to look at but now with her contacts, her hair all curly and it was natural too, wearing makeup, and her tan from the Yucatan, she looked actually beautiful. In the right clothes she would be sexy as hell. Wait until the girls saw the new and improved Nia. None of them had seen her since before her promotion and makeover. They had heard about it and Eleanor made sure they knew about her new apartment that she had bought and the incredible deal she had gotten. Things like that paid off to spread the news for a realtor.

❧ CHAPTER FOUR ❧

At work the following morning Nia wasn't sure where to go, the old office or the new. She headed for her old one and was surprised when she opened the door to find an unfamiliar man working at her desk.

He looked up in surprise. "May I help you?"

She looked at him blankly for a moment and almost felt like he was trespassing. Looking around she realized that her things were gone from the office and then she realized that Colleen, her efficient assistant had done what she had said she would, she had moved their office. It was a relief because for a moment she thought she was out of a job. She smiled and said, "No, no, sorry, wrong office," and quickly closed the door. She was relieved he apparently hadn't recognized her but then these days she barely recognized herself.

She took the elevator up to the new level and breathed deeply to calm her nerves. She was suddenly excited and nervous all at once. Almost like the first time she had gone into court by herself. As she got off on the Executive level she turned to the left towards where her new office was located. As she walked down the hall the plush carpet under her feet even felt different as she passed the other offices heading for her corner. She opened the door and was surprised to see what Colleen had accomplished. It was warm, it was professional, and she loved it immediately. Colleen had obviously ordered furniture for her office to match Nia's taste and she liked what she saw. It spoke of class, it looked rich without being ostentatious, but the warmth from the dark woods make it appear like a professional attorney's office and Nia was thrilled, she couldn't wait to see her own office and walked across Colleen's to her own door and opened one of the double doors to enter. The furniture that had been ordered wasn't nearly enough to fill the large office she realized immediately but that was fine, what she had for now could be added to later. Right now the large desk with the matching credenza filled just one small section. Two large and deep seated chairs faced the desk and made it feel professional. A sectional sofa lined the corner of the two windows giving it a comfortable homey feel. A large coffee table in front of it could serve dual purposes when they had to spread out their paperwork. Colleen had either bought plants or brought them from home, Nia knew she grew her own and had a green thumb, but their added touch made the room feel good. To the left bookshelves lined the wall and she knew she hadn't ordered so many, she was pleased that Colleen had taken the initiative to order extra and they looked fine with the spines of her various law books filling the shelves. Plants here too, an antique clock, and a few knick

knacks completed the look. Nia was very pleased as she looked around. A door to her left led into her private bathroom.

"Oh you're here," the pretty little soprano voice said behind her as she stood looking around her new office. Nia whirled to smile delightedly at her assistant.

"It's beautiful!" Nia said with arms spread wide to encompass the whole office.

Colleen smiled in relief, she had worked so hard with the delivery men, the I.T. people, and accounting to have as much of the offices ready as possible for Nia's return. It had been a chaotic couple of days when she first got back from her own vacation and the things she had ordered that had already arrived had just been dumped in the two offices. She had moved their personal things herself and it had taken numerous trips but she had steadfastly refused to let anyone touch her boss's things and knew just where to put what. She was excited at the new things that were in her office too and it was a real pleasure to work in the beautiful new office, there would be room for a second desk when Nia deemed it necessary to hire a second assistant. "I'm so glad you like it. If you need me to order anything else, let me know."

Nia shook her head. "I can't think of a thing we need right now," she smiled. Colleen didn't accept compliments well but she deserved them. She did a fantastic job and this was obvious in so many ways.

"You look like you had a wonderful vacation," Colleen admired her tan and her new look.

The suit she was wearing was a lot better quality than what she had worn in the past. Her cheap suits were all delegated to the Goodwill bag, she had realized she couldn't mix or match those anymore now that she was in a more elite crowd. The suits she now wore were expensive and mixing the materials wasn't possible. A few of her blouses had survived the purge but not many. "Oh it was marvelous," she said. Her deep tan made her whole new look come together. The sun and the salt water had bleached the ends of her hair to a red tone and it looked totally natural. People paid hundreds of dollars for this look and she had gotten it naturally. The contacts, the makeup, the expensive suit, she looked like a partner now and yet totally unique. She told Colleen all she had done and seen and they sat in the wonderful new office for nearly an hour as they caught up. Colleen poured her a cappuccino from the small machine on her bookshelf. Colleen was envious of the trip but she couldn't help but think that it all couldn't happen to a nicer boss although there were many that would disagree with her.

After speaking so long on a personal level they got down to business. Colleen kept a tight rein on Nia's schedule. "You have a partner's meeting at half past twelve in the conference room, lunch is being catered," she

informed her. "Alex Montieth called and wants to discuss his case the moment you get back," she gave her a hundred little details as she went down her list and handed Nia a copy so she could go over it again at her leisure. Discussing certain things they both set off for work in their respective offices.

Half past twelve came and Nia was right on time but only because at twenty after Colleen had popped her head in to give her a heads up on the meeting. Nia was knee deep in work already and surprised how fast her morning had gone. She stopped in her bathroom, ran a brush through her hair that she hadn't put in a bun in over two weeks, refreshed her lipstick, checked her breath with a mint, and headed for the conference room on the other side of the building. When she walked in she was pleased to see Stewart Dunham.

Stewart stared in absolute stunned surprise when Nia walked in. She looked incredible! The potential had always been there but with the right clothes, the contacts, the makeup, and her marvelous tan she was breathtaking. He had been right, she was sexy as hell. He was amused by the reactions of several of the partners, some of whom didn't recognize this young attorney despite having worked with her for years. Even her walk was different, more confident. He was very pleased with their choice. "Everyone, I give you our newest partner here at Chase-Dunham, Ms. Nia Toyomoto!" he stood up to acknowledge her and began to clap. Everyone joined in and those who hadn't recognized her took a second and even a third look. It was amazing the transformation that they saw. There had been a few that hadn't seen the possibilities at all. One or two thought this was a totally different woman. A couple of the women narrowed their eyes realizing there was now competition in the looks department. Nia had never been competition before and they didn't like it in the least.

Lunch was catered and the hot dishes didn't appeal to Nia, she filled her plate with fruits and vegetables. Drinking a Mountain Dew she got a caffeine surge as she told people about her vacation down in the Yucatan Peninsula. People were amazed when she told them about scuba diving, zipping lining off through the trees, the incredible scenery. They were even more amazed to realize that this previously demure and non-descript woman had done all that she described. Many shook their heads in amazement at all the changes. Stewart was very happy with her.

After their luncheon they got down to business and this went quickly. Nia really didn't have anything to contribute as she had just gotten back but she listened attentively and offered help where she could. After the meeting Stewart walked with his arm around her shoulders back to her office. He stopped and stared at the transformation first in Colleen's office and then in Nia's. "This is amazing," he warmly stated as he looked around admiredly.

"I just picked out some of the furniture, this all came together thanks to Colleen and her expertise," Nia shared. She never took credit for other peoples work.

"I should have her decorate my office," he joked. He knew the value of a good secretary. Sally had been with him for years and knew him as well as his wife.

Nia lowered her voice so Colleen couldn't hear them as they looked out the incredible view from her windows. "Since I've been promoted up here, shouldn't Colleen as a P.A. to one of the partner's get a raise as well?" She hadn't wanted to bring up this issue to Colleen but she knew the poor girl could certainly use the money with a husband like Cletus.

Stewart looked at her in surprise. "Of course she gets a raise; take it up with Human Resources immediately. We can't have that around the water cooler you know that we are short changing our secretaries." Stewart was old school and rarely called a secretary a personal assistant or P.A.

Nia nodded in acknowledgement. There would be a few things she had to adjust to including the power she now wielded as a partner. She had seen Annie was right when she parked her little Fiat in the parking garage under their building, her parking spot had been clearly marked and surrounded by BMW's, Mercedes, Porsches, Maserati's, and even a Ferrari and a Lamborghini, she had been embarrassed. Protocol must be observed.

One of the firm's legal assistants came in with a pile of research that he had for her and Stewart left her so she could get back to work.

That night after work, she had stayed later to get a little ahead on the piles that despite her absence would pile up regardless; she invited Colleen out to dinner as she had stayed late as well. As they walked through the parking garage where a considerable number of the cars were gone there were still enough that she remarked to Colleen that she had to get a new car immediately.

"I don't know, I kind of like your sporty little Fiat," Colleen grinned up at her now beautiful boss. She admired a lot about Nia. Her natural beauty she had seen before the makeover but now she fit what Colleen had seen before. She was one of the toughest litigators she knew. She was fair, she was honest, and she was unbending where right was. She might bend the law but she would never break it. The 'art of the technicality' was indeed an art with this woman. She had come out of law school running and never stopped. Colleen had come to work for her five years ago and knew of no woman or man she admired more.

"Yes, I love it too but it doesn't exactly fit in with corporate America," she spread her arms to indicate the expensive sedans and sports cars still parked in the garage. She unlocked her driver's side door and then got in

to lean across and unlock Colleen's door. She pushed her briefcase to the back where it barely fit.

"I'll help you if you want an objective opinion," Colleen grinned. Her car was always on the fritz and Cletus always promised to fix it but never quite managed it. She didn't know what he did all day with his time but fixing her car, or rather 'their' car was not on his priority list.

"That would be great. I just don't know what I want," she backed out and they were soon driving through Manhattan towards a little cafe she liked across the island.

As they ate over dinner Nia discussed with her what she thought she wanted in a car other than four wheels. She wanted it to be sporty but also luxurious. She didn't like the style of a Porsche, a Jaguar, a Lamborghini, or a Maserati. She felt the Mercedes too clunky and didn't like the bulkiness of a BMW.

"What about an Audi or a Saab?" Colleen asked

"The Audi I don't know if they would think it too low end although from the prices I've seen it's as expensive as a Mercedes or the others. I don't like the style of the Saab."

"Have you ever considered a Lexus?" Colleen suggested.

Nia admitted she never had and asked Colleen what she knew. Never having shopped for a luxury automobile she admitted she didn't know anything except for ads in magazines or on the television but would find out for Nia in the morning and Nia knew she would.

It was raining when they finished their dinner and Nia insisted on driving Colleen home so she didn't have to take the train despite the distance she wouldn't hear no from Colleen and secretly Colleen was relieved. They arrived at her house and Colleen invited her in since she had driven so far out of her way. They were soaked when they got inside the little house. Nia laughed as she pulled her silk blouse away from her body. Colleen was embarrassed as Cletus was laying on the couch in boxer shorts and his stomach hanging over the edge outside of his t-shirt. He looked disgusting and his snores reverberated around the small living room. Colleen rushed to get a towel so Nia could dry herself.

"Do you want a drink?" Colleen offered wondering in her head if the kitchen was still clean with Cletus home all day.

Nia was still laughing at herself and her appearance, so much for a makeover. "No, I just wanted to make sure you got home safe," she smiled. "I better be heading back."

Colleen was sad to see her friend leave but also grateful that she saw nothing else that would embarrass her further.

Colleen had a few things printed out for Nia the next morning on Lexus sedan's and their sportier cars. Nia was pleased with the research that was done by the time she came in and she read what Colleen had collected and the location of several dealers in the greater New York area.

"Hey, are you doing anything after work?" Nia asked her assistant as she handed her a file.

Colleen shook her head in puzzlement.

"Would you like to go car shopping with me? I'll buy dinner," Nia offered.

Colleen was pleased. She hated going home these days. Cletus was getting angry over being supported by a 'mere' woman and she bore several bruises that were the result of that anger. The idea of being out with Nia and getting a delicious dinner out of it made her day. She could tell Cletus she needed to stay late for work.

They started a little farther out since the prices at this dealership would certainly be a lot more reasonable than anything that could be found in or near Manhattan. Nia and Colleen test drove several models and Nia was pleased with what they found. She had a lot of fun with Colleen and they enjoyed themselves immensely. She finally found a model she actually liked. It as a cross between a sports car and a sedan and it was a new design for Lexus. Its golden color and matching leather seats were beautiful. What really sold her though was that it as a convertible with a hardtop that folded back automatically behind the back seats at the push of a button. She fell in love with it and talking with Colleen she let her talk the salesman down in price. She was amazed at how aggressive Colleen could be. Her normal mousy demeanor really disappeared when she was fighting a battle on her boss's behalf. Nia was pleased with the terms, wrote a check for the down payment, and signed the lease papers. She let Colleen drive her Fiat back to her apartment as she drove her new toy herself. Parking the Fiat, Colleen ran to get into the passenger seat of the Lexus and they drove off to have a wonderful dinner together.

"God I love that car," Nia smiled at her assistant over the table.

"It's awesome," Colleen agreed as she looked through the features in the small magazine that had come with it. The radio alone would require a bachelor's degree to operate it was so sophisticated.

They talked about their impressions and went over the whole process as they ate Italian and drank sodas. Nia refused to drink alcohol if she knew she was going to drive and Colleen followed her boss's lead at all times. Nia happily drove her home and asked, "You're not going to get into trouble with Cletus are you?" she meant the lateness of the hour.

Colleen assured her that she wouldn't and hopped out of the fancy new car. She couldn't hope to ever own something this nice but she was happy for Nia who she knew deserved it.

The next morning Colleen got a call from Human Resources, never a good sign, and she reluctantly went down to their offices.

"Colleen, come in," Betty motioned her into the office.

"Good morning Betty, how are you?" Colleen said politely.

"I'm good, how are you?" Betty asked wondering how someone as good at litigation as Nia Toyomoto put up with this little mouse. She didn't have much of a personality. She would have laid bets five years ago that Colleen would have been gone within the first week of working for someone like Nia. They had gone through a few secretaries that couldn't cope with Nia. But she admired Colleen for putting up with the dragon lady and for Nia for putting up with the little mouse.

"I'm good, what did you want to see me about?" she asked feeling nervous, she could feel some sweat trickling down her back and hoped it wasn't coming through her blouse.

"Oh, I wanted to give you this," she indicated an envelope she had on her desk and handed it to Colleen who opened it immediately.

Her first thought was that it was a severance check but nothing indicated it was final. Also enclosed in the envelope were a few brochures outlining increased health benefits for her and her family. What was this? "What is this Betty?" she asked confused.

"Oh, it's your back pay for this month, I'm sorry; I didn't realize that no one had put in for your increase until Nia mentioned it to me yesterday. That catches us up and those benefits are retroactive to Nia's promotion date."

"I don't understand. Back pay? Why am I getting an increase?" she frowned, sure that somewhere there was a mistake.

"You didn't think with Nia's promotion that you wouldn't get an increase too? Top executives and their assistants get a different level of benefits than those of associates. Since Nia is a partner now and you are her assistant she wanted to make sure you were getting your full pay. I am sorry for the mix-up and I'd appreciate it if you didn't tell anyone of our mistake."

Colleen looked at the amount again and swallowed her surprise. "But Nia wasn't technically a partner until she returned?" she asked sure that there was a mistake being made and she would have to return this check.

"No, as soon as she signed the papers she was a partner and you her executive assistant," Betty assured her. "And please, don't tell anyone of the error?"

Assuring Betty she wouldn't say a word she rose and left the office going back up to the Executive level and her own office. Her thoughts were whirling at what this extra money could mean. She wondered for an instant if she could keep the extra money from Cletus and then realized that would be futile. He checked her paystubs and checking accounts. He kept track of almost every dime she spent. The few times she had managed to stash some mad money had made him angry and his confiscation of the extra money had been humiliating. She knew better than to keep things from him.

Colleen thanked Nia later for contacting Human Resources for her but Nia brushed it aside as she went on with her piles of work. She watched thoughtfully as Colleen went back to her own workload. She wondered how much of that increase Colleen would actually see. If it would allow her to buy new clothes or fix her car. At the thought of her car she got up and walked to Colleen's office.

"Colleen?" she waited until she looked up.

Colleen began to rise in preparation of following Nia into her own office but Nia waved her back to her seat.

"Are you planning on fixing your car or would you be interested in a new one?" she asked her assistant.

Colleen frowned in puzzlement. "I hadn't really thought about it but I can't afford a new one so I guess eventually we will fix my old one."

"Would you be interested in buying my Fiat?" Nia asked carefully knowing that Colleen could be prideful and not wanting to hurt her feelings.

"I don't think I could afford to buy your Fiat and I don't think Cletus would let me."

"Even if we arranged the payments to be taken directly from your check every week? Would you be interested then?" She watched her assistant carefully.

Colleen brightened for a moment before her face fell again, she couldn't do anything like that without Cletus' permission first. "I'll ask Cletus," she said resignedly.

Nia smiled and said, "Just let me know," before returning to her office. She felt bad now for having asked. She knew the phrase 'I'll ask Cletus' meant no. Even if the car had been given in an outright gift he wouldn't accept it. Anything, just to be contrary.

That night as Nia drove home she wondered how much longer until she would be in her new home. She was excited for it now and knew that it would be at least one or two more weeks and she was anxious after having seen it last Sunday with Annie. She wanted to have more space and as she packed up her books and small apartment she realized how much more 'space' she really would have. She could unpack the nine boxes she had

carted around all these years from her parent's home and finally live like a normal person instead of a hermit. She also wondered about parking space, it was at a premium all over but now with having the two cars she had to move every few days it was going to be a hassle, she hoped Colleen could take the Fiat off her hands to alleviate that hassle.

The answer from Cletus wasn't just a 'no' but a 'Hell no!' and she quietly told Nia a polite version of the conversation explaining that Cletus wasn't sure he wanted some foreign car that he couldn't fix. Nia was equally polite and didn't point out that the ancient Nissan Sentra that Colleen drove was made in Japan. She shrugged it off and proceeded to put the car up on Craigslist. It was gone within the week.

On Thursday Nia was due in court for one of their various clients. As she entered the courtroom she had forgotten her altered appearance. "Nia Toyomoto for the defense your honor," she called as she came forward on behalf of her client. The judge, his bailiff, and several other officers of the court looked at her in astonishment. She hadn't appeared in court in a month and what a month it had been apparently. She looked fabulous and it showed in so many ways. The judge actually found himself staring at her several times and caught himself in time to hear her argument to releasing her client on his own recognizance. She was vastly amused when the judge granted it sure he didn't really realize what he was granting but grateful she had one this small concession for her bad boy client. He was released and ordered to appear one month later which gave her time to build up a defense for his case.

Nia was surprised to hear Colleen on her intercom a week later. "Eleanor James to see you Ms. Toyomoto."

"Send her in."

Colleen did one better than that, she escorted Eleanor into the new office and watched as Eleanor's face lit up in delight at the decor and view in this office. "Can I get you anything Ms. James, coffee? Cappuccino?" she indicated the machine on the shelf but Eleanor declined and Colleen smiled and exited the office closing the door firmly.

"Wow, who died?" Eleanor asked when they were alone.

"Excuse me?" Nia asked confused but then saw the amusement in Eleanor's eyes as she looked around.

"Someone had to of died for you to get these digs," she continued.

Nia smiled and said, "Would you like to sit down?" she indicated the two chairs facing her desk but Eleanor shook her head and walked over to the windows for the view. Nia watched her amused as she looked down and out and even up to see every which way she could.

"This is something Nia," she smiled appreciatively.

"Yeah, ain't it though," she joked as she returned the smile.

"You really fell into it. From what I hear though you deserve it. How in the world did you get Dennis Fazzoli out?"

"How did you hear about that?" Nia asked surprised.

Eleanor looked at her knowingly and Nia realized the girls had probably gossiped. There was always someone who knew something.

"What can I do for you Eleanor?" Nia asked. She had a lot of work to do and playing games with her friend wasn't one of them.

"Actually I'm here to do something for you," she said and pulled a large manila envelope out of her shoulder suitcase and handed it to Nia.

Nia frowned and opened the envelope which wasn't sealed. Inside were contracts and other papers and a set of keys. As she began to scan them she realized she was now the legal owner of the apartment. She looked up in excitement at Eleanor. "That was fast," she commented.

"Not really, it's been more than a month you know," Eleanor pointed out.

"Has it really?" Nia had to think back and she realized that it had indeed been that long. With the promotion, her vacation, and her life altering she hadn't realized how quickly it really had gone by. She thought it would be another week at least. She was really pleased with this. "Can I move in now?" she asked unnecessarily.

"Yep, lock, stock, and barrel," Eleanor smiled.

"Damnnnnn," Nia said drawing it out as she realized she owned a home for the first time in her life. And what a home it would be! "Thank you Eleanor so much for your help."

"You're welcome Nia, I hope we will do business again someday." The commission she had gotten from this sale while not a full commission due to her friendship had still been a pretty penny. She pulled a bottle of wine from her case next and said, "Congratulations Nia, to your health, happiness, and prosperity!"

Nia thanked her and Eleanor was soon on her way, mission accomplished.

Nia sat there stunned for a moment as she looked over her papers. Some were copies of what she had signed a month ago. Some were between the bank and the law firm and were for the mortgage. Starting next month her payment would automatically be taken out of her salary and she needn't worry about on time payments. Her credit score would rocket to the moon.

"Nia, are you okay?" Colleen asked from the doorway. She was just sitting there; she didn't do that very often.

Nia looked up in startled surprise. She hadn't known how long she had been sitting there thinking about her new place. She smiled and said, "I just got the keys to my new home." She indicated the paperwork lying on her desk and the bottle of wine.

"Congratulations Nia, how exciting!" Colleen was thrilled for her; she knew how anxious she was to move. "When are you going to move, do you need help?"

Nia shook her head. "I have nowhere to park a U-Haul so I'm going to have some professional movers move my boxes, bed, and desk." How pathetic was that, she didn't own tables, chairs, or even a sofa. She could fix that though and the list was in her purse as she took Colleen up on her offer of help with promises of lunch and possibly dinner for her efforts.

❧ CHAPTER FIVE ❧

On Saturday the movers made quick work of the little furniture and the many boxes of books, few boxes of kitchen utensils, and the nine mystery boxes that Nia had stored in her apartment all these years. The price they charged her was outrageous but they must have figured Manhattan, she can afford it. Colleen had met her at her new apartment and helped her to change the locks. Nia hadn't even owned a screwdriver and Colleen showed her how to change them. The few boxes in their various spots looked pathetic and her mattresses while good needed a better bedstead than the one she had upstairs in the loft now. The desk was a disgrace and the small black and white TV an embarrassment and both consigned to Goodwill now that she has seen them in the space.

"Let's go shopping!" she said excitedly to her friend and personal assistant after the movers delivered her pathetically few things.

They had a blast going to the same stores that Nia had visited with Annie as well as a few on her own. Colleen was impressed with Nia's innate good taste, nothing too ostentatious or showy but good quality furniture and accessories. Nia hadn't had to buy anything in years and now had somewhere to put things, she had several somewheres and bought nothing on a whim, only after careful thought and a thorough consideration did she pull out her credit cards. The cards had rarely seen the light of day and were justifiably fatigued at the end of their day. Some of the stores promised same day delivery or next day and Nia knew she would be busy that evening and tomorrow. Since she was expecting the deliveries she couldn't go to more stores and she realized the few towels and dishes she had would have to be replaced or supplemented another day. Colleen volunteered to shop with her the following week after work.

Nia realized how much fun Colleen was outside of work. She had known on some levels after working with her for five years but this was different, this was social. She didn't know that Colleen had to lie through her teeth to get Cletus to allow her to work all these extra hours but Colleen was enjoying herself enormously and living vicariously through her lovely boss. She would have done anything for Nia. She was kind, she was generous, and she was a really wonderful person. The lightning swift litigator whose brilliance in the courtroom had garnered the firm an impressive clientele list was a different person these days and had always been different outside the courtroom. When others criticized Nia in the break room for her coolness and lack of warmth Colleen was her strongest defender.

On Monday they went shopping for new dishes, pots, and pans. Not that Nia cooked a lot but what she had was woefully inadequate. The dining room table she had ordered looked marvelous and she had no place settings or candles to set on it much less decent silverware or dishes. They ended up with two sets of dishware since Nia couldn't decide between the two different designs. She bought settings for twelve people since she figured she would be entertaining soon. Already word had spread at work that she was in a new apartment and Stewart had subtly suggested she have a housewarming party.

On Tuesday they went clothes shopping and Nia insisted on getting lingerie. She had never owned anything so fine and it looked glorious on her tall thin body. She found she had a yearning for lace and satin. She insisted on gifting Colleen with a couple of sets of nice lingerie for putting up with all the shopping. Colleen had refused at first but succumbed to Nia's gentle persuasion and accepted the gift. She tried to draw the line when Nia also bought her two suits that could be mixed and matched but trying to say no to Nia was very difficult.

"I can't afford this," she pleaded with her boss and friend.

"You're not buying it, I am!" she said cheerfully wanting to share with her friend and wanting to spruce up Colleen a bit. She knew how hard Colleen worked and she also knew that Cletus would never let her buy such nice things. That was confirmed when Colleen continued her arguments.

"I'm going to have the devil's own time explaining the lingerie to him as it is but I don't see how I can explain the suits," she pleaded.

Nia glanced at her and saw what a lovely women her assistant was, she looked very good in the suit she had tried on. "Tell him you need this 'uniform' for your new prestigious position in the firm. That might tell him that your increase in pay was so that you could buy such things."

Colleen looked at Nia guiltily. Cletus had been suspicious of the increase in pay and had accused her of sleeping with one of the partner's to get a leg up. If she hadn't worked for a woman he would have accused her of sleeping with her boss and made her quit. That thought made Colleen angry, that the only way she could get ahead would be to sleep around and not on her own talents. That was how Cletus worked though; he kept wearing her down and keeping her in her place. Things like this though tended to help her break out occasionally. She couldn't disappoint Nia. She was too kind to her, too generous, and she'd do anything for her, including defy Cletus. She accepted the present of clothes graciously.

Deliveries continued through the week. Nia couldn't be there for them all since she was in and out of court so she had a key made for Colleen. Colleen guarded the keys that included Nia's home, her offices, and her file drawers with her life. She loved being alone at Nia's apartment while

she waited for the delivery guys to buzz in and bring things upstairs in the elevator. She liked to pretend that she lived in this beautiful sun-filled apartment herself, and these beautiful things Nia had bought were really her own. She was so happy for her deserving boss. She saw how hard Nia worked. She didn't begrudge her one thing.

On Thursday morning Nia was brushing her teeth as she walked around her apartment looking at everything. The brown shades of the various Tiffany lamps gave the place a warm feeling. The display cabinets she had purchased had been delivered the previous day. It was time to unpack her nine boxes from her parent's home she had packed up so long ago. She didn't have time right now and it would have to wait for the weekend but she was actually looking forward to it. She didn't exactly remember what was in all of them any more after all this time. She realized as she looked down from the loft into the living room how nicely everything was coming together. It was then that she also realized that her beautiful place owed something to Colleens touch. Hung in antique hangers that swung out on either side of the windows were massive plants that put a finishing touch on the decor. Matching candle holders made it look homey. Nia knew she hadn't purchased either and she appreciated the touches that Colleen gave her beautiful new apartment. She would have to remember to water them sometime. She could imagine some night sitting on the beautiful set of couches she had purchased and lighting the candles and sitting there admiring the lights of the city that she could see outside her gigantic windows. The window treatments she had purchased were installed and hooked up so she could have some privacy if she wanted it.

She looked into the far corner of her apartment at the ridiculous electric fireplace she had allowed Colleen to talk her into. Its large wooden mantel was a nice contrast to the brick. It looked natural against the brick of the building as though it had been planned and Colleen had been right. She would love it on a snowy winter's day. She might even use it on a rainy day. The large flat screened television hanging on the wall above it looked modern and efficient, if she ever had time to watch it. Hooking up the speakers to her stereo and surround sound system she and Colleen had ended up in tears laughing over the complicated and yet so very simple directions. A prominent and brilliant attorney had been humbled by this simple set of instructions. The place looked almost lived in as she considered whatever other furniture and things she still needed to purchase. She thought perhaps she might purchase a fish tank, she enjoyed losing herself watching the fish swim back and forth but she knew she would have to hire a service to take care of it, she had no idea how to do anything with a fish tank, but it would look nice. It and a hundred other things were just the right touch for this immense space. There was still a lot of room despite her spending spree but she wanted to shop around and

now that she had the basics she was going to start antiquing, a guilty little pleasure that no one knew about.

She looked at the spare bedroom up in the loft. There was no furniture in there as of yet. In the master bedroom she had replaced her ugly bedstead and desk with new and solid wood furniture. She had almost duplicated the rich woods of her office for another office down under the loft of the apartment. She wanted to put up a wall to separate this space from the dining area since it was all open concept. Colleen had suggested she put up divider screens instead and she was thinking about that very idea. It would look very attractive if she could find the right designs. She didn't have a lot of time at the moment though; her busy court schedule had returned full swing since she had been home. Tonight would be the first night she got to see her girl group in over a month and she wasn't going to miss that.

Eleanor was the first to see Nia as she entered the restaurant. She smiled in almost evil glee as she anticipated the other women's' reactions. She had kept the group apprised of Nia's promotion and apartment purchase but she hadn't told them anything about Nia's makeover. The crisp business suit with chains holding the clasps across her stomach looked marvelous. Her hair which she now only wore in a bun for court was down and the riot of curls caught the lights of the restaurant in the red brown streaks that the sun had bestowed. Her tan was still evident and she looked sleek and healthy. Few of them had seen her without her glasses and with her new contacts and now with her wearing make-up she was stunning. Nadia and Millie were the first to realize who this knockout was as she made her way through the restaurant to their table.

"Oh my God!" Millie said as her jaw dropped open. Everyone turned to look and there were quite a few raised eyebrows.

"Holy Shit!" Nadia added.

"Nia?" Gail asked incredulously as she looked at the woman she had known for years. The change was unbelievable but yet Nia was easily recognizable or so Gail thought. She had just been hidden under a different look.

"Hi you guys, sorry I'm late, court ran over." She smiled as she sat at an empty chair slinging her purse and matching briefcase over the back. She looked around at the stunned looks. Six women stared at her dubiously. The seventh, Eleanor smiled at the surprise on everyone's face. Nia made up the eighth at their gathering that night. "Is something wrong?" she asked the table at large no longer aware of the drastic changes that she was comfortable with that had happened in the last month.

"You look incredible!" Nadia told her admiredly.

Several of the women nodded and Millie added, "You really do!"

"Well thank you!" Nia smiled at the compliments.

They excitedly began to ply her with questions about her promotion, her vacation, and her new apartment. Nia found herself manipulated into hosting next Thursday's gathering of their little group and throwing her very first dinner party. She wasn't sure how that came about really but it would get her feet wet when she had parties for work. When she mentioned it to Colleen the next morning she was thrilled when Colleen volunteered to help.

"I can't have a friend serve at my dinner party," she protested at first.

"Nonsense, you have that lovely kitchen. I'll whip up a few entrees and you supply the food and drinks. I'll give you a list or if you want I'll go out and get them for you," Colleen enthused, her eyes lighting up at the thought of that wonderful and modern kitchen she had so admired.

"Colleen, I'll pay you for it," Nia offered generously and then was immediately sorry for the offer when her friend's face fell.

"Nia, I want to help you as my friend. I think after all this time we both know you're not just my boss," Colleen explained, hiding her hurt feelings, then she brightened. "Besides, when else would I get the opportunity to cook in that lovely kitchen of yours!" she added excitedly.

Nia couldn't refuse, Colleen was actually enthused at the idea and besides, Nia couldn't cook. She hadn't bothered as a young child although her mother was an excellent cook and by the time she would have normally of learned she was too involved in her studies. School and then her career had kept her from learning other than the basics, she was sure she couldn't even boil an egg. Other than heating coffee every morning or making cold cereal her sophisticated kitchen hadn't been baptized. She would have bought platters from the market but that would have been lame and having it catered with the small gathering she was expecting would have been over kill.

She left it all up to Colleen and left her a credit card. At noon on most days when others usually were eating their lunches Colleen could be found at various stores picking up the makings for a veritable feast or so it seemed to Nia. She stocked Nia's refrigerator with things Nia frequently forgot to even bother with, simple things like ketchup and mustard. The cool little refrigerator for wine was now filled to capacity with cooling bottles of both red and white wines and extras stored in her walk in pantry on the specially designed shelves. Nia's bar was fully stocked as well. She hadn't realized she really had a bar but she supposed the countertop with the bar chairs she had assumed was a breakfast bar could second as a booze bar. The glasses underneath gleamed with the various bottles of alcohol that would please any connoisseur. Somewhere Colleen found a beautiful rack to hang above the bar and wine glasses hung upside down

from it. Nia was really pleased with her friend's ingenuity. She didn't have the time, she didn't always think that way, and she could see Colleen was enjoying herself so she didn't mind the expense.

Thursday night arrived and Nia had given Colleen the afternoon off so she could cook to her heart's content. Meatballs simmered in a crockpot. Deviled eggs were on a plate on the bar along with several other delicacies. Colleen had also baked and when Nia finally made her way into her apartment she could smell the rich aroma of cookies, cakes, and things she only smelled in bakeries. "What did you *do*?" she exclaimed when she saw the spread that Colleen laid out. It looked marvelous.

Colleen dimpled and said, "I know, I got carried away. But all ten of your girls will be here, apparently no one wanted to miss your little dinner party."

"Everyone is coming?" Nia asked incredulous. She couldn't remember when all ten of them had been together at the same time. Maybe for one of their weddings...

Colleen nodded and said, "Yes, Lila called the office today and she makes ten as well as a couple of them are bringing a friend."

Nia shook her head at her friend and personal assistant. "You *are* a *find*, do you know that?"

Colleen dimpled at the compliment and then smacked Nia's outstretched hand as she reached for a sample. "That's for your dinner party!" Colleen said to hide her embarrassment.

Nia was amused. Not since her mother had anyone dared to smack her. She turned to go upstairs and change her clothes.

The guests started to arrive and Eleanor was one of the first and handed Nia a large bottle of superb red wine. She insisted on giving herself a tour of the now furnished apartment. She admired Nia's exquisite taste in furniture and furnishings knowing there had been nothing in the apartment before. "You have *got* to furnish that spare bedroom," she commented as she accepted a glass of chilled white wine from Nia who was pouring.

Others showed up in one's and two's and Nia was busy buzzing them in to the secured apartment building. Talk flowed easily as it always did among these friends and as it was the first time all of them had been together in a long time they had a lot to catch up on. Nia was pleased to see her friends didn't treat Colleen as a servant and included her in the conversations. Her apartment was the main point of conversation and Colleen helped her remember little details that the others asked about. A few significant looks were shared by a couple of the women at this easy intimacy between boss and personal assistant but fortunately for Nia and Colleen they didn't see them.

"You need art for these marvelous walls," Nadia commented and several of the others agreed. That was what was missing and it lead to a

lively debate between the women about the various artists. Nia was pleased when Colleen contributed and was surprised to find her quite knowledgeable.

She served dinner buffet style and the women picked and chose from the various delicacies that Colleen offered. She threatened to poison Millie when she said that Steven Allen's work sucked compared to Harry Longard. The women complimented her on her dinner, it was absolutely delicious.

"Good thing too or you *would all have* been poisoned." Nia smiled, cooking was just not her strong suit.

"Maybe you should go into catering," Nadia said smilingly at Colleen as she sized her up speculatively.

Colleen laughed. "I happen to enjoy working for Nia. Cooking in this awesome kitchen was just a bonus."

Nadia's eyebrows rose in surprise, "You *like* cooking?"

She nodded enthusiastically. "With a kitchen like this who wouldn't." She went to put out the cookies, little cakes, and meringues she had made to go along with their coffees. Colleen wasn't so unaware of Nadia's interest as she pretended, it made her uncomfortable though, and she had never had a woman come on to her. She knew that she couldn't talk about it with Cletus though; he would accuse her of bringing it on herself, of having unnatural desires or worse yet he would encourage her to go for it, but only *if* he could watch. She didn't understand what women saw in other women but she could at least be accepting of their differences. She knew a couple of the women here were lesbians and partners and no one seemed uncomfortable with that fact. Others seemed to have a healthy appetite for men whether it be their husbands, lovers, or boyfriends. From the talk and their easy inclusion of her she enjoyed her evening fully.

"You don't have to do that!" Nia exclaimed as the evening was over and they were both cleaning up.

"Nonsense, just a few minutes and it will be all done." Colleen laughed as Nia sloshed meatball sauce on the counter.

It didn't take a few minutes but working companionably it was quickly accomplished. The leftovers in Tupperware that Nia didn't know she even owned, her kitchen was well stocked with leftovers and snacks.

"I want to thank you for all your help," Nia said as she watched Colleen wipe off the counters one last time.

Colleen looked up and smiled into her beautiful bosses face. "I actually enjoyed it very much. Your friends are terrific."

"Hey, I'd say you made a few friends of your own here tonight." Nia didn't mind. They were an eclectic group and Colleen had made a good impression and fit right in. It had helped that they were hungry and Colleen's offerings had been delicious.

Colleen smiled. It was getting quite late and she still had to grab the train out to her home. She rinsed off the dish rag and hung it to dry. Looking around the kitchen one more time to be sure all was spotless she headed to get her coat.

"Did you get your car fixed?" Nia asked as she watched Colleen getting ready to leave.

Colleen looked at her sheepishly and shook her head. "I don't think it's revivable."

Nia was annoyed. She knew that Colleen made a decent salary but with an unemployed husband such as Cletus it had to be draining her resources. Nothing showed on her face as she went to her own purse and pulled out her car keys. "Here, take my car and pick me up in the morning," she offered generously.

Colleen shook her head immediately. "Oh no, I couldn't..."

Nia took on the cold litigator's voice she used in court that brooked no interference or rebuttal. "It's dangerous to get on the trains this late at night, take my car, park it somewhere reasonably safe and set the alarm. I don't want you walking to the train and riding it back at this hour. Your other choice is to let me pay for a cab." She looked at her assistant in concern despite her cold voice.

Colleen warmed at the words of warning. She knew her friend was just looking out for her and had her best interests at heart. She hadn't been looking forward to the long ride on the train, the cab would be outrageously expensive and having Nia's car would be sheer luxury. She looked gratefully at Nia and enveloped her in a hug as she said, "Thank you Nia, I'll take good care of it."

Nia hugged her back warmly and said, "Don't forget to pick me up in the morning!"

Colleen carefully maneuvered the Lexus through Manhattan traffic. Despite the late hour, the city never slept. She went through the tunnel to get out towards the Bronx and head home. The train might have been faster, it didn't have to contend with late night traffic, but it would have been infinitely more dangerous at this late hour. She parked it in a little used alleyway behind their house and set the alarm. Driving it had been a dream and she had enjoyed it immensely. Her whole evening had been a dream. The women had been friendly and kind and Eleanor James had even offered her a job any time she wanted to leave Chase-Dunham. She loved her job too much and working with Nia was fairly easy and infinitely interesting. She also knew that Eleanor James had looked at her as though she were the entree instead of the offerings she had made and while she was flattered at the offer she knew she wouldn't be comfortable around a lesbian such Eleanor James. Despite the subtle hints she had received, offers really, she had had a wonderful evening and driving the

car capped it off. As she went in the back door of her home she was riding high and it all came crashing to a halt.

"Where have you been you slut?" a vicious slurred voice asked disparagingly.

Colleen looked up frightfully at the image of her husband as he staggered into the kitchen. He was wearing boxers that gaped open exposing himself and a t-shirt known as a 'wife-beater' that didn't quite fit him, his stomach hung over grotesquely as it gaped out the bottom. "I told you I had to work late," she said quietly. She didn't raise her voice; it would do no good if she did. Cletus didn't respond well to anger. He didn't respond well to anything these days. He blamed the world for his unemployment and not his own slovenly appearance or surly behavior. It was everyone else's fault that he didn't have a job that wasn't beneath him. The truth was that he could have had a job but wouldn't stoop to working in a fast food restaurant or sweeping floors. These were all menial jobs reserved for illegals or so he thought. Someone had to do it and it wasn't Cletus.

"Yea, but you didn't say this late!" he said harshly as he swigged a beer. The slurping sound disgusted Colleen.

She looked at him and wondered for the millionth time how she had come into this nightmare. It hadn't always been this way. He had been a good looking man at one time with a promising job at a garage. He was a good mechanic when he wasn't drinking or snorting cocaine. His problem had always been his ego though. He thought he was better looking than he actually was. He thought he was a better mechanic than anyone else. He thought he was above the law and anyone who had a better education than he did just didn't have his 'street smarts.' She wondered what he had seen in her when she had met him to have her car fixed, the same car that sat uselessly in their garage with the door hanging ajar, something else that needed fixing around this dump that they lived in. Having just come from Nia's immaculate apartment and its new furnishings it felt terribly run down walking into her own home. It stank too. Not just from the beer bottles lying around that she tried to stay on top of but from body odors from her husband and his untidy habits. "I'm sorry; I didn't know it would run this late."

Cletus looked out the side window where the Lexus was parked. "Who's that?" he slurred as he looked at it blurrily.

"It's Nia's. She didn't want me to take the train." She couldn't lie; it wouldn't do her any good anyway. She just wanted this conversation over so she could shower and go to bed. She didn't want to anger him further; she could see he was boiling mad over her late hours.

"It's Nia's," he mimicked in a strange voice. "Christ, you see that woman more than you do me!" his voice took on an ominous note and Colleen almost visibly cringed from it.

"I'm sorry Cletus but it's my job. With the promotion there is a lot more work to do," she tried to explain.

"Maybe you shouldn't have taken that promotion," he snarled as he turned back to her and started for her.

Colleen held her ground and didn't answer. Sometimes it was best to just not answer.

"You spend more time at that office than you do at home taking care of me! It's your job to take care of me!" he snarled. He reached out to touch her and Colleen barely avoided flinching. He noticed it though, his eyes narrowed through their blurry haze. "If I didn't know better I'd swear you were avoiding me," the menace in his voice was apparent.

Colleen tried very hard not to tremble as he gripped her hair in his dirty hands. Despite washing strenuously with soaps and detergents his hands always looked greasy from the work he did on engines when he wasn't eating the food and beer that she bought. He worked a lot for friends who paid him under the table but Colleen never saw a dime of it. She knew he spent a lot of time in bars and went to friends' houses to 'work' or share drugs. He had a fairly large friend base who she knew their only thing in common was a need for drugs and desire not to do any real work.

Cletus pulled her head back by her hair to look her over. She looked nice in the new clothes that Nia had bought her. He didn't like the improvements. He thought she should dress down but he couldn't argue with the 'uniform' that she had to wear to the fancy smancy Manhattan law firm she worked for. It provided them with enough money that he didn't have to work. With the money he made under the table from repairing cars and dealing drugs he thought they were doing very well. He had no desire to go back to work. What he didn't realize or was too stupid to see was that every month they lost a little more, fell a little more behind. Eventually it would catch up with them. He leaned over her and she looked at him frightened, in his beer soaked mind he thought she was looking at him adoringly and he ground his mouth down on her lips. His beer breath nearly gagged her but she accepted it stoically. His beer spilled down the back of her skirt as he took her in his arms and started to grind against her immediately in his rising lust.

Colleen didn't bother to fight. It wouldn't do to resist anyway, he would just over power her and enjoy doing it. She had found that out much to her detriment early on. He liked to hurt her sometimes, howling in ecstasy when he taught her 'her place.' She had thought of leaving countless times but knew her father wouldn't support her in her decision and her own mother was too beat down to help her. Her father was just

like Cletus and thought him a fine upstanding man. If his daughter needed smacking around a little to bring her in line well that was what husbands did.

"You think your better than me don't you bitch?" he asked as he began raising her skirt dropping the beer bottle on the already littered kitchen floor as he ground against her. Already his erection was apparent through his boxers.

Colleen tried not to shudder in disgust as she didn't answer. Apparently he hadn't just been drinking that night which would normally render him impotent much to his shame and anger; it would of course be all her fault and never his when this happened. He must have taken drugs tonight and she hoped he hadn't snorted cocaine or she was in for a marathon session of sex. Cletus never thought of using a condom or worried about her arousal, it was always about him and his needs. There were many times she winced at the dryness and he slapped her for not becoming aroused when 'he' wanted to screw.

Cletus lifted her skirt and tore at her pantyhose which thwarted him for only a moment. Colleen did flinch as they tore from her sensitive legs. He ruined the nice panties Nia had gifted her with in his haste to have his way with her. She couldn't consider it rape since she didn't resist but he bent her over the counter and thrust inside her grunting like an animal. She certainly hadn't been aroused and the pain of his invasion on her dry privates made her try to unconsciously pull away. He grabbed her arm in one hand and her hip in the other as he thrust into her sucking on her nipple through her blouse. She wondered if he even knew she wasn't undressed. It only took a few minutes before he felt relief and let her fall where she had stood taking his abuse. She must have her period since blood was on his penis and he looked down at it in disgust as he tucked it into his boxer shorts. "You dumb bitch, you might've said something," he said as he backhanded her across the face and watched her fall. He grabbed her arm painfully again as he pulled her up from the littered floor. "Clean this place up," he snarled.

Despite the pain from between her legs, despite the pain in her arm and hip where he had grabbed her, despite the fatigue from a full day's work and the trip back, she began to gather up the debris off the floor and on the counters. Cletus watched her satisfied that she was obeying him before he staggered off to the living room to watch television. "Cable's out again," he called as though nothing had happened.

'*Why hadn't he paid the bill?*' she thought as she worked but she knew any money she left to pay any bill would never see the right source. Her paychecks were now automatically deposited and the bills automatically withdrawn. She must have forgotten to set up the cable company on that and resolved to take care of that in the morning from work. She had to

make sure she took out the rent right away too before Cletus got a hold of the rest of the money with the atm card, if she didn't it wouldn't get paid.

It took her another hour to finish the kitchen to its normal pristine condition that Colleen liked. It had been a few days since she had cleaned it but Cletus must have had friends over with the condition it had been in when she got home. As she walked down the hallway to their living room hoping to finally make it to bed she realized what a mess the living room was in as well and hoped he wouldn't expect her to clean this too, but she was grateful to find he was sound asleep on the couch snoring away, his shorts exposing him again. She climbed the steps wearily hoping he would sleep the night on the couch as she made her way to the bathroom and took a shower. She would have taken a bath to soak her sore muscles but thought that unwise, she'd fall asleep in the tub in her exhaustion. She set her alarm giving herself extra time to get ready in the morning and pick up Nia. Putting the thoughts of what had happened when she got home aside she went to sleep dreaming about the party she had put together for Nia.

"Good Morning!" Colleen smiled as Nia slipped into the passenger seat of the Lexus parked in front of her building.

Nia smiled in return handing Colleen a cup that smelled heavenly from the rich cappuccino she knew it would contain. "Did you sleep well?" Nia asked in return as she strapped on her seat belt.

Not a feature changed as Colleen hid behind her sunglasses and assured her boss that she had. She didn't tell her that she hadn't slept after a horny Cletus came back to bed. The horror of the previous night was behind her and she looked forward to working for Nia that day and escaping the horrors of her home life for a few hours. It was sunny and a beautiful morning in Manhattan, what a glorious day it looked like ahead of them.

It was midmorning when Nia handed Colleen a new file for a new client she had just finished interviewing. Nia glanced down as Colleen reached and instead she dropped the folder to grab Colleen's outstretched arm. Colleen tried not to wince but the flinching she did told its own tale. Nia stared in horror at the bruise that showed under Colleen's long sleeved blouse. The blouse was white and went all the way down her arm to her wrist but had ridden up as she reached for the file. "What the hell?" Nia asked as she examined the bruise. It was obvious it was made from a hand gripping her arm as she could almost perfectly see the finger marks.

"Nia, it was an accident," Colleen said quietly as she tried to pull her arm back but Nia wouldn't let it go. A tug of war ensued and Nia stopped it with a look.

"You have to report this," she hissed as she looked into Colleen's eyes with anger.

Colleen took a deep breath. She had hid other bruises and worse before, she could manage these new ones. She didn't meet Nia's eyes when she lied for the millionth time. "Cletus and I like it a little rough," she said blushing at the thought. Cletus liked it rough, she didn't.

Nia didn't have enough experience sexually to debate that. She had heard her friends talk about playful rough sex but she wasn't certain. This definitely wasn't her area of expertise. She let Colleen's arm go as she eyed her suspiciously. She thought she and Colleen had such a good friendship, not just that of boss and employee, that she bought the lie.

❈ CHAPTER SIX ❈

That weekend Nia began to unpack the nine boxes she had hauled around for so many years. It brought pleasure and memories as she unpacked trinkets, pictures, and junk. A large ornately carved dragon in green jade was placed on the mantelpiece above the fireplace. It gleamed with the polish she gave it as she looked at it stretched out on the ledge like it belonged there, like it had always *been* there. It brought back pleasant memories of her proud Japanese father and his equally proud heritage as she remembered him telling her stories. He would have been proud of her success but unhappy that she didn't have a man or children in her life. She wasn't sure she could have both and her career. She wasn't going to worry about it though.

A large carved box contained a mechanism that looked like a scaled down model of a phonograph. Instead of a needle it contained a comb of teeth. Carefully wrapped plates beside it revealed saw like blades with little rises punched in them, she unwrapped one and placed it on the mechanism. She carefully wound a rather serious key in the mechanism and pushed a hidden catch. The plate turned and beautiful music came from the box. As the plate turned the little rises hit the teeth and pinged out perfect notes. She had always marveled at this box and her mother had only brought it out only on special occasions. The German words on the carefully wrapped plates reminded her of the other side of her heritage, her German mother. She was drawn nearly to tears remembering the big robust woman who she missed dearly. She changed the plates and turned the key periodically as she unpacked the remaining boxes and their contents. Listening to the pinging tunes that were on the discs brought back many childhood memories of both her parents.

There were figurines and vases that she had no remembrance of. They must have had some significance when she packed them up after her mother's death but she didn't remember them now. She placed them on the display shelves; they looked beautiful, she hoped she would have the memories come back, someday. Only after she had gone through all the newspapers making sure she had gotten every trinket, everything out of the packing material did she begin to gather it up using a garbage bag and throwing it all in her compactor. The boxes were in terrible shape after all these years of moving them about and storing them and she collapsed them and left them by the door to take them down to the recycle station at the back of the building.

She sat down to enjoy the photo albums she had unpacked and placed on her coffee table. The afternoon passed pleasantly as she went down

memory lane. She had had a pretty average childhood or so she had thought as she looked at the pictures. Frequent smiles were returned to the faces she saw smiling out at her from the albums. The memories were too much occasionally but she got through them all during her long afternoon. As she closed the last book and took a stack to the cabinet below her display she lovingly packed them away in order. They didn't have to be out all the time for her to enjoy them. The framed pictures she placed in order of importance, at least to her, on top of the book shelves. She loved that her parents could see her new apartment, they were a part of her, she missed them desperately but they had been gone a long time. It didn't hurt less that they had died so long ago, the pain was always fresh but she suppressed it and moved on with her life. She liked to think though that they looked out at her from their frames and approved of her new apartment and new life. The pictures of her in various stages of growth, her graduations, her achievements, she placed along with her parents. It gave the apartment a homey feeling or so she felt with her ancestors and her memories around her.

She lay on her couch sprawled out in the early evening as she watched the shadows created by the light coming through her beautiful apartment windows. The plants didn't need watering and she suspected Colleen had made sure of that when she was over the other evening. She was so efficient that way. Nia wondered what kind of rough sex she enjoyed that caused the bruises on her arms and occasionally her legs that she had seen over the years. She had thought Cletus was hurting her but Colleen had assured her many times that it was just part of their sex life and Nia bought it. She didn't wonder long as she lay there enjoying doing absolutely nothing. That wasn't a common occurrence for her and she dozed in the early evening sunlight and woke to being ravenously hungry. She checked out her now full refrigerator thanks to Colleen and chose some deviled eggs and a fruit salad for her dinner. She had just sat down to eat when she heard the door buzzer.

"Hello?" she answered from the kitchen pushing the button to be heard. She hadn't activated her television monitor to see who was standing there.

"Hey bitch, let me in," Annie's voice came over the tinny intercom.

Nia's face broke into a large smile as she buzzed her best friend in. This was a nice surprise! She hadn't seen Annie since they had gotten back from Mexico. They had spoken of course but Nia never made it to Connecticut and Annie made the trip to the city so seldom. She put out another plate, silverware, and a wine glass before she walked over to her front door and opened it having heard the elevator ding at the end of the corridor. She popped her head out to see Annie looking fabulous as she walked the hall to her apartment. "What are you doing in the city?" she smiled as she enveloped her best friend in a hug.

"I decided it was time to see this outrageous apartment," she said as she returned the hug and then slipped past Nia to go inside. Having seen it bare the transformation was incredible. Not just the beautiful furniture but the plants, the knick knacks. It looked like a home. She had seen the hovel Nia had lived in before many times and this was a vast improvement. It showed style, it showed sophistication. Not that she had doubted Nia having any; she just hadn't taken the time to enjoy it. This transformation was amazing as she nosed around. "You have to do something with this bedroom!" she exclaimed when she found the empty room.

"I know, I know, but I haven't found what I want to put in it yet. It's not like I have visitors or anyone," Nia shrugged.

"You do now...where the heck am I going to sleep?" Annie grinned.

"I do have a couch," Nia said dryly before shepherding her friend down the stairs. "Have you eaten?"

They shared a delicious meal together and polished off two bottles as they caught up. Not that they didn't speak often by phone but in person it was so much different to see each other's faces and nuances. As Annie went into the kitchen to help herself to something else she looked into the refrigerator and was surprised. "Who cooked all this?" she asked.

"Who says I didn't?" Nia asked blandly trying hard to maintain an innocent expression.

"Ah, babe, I know you too well and cooking isn't your forte." Annie looked at her with a sardonic look.

Nia grinned. "Your right, actually Colleen insisted on cooking for my little get together on Thursday, isn't it marvelous?"

Annie popped a cold meatball into her mouth and nodded enthusiastically. They stayed up late and chatted about everything that two old friends could. As Nia started to yawn she cut it off abruptly when Annie asked bluntly, "So what are you going to do about sex?"

"What?" she was startled.

"Well jeezus, you're not a nun. Taking the bar exam was not a vow of celibacy," Annie rolled her eyes.

"I've had sex." Nia grinned as she said it so primly.

"That fling on vacation was what the first time in years?"

Nia shrugged. "I'm choosy."

Annie rolled her eyes again. "You need to get out there honey and get a relationship. You have this great home and no one to share it with."

"I don't need a relationship to feel whole. Yes I do have this great apartment. I've worked many years to have things like this. Nowhere does it say I have to share it with anyone."

"That's just it hon, you've worked forever. When does Nia get to enjoy life?"

"I have a lot of responsibilities as a partner of Chase-Dunham. I can't slack off now."

"I'm not saying you should slack off. Don't you think you'd be well rounded if you got laid more often or someone was in your life to enjoy it?"

"I rarely have the time..." Nia started.

"You make the time when it's important. Look at your Thursdays. Look at the shopping you had to do. You don't have to work all the time Nia."

"Maybe I like to work, did you ever think of that." Nia was trying hard not to become angry at her well-meaning friend.

"Yes." She nodded. "I know you love your work. You deserve everything you have achieved because you worked hard for it. I just don't want you dying all shriveled up and an old maid."

"I don't need a man to complete me," she said sounding peeved.

"Who says it has to be a man?" Annie grinned.

Nia shook her head at her friend. "I haven't jumped the fence, I'll let you know when I do, okay?" She threw a couch pillow at Annie's head as she rose up from the couch to end the conversation.

Nia shared her bed with Annie and they giggled like schoolgirls. They had been best friends forever and although Annie might swing both ways she had never crossed that line with Nia and for that Nia was grateful and comfortable with Annie's sexuality.

On Sunday they went shopping together which Annie said was only an excuse to spend money and that was the reason she came to the city, not *just* to see Nia. She begged Nia to let her drive her beautiful Lexus but Nia, knowing Annie's penchant for speed and getting easily distracted wouldn't let her. Even taking her down to the train station at the end of the day she wouldn't let her drive the expensive automobile. She hugged and kissed her friend goodbye as she got out. It was the end of a nearly perfect weekend she thought as she went back to her apartment.

She thought about what Annie had said about her being alone. It wasn't that she wanted to be alone, she really didn't, but the few relationships she had over the years did nothing for her. She got more satisfaction out of her work than she did from people. The circle of friends she had was enough she felt and she didn't need to mess that up at this point.

Nia held several company and client dinner parties at her wonderful apartment as the summer progressed. The first time Stewart Dunham came to one he was suitably impressed. He thought this an excellent apartment for their young partner. It showed taste, it showed style and flair he hadn't thought she had. The plants and knick knacks made it homey. He particularly admired the jade dragon on her mantelpiece and

that's when it really hit home her Japanese heritage if her last name hadn't before. To look at her you would never had known she was Eurasian. The clients who came to her dinner parties always left very impressed with her casual manner, it created an illusion about the new partner that people enjoyed, no longer *just* the incredible attorney that everyone respected and admired.

Nia usually hired caterers when she had these parties no matter how small they were. She knew she couldn't impose on Colleen for them. She had appreciated what she had done for her and her friends, in fact she had invited Colleen to several more of those over the months but Colleen couldn't always get away to attend. She just didn't want her friend and assistant to feel she was being taken advantage of by doing all the work. She enjoyed getting to know her better within her circle of friends and they certainly welcomed Colleen whenever she could make it and a few of the other women brought friends they thought their group would enjoy expanding their circle.

❧ CHAPTER SEVEN ☙

Late in summer Nia was reviewing paperwork and the television was droning in the background. It was a rerun of ER and the new season wasn't due for a few weeks. She absentmindedly watched it as she considered the wording of the papers she was going over. She didn't really follow many television programs but this one occasionally caught her attention. Tonight it had an episode about Kerry Weaver and some blonde psychiatrist. She realized as she watched that they had introduced a 'gay' element to the show. She wasn't sure she felt comfortable about it as she began to watch. She found herself watching the psychiatrist closely. Once the episode ended she wasn't sure how it made her feel. She remembered various shows over the years that introduced the 'gay' element and their ratings suffered. She wondered if this one would lose out too. She didn't consider herself homophobic but she was certain mainstream America was. It was why shows like Ellen had gone under from pressure with the networks. She had heard of other shows as well but as she didn't watch much television she couldn't really tell any gay characters on it. The psychiatrist stayed in her mind for days.

Over the weeks and then months she found herself making sure to watch ER faithfully. She wasn't sure why but the storyline with the characters of Kerry Weaver and Kim Legaspi fascinated her. Not that she found Kerry attractive, the actress was pretty but the character she found annoying. It was the pretty blonde psychiatrist Kim that began to wear on her thoughts. It worried her though as she found herself eagerly anticipating any air time between the two characters and their ill-fated romance as the weeks went by. She found herself thinking about the character played by the actress Elizabeth Mitchell many times as she went to bed. It started to give her wet dreams and this more than anything disturbed her. When the reruns played out and the characters separated she didn't know if she was more upset by it than the characters were. It had gotten her thinking though. If I get this horny over a story, maybe I should do something about it. I haven't been with a man since Mexico, but when would I find the time? Then she thought about sex toys and taking care of it herself. But what to buy? If she mentioned it to the girls on Thursdays they would ask endless questions that would embarrass the hell out of her. Although Colleen was a friend as well as her assistant, they just didn't have that type of a relationship. Besides, Colleen came on Thursdays occasionally and while Nia was sure she would be discrete, she just didn't want to take the chance with those friends. Annie too would want to know details and never would she share the wet dreams and

restless moments she had been having for weeks. Although Annie of all people would understand, she just didn't feel comfortable discussing it with her.

She didn't know where to turn or who to ask. She thought about going into a sex shop but the thought of going into one of those places totally turned her off. What if someone saw her? Not that she really cared but some things must remain private. She began surfing the internet looking at the various toys available. It was an incredible amount of information and she was soon confused about it all. She thought if she chose one that looked like a man's penis at least that would be the way to go. Then she thought she should buy one that plugged in because she didn't want to have to be buying batteries all the time, that would be a giveaway. She finally decided on one and sent off for it. The thought of it had her horny. She felt herself getting wet at the thought that maybe this toy could give her that elusive orgasm she had always wanted and never achieved. It would be a shame to be over 31 before she had her first. She didn't want to die someday without experiencing it once.

When the package arrived she was relieved it was in a plain brown wrapper. They had promised 'discrete' packaging and they hadn't lied. As she unwrapped the package in her bedroom she wasn't sure what to expect other than what she had read on line. She only knew she was anxious and hoped that it would do what she wanted. It was exactly what the ad had said. Shaped in a man's penis it was an orange pink color, almost skin color, just not quite. It had a small plug in near one end where the cord plugged in like the plug on headphones and the other end into an outlet. At the base was a turn knob that made it vibrate higher or lower. As she looked at it she thought it looked a little gross but she had been thinking about this for too long not to try it out. She looked around her bedroom wondering if she should wait until dark but then thought who the hell cares or would know?

She got herself undressed from work and cleaned up the wrapping papers being careful to put the receipt aside in case it broke and she had to exchange it. That was an even more gross thought. She plugged it in and tried out the various settings and then put it aside to lay there and think. She could feel she was wet, hell she always felt wet these days, she had taken to wearing panty liners to protect the beautiful lingerie she wore. They ended up sopping wet quite frequently and not for any reason she could think of except when she had erotic thoughts. She knew her thoughts could help her achieve an orgasm, she had read that on the internet but she really had no idea when to insert the vibe. She lay there for a while thinking about it and then began to think about the characters on ER and what it might feel like to be with that person. The thought of wanting that person to touch you, to kiss you, to be against you did

something for her as she fantasized. It wasn't long until she began to feel aroused and wet. She reached for the vibe and gently inserted it between her legs. It felt very cold and she felt a little ridiculous. She imagined her lover inserting it and that helped. It finally was in as far as she was going to let it and she turned it on its lowest setting. The vibrations made it feel very uncomfortable instead of arousing as she had thought it would. She tried various settings but nothing worked, not the least arousing. After a while she gave up in despair and annoyance. She didn't know what she was doing and it wasn't helping the wetness that she did have. There was nothing happening that she could tell. Even less than the men she had allowed access to her body. Nothing happened then either as they poked or prodded her body. She felt like a failure on this level and then realized she just didn't know. Who could she ask though? She thought about it as she pulled the vibe out and unplugged it and then took it into the bathroom to carefully wash it. She tucked it carefully in her underwear drawer knowing how embarrassed she was by the whole situation. She felt frustrated as she threw out the package wrappings. She wouldn't be returning the toy, it wasn't defective, and she wondered if she was.

She powered up her home computer in her office under the spare bedroom. She still hadn't gotten those beautiful room separators she had imagined so long ago, she really hadn't had the time to furniture shop in the last few months, her case load, the parties; her 'social' life had kept her quite busy. She could ask Colleen to do it for her but she really wanted to find it herself. She clicked on AOL and checked her mail. Her pop up blocker clicked and she heard a tone indicating it was repelling something, she was grateful for that as well as her excellent virus blocker because she had heard that AOL had the most viruses on its network than any other but she liked it for a number of reasons. One of them was that easy access to chat rooms. It gave her an anonymity that she certainly didn't have in public. Certain circles in Manhattan were very small and as a partner in Chase-Dunham she had to keep a certain decorum at all times. The chat room gave her a freedom from that, not that she had been on frequently, she really had no time but she knew about where things were and headed there tonight. With the thoughts about the character Kim Legaspi swirling around in her head she clicked on the gay and lesbian chat sites, she figured what the heck, who would know? She was surprised at the amount of them that came on. There were ones created by AOL and ones created by users. She clicked on the ones created by users because that seemed more real to her, made by 'real' people. She steered clear of the ones that read 'butch' because for some reason this frightened her, she wasn't ready for that. She found one that read Lesbians 30's and went into that one and then watched the lines of text come up as people 'chatted' and she read. She was surprised when she heard a ping of someone trying to instant

message her. She looked at the separate box and saw that a 'foxyroxy' was trying to get her attention. She looked at the list of people in the chat room and saw that 'foxyroxy' was in the chat room too.

She clicked on the box and saw: "Hi there, you don't have a profile?"

She thought for a moment and then typed: "No, I don't have a profile, I'm new to this."

There was a moment while the user must have read her reply before she responded: "How do I know you're not a guy?"

Nia was surprised at the question and naively typed back: "Because this is a lesbian chat room?"

"That don't mean nothing," the rude response was typed back.

Nia didn't know what to type. She hadn't come into the chat room to be attacked or defend herself but for information. She thought perhaps she could ask someone how to use her new toy but hadn't felt brave enough yet to ask as she watched the typed conversations scrolling up. She didn't know who this 'foxyroxy' was but she was rude. Nia clicked out of the room and off the internet. She didn't know what to do but had a lot of thinking to do. She had better things to do than to spend time on the internet anyway.

Over the next few weeks Nia was too busy to worry about her sex life much less her lack of one with the caseload that she had. She worked long and hard, many was the time she had to get home late and fall into bed before dragging her butt out of bed early to start an equally busy day again and again. It was very tiring. She didn't give up her Thursdays and one night the conversation turned to sex and toys and she listened avidly, not contributing, but taking mental notes. There was much hilarity over the subject and she felt herself blushing as she hid it behind laughter but she didn't feel she learned much as the innuendo and sly remarks went over her head. She felt stupid and she knew she couldn't ask these sophisticated women about her problem. She went home that night feeling inadequate. It made her angry. She was an intelligent woman. She had graduated from Wellesley and Harvard law dammit, she could figure out how to have an orgasm! With determination she turned on her home computer.

The first thing she did instead of using the screen name that AOL had provided her with that read User13579 she created a new one. Thinking about 'foxyroxy' she couldn't think what she wanted for her own for a while and then she put in 'lawgirl' and hoped it wouldn't be too telling. It was easy to remember. She saw that you could have up to seven screen names in AOL. She wondered what someone would need with seven screen names? Next she went and signed on as 'lawgirl' and began to create a profile. She wasn't too revealing but she was honest. She knew it wouldn't be a good idea to tell too much after all she was a prominent

Manhattan attorney. When it asked for a picture though she was stumped, she didn't have one on any of her computers, she hadn't needed one. She skipped that part as she went determinedly into the chat rooms. She wanted answers tonight and she wasn't going to be intimidated.

Her first IM was from a user named 'Lesboliscious' which made her want to laugh. That was so obvious.

"Hey baby, have a picture?" she typed.

Nia typed back, "No, not yet, I'll try to get one up soon."

"What do you look like," came back on her screen.

Nia clicked on the screen name so she could look at 'Lesboliscious' and her profile. She looked really heavy and not at all like Nia had hoped. Her hair was dark black and shaved on both sides close to her head, from the many pictures she had a braid hanging down the back. Her makeup was heavy and her skin very pale. She didn't know what she was looking for in a lesbian friend but this wasn't it. Not that she didn't have many lesbian friends even in her small circle, Annie was bi-sexual, she thought one or two of the Thursday night group were lesbians, and after tonight's conversation she was pretty sure about that. 'Lesboliscious' was too obvious but Nia was desperate for advice. With the anonymity, the woman didn't know what Nia looked like, she thought, what the hell.

She gave Lesboliscious her particulars of what she looked like to keep the conversation going. Then she had not one but two more 'pings' on her screen of people who wanted to 'chat' with her. One was from 'Sasha1234' and another from 'Girlicker.' Man, where did people come up with these screen names she thought as she clicked on them both. Both offered 'Hello's' and Nia responded in kind. Soon she was talking with all three of them at the same time, trying to keep the conversations straight and actually enjoying the challenge. There was a sameness about the conversations when they started and she felt comfortable answering their questions. She clicked on both of the two new ones profiles to see what they looked like and they looked like normal women, not so obvious as the first one, Lesboliscious. She had been chatting with them all for about half an hour asking questions, being asked questions before she felt comfortable enough to ask about toys. Each had their own opinions. Lesboliscious thought strap on's were great and she'd love to show Lawgirl sometime. Sasha1234 thought dildo's were a waste of money and that only vibrators were good and Girlicker went on about many different types including a Hitachi 'magic wand' she thought was to die for. Nia took notes. It was during the various suggestions and innuendo's that they typed that she heard from Sasha1234 and Girlicker both about a 'rabbit' something she had never heard of before. She was tired after her long day at work and her night out and told them she had to go. She signed off soon after getting a :-(from her new 'friends.' She didn't know what that meant

but she thought about it and realized it was computer lingo for unhappy. She had heard of that but she wished her new friends goodnight anyway and signed off.

The next day at work she looked up on the internet what a rabbit sex toy was. There was a confusing and vast array of these toys. She felt out of her depth again with all the information she was given. She also looked up the magic wand and thought that was overkill but was intrigued all the same. It didn't insert but provided stimulation outside. She didn't understand how that worked but it did interest her. Swallowing her pride she ordered the wand and then looked at the rabbits again. She decided rather than get the basic rabbit she would order the second basic. She didn't know why, maybe an ego thing but she ordered it all the same. She carefully erased the history on her computer before getting back to work.

Both toys arrived the next week. The magic wand looked huge. It was white and about eighteen inches long. She could see why it was too big to go inside with its large bulbous head. This was what vibrated and could be used against your genitalia. The vibrations were incredible and it plugged into an outlet, she could see why it needed the extra surge. It would have gone through D sized batteries like candy. The rabbit was purple and had two appendages. The large one looked similar to a man's penis. The small one which vibrated had a rabbit's face and ears. She didn't understand its purpose but she had talked to her internet friends many times since she ordered it and they highly recommended a 'rabbit'. She tried out the wand first and it was strong, very strong even at its lowest settings. She could feel the power behind it and she wondered if her body just wasn't ready for such strength. She played it over her crotch and while she enjoyed it she didn't feel aroused by it at all. As a back massager though it was awesome so at least she didn't feel cheated by buying this expensive toy.

She tried the rabbit next inserting the batteries she had bought in anticipation of its arrival. It was difficult to get inside and she realized why one needed lube occasionally as she shoved it in carefully. The penis like shaft finally was inside and the rabbit face resting along her slit. It had two sets of controls on the shaft and she hesitantly began fiddling with them to find the proper ones. One controlled the penis like shaft and caused it to whirl in a circular direction bending and vibrating in ways no man's penis ever would. Next she turned on the vibrations of the rabbits head and then lay back on her bed to wait for the sensations she knew had to come. Nothing happened. She didn't understand it. She shifted the vibrator, she turned off the rabbit and left the shaft on, she tried turning off the shaft and leaving on the vibrating rabbit easrs, but nothing happened. She tried thrusting in and out and while wetter than she was before, again

nothing happened. She had read up on this or so she thought, what was she doing wrong?

Sasha1234 and Girlicker both had helpful advice. They suggested she rub herself against the rabbit or thrust the shaft in and out. They suggested just rubbing the face or ears against her clit. Now Nia knew she had the right appendages and had heard about the clit but she had thought the folds of skin along her crotch were her clit. Reading about the proper spots on a female's body made her realize how naive she really had been. The clit was a tiny penis like appendage that stuck up when a woman was aroused. Small and infinitely sensitive, Nia realized she had never known exactly that her's existed. Both of her on line friends insisted that she play and enjoy herself, don't put so much pressure on the 'orgasm' that it would come in time. Over time Nia could tell there was a difference as she played between her legs but still had no orgasm. She thrust away at herself with the shaft and enjoyed the friction but determined that she didn't like the sensation of the shaft rotating and bending and vibrating. The rabbit now had possibilities and she began to realize her clit did in fact exist. She even went so far as to place a mirror to look at it when she was aroused and see its tiny tip sticking out.

It still felt wrong though to be using these toys and she was still not achieving any results when she realized the story line on ER and the fact that she was talking with lesbians about sex might mean she was drawn to women. Not that she didn't like men, almost all the partners at the firm were men, and she had had sex with men, but something was missing. It wasn't until she had changed her appearance and become a partner that suddenly they seemed to notice her as a person and admire her. Some of the associates and paralegals had actually asked her out but because of her position or so she told herself she had always declined. Now she realized it was because she wasn't drawn to them. She began to wonder what it would be like to be with a woman. She could have a discrete and quiet affair and no one be the wiser. She lived in a city with millions of people, she had access to millions more on line and in the surrounding cities, she could find someone, somewhere, couldn't she? Neither of the two internet friends she spoke to frequently interested her that way, they had been excellent sources of information but she wasn't drawn to either one of them from their appearances. Nia herself had put an old picture of herself on her profile, one where she still wore her glasses and no makeup so at least they knew what she looked like and that she wasn't a guy, apparently a common suspicion in these chat rooms.

Nia began spending her evenings on her computer looking for a 'friend' that could teach her what she wanted to know. She wanted to know how to have an orgasm. She wanted to know what it felt like to be with a woman. That thought these days made the powerful attorney wet in

anticipation of what she knew not. She didn't stay in the chat room she had become comfortable with and instead branched out. She still stayed away from any 'butch' sounding chat rooms or ones that involved whips and chains. The thought frightened her and she knew she wasn't interested or ready for any of that. On a conscious level she realized she might never be interested in any of it, on a subconscious level it scared the hell out of her.

She chatted with many people, she felt herself becoming very adept at the 'lingo' and she felt very comfortable after chatting extensively with Sasha1234 and Girlicker. She had realized early on that Lesboliscious was too out there for her and too blunt for even an internet friendship. She realized there were people out there who were just into it for the titillation; they weren't really looking for friendship. Some were men posing as women to see what they could get. She began to be able to spot some of these posers and click ignore when she felt they were wasting her time. Some of the same people went into different chat rooms and she began to recognize their names. She still chatted with Sasha1234 and Girlicker as she cruised the other rooms but she needed something more and she knew that too. She began to chat in the rooms she went into and found the different opinions interesting. It was almost like regular conversations except that you had to type them. The different emoticon's such as the :-(gave a lot of information quickly. She read and she learned.

She was sitting and watching the conversation in a chat room called F4FMoms just to observe, she realized now that F meant Female. She wasn't a mom and she wouldn't pretend to be but the conversation was interesting. She got her usual IM's or Instant Mail requests and some she would chat with or X out of to delete them, especially those inviting her to webcam with someone and go to porn. She wasn't interested in those things. She wanted a conversation with someone that might lead to a relationship, a discrete one. She participated in the chat room a little and teased and joked with the people in the room when she received an IM from JustLookin.

"Hello," the IM read.

"Hello," Nia typed back and then clicked on the profile, nothing outrageous, similar interests in books and movies. She was a mom that was apparent from what Nia could read but no pictures. This sent up flags, this could be a poser.

"How are you tonight?" JustLookin typed.

"I'm good, how are you?"

"I'm fine, nice picture," she typed.

"That's not fair, you know what I look like but you have no picture," Nia typed back, she didn't think her picture was very good. It was plain

and unattractive. She had learned a lot this year about enhancing her natural good looks from make-up to clothes.

"I only send out pictures after I feel the person I'm chatting with is really a woman," JustLookin typed.

Nia had to consider that was fair considering the number of men she had met in the various chat rooms. "Well, last time I looked I was a woman," she typed back grinning.

"Lol," JustLookin typed which stood for Laugh out Loud.

"So where are you from?" Nia asked, the profile not providing any information.

"New York, and you?"

"Originally Connecticut and now I live in NYC."

"What brings you to the big apple?"

"I work in Manhattan."

"What do you do?"

Nia squinted at the screen frowning. Apparently JustLookin wasn't reading her screen name of LawGirl. "Can't you tell by the screen name?"

"Oh, lol, sorry, I didn't want to assume. So you're in the law? Are you a cop?"

"No, I'm an attorney," Nia grinned at her screen. She didn't have to brag that she was a partner in one of the best firms in the city after all she didn't want people to really *know* that.

Their conversation continued and Nia learned that JustLookin was a housewife from Long Island with three kids, two dogs, and two cats and a husband that she couldn't stand or at least that was what Nia gleaned. JustLookin learned that Nia lived in the city, was new to this on line thing and had never been with a woman, only talked a lot with them. It got late and they both had to be going but Nia felt something for this anonymous woman and was pleased when she asked if she could add her name of LawGirl to her 'friends' list. Nia said yes and then asked the same out of courtesy. They were both pleased with their initial conversation.

Over the course of the next couple weeks and into the New Year they spoke, not every night, Nia's schedule wouldn't permit that, but often enough that a friendship of sorts was forged. Nia enjoyed it, it was comfortable, it was anonymous, and she could confide in JustLookin like she couldn't with her real friends. She learned that JustLookin's real name was Justine and from then on she always greeted her with a 'Hello Justine' when she saw her on line when she was on under the LawGirl screen name. It actually gave her some pleasure in her gut when she saw her there almost waiting for her. She still chatted occasionally with Sasha1234 and Girllicker but it wasn't the same. They didn't stimulate her mind like Justine did. She actually thought of things during the day that she could share with Justine. Rarely, but occasionally she went on line with her

work computer to see if she could catch Justine on line during the day. It didn't happen often but she would send her an email that said 'just thinking about you.' It was pleasant and a real trust was building. Justine finally sent her a picture of her and her kids. Nia was disappointed at first having imagined a much more glamorous housewife but then as she gazed at the picture daily that faded and Justine's actual looks superimposed themselves on Nia's imagination. Something about her eyes fascinated Nia from what she could see. A second picture with her smiling fully entranced Nia totally. She had perfect teeth and Nia admired how her eyes sparkled when she smiled. She felt like she was falling in love and as this was a first she was unsure of herself.

They talked about anything and everything as time went on. Nia felt like she was wearing out her fingers as she typed away quickly. She actually had fatigue after talking with Justine endlessly for hours some nights. She gave up precious sleeping time so she could chat with her. Finally though it was catching up with her and she asked Justine if she wanted to talk on the phone some time.

"I'm not sure," JustLookin typed back.

"After all this time, you're not sure?" Nia asked surprised.

"Well, I do have my kids and family..."

"I assure you I'm not a stalker but then again I suppose a real stalker would say the same."

"Lol."

"You know almost everything about me, what's not to trust?"

"Maybe you made it all up?"

Nia felt a little hurt at that but then thinking about it realized it could be true. A faker would indeed have an elaborate story. She dealt with lies all day long and some of them were real whoppers. She understood Justine's trepidation. "I didn't, but if you're uncomfortable you can star sixty seven before you call. Here is my cell number," she typed. "You call when you feel comfortable. You know my hours. Feel free to text occasionally but if I don't answer I hope you understand that I can't." She waited to see what Justine would answer.

"Thank you, I will," she typed.

They got off the computer soon afterward and Nia wondered if she would hear from Justine. She shrugged, she could only try and if Justine didn't feel comfortable with the situation she at least knew she had a friend on the internet. Justine did know a lot of her innermost thoughts after all this time. Nia had confessed her feelings about the toys she had purchased and Justine was genuinely interested. She herself had never had problems orgasming but could explain how it felt to a degree. She pointed out that it was different for everyone and that Nia shouldn't give up. They had on occasion talked about what they would do if they had an affair. It was

titillating, arousing, and fun Nia found and she had enjoyed it. Many was the time that she tried with her rabbit but still found no satisfaction with it. She tried thrusting it in madly over and over, she had tried grinding it against her clit until it hurt, she had tried sitting on it with both the shaft and the ears vibrating but nothing happened, she got wet but nothing happened. It was frustrating especially with someone like Justine who assured her that it was easy. She actually broke her first rabbit and ordered another identical one to the first with all her 'trying.' She wasn't sure if she just wore it out or that sitting on it and grinding downwards had broken something inside. She would have been embarrassed if anyone other than Justine had known. When she threw it out she buried it deeply in the trash compacter hoping no one would ever see it.

"Hello?" she answered her phone. It was fairly late in the evening and she was sitting on one of her couches going over a brief. Her voice was unconsciously sexy and she was definitely distracted.

"Hi Nia," a higher pitched voice greeted her. Nia looked down at the caller I.D. but it said private, and that gave her the first clue.

"Justine?" she asked to make sure.

"Yeah."

"Wow, I'm pleased to hear from you." Nia sat back on her couch. She was genuinely surprised. It had been a week since she gave Justine the number.

"Did I catch you at a bad time?"

"No, not at all, just finishing up some work around the house." She glanced at the brief she had been working on.

"I thought perhaps you were angry since I didn't see you on line."

"No, not at all. I've been in court, long days, I needed my sleep."

"Oh, okay."

Nia frowned into the phone realizing the time. "Where are your kids?"

"I waited until after they were in bed to call."

"What about your husband?" This had been a point that Nia worried about, she didn't really want to have an affair with someone who was married but Justine had assured her many times that her marriage wasn't that great. It still bothered Nia but she wanted to know Justine at this point.

"He's snoring in bed, vodka helps," she said and Nia could hear the note of disgust in her voice.

"Where are you?" she asked.

"In a spare bedroom, no one can hear me and I can hear if someone comes down the hall."

"Oh, okay," Nia said hoping she didn't sound like she was grilling her. Unfortunately that could be a job hazard in her line of work.

"Where are you?" Justine turned the tables on her.

"I'm in my living room going over briefs for tomorrow." She leaned back further in the couch to relax her back.

"You work too much," Justine teased. She had figured out a while ago from the little she had said that Nia was a high powered Manhattan attorney.

"Probably, but that's why they pay me the big bucks."

They teased back and forth for a while and really enjoyed their first real conversation until it got really late. They were both tired and rang off. This was the first though of regular conversations, texts, and the continued emails that they shared. It was an odd friendship, born of a need both had been seeking. While they hadn't physically met they both knew they would eventually and over the course of weeks after that first telephone conversation they began to tell more and more intimate and private things as they fell in love. Nia had never experienced anything like this in her life and Justine hadn't either. Both of them were amazed, both of them pleased, both of them in love with the person they came to know on the other end of that line.

They had been IM'ing, chatting, phoning, and texting for months before Nia finally said to her late one night as she lay in bed on her cell phone, "We have to meet."

Silence greeted her announcement but Justine agreed with her. It was time. This had been going on long enough. They both wanted to know one another intimately.

"How do we arrange it?" Justine asked nervously.

Nia thought about it. "I could take a day off from work and come out to meet you."

"But where?"

"Do you think a hotel would be too sleazy?" Nia asked hesitantly.

"No actually, I think that would be good idea. I can't have you here," she said apologetically as she looked around the spare room where she lay every night having their conversations.

"That's okay, I understand," Nia said relieved.

They made arrangements for the next week. Nia would get a room at the local Country Inn and Suites for Thursday and Friday. She didn't tell Justine she would be arriving Wednesday night; she didn't want her to feel any more nervous than she did herself. She made the arrangements herself taking off on a well-deserved long weekend was to be expected after all she had been doing at work.

Wednesday morning she packed a small bag with clothes for the weekend even though she would be gone only two days and three nights she felt the need to have several changes of clothing. She brought along her toys which she and Justine had discussed. Justine was particularly interested in the Hitachi Magic Wand and Nia had enjoyed teasing her

with the joke that she was going to tie her down and use it on her. It had titillated and excited her but Nia had no intention of going that route. She wasn't confident to that degree by any stretch of the imagination.

All day she was jumpy waiting for three o'clock to come so she could get on the freeway out to Long Island. She had a pretty light day, meeting with a new client first thing in the morning, and plowing through mounds of paperwork until she broke for lunch. Even through lunch though she read paperwork and made notes. She had a small appearance in court at 1:30 and was back at the office by 2. She finished up some of the paperwork on her desk and carting it all to Colleen's desk and leaving it for her to file, to sort, to mail.

"Big plans for the weekend?" Colleen asked as she gathered the pile from Nia knowing that she was taking a long weekend.

"Oh, I'm going out to visit a friend on Long Island. I thought I'd go antiquing after that." She hoped she sounded believable.

"That sounds nice, I envy the antiquing part!" Colleen smiled at her boss. She had noticed a change in her, something indefinable the last few months. She moved differently, almost more alluring, but Colleen couldn't put a finger on it. What she didn't realize she saw was that Nia was becoming more confident in her own body, she felt sexy by talking with Justine, she wanted more from life than it was giving her and she had the body to do it with. She was coming into her own on several levels.

Nia was out the door of her office with it locked behind her at three on the dot. Her purse and briefcase over her shoulder she wished Colleen a nice weekend and headed for the elevator.

"Nia!" she heard and almost groaned.

Ralph Carter came hurrying up as she waited for the elevator. She turned to him with an inquiring look.

"Off for the day?" he asked trying to be charming.

Nia sighed but not so he would notice. He had been coming on to her for months and she was just not interested. He had a big belly and liked his beer; his rounded face from the extra weight gave it an unappealing fleshiness. He could have been attractive but given her interests these days she was just not going to go there. She smiled though, her lawyer training an act that was hard to follow. "No, I'm off for the weekend."

"Oh, where are you going?" he tried so hard. She felt sorry for him. She knew of his interest, she didn't return it, and being pleasant to him was all she could offer. As a partner, technically she was one of his bosses, but she had always treated the other lawyers as equals when she could.

"I'm driving onto Long Island to visit a friend and then probably shopping," she answered brightly.

"That sounds fun, what kind of shopping?"

This boring conversation was going to go nowhere and she was never so grateful as to hear the bong of the elevator. "Sorry, got to go." She smiled as she pushed the button to close the doors on his eager face.

She felt bad about the man but how many times must she turn him down for him to get the hint? She wouldn't let it ruin her mini-vacation in any way though as she unlocked her Lexus and slid onto the cool leather seat. She stored her briefcase in the back; it contained her laptop as well as several important documents of cases she was working on. She thought better of placing it there but then putting it in the trunk didn't make sense either if she got carjacked. Her laptop was backed up daily when she went home anyway, automatically. It was an Apple computer and she used it because it was practically impervious to viruses and she didn't have the patience or the time to waste on things of that nature. She strapped herself in and drove carefully through the always congested New York streets and made her way to the Long Island Expressway. She felt great flying down it. It was just before rush hour and she had timed it so that she wouldn't sit for hours in the congestion. She still hit pockets of slow traffic but nothing like it could be. After a fifty minute drive from the city she saw her exit and made her way over towards it pulling off and a short drive later she arrived at the hotel and checked herself in.

The room was nice with a little living area, a kitchenette, and a large bedroom. She looked around nervously for a moment and then realized she had nothing to be nervous about. She got out her swim suit and made her way to the pool. A family who were obviously on vacation were the only ones in the pool and she swam laps to relieve some of the self-imposed tension she had created. She didn't swim often but maybe she could join a gym and do that in the city. She was naturally thin but not naturally toned. It would be a great stress reliever she though as she sat in the hot tub afterwards. That was a mistake as it made her warm and think about Justine who was to meet her in the morning after she dropped her kids off at school.

Nia had trouble sleeping that night as she was wondering what the morning would bring. Justine had threatened to 'rip her clothes off' once and while Nia was certain she wouldn't do that, she was nervous all the same. She had texted Justine in response to her own text, assuring her she would be there in the morning. Nia gave her the room number she had reserved. It was late before she finally got to sleep. In the morning she got a continental breakfast that the hotel served and taking an extra Danish and cup of coffee back to her room, she left them on the bar of the kitchenette before hoping in the shower and washing herself extra carefully and making sure her legs and underarms were shaved and clean. She applied anti-perspirant and dried off the rest of her body. Her long curly hair she partially dried but before it could dry out or look windblown

she applied a conditioner and rubbed it in. Carefully she applied her makeup and perfume and dressed like she was going to court. She had thought about that long and hard for her first meeting with Justine and thought she would be more comfortable in her normal clothes. She rarely wore jeans and never t-shirts so she hadn't been sure what the proper attire would be to meet her potential lover.

Nia answered the door wearing a power suit with blouse, jacket, and matching pants. She hadn't bothered to put on shoes yet but her stockings were black. Justine stood there before her looking casual and relaxed in jeans and a blouse and carrying her purse, Nia felt ridiculously overdressed.

"Hi," Nia breathed looking down at the woman. She hadn't realized she would be so short!

"Hi," Justine looked back surprised at how elegant and powerful Nia looked. The makeup alone changed a lot about her looks from her picture.

"Come on in," Nia said gesturing. Justine walked in looking around curiously at the suite. "Would you like something to drink?" Nia asked. She had brought along small bottles of liquor but knowing it was too early in the morning she had also brought fruit juices. "There is some coffee we can re-heat," she indicated the cup on the counter next to the Danish. "I didn't drink it at all and it has sat there about half an hour..." She was babbling and she knew it.

Justine answered, "The coffee sounds fine let me see if it's still warm," she touched it and brought it to her lips. "This is fine."

"Would you like to sit down?" Nia asked. She hadn't felt this nervous in years and didn't understand why she did now. She was a litigator for crying out loud, she should be able to handle meeting a potential lover.

They sat on the couch together and neither said anything. Nia had sat at one end and Justine sat close to her, their shoulder's brushing. Nia felt dry mouthed and unsure of herself for the first time in years.

"How was your drive?" Justine asked as she examined Nia. She was lovely. So different from the unattractive picture she had sent. She had warned Justine that it was an old picture but Justine hadn't been prepared for *this*.

"Actually, I came out last night. I didn't want to have to contend with the traffic," Nia confessed glancing at Justine and feeling a little better, at least they were talking.

"Oh, you didn't call..." Justine left off as she took a sip of the luke warm coffee.

"I know, I was feeling nervous," Nia confessed feeling braver as they talked. This was Justine, the woman she had talked to about absolutely everything for months, why was she so nervous?

Justine smiled. She had felt the same way when she realized this was it. Nia would be out here for two days. She had arranged for the kids to be picked up after school so she had until seven that night until she had to be home. It was only nine am. "Would you like to go somewhere first, drive around maybe?" she asked to calm her own nervousness.

Nia shook her head and then thought again, "If you want..." but they could both tell by her voice that she didn't really want to.

"Relax, we don't have to do anything you don't want to," Justine said but she was unobtrusively rubbing her shoulder against Nia's as they sat side by side together. Nia hadn't noticed that half the couch was unoccupied.

Nia looked into Justine's eyes and was lost in them. She thought for the thousandth time how beautiful they really were with their long eyelashes. Justine had double rows of eyelashes and they just captured Nia's attention as she looked deeply into them. Taking a deep breath she asked, "Have you changed your mind?"

Justine was just as affected by Nia as she was. Nia was a lot more striking than her picture and Justine was feeling a little intimidated. She shook her head at the question and gently took Nia's hand in her own and squeezed. "It's okay, let's just take it slow," she said in a soothing voice.

Nia wanted to desperately kiss her but had no idea how to proceed. She had visions of straddling this woman's lap and grinding against her, in fact in the anonymity of the internet, in the phone calls they had shared where they didn't need to face each other she had spoken her fantasies to this woman and more. Justine knew everything about her, what she had wanted, what she was fantasizing about, her passions, her innermost thoughts. In fact Justine knew things that Nia had never shared with another human being. She didn't know why she had shared so much but Justine had shared just as much and she had felt comfortable with her. She sat up suddenly and said, "Yes, let's take a ride, we need to relax together." She stood up and nearly knocked the coffee into Justine's lap.

Justine looked up in amusement. Getting up herself she looked down at Nia's feet and asked dryly, "Own any shoes?"

Nia laughed as she went to find a pair. They were soon out the door and Justine was thrilled to get into the luxurious Lexus. She hadn't wanted to take her own car in case it was recognized. This area was heavily populated but no one she knew would see her with the tinted windows of the Lexus. She had parked her own mini-van around the back of the hotel. Justine was soon playing tour guide as they explored the South Shore near where Justine lived. Justine showed her the neighborhood where she lived and the house but they didn't stop or go in. By then they had both calmed and were talking and joking as of old. It had relaxed both of them and they headed back to the hotel. Nearby was a park and impulsively Nia

asked if Justine wanted to take a walk. It was a fine fall day for it and Justine enthusiastically agreed.

They walked along talking just as easily as they did every night on the phone and Justine turned around and walked backwards as she made a point. Nia tried to warn her but she crashed into a bench before she could say more than two words. "Oh my God, are you okay?" Nia asked concerned as she held out her hand to help her up from her fall.

Justine grabbed her hand and between the two of them they got her on her feet and Nia looked at her wondering if she was going to be okay when Justine started laughing. "Come on, let's head back before I hurt something important." They laughed and joked all the way back to the hotel.

Justine was limping slightly though as Nia unlocked the door to her suite. "Can I get some ice for your foot?" she asked solicitously.

Justine shook her head. "It's not my foot; I think I scraped my back."

"Want me to look?" Nia asked as she placed her purse on the counter and took off her suit jacket.

Justine watched the body that was revealed under the jacket. Nia had high firm breasts and despite not working out her body looked inviting under the silk blouse. Justine was definitely interested. She nodded and answered, "Yeah, could you?"

Nia's touch was tender and the perfume she used inviting as she got close to Justine. She softly lifted the t-shirt and saw an angry red streak across Justine's lower back. "Yeah, that looks nasty." She touched slightly with her fingertips and Justine flinched.

"Do you have something we could put on it," she tried to crane her neck over her shoulder to see.

"I have some lotion but I doubt that will do much. I think you need one of those deep heating things," Nia answered.

"I'll do that when I get home then," Justine answered realizing how close they now both were.

Nia looked disappointed. She was leaving already? It was almost noon and they hadn't done anything they had planned except spend time together. She hadn't minded that but she knew they had both planned for more.

"Do you mind if I lay down and you put the lotion on for me?" Justine asked as she watched the expression on Nia's face. It changed immediately as Nia agreed.

Justine lay on the end of the bed kicking off her shoes as Nia went to grab her lotion. She pulled her t-shirt up so that Nia could reach the affected area. She turned her head towards where Nia was walking. She saw Nia kick off her own shoes and fetch the lotion. She unbuttoned the sleeves of her blouse and pushed them up before grabbing the lotion bottle

and pumping some into her hands. She put it down next to the bed before sitting next to Justine and rubbing her hands together to warm the lotion. She gently placed her hands on Justine's back and saw Justine stiffen up from the unfamiliar touch and coolness of the lotion. Gently she began to touch the affected area before lightly applying both hands in a soothing rub. Justine arched slightly enjoying the firm warm hands. Nia began to rub all over Justine's lower back and began to rub higher as she noticed the response. Pretty soon she found herself giving Justine a backrub. It allowed her to touch her all over and she found she enjoyed it. She could tell that Justine was enjoying it and she kept it up for quite a while until her hands felt tired almost. She knew her shoulders were from the odd angle she needed to give the rub. She lay down next to Justine on the bed and continued rubbing with just one hand.

"Scratch, oh please scratch," Justine said as Nia accidentally used her nails. So Nia scratched Justine's back lightly all over only to hear, "Harder," as she arched into Nia's nails.

Justine turned her head to Nia and looked deeply into her face. Quietly she asked, "Can I kiss you?"

For a second Nia's heart stopped, this is what she had been waiting weeks for, months. In that split second she knew she wanted to kiss Justine and couldn't say a word so she swallowed and said, "Mmmhmm," as she leaned in for that first kiss. There are times in your life when you know you're doing something just right. Nia knew at that moment that this felt very right. It wasn't like 'Oh wow, I'm kissing a woman,' it was more like 'Oh wow, I'm *finally* kissing Justine.' She really enjoyed that first kiss, putting her all into as she gently touched her lips to Justine's. She could tell almost immediately that Justine didn't kiss as well as she did. It wasn't a competition but Nia had enjoyed kissing the few people she had over the years and was good at it. Justine wasn't but that didn't stop them both from enjoying that first kiss. Nia deepened it as she opened her mouth and gently slipped her tongue along Justine's lips. Justine liked the feel of the tall woman's lips against her own. She wanted more, so much more as she leaned in deeper for it, finally though she pulled back enough to quietly ask, "Are you okay?" After all Nia had never done this before and while Justine had, she didn't want to scare off the beautiful woman she wanted so much.

Nia repeated herself "Mmmhmm," before feeling more confident and leaning in for another kiss. Her hand made lazy circles on Justine's back caressing and scratching at the same time in alternate strokes. Now that they had started, Nia wasn't going to stop. Her right hand was doing the caressing and her left was propped up holding her head up as she kissed Justine. She brought her right hand to cup the side of Justine's head in a caress that brought her into closer contact with Nia's heady perfume.

Justine breathed deeply of it and felt a gut wrenching feeling of desire. Her own hands wrapped around Nia's body in an embrace. Nia opened her mouth wider to explore Justine's deeper. Her tongue was playing with Justine's, caressing it, and fencing with it. She loved the feel of it as she played. Her hand caressed beneath Justine's ear, her fingertips brushing along her neck and Justine arched slightly into it, letting Nia know how much she enjoyed the feeling, the caress. She made lazy little circles down her neck with just her fingertips as she made her way to Justine's shoulder and caressed the length of it inside her shirt. Justine brought her body close to Nia's letting her know unconsciously how much she wanted her, how much she wanted to be in contact with Nia.

Nia let her hand slip deeper into Justine's shirt, never letting her lips break contact as she kissed her over and over again, expertly playing with her tongue along Justine's lips and into her mouth. Justine's breath caught slightly in anticipation when Nia reached her bra and hesitantly slipped her fingertips inside. When she touched Justine's nipple for the first time the gasp that Justine let out had Nia pulling back slightly in alarm worried that she had hurt her but then she looked deeply into Justine's warm eyes and realized it was a pleasurable gasp which reassured her and allowed her to continue. She smiled slightly as she leaned in for another kiss, her fingertips gently caressing Justine's erect left nipple. She began to apply firmer pleasure and Justine began to rub against her in response, encouraging her to continue.

Nia's lips left her partner's as she kissed along her jawline and began to head for her ear and neck. Justine's head fell back in response, encouraging her to continue, to touch and be touched as her hand came up to cup the back of Nia's head and then touch her own fingertips along Nia's delicate neck. Tingles shot down her spine at the touch. Nia's lips continued to nibble, kiss, and suck slightly as she tongued along Justine's sensitive neck. Nia could hear by Justine's breathing how much she was affected. Nia kissed down her neck, around her shoulder blade, sucking lightly at the indent at the base of her neck, feeling Justine arch into her in response as she played with her nipple with her fingertips. She kissed her way determinedly towards Justine's nipple which was standing at attention begging to be kissed. Justine let her breath out in a hiss as Nia's mouth closed over the stiff nipple. A little strangled cry escaped her lips as she arched her breast into Nia's mouth, encouraging her. Nia's tongue gently circled the erect nipple as her hand kneaded the breast, Justine's response encouraged her as she gently took it in her mouth and sucked on it watching to see that Justine fully approved as she arched and her hand encouraged behind Nia's head.

Her tongue and the suction were driving Justine insane as she leaned hard against Nia's tall body. For someone who had never done this before,

Nia was doing marvelously thought Justine, but then they had talked extensively about what they would do when given the opportunity, the opportunity was here now and they were going to take full advantage of it.

Nia's hand continued to massage Justine's breast until it was hard beneath her, she wanted to feel more though, her own arousal was apparent to her and she wanted more, much more. Her hand left the breast and slid down Justine's body and under her t-shirt which was still raised high from her backrub. The touch of her hand on Justine's warm body delighted her and Justine approved as she hissed in at the contact. Nia began to raise the t-shirt, lopsided with her right hand as she tongued the eager little nipple. She leaned back and pulled Justine over on top of her own body, relishing the feel of her weight against her. She raised the t-shirt completely up her back as she whispered, "Remove this," and continued sucking and tonguing on Justine's nipple until the t-shirt got in the way as she raised it. She didn't like losing the contact but there was no other way to remove the shirt. The shirt was soon flung to the floor of the hotel room and Justine captured Nia's lips. They both enjoyed the sensation as they kissed deeply, hungrily, communicating their desires in an old fashioned way.

Justine began to unbutton the blouse she was laying on, her fingers enjoying the sensation of the silk beneath them. The fine buttons proved worthy adversaries but she finally managed to get most of them through their little holes one handed. As Nia's body was exposed Justine became even more excited, she was a beautiful woman and Justine couldn't wait to be with her, to have her, to be her first. It had been one of the many reasons she had pursued this relationship, God knew the picture of Nia hadn't done her justice. Something about her though had appealed to Justine and she had wanted the woman, she was glad she had hung on because now she would have her. She pushed the silk shirt back and exposed Nia's narrow shoulders. She looked beautiful lying there with her hair spread out beneath them. Justine wanted to enjoy the view but knew that Nia was impatient. She pulled back to remove Nia's arms from her blouse and Nia rose up to let it fall from her back. Justine, out of respect for the costliness of the fabric threw it on a chair before turning back to straddle Nia and begin her assault in earnest.

They both lay there in their bras and caressed each other as their mouths got to know one another. It felt so good, it felt so right, and both couldn't believe how much enjoyment they got out of a simple kiss. Nia reached above her to Justine's back and released the bra. Justine rolled them so she could do the same but then had to laugh when she realized Nia's bra fastened in the front. The laughter loosened some of the tension that had been building. As both examined the other they shared a smile and Nia reached for Justine's pants button as Justine reached for hers. They were soon down to panties and stockings or socks. Each rolled the

other's off sensuously, slowly, and with infinite care. Nia was beginning to feel a little shy and was grateful that Justine was more experienced than she. Once she was naked before Justine she felt so vulnerable but the appreciation she saw in Justine's eyes made her feel beautiful and less shy. Justine had nothing to be ashamed of. Her body was small and compact, a slight rounding around the hips from childbirth, but still a desirous body and Nia enjoyed touching it, feeling it, bringing gasps from Justine's mouth as she found a particularly sensitive spot.

Once naked though Justine lost any shyness and seemed to begin her attack on Nia's body lovingly and determinedly, she firmly caressed her way down Nia's long body. Nia was kissing her when she realized Justine's soft hand was on her hip. She desperately wanted Justine to move it to the V of her legs, to feel it on her mound, to begin what she had promised on the phone. Nia had no idea how she was going to orgasm but Justine had promised she could bring her to this unfelt state. Nia was holding her to that promise as she kissed her deeply, felt her naked body against her own, and enjoyed the sensations that she was causing. The first touch of Justine's hand on her crotch surprised and delighted Nia. It felt different from a man's, it felt softer somehow, more loving, and infinitely more desirable.

Justine began exploring the beautiful woman's body, enjoying the trip. Nia had no idea how excited Justine was at the opportunity before her. Justine had never been with a woman who was essentially a virgin in this arena. Her past affairs had been with women who knew the score, who had been around a bit. None had begun like this or proceeded like the relationship she had with Nia. Nia had unknowingly aroused lust in Justine with her simple words on the computer and phone. She had no idea how much Justine wanted her. To find she was a beautiful woman had been icing on the cake. Justine was hard pressed not to take her pleasure and be done but she wanted to savor this, she wanted to hear Nia cry out in passion, she wanted this woman like no other in a long time. She was willing to be patient with her and teach her what she liked; she was already proving to be an adept pupil. She had taken the lead with touching her breast and licking it. Justine's nipples were particularly sensitive and her clit was standing on its end waiting its turn but she could be patient. She could teach Nia. As her hand caressed her smooth skin she slowly brought it to the juncture between Nia's legs. She wasn't as wet as Nia had told her she could get over the phone. She explored the folds with her fingers, played with her clit, but she didn't get wetter. That didn't matter, Justine could correct that. She began to kiss her way down Nia's body.

Nia eagerly anticipated the first touch of Justine's tongue on her clit. She thought that was all lesbians did and while she had been worried about

doing sixty nine she and Justine had agreed to 'take turns' until they both felt more comfortable with each other. The first touch was disappointing. There wasn't like a light that went off indicating that she would get an immediate orgasm. Nia knew then the romance novels she had read since she was a teen, lied. She enjoyed the warmth though as Justine examined and then began to play with her clit, her folds of skin, and what little wetness there was, her tongue making up for the lack that she wondered at.

Justine realized Nia was dry because of nervousness. It was her first time after all. She lay there and accepted whatever Justine did to her, accepting anything Justine wanted to do. The thought was heady but Justine knew Nia wasn't ready for anything more sophisticated at this point. She slowly wetted her finger with her mouth and gently inserted it inside Nia. She was dry inside as well except for a small amount of natural moisture. She gently began to finger her hoping to elicit a response as she began to nuzzle and lick the folds of skin and make her way back to Nia's clit. The clit was not standing at attention and Justine looked up to see that Nia was laying there waiting, anticipating she knew not what. Justine realized she wasn't aroused like she should be. Certainly wasn't wet like she complained about over the phone. She didn't realize yet that she had to participate fully for this to work. Gently Justine began to thrust her finger inside; a small amount of wetness was released and helped her to add another finger. She licked and nuzzled, caressed and played but the clit did not get erect and no further wetness came out. After a long time Justine heard Nia say, "give up," and sigh. Justine climbed up her long body and lay next to her, their warmth feeling good as she lay there wondering what had gone wrong.

After a moment Nia decided to get her mind off the terrible disappointment she was feeling and turned to her and began to caress Justine. At first Justine wanted to object but then she figured why not, at least one of them would cum in this debacle. Nia, despite being a novice or even a pre-novice in making love to a woman was getting results if the puckered nipples were any sign. She lowered her head to Justine's erect nipples and began tonguing them and sucking on them hard. "Gently," she heard Justine rasp out and she began tonguing them fiercely, first light almost ticklish laps and then harder ones, judging Justine's reaction as her hands caressed up and down Justine's body. When Justine began to squirm against her to a degree she began kissing her way down the blonde's body. Justine's breath caught in her throat hoping that the novice wouldn't stop. Nia stopped for a moment at the V of Justine's legs. First she noted that Justine was definitely not a natural blonde if the darkness of her curls were any indication. Next she noted the scent coming from between her legs that indicated her arousal. This is it she thought, if I'm going to be a lesbian I have to be able to go down on a woman. I could

back out now, but she hesitated, she wasn't a coward, and she was curious. Could she give pleasure to another woman?

At the first touch of her tongue to Justine's clit Nia felt a lot more confident for having done the deed. The first hurdle was over; she looked forward to the rest. Her hand came down to help her, first to feel the folds of Justine's pussy and then the wetness. Tasting that wetness was an eye opener for Nia. It had a smoky salty flavor. Not unpleasant but nothing like she had tasted before. It didn't bother her at all as she dipped her head to run her tongue among the folds. She noted that Justine's clit was standing on end, a tiny appendage that was supposed to bring so much pleasure to a woman. Nia used her hand to spread the folds, showing more of Justine's charms to her view and letting her see how wet Justine really was. It was a clear thick fluid with a hint of white that also reminded her almost of glue with its stringiness as she parted the folds. She leaned in to taste some more and found herself licking the folds thoroughly, to get every drop. It didn't work though as Justine became more aroused and produced even more than Nia could handle. She began to concentrate on licking and gently sucking on Justine's clit, remembering the admonishment to 'go gently' she licked at her erect clit like an ice cream cone. As she watched Justine's reactions to her ministrations she realized if she licked on the left side Justine reacted a little more aggressively than if she concentrated on the right.

Enjoying the power, such as it was, she experimented until she sensed Justine needed and craved a release. Her hips were bucking against Nia's face, more violently if she happened to be playing on the left side of Justine's clit. She concentrated there for a long time and wondered when or if Justine would cum, she had never seen a woman cum before and having no experience in it herself she had no idea. She watched as Justine played with her own nipples and wondered if she was failing her 'job' at not playing with them too when she felt the first signs of Justine's orgasm. Her body rose slightly and she caught her breath in a series of gasps as she convulsed. Nia kept up the licking and caressing all through the orgasm, figuring this was the best idea since an abrupt withdrawal might prematurely end the spasms. She watched as Justine's body seemed to convulse over and over again, it awed her, it caused her envy since she had never experienced it herself. As Justine's body calmed the spasms slowed and she gasped air into her lungs. Only when Justine brought her hand down and tried to pry Nia's lips and tongue away from her clit and gasped, "Enough," did Nia stop. She grinned; she had made a woman orgasm! It was heady power. She kissed her way up Justine's body, wiping the cum off her chin and face in kisses designed to do so. She settled next to Justine to wait for what her lover would say, she wasn't waiting for compliments or accolades but she wasn't sure of the protocol at this point.

"That was awesome," Justine gasped after a while as she rolled and looked deeply into Nia's brown eyes.

Nia grinned, still unsure of what to say.

"Are you okay?" Justine asked, she was a little concerned. The point had been to get Nia to orgasm and that hadn't happened.

"I'm fine," Nia assured her with a little smile, trying to hide her own disappointment.

"I'm sorry I couldn't make you cum," Justine said as she turned more fully on her side to touch Nia. She really had a very good body and Justine was thrilled to be able to play with it. She gently tweaked Nia's right nipple.

Nia watched her amused and answered, "Maybe I'm broken. Maybe my clit is broken."

Justine shook her head. "It's like anything, you need to use it. It hasn't been used properly before, it might take time."

They played on and off for hours and Nia enjoyed herself. She really liked when Justine used her fingers and thrust them inside hard and fast but even that didn't make her cum. They showered together late in the day and Nia realized a fantasy she had shared with Justine as she knelt before her and tried to make her cum from standing. Justine loved the sensation and the visual but couldn't cum standing up. Nia insisted on taking them to an early dinner before Justine had to get home to her husband and children. Nia spent the evening watching a movie on cable and thinking about her day. It had been very disappointing but she had learned a lot. Justine was right, it would take time and patience for her to learn how to cum, but how much time and how much patience would someone like Justine have? Nia went to sleep fairly early.

Justine showed up on Friday ready and willing to 'teach' Nia even more about her body. She had thought a lot about the previous day and it had aroused her again and again throughout the night, she was determined to try again to make Nia cum. It took on a familiarity as they had the same results as the previous day. Justine insisted that Nia show her the toys and loved the feel of the Hitachi Magic Wand. She thought the electric dildo gross but was intrigued by the rabbit. Nia learned to use it on Justine and watched her have an intense orgasm from their love play. It was awesome to see the woman lose control for only a few minutes as her body convulsed. She wasn't loud at all but Nia wondered what made a woman loud. Justine used the toys on Nia as well and while Nia enjoyed it her mind betrayed her time and again. It was late on Friday when she felt an inkling of *something* but dismissed it as being overly anxious. They kissed longingly before Justine left, promising to meet again whenever they could arrange it.

The next day Nia was on her own. She used the time to go antiquing in shops she would never have visited otherwise. Everyone said Upstate New York was the best place to antique and she was sure they were right but she was enjoying the stores she went into. She found a delightful set of end tables that she wrestled into the little back seat of the Lexus. There were wonderful finds but she found nothing else she wanted to have or absolutely had to have. It was a quiet and reflective time. She tried unsuccessfully not to think too much about the last two days. She had enjoyed Justine, she loved her, but she was concerned that her body couldn't orgasm. She wondered if she should see a doctor but then thinking about how humiliating that would be to tell a perfect stranger that her clit appeared to be broken she decided against that course of action for now.

She returned to the city fairly early on Sunday to avoid the traffic. She found she had missed the hustle and bustle of the masses. She pulled into her parking spot behind the apartment building and lugged her briefcase and suitcase to the elevator locking the Lexus with the button on her key chain. She got them into her apartment before she returned for the tables. Placing them on either ends of her couches she thought she might move them several times before she found a place for them. It didn't really matter, they were beautiful and she was glad she had found them. She put her dirty clothes in the stacked washer she had in her kitchen and checking her pockets she put her suit in the dry cleaner's bag ready to be dropped off the following day with all her other laundry that read 'dry clean only'. Her mundane chores done she unpacked her briefcase and double checked that the work she had brought with her was meticulously done and waiting for Monday morning.

On Monday she would hand it all off to Colleen to type up her notes, letters, or file as the case may be. She had paralegal's to research things for her although in this day and age her computer came in very handy. The associates who worked on cases for her did so to learn from her and while they were all only a few years younger than she and a few even older, the fact that she was a partner in the firm tended to awe them and keep them in line. They learned a lot from her and Nia, while fairly young, had learned a lot over the years herself and had observed wiser men and women and absorbed their knowledge like a sponge.

After her work was done she didn't really know what to do with herself, she had most of the afternoon and evening. She decided to take a walk. This was when she wished she had a dog. Several people in the building did and she had seen all different kinds, but with her lifestyle and work hours it didn't make sense since she wouldn't be able to devote the time to a pet. It also made her think she wouldn't want to have children someday, she just didn't have the time; she watched some playing at the

park during her walk. She walked all around the long blocks that constituted her neighborhood. She liked this section she had chosen to live. There were small family owned shops that still resided in the bottom of a lot of buildings. Offices were usually on top of many of the high rises but some, like in her building had living space. She appreciated the convenience of having stores close and while they didn't supply all her needs, if she needed a loaf of bread or a pint of milk there was always something nearby.

She grabbed some Chinese food for dinner and was sitting down at the bar with a glass of wine when her phone rang. She heard the caller I.D. announce 'Annie' but she didn't budge from her seat. Annie had this uncanny sense of friendship. She knew when to call or something like that. It had happened many times over the course of their friendship and annoyed Nia no end sometimes. Nia didn't want to share her weekend or her inclinations with anyone and yet Annie was the only one she could share with who would absolutely understand. She didn't move though as she ate her cashew chicken and listened to Annie's message, "Hey, you there? I'm sure you are, you don't *do anything*! Pick up this damn phone, I know your listening." A small silence followed by, "Okay, maybe you do have a life, when did *that* happen?" she teased. "Call me when you get a free moment," and hung up the phone. Nia laughed. Annie knew her hectic schedule and the fact that she had no life outside the office. Even the parties she had thrown over the summer had been mostly work affairs. Annie could wait though as she wanted to finish her dinner.

When Nia sat down on her comfortable couch and was on her second glass of wine she hit the callback feature on her phone. When she heard Annie's voice she smiled. "What makes you think I have no life?"

Annie smiled in return and responded drolly, "I know you remember?"

"So what have you been up to? I'll live vicariously." Nia laughed. Only a good friend could insult her so much and still care so deeply.

Annie told her about the latest fling she had with a man, a *married* man.

Nia frowned and wanted to criticize but then she was involved with Justine who was married.

When Nia didn't criticize though Annie was surprised. "What's up with you?" she asked suspiciously.

Nia shrugged and said, "Nada, why?"

"Come on, I know you chica, what is going on?"

Nia blushed, this gal knew her too well but that was what happened with long standing girlfriends and Annie was her oldest friend. They had grown up together in Connecticut. Long gone were the days she helped Annie with term papers though. "Not much," she tried to hedge but knew it was fruitless; Annie could and would ferret out every detail.

"Don't give me that, something's up, I can tell, tell Aunt Annie all!" she demanded playfully.

At the reference to Aunt Annie, Nia laughed. It was an old joke. Nia was taller, she was older, and they looked nothing alike. Aunt Annie indeed! "What makes you think something is up?"

"Hmmm, you haven't really spoken to me in weeks. I call you to tell you about this absolutely delicious married man I'm seeing and you don't give me the riot act about morals and scruples...."

Nia grinned, she had been a little quiet lately but then all her energies had been centered on Justine and their nightly chats, add her workload and she just hadn't had the time. "I'm not your conscience Annie; you know it's wrong, that it will end badly. It's up to you to decide, not me."

Annie was astounded. Now she knew something was up. Nia should have been reading her the riot act. "Ok, spill, there is something going on with you and don't give me that lawyer routine of doubletalk," she demanded as only a close friend could.

Nia laughed, she shook her head, only Annie could talk to her like this and get away with it. "Okay, okay. I met someone," she smiled knowing that wouldn't be enough for her nosy friend.

"What's he like?" Annie asked excitedly. This didn't happen often and she wanted the details.

"She's pretty nice," Nia said innocently waiting for the explosion that was sure to come.

"*She!?*" Annie screeched. The miles between them on the phone didn't seem far enough at that moment as Nia pulled the receiver away from her ear.

Calmly as though she hadn't just shocked the hell out of her best friend she answered, "Yes *she*."

"How did *that* happen?" Annie asked confused. "Last time I checked you were pure and untouched and hetero!"

"I met her online, in a chat room," Nia confessed.

"That's such a cliché! Have you met her in person? I bet it's a guy pretending to be a girl," Annie said wisely.

Nia laughed at her paranoid friend. Like she hadn't been cautious? "Not only have I met her in person, we spent two days together and had sex," she added knowing that Annie's head was going to explode.

"Holy shit, you had *sex* with a *woman*? How was it? Did you enjoy it? Are you going to see her again? What is she like? Is she butch?" The questions came fast and furious from her well-meaning friend.

"Jeez Annie, take a breath," Nia advised and when she had calmed enough to listen she began telling her from the beginning. From the TV show ER to her feelings for Kim Legaspi she continued on to the toys she had bought. There was a long discussion about them and their uses as

Annie had a lot of questions and a lot of opinions, then on to the chat rooms and talking to Justine and finally meeting her.

"Well, not everyone orgasms easily, especially with a new partner," Annie told her wisely. "You're new at this, you have to patient," which was what Justine had advised as well.

"Yeah, but I was hoping she could teach me how to have one, it was awesome to watch her having them and she had assured me she could make it happen for me," Nia said disappointed.

"Have you ever had one on your own?" Annie asked, knowing the answer before Nia confirmed she hadn't. "How can you expect someone else to give you one when you can't even do it to yourself?"

Nia had to admit that was a good point. She was relieved to have someone other than Justine to talk to about her problems. Annie had a lot of experience and while not particularly discriminating in her choice of partners, she had a few do's and don'ts that she passed on to Nia. Nia listened, sometimes amused. Aunt Annie was doling out the advice in buckets this night but it wasn't all bad. She rang off feeling at least that Annie was in her corner. She hadn't been judgmental or unkind. In fact she had applauded Nia exploring this side of her and while she didn't think Nia had lesbian tendencies, she did feel she should give Justine another go and see where it led.

Nia hadn't even thought of not speaking to Justine again. They had texted; she to tell Justine she was home and Justine to tell her she was out with her family, so each was looking forward to 'chatting' that Sunday night. After talking so long with Annie it was already getting late but Nia fired up her computer. She was almost immediately hit with a 'ping' indicating an instant message. She clicked on it seeing JustLookin and knowing it was Justine.

"Hi," it read.

"Hi," she responded.

"Thought you weren't going to be on tonight, had just about given up," she typed.

"Sorry, had a phone call that ran long."

"Are you angry?" Justine typed.

"No, why would I be?" Nia responded.

"I thought after you thought about what happened on Thurs and Fri you might have changed your mind about us."

"No, not at all."

"Willing to meet me again?"

"Sure, when?"

"I can come into the city on Saturday, would that be okay?"

"Great, I'll show you my apartment." Nia saw that it was taking a while for JustLookin to type back so she typed, "Is that okay?"

"Yeah, sure, sorry, kids."

Nia looked at the clock. She knew that Justine's kids always went to bed by nine pm and as it was well after ten she wondered why Justine was lying but shrugged it off.

"Is that okay? Meeting at my apartment? Would you rather I got a hotel room?" she typed quickly.

"No, that's fine, hey I gtg, hubby," and she quickly signed off.

Nia stared at the screen for a moment before signing off and turning off the computer. She wondered if she had somehow made a mistake, but inviting Justine to her apartment didn't *seem* like a mistake. She read people all the time and Justine was a loving and caring individual. They had fallen in love with each other which was why sex had seemed the natural course to take. Just because it hadn't been mutually satisfying didn't mean that ended their love. Nia wondered what Justine was thinking.

She thought a lot about Justine the next day as she sat in various meetings. They wanted her to travel more for the firm and she didn't mind as long as they were cases she was interested in. Some of the travel she felt would be unnecessary and she was arguing her point. It was an uphill battle with some of the partners who were older men, and thought of her as a young upstart despite her brilliance. Nia brought a lot of business into the firm and the change in her for her position had been a positive thing for both her and the firm. It paid to listen to her.

She texted Justine, "Are you okay," at one point but another meeting interrupted and she didn't see the response for hours.

"Do you think we could just be friends?" was on her phone when she got back to her office.

Nia stared at the text feeling panicked. She loved Justine, she was sure of that. She wanted to know what was going on. "What happened that you would ask that?" she texted back. When she didn't hear back immediately she worried that something dire had happened and their relationship was over.

Nia finished her work for the day and went home hoping to hear from Justine. She didn't know what was going on and Justine had a lot on her plate. Being a housewife and homemaker she was always running around for her family, not that she didn't love Nia but she had other priorities. Not that being a top litigator wasn't important, it was just…different.

Nia was relieved when her cell rang with Justine on the other end of it later that evening. Her mind had been playing on her nerves and she had thought the worst. The bad thing was she didn't know if she could or should call. "Hello?"

"Hi Nia, sorry I couldn't call earlier," Justine sounded relieved.

"What happened?" Nia asked concerned.

"Rod found out, don't ask me how, I think he might have put a key logger on the computer."

"Found out what?"

"About us," Justine said miserably.

Nia felt distinctly uncomfortable. She hadn't anticipated this. Justine had told her that their marriage was in name only, that she wanted to file for divorce but that she hadn't because of their children. "Oh my God, what happened?"

"Apparently he's been suspicious for a while, you and I talking on the phone for hours or the IM'ing hasn't gone unnoticed. I didn't think he cared or anything." She sighed deeply. "Then yesterday when you and I started IM'ing he laid into me with accusations. He thought I was having an affair with a man. I lied about an affair but I could truthfully say that it wasn't a man," she laughed miserably. "The dumbshit has been on my case all day calling from work to chew me out a little more each chance he got. The kids realized something was up and have been acting up too so it's been one of those days. I'm sorry I sent you that text about just being friends, I don't want that, I want so much more," she sounded unhappy.

"Maybe we should just take a break, calm down, and relax. It will blow over if he's not suspicious," Nia said. She didn't *want* to take a break, she didn't want to calm down and relax.

"Nia, I love you. I no longer love him; I fell out of love with him a long time ago. You make me feel so good, I don't want a break but if you don't want the hassle I will try to understand," she offered generously.

"I'm okay, I'm worried about you though," Nia said and the concern was apparent in her voice.

"I really blew my top at him and moved some of my things into the spare bedroom. It gives me my privacy and space."

"Jeez Justine, this is a mess," Nia answered.

"Your right, it will all blow over." She waited a few seconds before asking, "Do you still want to see me this weekend?"

"Yes, of course, but what about your kids and him?"

"Well, I told them about it like it had been planned for a while and he even thought he discussed it with me, the dumbshit, and the kids will be fine for a day. He is their father, he can have them for the day!" she said it almost angrily.

"Okay, what's the plan then?" Nia asked. She didn't want to discuss Justine's husband, it made her distinctly uncomfortable. She didn't want to think she was breaking up a marriage even if Justine had reassured her repeatedly that it was over. Moving into her spare bedroom made Nia a little more comfortable that they weren't having sex. Sharing Justine just didn't sound good to Nia with what she had come to feel about her. It amazed her how protective, how possessive she felt about this woman.

She wanted to help her, had even spoken about helping in a divorce not that she would take it on herself she did have other lawyers in her firm, but Justine had refused.

They discussed a few more of the details for meeting up on Saturday and then Justine made a totally outrageous suggestion, "What do you think about the idea of us having phone sex?"

Nia was surprised at the suggestion. She had never considered it. Sure they had talked pretty racy over the weeks leading up to them finally being together and she had been left feeling pretty horny after those phone calls but she hadn't really done anything about it. Justine had confessed to masturbating many times after their conversations and Nia had found herself intrigued at what Justine did to get off. She made it sound so easy and simple and Nia was disappointed that she couldn't just as easily. Nia wasn't so sure about phone sex though, she needed to think about it.

❖ CHAPTER EIGHT ❖

Saturday morning she met Justine at the train station. They linked arms after a friendly hug and began walking. Justine loved the Lexus again, it was so stylish, so classy, so…Nia. "Do you want to get brunch or lunch or something?" Nia asked as she maneuvered through traffic.

"How about afterwards?" Justine asked, her eyes twinkling. She fidgeted in her seat.

Nia glanced at her realizing that Justine was as horny as Nia and glad to know that fact. Nia had actually thought something was wrong with her with how much she thought about Justine, how wet she got over her, and after what had happened with their weekend together.

Justine was surprised how non-descript the building Nia lived in was. There wasn't even underground parking but instead there were assigned spots behind the building which surprised her as space was at a premium on this small island. Apparently there weren't many apartments in this old converted factory and from Nia's descriptions the apartments were pretty nice. She followed Nia through the back door next to the elevators and Nia pressed the tenth floor. Her apartment was one of two on this floor. On the sixth through ninth floors there were four apartments each. On the fifth again only two, on the second, third, and fourth they were divided into four. Or at least that was what Nia had been told when she bought the place. The first floor was taken up by stores. As Nia unlocked her apartment she gestured for Justine to proceed inside and she walked four steps before stopping dead at the beautiful huge apartment before her. Twenty foot ceilings faced her with huge sixteen foot windows. Nia hadn't even used all the wall space. Her furniture looked expensive, well made, and warm. Justine saw across the great expanse the fireplace Nia had spoken of with a wide screened television hanging above the mantle which had a large expensive looking jade dragon reclining on it. The windows had coverings that she could see were electrically controlled by the discrete buttons on the side, with windows that tall it was to be expected. Plants lined along each side of the windows hanging from beautiful antique looking hangers their leaves leaning towards the incredible amount of light that came through the windows. Matching candle hangers corresponded on the walls between the plants. Beautiful display cabinets contained trinkets and knick knacks under their glass. Pictures lined the tops of these cabinets. She could see beyond the living space to the left an ultra-modern kitchen and the bar that she knew Nia ate at often declining to use the dining room set to their left. A set of stairs curved down from the loft that held Nia's bedroom and a spare. Under the

spare bedroom was her den or office but Justine couldn't see it beyond the steps. It was lovely, it was immense, and it was Nia's.

Nia had been watching her face and didn't say a word as she helped her out of her coat. She waited until she turned back to her and asked, "Well, what do you think?"

"You need art-work on the walls," she said with a smile.

"I know huh, I never have time to shop for it though," Nia said laughing. It had been commented time and again with these huge bare walls she should put something up on them. Someone had even mentioned putting a hanging like some medieval knight to fill the spaces. She knew it wouldn't go with the decor but she had thought about an oriental rug perhaps.

"Maybe I should come into the city more often to help you shop," Justine smiled; they both knew she hadn't come into the city to shop as Nia took her in her arms.

The kiss was very satisfying. The feel of Nia's body against Justine made them both happy. It became heated almost immediately and Nia was soon leading Justine up her stairs to her bedroom where they 'practiced' time and again as they taught Nia to know her body and Justine demonstrated time and again. They spent a delightful day together and it wasn't until the sun was nearly down that they came up for air.

"That was a lot better don't you think?" Justine asked hesitantly, she knew from the responses that Nia had been a lot more relaxed this time.

"Yes, but still, *nothing,*" Nia lamented.

"Maybe you should just stop trying so hard for an orgasm and let it come naturally. I'm not going anywhere. You were a lot wetter this time," she smiled as she pushed hair from Nia's face that she was looking down into.

Nia loved to see Justine smile, it was such a wide and perfect smile, and it transformed her face into something beautiful. Her eyes though captivated her with their double lashes. She knew why she desired this woman; she just wished she could share in that special feeling that seemed to come so easily to Justine.

They went out to dinner at a nice little Greek restaurant. They enjoyed the time they had together and walked through a little mall so that Justine's excuse of coming into the city was legitimate. They shopped but bought nothing except for Justine buying a few trinkets for each of her kids. Neither wanted to say goodbye and Nia wanted desperately to wake up beside Justine, she wanted to sleep with her and knew there was no way to arrange it. Or was there?

❧ CHAPTER NINE ❧

A month later Nia was due to fly to Florida to meet with Allison Gottfried the head of a pharmaceutical company whose business that Chase-Dunham wanted to handle. Nia was lucky enough to get an interview with the busy woman for Friday. She was flying in Thursday and she handled all of her arrangements herself because she had also called Justine about it and arranged for her to fly in on a different flight. Justine had used the excuse that she needed to visit her sister who also lived in Miami. While Nia was in meetings with Allison Gottfried, Justine could visit with her sister. The rest of the time and their nights would be together.

Nia had given in and they had started having phone sex together. She had bought a headset to attach to her cell phone so that her hands could remain free while she played with herself. While she still hadn't had an orgasm, or thought she hadn't, she had come farther with relaxing and listening to Justine's coaching. The soothing tones of Justine's voice telling her to 'relax' were more exciting and stimulating than her toys sometimes. She had gotten wetter and more excited as time went by and she learned her body's responses and imagined Justine touching her so. Justine could tell by the panting and excitement in her lover's voice how close she was to having that actual orgasm she so sought. She was looking forward to being with her in Florida. They hadn't managed with Nia's schedule and Justine's to be together since that day when she took the train into New York. They were both looking so forward to seeing each other in Florida.

Nia waited in the terminal for Justine's plane to arrive. She knew Justine hated flying but had managed to convince her to come for this vacation. She had arranged a beautiful hotel suite overlooking the Atlantic Ocean and couldn't wait to be in Justine's arms after all their time apart. Their planes had arrived within forty five minutes of each other and she didn't mind the wait. It had been too long apart and she wanted to practice what she had learned on Justine's body. She wanted to share her own body with this amazing and exciting woman she had come to love. Their conversations had really excited them both and living so close and being unable to see each other had really increased their wants and desires. Telling someone you want them is nice; telling someone what you're going to do when you are together is nicer. It was easier to tell Justine the sexual things she wanted to try over the phone than it would be in person, now they both wanted to try those things in person. Her plane was late and Nia was getting impatient. She had to stay in the terminal because once

she left it to go get her luggage she couldn't come back in because of security. She paced, waiting until the doors opened and the first passengers began to walk out. She stood there silently waiting as she looked anxiously for the short blonde. She smiled broadly when she saw her walk out looking the worse for wear, she *really didn't like* flying. She saw Nia waiting for her and returned the broad smile. She walked right into Nia's welcoming arms and a big bear hug.

"Christ that was awful," she said by way of greeting.

Nia pulled back to look down at her friend, "Why? Did you hit turbulence?"

Justine shook her head, she just *hated* flying. They chatted animatedly as they began walking down the concourse towards the escalators that led down to the baggage claims. While Justine waited for their luggage to go around Nia went to security to claim her bag which had arrived an hour before with her flight. They met up at the car rental desk where Nia had reserved a nice sedan and they took a bus out to the outer lots where the cars were all parked. Nia made Justine choose the one from the row they were let off at. They had a nice little maroon sedan that they piled their luggage in. Nia drove it to the exit where they checked it off and they were soon on their way. She had a GPS and they drove off the freeway towards the Atlantic Ocean. The hotel had valet parking and they took their luggage inside and checked in. They were on the eighth floor overlooking the beach and had the tiniest balcony either had ever seen. The room had two twin beds though.

"Um, I requested a room with a king sized bed," Nia said to the bellboy questioningly.

He looked immediately uncomfortable as she looked at him waiting. "I'll phone down and see," he said as he turned his back on her.

Justine looked at Nia incredulously. She wouldn't have said a word but Nia was annoyed. She had paid for a room to overlook the ocean and for it to have a king sized bed.

He was soon off the phone and said, "Um, this is all they have, I'm sorry," but didn't look in the least bit sorry.

Nia's eyes narrowed. "I made this reservation myself. I have a confirmation for exactly what I ordered. I suggest you get your manager on the phone and tell him I am here on business, I am a lawyer, and I'm not going to dick around with this type of service."

He immediately got back on the phone. The tall brunette had cowed him with her tone.

Justine stared incredulously. She had never seen Nia in her 'lawyer' mode.

The bellboy handed her the phone reluctantly.

"Hello," she said impatiently.

"Yes ma'am, this is the manager, I'm sorry but there has been some mistake. We don't have another room to put you in."

"Well then since it's your mistake I expect you to correct it or accommodate me in some way. I requested a king sized bed, these are twin. I don't think that's the kind of mistake you want getting out."

"I'm sure you can understand that mistakes do happen madam," he said in an unctuous tone.

"Sir, I agree that mistakes do happen. It's why I'm good at what I do. I am a lawyer. I am also a partner in Chase-Dunham of New York. I'm sure my firm and every other firm I deal with would love to hear the story of how unaccommodating your hotel was to me while I was down here on business. Now, either you get me what my reservation was for, you provide me with better, or find me accommodations in another hotel that can provide me with what I reserved in your establishment," she said it all matter of factly, not threatening in the least but clearly pointing out his options.

At the name Chase-Dunham though the manager had been frantically looking at their reservations and availability lists. He quickly moved some things around and said, "Yes ma'am we will move you immediately. Could you please give the phone to our bellboy?" he asked pleasantly.

She handed the phone back to the utterly cowed bell boy.

"Get her up to the penthouse suite immediately," the manager hissed to the bell boy. "I'll send someone up with a key."

"This way ma'am," the bell boy gathered their luggage and headed for the elevator.

The penthouse suite was huge in comparison to the room they had been originally shown. At least four times the size it had room for a full couch, a piano, a bar, and an extended sized balcony overlooking other hotels as well as the Atlantic Ocean. "This is what my reservation was for?" Nia asked the bell boy amused.

He grinned, she was a lot less intimidating now that she was being accommodated, he shook his head, "No ma'am, I'm sure the mistake bumped you up a bit, I hope you enjoy your stay," he began to back out of the room.

"Wait a minute," Nia stopped him and took a ten-dollar bill out of her pocket to tip him. For two bags and the hassle she figured that was adequate to show them to their room.

"Look at this," Justine said as she twirled around the luxurious room.

Nia smiled at her antics as she took off her suit jacket and hung it up. She walked over to the bedroom double doors and opened them wide. This was about the size of the room they had been in earlier. She opened the balcony doors in here and let the warm tropical breeze into the rooms. She leaned back on the bed and said, "Wow, this is nice."

She was surprised when Justine straddled her hips and said, "Yes this is nice," and leaned down to kiss her.

Their kisses got rapidly hot and heavy. Nia was reaching under Justine's blouse when Justine's phone went off. "I've got to get it," Justine gasped as Nia tried to hold her back. Neither wanted to stop but Justine answered her phone anyway, "Hello?" Nia tried touching her and Justine pushed her hands away as best she could one handed. The conversation was rapid and Nia raised her eyebrow when she finished with "We'll be there." Justine looked down regretfully from her perch on Nia's hips. "That was my sister; we are expected at her house for drinks before going out to dinner."

Nia looked at her incredulously. "I thought we were down here for us?"

Justine got up off her lover and looked down on her and said, "You are here for work, I'm here to visit my sister, and we are here to have some fun."

Nia rolled her eyes but got up off the bed to pull on her shoes and jacket. Justine knew the way and drove them to a small suburb near Miami. To Nia the houses all looked the same, quickly built and the reason why a good storm knocked out whole sections of Florida. They were inexpensively made and of modular design.

The woman who answered the door looked only artificially like Justine. Jenn was a prettier version of Justine who was the older of the two. She also looked like an adult Barbie doll, all boobs and no personality. The two sisters, after introducing Nia, were soon involved in catching up. 'Had they never heard of a telephone?' Nia thought wryly as she declined a drink from Jenn's husband Rob. Their conversation excluded everyone until it was time to go out to dinner.

Rob and Jenn had chosen an authentic Italian Restorante. Nia was grateful as the food was delicious even if Jenn insisted her Italian husband order for the table. Nia found this a little rude as they had no idea of her tastes but Justine accepted it and Nia said nothing. She listened as the two sisters excluded everyone out of their conversation until Rob surprisingly asked her what she did.

"I'm an attorney in New York," she said modestly.

"Don't let her fool you," Justine put in having heard them begin a conversation. "She's a partner in a law firm in Manhattan. She's the youngest woman to have done that," she said proudly.

Nia's cheeks pinked slightly but she could see Rob was impressed and Jenn finally looking at her with some interest. "What kind of law do you practice," was the inevitable question. Everyone asked that.

"I'm a litigator. I don't specialize. I actually handle several types of law depending on our client's needs." She didn't like to be pigeonholed.

"Does that mean you handle divorces and stuff?" Jenn asked.

Nia looked across at the blonde calmly. She could tell that Jenn's question came not from a genuine interest but rather because Rob's interest had strayed from Jenn's conversation with Justine and she wanted to be a participant. "I handle divorces occasionally but I don't specialize in them. Whatever my client needs we have services for or can find for them. We have many associates who specialize so we can utilize them."

"Then you just coordinate it?" Jenn said, there was a note in her voice that Nia recognized as jealousy. As a housewife she was frequently bored and Nia had an important and exciting job in Manhattan. She needed to be the center of attention and while Nia hadn't asked for it she had taken away Jenn's moment from the table at large. Rob's interest in the tall woman on a social level needed to be curbed immediately, minimalized.

Nia smiled almost condescendingly, she wouldn't be put in her place by anyone. She didn't have 'a place' and wouldn't let this jealous little Barbie snipe at her. She shook her head. "No, if I need assistance I use my associates as a second chair if the case goes to court but I handle my own cases."

"Would we have heard of any?" Jenn asked.

"I don't know that it made the national news, probably not down *here*," making it sound like Miami was too small a burg to warrant the news. "But I won the Halmond Phere case last fall," she said modesty.

Justine looked at her in amazement. Everyone had heard of that case. Jenn's mouth barely kept from falling open. Rob enthused, "Of course we heard of that. Everyone did! You were involved with that?"

Nia nodded not adding anything.

"Can you tell us anything about it?" Jenn asked her eyes sparkling in malicious glee.

Nia shook her head. "No, I'm sorry, except for what you may have heard on TV or in the papers I can't reveal anything. Attorney-Client privileges and all that," she dismissed and waited to see what Jenn would do.

She could see that the Barbie was annoyed, she thrived on gossip from what Nia had overheard but Nia certainly wasn't going to provide her with more details. Not only would it be unprofessional but unethical. Nia never let anything out that they didn't want out for the client's benefit. She had been learning for years how to manipulate the press and she certainly wasn't going to reveal anything she didn't wish to reveal.

The rest of the meal was snippets of conversations. Jenn dominated it and Justine followed along, seemingly enthralled but Rob and Nia barely contributed. Nia was amused that Jenn obviously felt that she was 'all that' and that she had put the Manhattan Attorney in her place somehow.

"Well, shall we go shopping or something?" Jenn asked as they waited for their cars to show up from the valets.

Nia went to make an excuse but Justine jumped in, "Oh no, how about tomorrow, you can pick me up, I've got to get some sleep, between that flight and that delicious meal I'm beat!"

Jenn must have accepted the excuse at face value but Nia wasn't fooled and glancing at Rob, neither was he.

Nia didn't care as they were soon on their way; it was a lot quieter in the car as she maneuvered through traffic back to the hotel. After the gossipy chatter of Jenn the silence seemed deafening.

They were about five minutes from the hotel when Justine said, "I'm sorry for Jenn, she's normally not so snippy but she's jealous."

Nia looked over in surprise. "What has *she* to be jealous of?" She thought about her perfect little Barbie body and pert breasts.

"You don't see it do you?" Justine asked.

Nia glanced down to see if she had a spot on her suit or something as she shook her head.

Justine laughed. "You're a successful and attractive woman; she was pea green with jealousy!"

Nia glanced over to see if Justine was pulling her leg. "You saw what I looked like before my makeover," she thought about the Barbie looks. "What has *she* to be jealous of?"

Justine snorted through her nose. "She is stuck in her no end job in her house as a housewife and you are out there doing things that she can only *read* about!"

Nia felt uncomfortable and dropped the subject as they pulled up in front of the hotel and the valet ran out to take the keys. She escorted Justine inside and up in the elevator, taking advantage of their moment alone to kiss Justine in public despite being in an enclosed elevator…she knew the camera's would be on. Justine didn't seem to mind as she kissed back and smiled through the kiss.

Nia could look back on her weekend with Justine and her meetings with Allison Gottfried and smile at the wonderful time she had spent in Miami. Justine and she had explored more of their relationship, there was only the bothersome meetings that Nia had to attend but those put her in such a good mood that it translated when she met up again with Justine. Allison Gottfried either had the most inept attorneys or she hadn't ever met someone of Nia's caliber before because before the meetings ended Allison signed an agreement with Chase-Dunham and in particularly with Nia Toyomoto as a representative of her firm. It brought a lot of business into Chase-Dunham and everyone was going to share in this one.

Justine and Nia celebrated her success with nice meals out and countless hours in bed getting to know each other better, experimenting, and for Nia searching endlessly for that elusive orgasm that she knew was there but couldn't seem to find. Neither one of them seemed to mind though as they played to their hearts content, until they were happy and exhausted. Something Nia realized though was that despite not having an orgasm she was happier than she could remember ever being before. She loved Justine, and she was certain Justine loved her just as much. An orgasm didn't mean the everything, sometimes the journey was just as fun. As they tried out various toys and positions, learned each other, each kept their thoughts to themselves as to why Nia hadn't orgasmed.

Nia returned to New York on the same flight as Justine, something she had arranged so they could spend their last few minutes together, neither wished the weekend to end but Justine had to return to her family and Nia to her work. The weekend was a wonderful interlude and both would remember it fondly in the years to come.

"Allison Gottfried called and raved about you!" Stewart stopped Nia as she headed for her office.

"She should rave about me, I rocked," Nia joked as she smiled up into Stewart's delighted face.

Stewart pulled back in surprise at her cocky answer and smiled, "I'm sure you did."

"Seriously," she took his arm to lead him to her office since they seemed to be headed that way anyway. "Whoever represented her before was doing a very bad job."

Stewart escorted her back to her office and past Colleen who smiled a good morning as she typed away at her computer. Nia nodded as she continued into her offices with the head of the firm who let her arm drop and admired her taste in office decorations once again.

"You do know who used to represent her don't you?" He then mentioned another firm that they had been in competition with forever.

She raised her eyes in surprise and yet she wasn't that surprised. She knew what direction she wanted to go with Gottfried Pharmaceuticals and their current litigations. She had studied them extensively for the meeting and knew they could do better. She was just surprised the previous firm hadn't done anything like what she was planning before.

She and Stewart discussed the meeting for a while and he left pleased with her news and view on how it should go. She was going to put together a team from their own firm to handle the various aspects of litigation and go over the files that they were going to requisition from the previous firm as well as from the company and the various lawyers

involved in suing them. They would bury the competition in paperwork if they could but at the same time it would provide them with a lot of work and show that they were doing the job that would bring in a lot of business and money to the firm.

❧ CHAPTER TEN ❧

"Okay, here is the stack that needs to be done today, these can wait until tomorrow, but no later, and these get to when you can," Nia gave Colleen the stacks placing her hand on each as she emphasized their importance and set them on the table so that they remained separate and in order as Nia liked it. "Let me know if you need help on this," she slapped one of the stacks that had been piling up.

"Actually I think I do, contending with all this new stuff and keeping up on your older things is becoming a bit much," Colleen answered and blushed to admit she was falling behind, this hadn't happened before, but as Nia's work load had increased so had Colleen's exponentially. She had used the secretarial pool but as they were overloaded as well she really needed someone dedicated to just Nia's work as she was.

Nia wasn't surprised, her job had become horrendous and she had wondered how Colleen was coping. She noticed a bruise on her arm that her short sleeved blouse didn't quite hide and wondered momentarily if she should say something but then returned to the issue at hand. "Let's get a secretary or two assistants from the pool to help, maybe an intern, gawd knows I keep the legal assistants busy enough with research," she smiled.

Colleen laughed, complaints had been heard but she wasn't the only one busy these days, Nia and a few other lawyers had been bringing a lot into the firm. She felt confident having been with Nia for years that her job wasn't in jeopardy from the increased workload and knew that Nia had her back on it and utmost confidence in her. "Do you want to mention who you might want…" she began.

Nia shook her head causing her beautiful hair that was down today to wag in an attractive swing. "No, I want you to decide who and what you need. Maybe it's time to keep another assistant on full time, put another desk in the outer office, I'll leave that to you since you will have to work with him or her more than I will and I want you to supervise. I'll call personal and tell them you will be making a choice and to fully cooperate with you."

Colleen was thrilled at the unintentional praise and raise in status. Many lawyers made all the decisions in their offices and she appreciated Nia's confidence in her.

"Are you going to make it to Thursday's dinner?" Nia asked changing the subject as her mind worked in its multi-tasking mode.

"Did you need…" began Colleen hesitantly thinking she had forgotten something and trying to wrack her brain.

"No, nothing." Nia grinned realizing Colleen didn't get it. "The girls were asking if you'd be there."

"Ohhh," Colleen laughed at herself, she didn't realize this was social and then she realized that she might not be able to make it. "I have to get home but maybe next time."

Nia remembered the bruise on Colleen's arm and wondered if perhaps that was causing her to hesitate. She had tried to help her on numerous occasions but Colleen still denied that anything was wrong. "I hope so 'cause otherwise they are going to think it's my fault you don't come out for drinks," she said with a joke.

Colleen laughed buying it.

"Mr. Stephanos, I will be unable to represent you in this case, I am sorry to of wasted your time," and with that Nia rose to leave the room leaving behind an ominous quiet that the other shocked attorney's didn't or couldn't break.

The man rose to stop her from leaving the office and grabbed her arm to ask, "Why not?"

Nia studied the genuine puzzlement on the man's face, he had no clue but she looked pointedly at the fingers restraining her until he looked down too and removed them looking back up apologetically and waiting for a reply to his question. She looked him straight in the face and said, "You sir are an elitist, I'll help you GOOGLE that word if you can't spell it, but your remarks are hurtful to the average man and that's why these people feel you owe them. You can't keep your big mouth shut long enough to prevent another lawsuit from cascading over the others that are pending. You compound matters because you can't see that an average Joe can't afford $100 tickets for seats in the nose bleed sections of the stadiums just so he can see your precious self perform, badly I might add, you certainly are NOT worth the hundred million dollars you're asking over the next five years." As Nia talked to the man she backed him down, he wasn't used to such tall women and she slowly advanced on him as she got in his personal space until he sat down abruptly and looked up at her towering over his chair. "Furthermore, going on national television and crying over the high rates you have to pay for insurance on your Lamborghini is not going to win anyone to your side in any of these cases. People hate you, for those reasons and more. I won't represent an idiot and you've been not only playing like one but acting like one. You won't listen to me, you won't listen to them," her arm swept the room of lawyers, paralegals, secretaries, and agents. "Since you won't, why waste either of our time." With that Nia turned and swept out the room with Colleen hurrying after her.

LAWYERED

Pete Stephanos turned to his agents and said, "She's the one!" The agents and other lawyers exchanged wary glances and then got down to business as to a plan of action.

"No Stewart, I won't represent Pete Stephanos, he's an arrogant prick who won't listen to anyone," she told the senior partner.

"Yes, he *is* an arrogant prick." He wanted to smile at her choice of words but didn't as he continued to try and persuade her to take on this difficult and profitable client. "But he is also an arrogant prick whose money means a lot to this firm. He has also assured me personally that he would listen to you, you will call all the shots," he assured her.

"Yes, until he gets out of this dilemma and gets into another one, do you really want to babysit this overgrown idiot?"

"Since when have we been choosy about who we represent?" he asked in a no-nonsense voice.

Nia took the tone for what it was worth, this was after all the senior partner, her sponsor, and he obviously wanted her to take on this difficult client. "I just want it known though if he continues to behave the way he has in the past that we can eliminate him for cause and keep the outrageous fee I intend to charge!"

"I'm sure you will word it in legalese," he smiled knowing he had won.

Nia did just that, pouring over books and getting the wording just right, it certainly wasn't a standard attorney-client contract but rather one that one Mr. Pete Stephanos would pay to heed or they *would* break him or rather Nia would.

"I wouldn't sign that if I were you Pete," his other attorney's recommended as they glanced at Nia, almost fearfully.

"You're not me and I like her," he said petulantly as he looked down at the paperwork and read through it, although he didn't completely understand it Nia had explained the critical paragraphs telling him exactly what she would do to him if he reneged on their agreement and what she was prepared to do to him in that case. She also had a plan of attack regarding the latest allegations against him and how to fight them; he was pleased all around at what she was telling him and what she had threatened him with. He respected that about her and was willing, for the moment, to listen to her and behave. They both knew it might be a matter of time before he fell off this particular wagon but they were both willing to give it a try, him because he had run out of options and she because she knew the amount of money it would bring into the firm either way.

"Cleaning house?" Stewart thumbed at the additions in the outer office as Nia looked up from the couch where she was reading briefs.

"What?" she asked puzzled before the sense of what he had said penetrated and then she smiled and shook her head. "No, I needed another assistant and Colleen got them a desk," she answered.

"About time too," he said knowing she had been borrowing from the pool and while they were good she needed someone loyal. "Who'd you hire?" he asked as he came into the room to head for her cappuccino machine.

"I don't know, you'll have to ask Colleen," she said absentmindedly as she put her finger on the line she was reading to hold her place.

"Ask Colleen?" he asked in surprise as he poured himself a small cup.

She looked back up and nodded. "Yes, she was the one that is doing the hiring; she has to work with whoever it is."

He nodded musingly realizing her argument was valid, he hadn't thought about it when he got an assistant for Sally. It made sense; he wondered if Sally got along with Bette, it had never occurred to him before. "I hear you have a meeting with Lawrence Catwood this afternoon?"

She nodded as she stopped reading again wondering why Stewart was bothering her and realizing it was probably about that very issue and not her delicious cappuccino.

"Do you know what you are going to say?" he asked hoping for some details into her fine mind and how she was going to handle such a difficult client.

She nodded again as she out waited him. He grinned realizing she was too good at her job to show her hand, to anyone. Saluting her he took a gulp of the excellent cappuccino and left the office as Nia returned to her reading.

"Colleen?" he stopped at her desk.

"Yes sir?" Colleen made to get up from her desk but he gestured her to stay.

"Could you make sure Sally has the name of that excellent cappuccino and where we can get that cappuccino maker," he gestured with his thumb back into Nia's office.

"I can get you the cappuccino maker and where I got it but Nia buys her own cappuccino," she told him.

He smiled. "I bet she won't tell either," he shook his head despairingly and Colleen nodded knowingly.

"Are you saying I should lie? Disappear?" Lawrence Catwood asked despairingly.

"No, absolutely not, I am never going to tell you that. But what I am saying is that you don't have to make this so easy for them. They are suing you. Make it as difficult as you can for them. Don't volunteer information; don't give them anything they don't compel you to show. Rather than hand them their case on a silver platter, make them earn their money." She shrugged. "Maybe if you make it hard enough for them, *costly* enough, they will give up." She rose to leave the room.

"Wait a minute," Lawrence halted her from leaving.

She looked back waiting patiently, the picture of innocence.

"You're hired," he said realizing that an honest attorney was hard to find and this one at least would bend the rules without breaking them.

❧ CHAPTER ELEVEN ☙

"So what are *you* wearing?" Colleen asked seductively into the phone.

Nia stared at her in shocked surprise. She didn't *talk* like that. She wasn't sure she hadn't heard it wrong. She had asked her to answer the phone for her but was stunned to overhear that line. She looked around the edge of the bedroom door and down into the living area where Colleen had picked up the house phone.

Colleen hung up the phone and laughed murmuring, "That will teach you to call during 'optimum sales hours'." She laughed again as she went into the kitchen to continue prepping for the party.

Nia relaxed and laughed to herself realizing it must have been a phone solicitor, what a clever way to handle them! Colleen was such an excellent assistant!

"Just because you *think* you have me by the short hairs, don't assume I won't go for the full Brazilian!" Nia towered over the opposing council in her anger and their smug little client. Her own client was visibly cowering at what they had just pulled.

"There is no need to get crude," opposing council returned a little prudishly.

"No?" Nia's expertly plucked eyebrow rose in an otherwise stony face. "After what you just subtly implied, I do think it's apropos."

"Look, your client is clearly guilty," she gestured to the squirming man seated beside Nia.

"Clearly?" again Nia's eyebrow rose only this time in astonishment as she interrupted. "I don't think so; I believe that is all up to interpretation. A jury surely wouldn't think so."

"A jury?" the other lawyer returned haughtily attempting to bluff Nia. "I thought we were here to work out a settlement or agreement so this didn't have to go to trial?"

Nia however wasn't about to be bluffed, she knew their case wasn't that strong but the nastiness of the other attorney on behalf of their slimy client had pissed her off and she had lowered herself to her own version of crudity. She wasn't going to be cowed by them and she smelled some information hadn't been disclosed. With apparent disregard she answered, "I'm sure the courts would appreciate us not tying up their time with this." She gestured at the paperwork spread out on her oversized table; she knew her office alone had intimidated both her client and theirs. "But if it's necessary, I'm prepared to go to court and prove my client has been

slandered, smeared with that," she indicated the opposing council's client who had lost his cocky grin at her words. "And we will of course be suing for costs including defamation of character and all that as well as those costs involved in investigating this further including disclosure."

The attorney exchanged a look with her client and turned back to Nia and her client, "Could we have a moment?" she asked.

Nia immediately nodded and indicated to her client that they would be leaving the room for a moment. As they came through the office door she caught the edge of the door frame momentarily as she pulled the door firmly behind her. Colleen looked up from her desk in surprise to see Nia standing there with her client. "Can I get you something to drink while we wait?" Nia asked her client cordially and saw out of the corner of her eye as Colleen made to get up and fetch it.

"Ms. Toyomoto," her client began nervously, he had an awful habit of slicking back his greasy comb over on his balding head with his hand and it grossed Nia out.

She interrupted raising a hand in objection, "Please, call me Nia," for the umpteenth time.

"Nia," he started again, just as nervous as before. "I thought, we didn't *want* this to go to court," he whispered.

Nia smiled reassuringly. "No, we don't but *they* don't *know* that do they?" She thought back over the last hour and a few key things stood out. "There is something there though, they don't want us to know and if they think we know of it I believe this may work out for us."

"But what if they call your b b bluff," he stuttered as he whispered.

Nia shrugged. "Then we go to court," and watched as the rest of the color drained from his already perspiring face. "Trust me." She smiled and put a hand on his arm before it could make the now familiar gesture of going through what little hair he had left. "There is something there and with all criminals they fear being found out, you just need to have patience."

Colleen watched fascinated as Nia calmed her client. This man had been so nervous about even approaching Nia to defend him in his case. He had almost bolted waiting for the first meeting. In the ensuing months as Nia worked the case he had become increasingly agitated in worry over going to prison. Colleen had seen the other client and his cocky demeanor made you think he knew it all, that he couldn't possibly have done what they were accused of.

They waited fifteen minutes as the client nervously drank cup after cup of water and paced. Nia went over a couple of files that Colleen handed her while she stood there and glanced up as the client took yet another drink from the water cooler and then returned to pacing. Occasionally she exchanged a glance with Colleen. Finally though the door opened and

opposing council smiled at Nia, "Thank you for your consideration, we are ready to continue."

Nia closed the file she had just finished her notes on and handed it without a glance to Colleen.

They had won. A lot more than expected, in fact no one had thought they could win this case. They had a large check that had been messengered over and they were just waiting for their client to come in and pick it up and sign the final papers. He had promised to write a check for the firm's percentage on the spot. They would wait a couple of days and cash it. She looked at the cashier's check and the many zero's on it and smiled. She knew there had been something there, she couldn't put her finger on it and while curiosity teased at her she didn't really want to know, it was healthier not to really know the whole truth.

"Won another one for us Nia?" Stewart stuck his head in a few days later as Nia sat working diligently at her desk.

She looked up in pleasant surprise to see him walk in as he headed for her cappuccino machine. He indicated it and silently asked as she nodded. "Which case would that be?" she pretended ignorance but she knew, and he knew that she knew. The whole firm had buzzed about it because this case, this particular case meant a ton of new business that had walked into the firm with the hope that Chase-Dunham and particularly Nia Toyomoto could help them. In fact Stewart had just checked with Colleen and Nia's schedule was so full that she really had no room for new appointments. She had commandeered some of the best first and second year lawyers the firm had and they had all complained at the high expectations she had for them and their work. Stewart had laughed when he heard. Nia had high expectations of herself; there was no sin in expecting the same from her co-workers. She had given the family law and finance law department a ton of referrals and not just in the past few days either. Only two other lawyers in the firm had billable hours even close to Nia's and he wasn't going to let complaints go any further than they had.

He grinned in response to her innocent question. "Nia, you never disappoint," he answered.

"I actually am pleased with myself on this one as well, I couldn't put my finger on it but there was just something there and we needed to play it out."

He shook his head at her modesty, she was good, she was just *that* good. Brilliant, attractive, and lethal, a heady combination and they had benefited. As a partner her share in the firm would make her very rich, very rich indeed. "That last party was spectacular, I hadn't expected to

meet Senator Ellington in this lifetime," he commented, he had been impressed despite himself.

"He actually knew my father and I didn't think he would come but I sent an invitation anyway, he knows the mayor and invited him," she remembered the party he was referring to. It had been a good one connection wise. Colleen had out done herself and Nia had made sure to compensate her with a bit extra under the table, she only hoped she had been able to keep it from her husband's greed.

"That Graber Van Lines case he referred us to is going to be a monster," he added admirably.

She smiled at the challenge it represented, it had taken up a lot of the firm's resources and the billable hours had been horrendous thus far. "I think this will put us on the map," she joked.

Stewart laughed, they were already on the map, hell with this they made the maps. "Don't you be getting sick on us or anything," he shook a finger at her as he took a sip of her most excellent cappuccino.

She laughed, she didn't have time to be sick and other than an occasional three day weekend she didn't take time off. They had been curious about her personal life but as far as anyone at the firm was concerned she didn't have one. Work, work, work was what Nia Toyomoto was known for. "I'm not planning on any sick days."

"Is there anything you need?" he asked sincerely, it paid to keep all their lawyers happy but this partner of theirs had proved to be a brilliant addition to the firm's roster.

"I'm fine," she told him immediately wondering if there was anything else she should be aware of, she listened for things like that but everything had been working out smoothly lately.

"You'd tell me if there was something?" he asked fatherly, he liked this partner of theirs, she was good, she hadn't let the 'conditions' of her partnership undermine her in any way. She had risen to the occasion admirably and excelled at it beyond their wildest hopes and dreams. Several of the senior partners had commented on what a wise decision it had been to make her a partner. The money didn't lie and the subsequent sharing of wealth as well as additional business for them all had been appreciated.

Nia gave him her full attention wondering if there was anything she wasn't picking up on. Her intuition told her that Stewart was just checking in on her to make sure she was happy. She was. She had a personal life she enjoyed that wasn't too intrusive on her time and her work fulfilled her in so many ways. Was there more? "Is everything okay Stewart?" the lawyer in her turned the question on him.

He laughed shaking his head knowing exactly what she was doing; he had been a lawyer for too many years not to recognize the same in another.

"Everything is fine; I wanted to thank you for winning that case and make sure everything was fine here. I also heard you blew up at Cayla Burns the other day and wanted to make sure you weren't stressing out or anything."

"Cayla Burns should thank her stars that she hasn't been fired for incompetence. I merely pointed out to her that her job was not to accommodate a client in so *personal* a manner but merely that she *do* her job."

Stewart laughed to himself, he had thought it was something like that but wanted to be sure before proceeding. Cayla had filed a report with Human Resources. "I hate to ask..." he began but Nia was ahead of him and held up a hand.

She reached into her desk drawer and pulled out a file. "I believe this is the report of the incident you were just about to ask for," she told him blandly.

Stewart reached for the file not in the least surprised that she had it ready for him and typed up. He glanced over her version of the events and nodded sagely. "I'll file this with HR personally," he replied.

Nia wanted desperately to get back to her paperwork; she had real work to do and didn't have patience or time to deal with trifles. People like Cayla Burns were trifles and a waste of time. She watched as he put the cappuccino cup in the sink before looking back at her. "Was there anything else?" her eyebrow raised in question.

He smiled and shook his head. "No, not at all," he hesitated before adding, "Thank you Nia, good job," he indicated the paperwork piled on her desk that he himself knew he would want to get back to as well as he nodded and left her office.

❧ CHAPTER TWELVE ❧

The months had flown by, new clients, old and established ones, Nia was living the life she had wanted for a long time, if something was missing she wasn't sure she missed it. Justine was still in her life and they enjoyed each other fully.

"Can you help me with the divorce?" she had asked finally as they lay on Nia's comfortable bed one afternoon.

Nia shook her head. "No, that would be a conflict of interest and I would prefer to stay completely out of this if you don't mind, I can refer you to one of our other attorneys or another one out on Long Island that might be less expensive."

Justine sat up feeling a little hurt that her girlfriend had refused to help her. Nia looked at her calmly feeling more in control of herself than she had in a long time, she had gotten used to having Justine in her life and she wondered at the love she felt for this woman. She felt confident in it. "You won't help me?"

Nia sighed inwardly, sometimes she felt a little irked by Justine, she was a brilliant mother, a fantastic lover, but she sometimes knew their relationship wouldn't be forever. That thought alone scared her, she didn't want to be alone, she had just found her, she was learning so much about herself through her relationship with Justine. She had just experienced her first orgasm, or so they thought, they'd have to work on that one and both were willing to 'experiment' until they were sure. "I am helping you by not taking it on myself, if your husband realizes I'm involved I could get in a lot of trouble, embarrassment not the least of my worries…"

Justine realized that was true and appreciated that Nia would help her find an attorney. "Well, make sure she understands my predicament!" she said annoyed.

Nia wanted to laugh, first at Justine's assumption that it would be a woman, second that she was so easy to annoy. She knew how to tease her out of her annoyance though as she pounced on the other woman's body and began to make love to her.

Justine loved Nia's body and reached into the robe she was wearing to touch those breasts she adored, they had learned a lot together in the past months and she couldn't help but respond.

"What the hell was that?" Nia asked as she realized she must have peed.

"Relax baby, you just ejaculated," Justine rushed to assure her, wanting to laugh at her lover but pleased for her.

"I though only guys ejaculated," Nia asked but remembered things she had read and realized how dumb that sounded.

"You should be proud of yourself," Justine stated. "Not everyone can do that, I know I can't," she said ruefully.

"I'm going to have to keep a towel near the bed when we make love then," Nia complained good-naturedly.

They laughed and played the afternoon away learning more about each other physically and talking for hours.

"No, we don't want a trial date on a Friday," she assured the group, the client looked at her questioningly and Nia explained, "It's the night after," she named a popular television show. "And the lawyers who follow that show tend to be more aggressive the day after it airs and the judges who watch it tend to come down a little harder as a result."

"You're kidding!?" the client gasped in amazement.

Nia shook her head. "Furthermore, if this goes bad, you don't want to be stuck in jail over the weekend when there is no way to get you out until Monday, everyone they put in jail over the weekend, from drunks to who knows what has access to you."

The client shook their head at Nia's reasoning. Thinking about it though they realized her arguments were valid and while they sounded outlandish could possibly cause them a lot of unnecessary problems. "Okay then, no Friday hearings!" they agreed.

"Why did you tell them that," one of the other attorney's questioned Nia later.

"Because it's true and the client needs to know there is a strategy to their defense, I'm not in this just for their business but to actually win," Nia said with a sardonic look in her eye.

"But that nonsense about the TV shows…"

"It's not nonsense; statistics show that people are influenced by what they watch on television, whether they allow their behavior to come out from it or not, whether they know it's real or not, they make assumptions. Even those of us who know better tend to get a little pumped when their favorite characters have something happen to them."

They stared at Nia like she had lost her mind but then as the words penetrated they had to concede she was right.

"She's defending what?"

"Our client is being sued for having a dog," Stewart answered blandly.

"How did you allow it to get this far, why wasn't it settled?" one of the partners asked incredulously.

He shrugged not knowing Nia's strategy. He did wonder though that this was actually going to trial. Stewart slipped into one of the back chairs of the courtroom to watch their young partner defend their client.

"And sir you are certain that it was Mr. Jenkins's dog that was keeping you up night after night?"

"Yes ma'am, the police were called on several occasions."

"Your Honor, I submit the police reports that the plaintiff is referring to," Nia pulled a sheaf of papers from the file folder on her table, handed the copies to the defense attorney and submitted them to the clerk who handed them to the judge for reference.

The judge nodded after perusing them for her to continue. "Now, the police refer to this as a nuisance violation, is that correct sir?" Nia asked politely.

"Yes, that damned dog is a nuisance," the witness testified annoyed as he spat it out and then cringed at the judge's admonition.

"Language," the judge said solemnly.

Nia was done playing with him; her client had gotten what he wished out of the suit, adequate representation, a decent fee, and the documents she had prepared in the file folder. "Sir, are you aware that Mr. Jenkins does not own a dog, nor has he owned a dog in seven years?"

There was muttering in the courtroom for the waste of time that the plaintiff had caused the court. Stewart sat up wondering what she was going to do now.

"But I *heard* the dog, many times!" the defendant sputtered.

"What you heard sir was the neighbor behind your properties, you have sued the wrong man out of sheer spite." Nia turned to the judge, "Your Honor, my client has denied this suit from the beginning. The defendant refused to drop it or discuss it." She shrugged dramatically. "I would like to put forth this counter-suit for damages including attorney's fees and a waste of the court's time!" Nia picked up the prepared documents and handed them to the clerk who then handed them to the judge.

"Objection your Honor!" the prosecuting attorney stood up outraged.

The judge waved him down as he read over the documents and looked over his half-moon spectacles at Nia's client, Mr. Jenkins. "Sir, is it true that you do not own a dog?"

Mr. Jenkins stood up as Nia had prompted him in preparation for this moment today and nodded politely. "Yes sir, I do not own any pets, I did try to tell him," he gestured helplessly at the plaintiff. He shrugged. "I'm allergic. He wouldn't listen," he finished with disgust.

The judge was angry and cast a glance at Nia to see her reaction. She stood there looking tall and proud but no reaction went across her face.

Beside her the plaintiff's attorney was looking apoplectic, ready to explode, realizing he had been outmaneuvered and outsmarted by this woman. The judge looked down at the paperwork seeing it was all in order. He looked over at the plaintiff and said, "Sir you may go sit down." Some of the court's time was further wasted as he looked to see that the paperwork was in order. "Ms. Toyomoto I am dismissing all charges against your client, in return I grant your request for all charges to be levied against the plaintiff on behalf of the defendant. It seems the nuisance charges were misdirected," he finished wryly as he brought down his gavel with finality.

Nia nodded her thanx and turned to approach her client who shook her hand in gratitude.

"Thank you Nia, I didn't think you could pull this off," he said softly under the conversation that had arisen immediately all around them after the judge's pronouncement.

"Shhh, right now act relieved and pleasant, no emotions," she warned as the judge left the courtroom. Nia sensed rather than saw the plaintiff's attorney behind her as she packed her briefcase. Glancing up at her client who waited patiently she saw him looking beyond her and she turned with paperwork she had prepared in her hand.

"Well Nia, I didn't think you could pull this one off, just goes to show you how things can surprise you," he said holding out his hand to be shook.

Nia shook his hand with her right hand holding the paperwork in her left. "Well Mike, it just goes to show you that you can teach an old dog new tricks," she grinned at the wordplay and then handed him the invoice for his client. "I'm sure you can explain this to your client," she smiled as she slung her briefcase strap over her shoulder and gesturing to her client to follow her she pushed the swinging gate and held it for her client as they walked out of the courtroom leaving a very angry plaintiff with his attorney.

Outside the courthouse the client shook her hand warmly. "Thank you Nia, that was the silliest thing I've ever heard and I appreciate you making him the fool!"

"Just remember, it's a game, we will win but only if you keep your cool and do not respond with emotions," she warned him again as she smiled.

"You are worth every dime," he said enthusiastically as he nodded to her and spotting Stewart watching them gave a little salute and sauntered off to catch a cab.

"What was that about?" Stewart asked as he came up behind Nia.

Nia turned having spotted him in the courtroom but playing her part to the hilt had ignored him. "Good Morning Stewart, don't you have anything better to do than to check up on the partners?"

He laughed as she had expected him to. Gesturing at the departing client he asked, "What was that about?"

"Do you have your car and driver? I could use a lift, I will tell you on the way," she said mysteriously with a gleam in her eye.

He nodded and escorted her to the Lincoln Town Car that waited for him opening the door for her to get in the back with him. "Back to the office," he directed the driver before closing the window between them. "Now?" he asked with a raised eyebrow.

She grinned. "Mr. Jenkins came to me with a lawsuit for having a barking dog. He had tried to tell the police he didn't own a dog but still the complaints came in and the reports. He wanted to go to court with it. You know Mr. Jenkins," she said with a grin.

He nodded; he did indeed know Mr. Jenkins, a real pain in the ass about lawsuits. "But why would you take this to court?"

She smiled. "Because his neighbor thought he had him on something small and something petty in order to hide the bigger suit he would be shortly attempting. He wants to own all the property on the block and has started these nuisance suits before. In fact, if you look at the history on his small section of New York, he owns a pretty good chunk. Mr. Jenkins has decided it's time to pay him back and take back some of the properties he has won through lawsuits. He starts with something small like this dog barking, by the way Jenkins really hasn't owned a dog in years, and then he bankrupts the owners with other equally stupid suits and their attorney's fees. That's why today we had the paperwork for the counter-suit ready and the judge, who was already angry, was willing to read what we requested. I get paid a lot of money that will not be coming out of Jenkins pocket even if he can pay. This time Renaulds is going to pay and he is paying *a lot*. Once that is paid Jenkins has a few other suits up his sleeve that he would like me and the firm to look into. He wants revenge, he can afford it, and Renaulds barked up the wrong tree," she finished with a grin, enjoying her pun.

Stewart shook his head. He should have known Nia Toyomoto wouldn't waste valuable company time and resources on a mere dog barking suit for one of their important clients. She looked at the long range possibilities and Renaulds properties would be quite valuable to Jenkins. Jenkins various properties were all handled by the firm. It would in turn become very profitable to everyone involved. He smiled at her and her astute handling of the client. "You know, you are amazing," he complimented her.

As the prosecution got louder and louder in their rants Nia got quieter and quieter. Many in the courtroom wondered at this as they watched the

judge lean in to hear her over the prosecution's rants, often asking her to repeat herself. As Stewart watched he couldn't help but wonder why she didn't blow, the prosecution was rather vile. He with everyone else in the courtroom was therefore shocked when the judge ruled in favor of Nia and their client. He was obviously guilty but apparently the judge thought Nia's quietly spoken arguments to be valid as he hammered his gavel in their favor. The prosecutor looked on disbelievingly, his mouth hanging open in surprise. The firm's client shook Nia's hand happily as his wife came through the barrier gate to give him and then Nia a hug. Stewart was amused to see the impeccable Nia Toyomoto look uncomfortable at the gesture but happy over the win. She escorted the client and his wife out of the courtroom nodding to Stewart who made a gesture. Nia halted outside of the courtroom waiting patiently as Stewart spoke with a few people he recognized. She looked pointedly at her watch as she looked at the spectators streaming out. Stewart caught her amused look as the prosecutor gave her a dirty look on his way out of the courtroom.

"You want to explain that technique to me?" he asked quietly as they began to walk down the hall together.

"What?" she asked innocently.

He grinned, not fooled in the least. A lot of court action was about posturing, acting, and knowing your stuff. Nia had the stuff but he hadn't seen this particular ploy before and was interested in hearing what that was about. "That case wasn't really winnable," he said wryly. "The most we could hope for was a settlement; I'm surprised you took it to court."

"When I heard which judge had been assigned I bluffed to the prosecution knowing what he would do in court and played it accordingly."

"So why were you so quiet?" he asked truly puzzled. He still didn't get it.

"Look, Barney over there gets way too upset over things, he is all bluster. Judge Owens doesn't like a show. He wants professionalism at all times. I was courteous, quiet, and I argued well. I won because I didn't piss him off as I knew Barney would."

Stewart looked at this partner with genuine appreciation, she had played it well. "You did your homework," he commented.

"Damn straight," she murmured as they left the courthouse.

Stewart laughed, his confidence in her well founded and he couldn't wait to tell the other partners about what he had observed. "Do you need a ride back to the office?" he asked.

Nia shook her head. "Nope, since I got out of there much sooner than I expected I'm going to take a longer lunch with some friends." She waved as she headed off down the sidewalk.

Stewart wondered briefly at who her friends were but having known about the realtor Eleanor James he was certain her friends were high caliber.

"This is a copy of the defendant's book that you are suing said defendant over? Is that correct?" she asked.

Gavin McCord looked at the cover and nodded.

"I'm sorry; you must speak a yes or a no for the court."

"Sorry, yes, that looks like the book," he answered leaning into the microphone so everyone could hear him clearly.

"Tell me, how do you know this is a copy of the book?"

"It has the two men on the cover and it says her name right there," he gestured.

"Let me enter this into evidence your honor, a copy of the book, 'Savage Pleasures,' by my client Ms. Emily Dante." The purple covered book showed two men wrapped around each other as though they were struggling but portraying passion with their strongly muscled bodies that wore no shirts, their eyes locked on each other. One of the men looked similar to the defendant who sat fully clothed in an Armani suit on the witness stand. Fluttering from various pages on the outer part of the book were post it notes.

The judge nodded to his clerk and the book was entered into evidence.

Nia opened the book and went to a tagged page. "Could you read this aloud to the court please?" she asked Gavin as she handed him the book.

He took the paperback in his big hands and looked down at the passage that she indicated. It was obvious he wasn't comfortable reading aloud as soon as he began to read, "PUBLISHER'S NOTE This is a work of fiction. Names, characters, places, and incidents are the product of the author's imagination or are used fictitiously, and any resemblance to actual persons, living or dead, business establishments, events, or locales is entirely coincidental." He finished with a flourish as though proud of his accomplishment, he had read the entire passage a loud and clear, if painfully slow and halting.

Nia waited a moment to let that sink into everyone's consciousness. It was obvious the defendant had no idea what it meant. "Do you understand what you just read Mr. McCord?"

He blinked a moment as he thought about it and shook his head.

Nia retrieved the book from his hand, gently taking it back as she read aloud what he had just read to the court. "This is a work of *fiction*. Names, characters, places, and incidents are the product of the author's *imagination* or are used *fictitiously*, and *any resemblance* to actual persons, living or dead, business establishments, events, or locales is entirely

coincidental." She emphasized certain words for effect. She looked up at him to see if it was sinking in, if he understood what she had just read to him. She could see the reactions of the juror's as well as the judge who despite his solemn demeanor she could see was incredulous at the stupidity of him as well as his lawyer.

"So you don't understand what you just read to this court or what I read to you?"

He shook his head again and the judge instructed him to say yes or no. He leaned forward to speak into the microphone again and said, "No ma'am."

"It means Mr. McCord that my client can use made up names and that it is just a coincidence that yours was used," she gently explained. She saw several jurors nod their heads as though to explain it to him.

"She can't use my name though!" he said indignantly.

She smiled as she shook her head, "But she can, she can make up any name she wants."

"But not *my* made-up name!" he emphasized to make his point.

She seized on that, "Are you saying Mr. McCord that your name is made up?"

"Yes, I made it up myself!" he said proudly as though he had done an amazing deed. He didn't see his lawyer slowly shaking his head in the background hidden by Nia's body as she grilled him.

Nia turned to the judge and asked, "What are we doing here then your honor? This is a waste of the court's time, this is a waste of resources, it is obvious this is a frivolous lawsuit brought for the sole purpose of getting someone's name in the papers and on the television. I ask that all charges be dismissed against my client." She gestured to the table where Emily Dante sat.

The judge agreed and before the other lawyer could fully voice his objections the judge dismissed the case fully and admonished Gavin McCord and his lawyer for wasting the courts time. He also imposed all court costs to be paid by them. He apologized to the jury and dismissed them, thanking them for their wasted time.

Emily shook Nia's hand emphatically. "I didn't know how you were going to get me out of this one!" she said gratefully.

Nia shrugged off her thanks, something about this case in general had stunk from the get go but Emily Dante was an important client of the firm and she was required to take the case. As she left the courthouse though she went down a little used hallway instead of taking the elevator intent on using the stairs. She saw Emily Dante and Gavin McCord in animated conversation. She shook her head as they shook hands and parted.

"So you won another for Emily Dante, that woman sure winds up in court more often than not!" Stewart said as he greeted her back at the firm as she got off the elevators.

"If she didn't write such provocative fiction she wouldn't ruffle so many feathers. This time though I think she set us up," she informed him.

"Set us up? How?" he asked concerned as he escorted her to her office.

She waited until they were behind closed doors to confide what she saw and suspected. "If she did pay him to create this lawsuit, she used artwork that looked very much like him. The newspapers and other press ate this up. That could mean millions in sales of her novels as well as getting his name plastered all over the place. Both of them win in this case and even the court costs that the judge imposed weren't that much."

Steward shook his head at the idea that their client had used them as a publicity stunt. He trusted Nia's instincts though. "I take it you don't want to represent her next time?" he asked.

Nia grinned. "I don't mind representing her but that three ring circus she just enacted; let's make sure she knows that we know *next* time!"

"I plead the fifth! Nah, who am I kidding, I drank it!" he joked but no one was laughing. Especially not the snobby lawyer who towered over him. "You hate me don't you?" he asked with a bit of a sneer.

"Just because I hate you doesn't mean I can't represent you," Nia said with a sarcastic little smile.

The client looked at her startled and began to laugh; his laughter was deep, sincere, and lasted a long time.

Nia exchanged looks with Howard wondering if her 'smart' mouth had cost them this account.

As the client's laugh wound down he wiped the tears from his eyes and said, "That's right it doesn't and you are hired if you are still willing to take the case?"

Howard looked at Nia incredulously and then was all smiles as he rose to shake hands with their difficult client.

"You may wish to settle this out of court," Layton Orion suggested to his client.

"And why would I wish to do that?" he was asked.

"Because the woman suing you is represented by Nia Toyomoto and she will be probing into every aspect of your life and using it against you in court," he answered with devastating effect. He watched as what he had said sunk in, the nuances taking a little longer.

"So you are afraid of this other lawyer?"

"No, I could probably beat her. But she is good, she is *very* good, and she is one of the most thorough attorney's I've come across in a long time. Her reputation is such that you may wish to consider every angle of this entire case before you decide. Before you proceed with this, and it is *your* decision, I suggest you think about it and what she might uncover before we continue. Everything she uncovers could come to light in the course of the trial and testimony."

The client thought it over for a few moments and nodded slightly. "Fine, offer them a settlement." They then proceeded to hammer out an agreement that Layton could present to opposing counsel that might settle this case before it even came to court.

Nia wasn't surprised when they asked for a meeting to discuss a settlement. What did surprise her was the amount and she argued with them using the threat of a trial to hold over them until they more than doubled it for her client.

❖ CHAPTER THIRTEEN ❖

"I have an Alice Weaver to see you?" Colleen intoned over the intercom.

"Did you say Alice Weaver?" Nia asked in surprise as she stared at the phone speaker.

"Yes ma'am, shall I ask her to wait?" she asked unsure of the protocol. The woman standing before her was rather…intimidating with her blonde good looks and odd yellow colored eyes.

"I'll be right out," Nia told her a she dropped everything she was working on to go to the door of her office and open it. She smiled in surprised delight at the petite woman standing in her waiting area. "Alice? What in the heck are you doing in New York?" she held out her arms in delight as the smaller woman walked into them for a hug.

"I have a few things to discuss with you if you've got some time," Alice murmured into her shoulder as she returned the hug.

"I'm sure I do," she looked at Colleen meaningfully and her secretary nodded imperceptibly as Nia escorted Alice into her office.

Alice looked at the corner office and around at the rich and warm décor. Looking out the windows she murmured, "Nice, very nice."

"Yeah, I've come up in the world," Nia teased.

Alice turned around with a smile. "I want to update my trust and add a few things," she said as she sat down on the comfortable couch.

Nia joined her on one of the seats across the coffee table from her. "Can I get you some coffee? Cappuccino? Juice?" she asked.

"Juice would be good," she answered as she glanced up at Colleen who had followed them into the office and quickly went to a hidden refrigerator and retrieved two apple juices for her boss and her guest. She handed them to her boss who nodded in dismissal. Colleen closed the door to the office firmly behind her as she wondered at this odd client and her relationship with her boss.

"Can't your LA lawyers handle that?" she asked curiously as she unscrewed the top and took a sip to wet her whistle.

Alice nodded as she took a sip of her own. "Normally yes, but my wife and I have separated and I wish to add in a few things to the trust that weren't addressed before. I also want a few things handled by you instead of them."

"You don't trust them to handle it?" Nia asked interested. "Is the separation permanent?"

Alice shrugged. "I don't know if it's permanent but I'm here on the east Coast and they are out there, I don't want to do this via fax and as I

trust you to do it efficiently and discretely. I wanted to see that it was taken care of for me."

"Are you staying at your apartment?" Nia asked.

Alice nodded. "Yeah, Simone took care of it for me all these years."

"Simone is still around? I haven't seen her in years!" Nia smiled.

"Yes, she lives at the apartment on and off. I've got a few things to give you," she stressed indicating her folder.

"What did you have in mind?" Nia asked as she got down to business.

Alice pulled papers out of the folder she was carrying and handed them over for Nia to peruse. Reading quickly she saw nothing out of the ordinary but with a client such as Alice Weaver, one never really knew. She re-read it to be sure and saw the tiny bit of information she was looking for. "You want your wife to have this?" she asked as she pointed out the discrepancy.

Alice grinned, there was no pulling the wool over Nia's eyes, she was too astute to fall for such tactics. "Yes, I want her to know about that when or if the time is right. Now that our marriage is legal in California I want to make sure she knows everything that I own in the event of my demise."

"Planning on dying any time soon?" Nia asked sardonically as she sat back and relaxed over the tiny issue.

Alice shook her head and laughed, her cat like eyes narrowing as she genuinely and sincerely laughed. "Who knows, it's pretty dangerous on the streets of New York you know."

"I've been to Los Angeles a few times, it's just as dangerous," Nia rejoined.

They bantered back and forth as they caught up and Nia heard about Alice's kids with her wife as well as her adopted step-daughter. She was the most surprised that Alice would have married much less had kids. The things she suspected about her client and friend she kept to herself. Alice was a good friend to have and had helped out when Nia first started practicing law but she was a bad enemy and she had seen a very angry Alice verbally decimate someone when her ire was aroused. That person had disappeared weeks later and Nia had her suspicions but New York was a dangerous place and it was possible that the person's disappearance was a coincidence.

"Okay, I can have something for you in a few days, you know I have to contact your attorneys out on the coast so I don't step on anyone's toes right?"

"I figured," Alice answered as she finished her juice and stood up, signaling the end of their meeting.

"Leave your number with my receptionist so I can let you know when I'm ready for your signatures," Nia told her a she escorted her to the door and opened it.

"Okay then, you should drop by and see Simone when you get a chance," Alice suggested.

"Annie is in town next weekend, maybe we will."

Alice smiled brilliantly. "Yes, *do* bring Annie; we'd love to see her."

Nia watched as Alice left her number with Colleen and then she turned back to her work. Looking over the paperwork she sent off an email to Alice's attorneys in Los Angeles asking for a current copy of the trust and will so she could make these additions and suggestions that their client wished. She knew the firm would be worried at losing Alice Weaver's business but really it was prudent of their mutual client to keep things current for her wife and family.

"Is it true?" Stewart stuck his head in Nia's office a few weeks later.

Nia looked up from the mountain of paperwork she was trying to weed through. "Is what true?" she asked as she tried to focus on him.

"You not only landed one Alice Weaver but that netted us Sasha Brenhov?" he said barely constraining his excitement as he came into the room with a newspaper in hand.

Nia chuckled. "Yes, they both have a business deal that they want me to look over the legalities of. I'm handling Alice's trusts and will updates and Sasha thought I should look over hers as well," she told him.

"Alice? Sasha? You are on first name basis with these clients?" he asked surprised.

"Alice I went to college with and when I first started here we handled some business for her," she reminded him knowing he would know nothing about it or wouldn't remember. "Sasha insisted I call her by her first name once we had met and on Alice's recommendation." They had gone out on several occasions, Alice had insisted so that a more 'social' Nia could get to know Sasha on another level. It had allowed the Russian to trust the lawyer who would be handling their legal work and to become her friend. The pictures of the women partying together, Nia, Alice, her friend Simone, Sasha, her girlfriend Lexi, had been in the society papers many times.

"Do you know how much business that could generate for the firm, we are going to have to take on more associates, possibly more partners," he spoke his thoughts aloud and wondered if this was actually beyond this partner's capabilities.

Nia could almost read his mind and she had thought of the same things. She put up her hand to calm him. "It's just one business transaction and two wills right now, don't go renting more office space," she advised him.

He laughed at himself. It was like being a kid in a candy store. Sasha Brenhov was rumored to be one of the richest women in the world. Her business alone could make or break a firm. They would have to consider expanding into other cities just to handle business like hers if she gave them more. "It doesn't hurt to be prepared," he defended himself.

"Way ahead of you on that score, I've outlined some plans when or if she gives us the go ahead on other projects," she told him in her courtroom voice to calm him. She was ready for him; she was ahead of the ball on this game. She had to be, Sasha Brenhov's businesses were like nothing any of them had seen before.

"You have?" he blinked and then realizing who he was talking to he smiled and nodded. "You never cease to amaze me. I look forward to the status meeting later this week with the other partners," he told her before saluting her and heading out the door of her office.

Nia laughed silently as she watched him go. She wondered if the other partners or associates got as much personal attention as she garnered from this partner. She had seen many meetings with other partners but Stewart was special and she was grateful for his sponsorship.

"Now you realize this supersedes all the other trust papers and this is revocable," Nia explained as she signed the trust papers.

"Yeah, we don't want a non-revocable trust," Alice had said wryly. Nia had long ago explained the pros and cons of such trusts and the nightmare it could be if she wanted to change anything in a non-revocable one but since then Alice had done many such additions and changes over the years.

"This is getting to be a book," Nia commented teasingly to Alice as they met to go over the business deals. Colleen who was in the room helping out and getting drinks for the two of them stared in surprise at how easy it was for her boss to tease this intimidating woman. She had heard that Nia had gone out with the client as well as how she had been introduced to Sasha Brenhov. She had overheard from the other secretaries how impressed their bosses were with Nia's contacts and how much money they could potentially make if Nia managed to land the business interests of Sasha instead of just this one deal which alone had generated a lot of money for the clients as well as the firm.

"Which, my trusts or these deals?" Alice kidded in return noting that Sasha had already signed the documents. The piles were thick, very thick with legalese which was why she was glad she trusted Nia.

Nia smiled. They had worked hard and quick on both the trust and the deal for Alice and Sasha. A lot of midnight burning of the oil was taken on by Nia, law clerks, interns, and other partners she brought in on the deal to make it happen and make sure they were covered. With Sasha being a Russian citizen there were a lot of legal loopholes that had to be considered to make even the simplest deals which these were, happen.

"Is that it?" Alice finally asked much later as she perused the last of the legal mumbo jumbo and Nia had explained anything that caught her eye and how affected her.

"That's it," Nia said as she began to gather up the reams of paperwork that had been involved and to make sure they were in the appropriate stacks.

"Are you coming to the party next weekend?" Alice asked as she watched her friend and sipped the drink Colleen had handed her.

"And miss my second most important client's party?" Nia joked as she grinned at Alice in return.

"Second most?" Alice asked distractedly.

"Well, after you of course," Nia said smoothly.

Alice was pleased. "Are you going to bring anyone?"

Nia shrugged. "I don't think Annie can come back to town, I know a few of the other partners would love to come," she answered and didn't mention that her girlfriend was furious that she would be out on Long Island for the party but she couldn't see her. Nia preferred to keep her private life, private.

"Bring them all," Alice said generously. "You have to impress the bosses and with the people I know that Sasha has invited it should be a very impressive cast of characters, the crème de la crème."

"Don't you think Sasha should do the inviting?" Nia asked, she didn't want to step on someone as important as Sasha Brenhov's toes and perhaps jeopardize what could be potentially a very lucrative client. Sasha had already turned some business onto the firm that had her partners buzzing besides this deal and hinted at even more. Nia had gone over her latest will for her as a courtesy and suggested a few changes that Sasha had approved.

"Sasha was the one who suggested it to me when I last spoke to her," she answered. "I think she is hoping that Lexi will stay longer if she makes business contacts, as you did."

Nia nodded understanding. It had been obvious how crazy for Lexi that Sasha was. It was interesting to her to see how high powered women, lesbian women coped with being out and public. She herself was new to the lesbian scene and kept her girlfriend who happened to be married to a man well hidden. Even her closest friend Annie knew very little about her

affair. "I'll be sure to invite them, short notice and all but I'm sure they will drop everything and run," she grinned.

Alice shared that grin, she knew how kiss ass the partners in such a firm could be. It was really a coup for Nia and she was pleased to help as she was pleased with how fast Nia had done the work she hired her for. "Do you have my bill?" she asked.

Nia was surprised and shook her head. "No, I have another department that handles billing; did you want it now for some reason?"

Alice shook her head. "No, just making sure things are in order. I'm thinking of visiting with Sasha since I don't really have anything to go back to in California other than the kids." Talking to her estranged wife Kathy on the phone had become impossible and she really missed the kids but she was going to be selfish and travel for a while. Sasha had suggested she check out some of her more 'interesting' businesses in Russia and abroad. Alice thought perhaps a change of scenery once again was in order.

"I'm sorry Alice, about Kathy," Nia said sadly. She could tell how much Alice missed her, how much she loved her despite the separation. She suspected the reasons but hadn't told anyone or would voice them aloud to her client and friend. There was just…something about Alice that forbade it and she didn't want to cross that line, however indistinct it was.

Alice shrugged as she finished her drink and stood up.

Nia gave her a hug, promised to see her on the weekend for the party and sadly watched her go. She wondered if Kathy really knew how well Alice had taken care of her and business for their family. The trusts she had worked on diligently with her associates, pushing aside other clients work to get this done quickly and efficiently had meant a lot of long hours. This was only one aspect of Alice's holdings she knew but wow, the work that was in that woman's head was impressive. Seeing the lucrative deal that she and Sasha had come up with made her lawyer's head spin. They could now proceed with clear sailing and without any governmental interference.

"Colleen, let's get the copies to the appropriate departments and file this, this, and this," she indicated from the piles on the coffee table where she had separated them as she got back to work.

Colleen came up to assist her and Nia's perfume assailed her nostrils disturbing her train of thought for a moment. She ignored it thinking she was going through 'the change' early in life, she had heard it made a woman a little absent-minded. It never occurred to her that she was attracted to her boss.

"And with this we are finished with Ms. Weaver and Ms. Brenhov's wills and first business transaction. In celebration we are all invited to Ms. Brenhov's yacht out on Long Island," Nia finished with almost a flourish. She was proud of all their hard work. She had made sure that everyone involved, from the lowliest secretaries, clerks to the associates and partners all were mentioned and garnered praise from this monumental task but it had garnered them all new business, future business, and definite bragging rights. The long hours they had all put in had paid off, big. Since several partnered lawyers had been involved in the creation and implementation of the work that Nia had for them the billable hours had been higher and netted all of them a tidy sum. Billable hours for partners were always higher than associates.

"All of us?" one of the partners clarified.

"Yes, Ms. Weaver asked me personally to invite all of you and your wives to the yacht." Here Nia grinned a little. "She knew how important it is to make contacts at social events such as hers and Ms. Brenhov's for law firms such as ours. She is very pleased at how quickly we did the work, the quality of the work and how efficiently we handled it."

The partners all swelled at this information. The status meeting took on a different tone from then on as they all felt personally responsible in some way for this coup. Each was thinking of possible clients and transactions that could start at such an event.

"I'll have Colleen memo all of you the information for the invite including directions out the house where the yacht is anchored," Nia finished as she sat down for the next partner to contribute.

No one else felt like contributing after that as they discussed the party and possible contacts. Nia watched as they gossiped like old women and caught Stewart's eye a couple of times as she sat quietly and only occasionally contributed when she was asked a direct question.

"You know, the firm is going to have to name you a partner with a plaque on the wall if you keep this up," Stewart said as he escorted her back to office after the meeting. It had lasted longer than any other status meeting in a long time and he was proud of his protégée. She deserved it. Knowing someone like Sasha Brenhov really was a coup.

"A named partner eh?" Nia teased back knowing he was only a little serious. The firm was called Chase-Dunham and had about six other names tacked onto it but was shortened to the founding names for convenience. She was sure Toyomoto would look fine on the stationary if they ever got that far.

"You'll be bringing a date?" he pressed.

"A date?" she looked at him in surprise. "I hadn't thought to," she answered before she thought.

"You should really start thinking about those things you know," he advised. Since they had given her the partnership all she had done is work, but what work, she was more than worth the deal they had given her nearly two years ago.

"When do I have time?" she teased thinking he was.

"Well, all work and no play makes Nia a dull partner," he advised as he stopped to let her walk a few feet and she turned back to look at him enquiringly. "You should think about that, it would be a shame not to pass that brilliant mind off onto offspring at some point."

She nodded thoughtfully wondering what he would say if he knew she was a lesbian. She had realized a long time ago in her relationship with Justine that she was indeed a lesbian, this wasn't a phase she was 'trying out,' she much preferred the touch of a woman over the touch of man. It was so much more than the touch of a woman though, it was a meeting of the mind, the soul really that touched her in ways she hadn't expected. It had surprised her and ultimately, once she had come to terms with her own sexuality she realized many other things about herself.

"I don't see why I couldn't just go and be another guest of the masses," Justine complained about the party.

"I know baby, it would be easy to slip you in but all my partners are going to be there," she tried to explain as they lay in bed together a few days before the party.

"All the partners?" Justine asked surprised. Nia had explained some of their foibles over the year they had been together; she knew many of their names as well.

"This is a golden opportunity for many of them, they will be sure not to miss it," she told her unknowingly making her lover jealous.

"They won't even know I'm there," Justine sat up and unconsciously revealed her nudity.

Nia looked her body over appreciatively. She had learned a lot since they had become lovers, not the least of which was to orgasm with her lover. Justine and Annie both had been right, it wasn't the goal of an orgasm that was paramount, it was the journey. She also realized that she had learned everything she could from Justine, she wanted more, she needed more than she could get from this woman. She didn't know how to break it off though. Justine was in the midst of what had become a very nasty divorce and had to be very careful when she came into town to meet with Nia. They no longer went shopping together or anywhere else in public in case her husband had them followed and photographed. She was beginning to tire of it though and while she knew she loved Justine she had outgrown her in some ways. They had enjoyed each other and their bodies

and experimented as each learned but their time had come to an end. The only problem was, Justine didn't see it that way. Coming back to the business at hand she reached out to caress her lover and said, "Babe, not this time, not this party." She tried to appeal to her sense of fair play.

Justine, knowing she was being petulant allowed Nia to seduce and convince her about the party. She looked around the apartment later after they made mad and passionate love with a sense of propriety. She looked forward to making her 'home' part time here in the city once her divorce was final. She wasn't sure she would have enough to live on with the children but her lawyer, one Nia had referred her to assured her that her husband would be reasonable. The weekends when he had the children she was going to spend here in the city with Nia, she had it all planned out already. She felt so at home here in the apartment she had begun to think of it as her home away from home.

"Shall we order out?" she asked her lover as she looked down into the living room where Nia was sitting looking at some work she had pulled from her briefcase. She came downstairs buckling her belt from where she had gotten dressed after her shower in Nia's beautiful bathroom.

"I thought you had to get back home?" Nia asked as she looked up from the brief.

"Not until late, I'm 'shopping' remember?" she asked making quotation marks to emphasize her word. "I thought I'd order from that little Italian place on Grant," she said as she came down the stairs and headed for the kitchen for the menu they kept stored there.

Nia was annoyed. They had spent the night and most of the day together. Justine knew she had to work and had not done any since she had met the train the previous night. She had become worse about Nia's job and the work it entailed, especially when she travelled. She complained bitterly about the time apart and then when they were together she clung desperately. Nia was tired of it. "Babe, I have to work, there are leftovers from last night and other things in the kitchen," she told her.

Justine was disappointed, Nia had all this money, as evidenced by this apartment, her car, and by the career she had and she spent all her time, any time working. They hadn't had a 'good' time in so long because of the divorce she was tired of it all and wanted some fun. Some of the places they ordered from and had previously gone out to were only one of the perks. She never paid for anything except for her train ticket into the city. Nia had given her gifts, many gifts, over the time they had been together. Christmas had garnered her a beautiful gold pendant, she had hoped for a 'promise' ring or some sort of indication that they would be together *forever*. "Aren't you hungry?" she asked disappointed.

"Yes but really I hadn't thought about it. I thought you wanted to get back to the train station after your shower?" she looked up again from her brief.

"I just said I was staying in town later," she nearly whined but kept it in, barely. Nia was a complex woman, brilliant, but even she sensed that their affair was coming to end. She didn't want an end, she wanted a beginning. With her divorce coming to an end she wanted a relationship with this woman. "Do you want me to order?" she asked.

"Yeah go ahead, I have to read this though and make my notes," Nia said resigned as she looked back down at the paperwork.

Justine tried not to show her irritations as she gathered the appropriate menu and looked for the cordless phone. Placing the order she didn't consult or interrupt Nia again since she knew her preferences. They had her credit card on file at the restaurant and Justine went upstairs to watch television as she waited for them to deliver the dinner.

Later, after dinner Nia drove Justine to the station in the pouring rain. "So when will I see you again?" Justine asked before she got out of the nice Lexus.

"Well next weekend is the party," she immediately was sorry for bringing that up again. "I've got court the following week and the week after that I'm to go to..." she began but Justine interrupted.

"And when will I see you again?" she asked trying to put things in perspective.

"I'm not sure babe, I'm sorry," Nia said tenderly as she reached out to caress her lover's cheek. "I just have so much damn work. You have to concentrate on your divorce and keeping the kids in check," she advised carefully. "I'll call you when I can, text me when you can," she offered, they had had that for over a year. Despite only living fifty or so miles away from each other getting together had been difficult and didn't happen as much as either had wanted in the past. Offering her the same old platitudes had a note of finality, resignation to it. She loved Justine but it just simply wasn't enough to maintain this relationship and she didn't know how to end it either. Maybe she just should stop seeing her, finding excuses to see her until Justine got the hint. It was cowardly but Nia didn't want to hurt her.

Justine sighed. Nia didn't lie to her but she sensed the withdrawal anyway. She knew she was busy, she had gone on that trip last year to Miami and a few since but they were so rare and so far between that their weekends at Nia's apartment had been her only time with her. "I know babe," she returned trying to be the understanding girlfriend. She leaned her face into Nia's soft touch. "I know," she sighed. It was frequently like this and she hoped with the divorce final that they would have more time together.

LAWYERED

Nia kissed her tenderly; she knew the tinted windows and dark of night would keep anyone from seeing them. She wouldn't accompany Justine onto the platform just in case but she worried whenever they had to wait for the train too long. She watched from afar as Justine climbed the steps to the train she looked miserable as she left. Once Justine was out of sight she waited for the train to arrive and turned on the heat and defogger in the car. She watched sadly as it finally arrived and evidently loaded and offloaded passengers. She couldn't see them and she waited until she saw the train leave feeling the loss of her girlfriend and the relief of her going. She turned the car around and headed home.

❧ CHAPTER FOURTEEN ❧

The party was out on Long Island at one of the many homes that Sasha Brenhov owned. Nia arrived with a couple of the partners and their wives from work having met at the office looking all impressive in tuxedos and gowns. Nia herself wore a womanly tuxedoed gown that showed off her tall good looks and with her mother's pearls made her look quite striking. Her hair was down and brushed out and when it caught the lights looked beautiful. The partners she rode with silently approved and their wives took the opportunity to get to know this partner better in the ride out from the city. They were all impressed with Sasha's house. A heliport was out back and in use for arriving guests. One or two of the partners were coming out this way. The yacht was very impressive and could easily accommodate the amount of people that showed up to gawk and look at the many possessions of the multi-billionaire. Motorboats took guests from the house out to the yacht which after a while went further out. It was a beautiful night if a bit choppy.

Alice and Sasha were introduced to some of the partners who hadn't had the pleasure. They in turn introduced everyone around them to the partners. Soon people were talking to others and not monopolizing their host's time. Nia smiled and shook hands with Lexi, Sasha's lover and longtime girlfriend. The woman fascinated her as she had kept the powerful Russian intrigued and in line for years, refusing to live with her for anything more than a month at a time as she lived in the Midwest and met her lover all over the world. She refused to be kept by Sasha and this seemed to keep the wealthy Russian fascinated as she resisted all efforts to do so. She said she would not give up her family and Sasha, while annoyed at the inconvenience kept coming back for more and would take any time she could get with the attractive and sophisticated woman. As they had all gone out together from time to time Nia really enjoyed being included in this group. She tilted a glass to Eleanor James who she knew would forever be indebted to her for being included in such an illustrious party, she would probably have gotten invited on her own but because she was Nia's friend, Nia had tendered the invitation personally to include her. She smiled as she watched her smoozing with the powers that be and talking animatedly. She wandered away though after meeting many important people who, by association, wanted to meet the attorney of these powerful women.

She looked out over the moonlit water and was suddenly joined by of all people, Annie.

"Hey you, imagine running into you out here," Annie grinned at the irreverence in her own tone.

"I thought you were invited," Nia said pleased to see her best friend as she gave her a hug. She looked at the gown her best friend was wearing and saw how beautiful she was when she cleaned up.

"Yeah well, this is a helluva party not to miss," she said as she took a sip of bubbling champagne and looked around at the elite guests milling about.

"It sure is, I must have four new appointments in the coming weeks from just being associated with Alice and Sasha," Nia laughed knowing it wasn't what you knew but whom.

"This is the place to meet and greet," Annie nodded understandingly as she watched Alice's friend Simone escort two lovelies downstairs for what was obviously a tryst. She grinned remembering a time long ago that Alice and she had hooked up and enjoyed each other, a *long* time ago.

The press were having a good time socializing, taking pictures, talking with the guests who wanted to be seen in the society papers tomorrow as well as various newspapers, magazines, and independents. Pictures would sell at a premium and Sasha had allowed specific journalists on board for this purpose. It was much better than having them buzz around the yacht in their boats snapping unwanted pictures and implying more than there was, this way it was in a controlled environment. The society pages would be well covered as people preened and posed for pictures as light bulbs went off lighting up the dark night. The moon made an appearance and provided an excellent backdrop to the fancy party. The wind was light but the ocean a little choppy which was hardly noticeable on the large yacht.

The motorboats that Sasha had arranged to ferry her guests to and from the yacht came and went. Some went back to see the impressive house she owned, the art contained therein and to gawk at the possessions that Sasha owned in this house. Enough security, many disguised as servants roamed the grounds and the house that she wasn't worried about giving them free reign to come and go. The yacht started up smoothly and began to take them farther out to sea, the motorboats would have to ferry the guests a little further from then on.

Nia watched as Simone went downstairs as well and wondered how one woman could enjoy so many different women all the time. She had seen her in the clubs her clients introduced her to and she was what people called a 'babe magnet' and while very attractive, she wondered how she did it all without upsetting the various women who flocked to her. She was honest that she didn't want a commitment and they seemed to accept her on that basis. Nia wondered though, how did she do it? How did she have one woman and go onto another one so easily, without a care, without hurting feelings? She wondered what Justine was doing at this

moment and how she would have acted had she allowed her to be here with her.

"What are you thinking about that you are frowning at that stairwell so hard?" Annie asked her with a grin as she watched Alice head for the quiet back of the boat away from the throng of guests who were arriving or heading back to the house from the front where a motorboat had just docked.

Looking around to make sure they weren't overheard she turned slightly away from the journalists, some of whom she knew read lips to get their stories. "I'm wondering how to break up with Justine," she said quietly.

"Why, did she piss you off?" she asked intrigued. She had only heard about the mysterious housefrau, she had never met her. And while Nia had solved some of her own sexual problems she wasn't quite sure that the woman would be her one and only. This was the first time she had heard that her friend didn't want a happily ever after with the woman.

"Not pissed off really, it's just changing. Maybe I'm changing, I don't know. I love her but I'd rather have her as a friend and see what else is out there."

"Uh oh, sounds like you've outgrown her," Annie said wisely.

"I think that's just it, I have." She continued to stare at the stairwell and the glanced out over the water as one of the motorboats left with some guests to return to the shore. She saw a strange mist in the distance that looked like a cloud cover might be coming over the horizon but the sky which looked absolutely beautiful had no clouds in it. It was nice to get out of the city where you could barely if ever see the stars because of the intense and numerous city lights. The moon looked fabulous, as though it was showing just for this marvelous and elite party.

Nia watched and observed the different human interactions, some joined her at the side of the yacht, some came and went. She was fine about not seeking anyone out specifically and she watched as Simone returned from downstairs, a smile on her face as well as on the faces of the women who followed her back to the aprty. She and Annie both shared a smile of mutual understanding over that.

They both watched as their hosts discretely broke off from the masses and made their way to the back of the boat chatting quietly. Nia wondered what two such powerful women would have to talk about among this mass of humanity they had invited.

"Are you enjoying yourself?' Sasha echoed her thoughts much later as she admired the view from the back of the large yacht and gazed out to sea.

"Oh I am," Alice told her sincerely.

"This is goot," the Russian answered as she handed Alice a wine glass. "You have seemed up and down in the veeks I have known you."

"Yes, I am missing my wife and children, it's time I went home and took care of things. I'm leaving on Monday to do just that," Alice informed her.

"Goot, it is better that you be happy eh?" she smiled as she looked out over her boat full of guests as a fog started rolling in. "I guess ve vill have to go back soon or deal vith this eh?" she indicated the odd cloud rolling towards them.

Alice looked and thought she saw other boats but this was Long Island, boats were everywhere although not as many as one might think as they had come farther out. "Where is Lexi?" she asked.

"Bah, she is showing someone that painting I bought last year in Venice," Sasha told her in disgust. "She took them back on vun of the motorboats, she vill be back."

Alice laughed. Alexis didn't often do what Sasha expected of her but she did it with such grace and style that you couldn't help but love her for it. She let Sasha's peevishness roll off her without a concern in the world, she knew Sasha loved her.

They talked business, wrapping up a few minor details of their business deal together and discussing possible future ventures. The lawyers from the firm that Nia worked for would be pleased if they used them again. They were very eager for both Alice and Sasha's business and had made that perfectly clear in no uncertain terms to the two power women. Nia had laughed with them earlier over it but thanked them both for coming to her and her firm and allowing her to invite all the partners and her friends.

Their friendship had delightfully surprised both of them and Alice didn't find that too often but she respected the Russian and while she was certain not everything that had made the woman and her now deceased father billions in the fall of the communist empire was legitimate she liked the ethics of the woman and respected her fine mind. She hadn't had a problem writing a check for millions of dollars to go into business with the woman as they shared the risks of the business deals.

Just then a tremendous roar blotted out everything. Nia felt herself thrown into the water. Debris rained down around her and she looked about wondering what had happened. She had heard the explosion and she saw people all over.

"Annie?" she called and to her relief she saw her best friend not far from her, a shocked look on her face but otherwise okay.

"I'm here," she answered sputtering and spitting the salt water out of her mouth. "What the hell happened?"

"I don't know," Nia answered honestly. She looked around to see who else she could see and treaded water. They could see the yacht was burning and sinking rapidly. There were calls for help all around them, some crying, and some shouting as people began to look for their companions and friends. People began to help each other as they began to swim or grab debris to keep afloat. Fine gowns and rented tuxes were ruined in the salt water. No one cared, instead they began heading back to what was left of the boat that was afloat, their only hope in the vast ocean off of Long Island. The fog continued to roll in making it hard to see. From their bobbing heads it was already hard to see over the small waves that were out on the ocean, it had been a nearly perfect night for the party but the wind was causing the choppy water.

"Let's get back to the boat," Annie said firmly.

"No wait, it's sinking, there might be some suction," Nia cautioned as she remembered that movie where the suction pulled people in and while the yacht wasn't that big it would still have sucked some people in. Just then another explosion rocked around them and blew more debris into the water raining down on them and cutting into exposed skin. "OW!" Nia said at the unexpected pain of the debris hitting her.

"You okay?" Annie asked concerned as she grabbed something to help her keep afloat.

"Yeah, I'm fine; can that hold us both up?" Nia asked as Annie shoved whatever the piece was, it looked like part of one of the cabins towards her.

"I don't know but if this is like Kate Winslet and Leonard DiCaprio, I'm playing Kate," Annie said irreverently.

Nia snorted in the water at the unexpected and inappropriate joke. There were people crying and shouting around them but there were others, they both could see them that were floating face down in the water. "Oh my God," Nia said as she looked around from what she could see as they floated there. She saw a couple of the motorboats faintly coming towards the scene and hoped they saw the people and wouldn't mow them down.

"Help me! Help me!" they could hear the screams.

The carnage was terrible. Nia wondered who had lost their lives in the actual explosion and who would be maimed for life. They spent a long time in the water and if not for Annie and her irreverent humor, she wondered if she would have gone off into a panic as she saw several others do. The wait for help seemed interminable as finally they were fished from the waters of Long Island. Nia in pants had fared better than some of the female guests in gowns which had hung on them and for some possibly dragged them down in the water. Her analytical lawyer's mind, while

answering questions for the authorities was also wondering at the lawsuits against her firm, her clients Sasha and Alice, and whomever else people could find to sue. She had invited *all* the partners; somehow, someway she was going to be held accountable to some of this although it was clearly no fault of her own.

"You okay?" Annie asked her innumerable times as the authorities treated them and others asked questions about what they had seen and heard. They really knew nothing other than the social aspects. No one had seen anything.

As they were treated at the hospital for exposure and cuts and bruises Nia's silence bothered her good friend and she stayed with her. It was only when they finally found a ride back the city in one of the many limos taking guests back that Nia began to relax a little. She was dressed in a hospital set of scrubs, her fine tuxedo suit thrown out along with the matching shoes. Her pearls and other jewelry looked odd with the outfit but what choice did she have. She looked like a waif and as her purse had been left with her coat in the house she was able to retrieve her keys and get into her apartment where she and Annie collapsed on the couches, numb for their ordeal over the many hours since the explosion.

"Holy shit, what a horrible night," Annie said understating it.

"And then some, the lawsuits are going to start coming in on Monday," Nia answered.

"Can't that go under something like an act of terrorism or something," Annie asked not looking over at her friend.

"Oh hell no, those greedy vultures will be hitting up Sasha's estate as it was her yacht, her party, her home, whatever their lawyers can come up with. I better get a few hours of sleep and head into the office," she said sadly. She had already heard from the police that neither Alice nor Sasha's bodies had been found yet and if that was the case Nia had to be prepared not only for the lawsuits but implementing her will and Alice's.

"Don't you get a weekend off?" Annie complained good naturedly but knew her friend too well to know she would behave irresponsibly at all.

"Weekend off? What's that?" Nia said wearily. She slowly dragged herself up and noticed her phone flashing from a missed call. She had turned it off when she tucked her purse in with her coat at the mansion. She didn't want to bring notice to anyone that she was leaving her purse with her coat but she didn't want it out on the water where it might get dropped in the water, now realizing that thought again she thought it ironic. She pulled the phone to her and saw she had several missed calls, a few from Justine, one from Stewart and that from several hours ago when she was in the hospital getting checked over.

"Anything important?" Annie asked seeing her look at her phone.

She shrugged but wondered if she should return Stewarts call now. She looked at the clock and decided against it for now. "I'm going to go take another shower. The one at the hospital smelled of that soap they use and I want my creams and lotions," she said as she stood up wobbly.

"I'm heading to your other shower," Annie told her as she followed the taller woman. They might have washed at the hospital before donning the scrubs but both would feel better in regular clothes.

Annie joined Nia in her bed after both had pampered and primped themselves in the bathrooms. Both slept like the dead until Nia's home phone went off several hours later.

"Hello?" Nia answered and sounded gruff.

"Oh thank God, you're alive," Justine gushed.

"Hi babe, sorry I didn't call you, it's been a rough couple of hours," Nia told her as she glanced at the blurry eyed Annie staring at her from the other side of the bed. She took the cordless phone with her as she got out of the bed. It hurt to stand, her joints hurt, she had aches and pains in spots on her body in various places. The bruises had already begun to appear on her skin. She hadn't needed stitches but the scabs they had covered in bandages felt like they were pulling already.

"Are you okay?" Justine said relieved. She had had a frantic morning. It was all over the news about the yacht explosion that had killed several people including the yacht owner some Russian chick and some other woman from California. She knew that they were clients of Nia's and that had been the party that Nia wouldn't take her to because of her partners. Not all the missing had been accounted for. Not hearing from Nia and no returns on her phone calls or text messages had made her feel frantic.

"Yeah, just tired and a bit banged up," she answered sleepily as she tried to force herself awake.

"Should I come into the city and take care of you?" she offered but they both knew that wasn't going to happen. She didn't have anyone to watch the children and even though she was divorcing her husband they still lived in the same house.

"That's okay, I'm going to head into the office in a little while," Nia told her as she headed to the kitchen for something to eat.

"The office? Why?" she asked.

Nia was already tired of the conversation. She didn't have to answer to Justine and yet after being together all this time she felt like she did. She knew she was tired still from last night but she needed to work to prepare, in case. She also had some other things she had intended to work on this weekend anyway. "I've got work to do and I've got to go to the office in case the shit hits the fan with this," she answered wearily.

"Well they can't do anything over the weekend can they?" she asked as she watched her children in the backyard. She had no concept really of

what Nia really did for people. All she could see was the nice apartment, the nice car, and the nice clothes.

"There will be dozens of lawyers all revving up this weekend to file lawsuits on Monday against my client so I have to be prepared for it," she said as she poured herself some orange juice.

"Well you need time to rest too," Justine said unnecessarily.

"Yeah I know, hey I got to go and get ready, I'll call you or text you when I can," she said trying to get off the phone. It still took her another five minutes or so as Justine apparently had time to talk and wanted to touch base. Nia was definitely annoyed by the time she got off the phone. She was equally annoyed at the various texts and a few calls she got interrupting her work as Justine 'worried' about her.

"Dammit Justine, I have to work!" she shouted into the phone much later from her office. "I can't be answering your texts every few seconds or your calls! I'm WORKING and I NEED to concentrate!" she said hurting her feelings and rubbing her scabby forehead where one of the bandages had come off already.

It wasn't pretty and Justine's feelings were definitely hurt. She pouted and whined until Nia finally said, "This isn't working for me anymore Justine. I think we should stop seeing each other. I'm not going to argue with you about this anymore!"

Before Justine could answer that she hung up the cell phone. It was nearly dead from all the texts and phone calls she had been bombarded with, mostly from Justine. It immediately began to ring again and she let it go to voicemail. It did that five times before Justine simply gave up for a while.

Nia was going through case studies and law books in preparation for the potential lawsuits that would be filed on Monday morning. She also caught up on several other cases pending in anticipation of the possibility that Alice Weaver might not be found and her will enacted, she would have a lot of work ahead of her including dealing with Alice's wife Kathy. She also prepared for the possibility that Sasha's will would have to be fulfilled as well, she knew that Lexi, Sasha's long term girlfriend would be shocked to find out she was the sole beneficiary of that.

She spent many hours over the weekend preparing notes and work for her clerks, paralegals, and secretaries so she was well-prepared for Monday morning when it arrived.

"What did you do, work all weekend?" Colleen asked when she saw the amount of work on her own desk much less Suzette the other secretary that worked for Nia.

"Yes, we need to send out these flowers to the partners that are still in the hospital, I started yesterday. Thank God none of the partners were killed," Nia said unnecessarily. Already the office was abuzz with what

had happened over the weekend. She wasn't the only partner that had worked and of course everyone had seen the news broadcasts. She had made many calls to the various partners, making sure who was in the hospital and who was in what state. She was grateful that Eleanor had survived the blast. She was worse for wear but alive and well and Nia had sent her a huge bouquet.

"This is a nightmare," Stewart said at the emergency meeting that was called later that morning for all the partners. Nia wasn't the only one sporting scabs and bandages. One had a sling on his arm, another was on crutches. Others were grateful they hadn't gone or were in the house when the blast went off.

Nia explained what she had accomplished over the weekend and what she had her clerks and associates working on and preparing at the time. They expected some of the lawsuits to begin filtering in this afternoon.

"Has anyone found the bodies yet?" someone asked in reference to Sasha and Alice.

No, they hadn't and no one had any word on a few other guests that were still missing after two days of intense searching, they were presumed dead.

After leaving the meeting, Nia felt drained. She was still recovering physically, she was exhausted of course, but mentally she was getting fried. She wasn't surprised to see Alexis or Lexi as everyone called her waiting for her in Colleen and Suzette's office.

"Have you heard anything?" Lexi asked concerned. She had been on one of the motorboats when the explosion went off.

Nia indicated her office and escorted her inside closing the door firmly behind the elegant woman. "No, the authorities haven't found any sign of them at this time. I've called regularly, I've left messages, they know who I am."

"I know, I've done the same," Lexi said as she sat down on Nia's couch. "I don't know what to do really," she said helplessly.

"This is going to sound lame, but really all we CAN do is wait and hear," Nia said as she too sat down across from the woman. She would have offered comfort but she herself wasn't comfortable with hugging another lesbian, not at this point, but even her friends she didn't hug too often.

"I know," Lexi sighed as she leaned her head against her well-manicured finger tips and looked out at the excellent view of New York that was beyond Nia's windows. "I don't know what to do with myself at this point. I can't call them all the time and after limiting myself to once or twice a day I really just sit and think."

Nia leaned forward. "I know, it's hard. I can only handle things from a legal standpoint. We are prepared here," she told her client's girlfriend.

"What do you mean?" Lexi turned back to the lawyer to look at her.

"You have to realize that all those people that were on the boat, even some that were just there can and many of them will file lawsuits against Sasha. She is a very wealthy woman and they will think they can get what they can out of her."

"You are assuming she is alive after all this time?" Lexi said sadly, there was a hint of tears in her eyes.

Nia had been careful how she worded that. She smiled wryly but knew that Lexi understood. "If not her personally then her estate," she said quietly.

"She just finished that damn will with you a few days ago didn't she?" Lexi asked to confirm, she remembered Sasha telling her about it.

"Yes, it's all legal and ready to go but hopefully we won't need it," Nia said carefully. "She will have to be confirmed dead," she said and then cringed seeing the devastation on the other woman's face. Nia dealt in facts, cold hard facts, and while she had enjoyed meeting and working with Sasha, she was her attorney, she couldn't allow her own feelings to enter into this.

"Damn, I hope they find something and soon. She's so…" she couldn't finish. She missed her so and the worry was killing her. The thought that she was dead was unbearable. She had mentally beat herself up all weekend long thinking of 'what ifs' and 'shouldas.'

"They will let us know," Nia told her.

"Don't they have to wait seven years to declare her dead?" Lexi asked naively.

Nia shook her head. "No, enough people can confirm that they were on the yacht when the explosion occurred. If the authorities can't find their…" she swallowed not wanting to say the word, "bodies they will be presumed dead." Although she couldn't at this point tell Lexi she was the sole beneficiary of Sasha's massive estate she could give her some clues. "You may wish to be the one that has her declared legally dead at some point after the authorities stop looking," she told her sadly knowing that this was hard for all of them involved.

"Declare her dead? Without a body?" Lexi said in a shocked tone.

"They may never find her," Nia told her quietly. She waited for Lexi to nod and gather herself before she continued to explain. "A person can be declared legally dead based on the evidence we would present to a judge. Just because they don't find the," she hesitated to add, "Remains she would be declared dead in absentia or on the legal presumption of death from the explosion. We will give it a few more days so that no one else can lay claim to her estate and we can see who is going to be suing her for the accident."

Alexus stared at her as the words sunk in. She was trying to be brave, so brave, but the thought of Sasha actually being gone was hard to fathom. They had spent a lot of time together but an equal amount of time apart and it was as though Sasha was just in another part of the world and she was waiting for her call.

"The circumstances of her disappearance overwhelmingly support the belief that the person, in this case Sasha didn't survive the explosion on the yacht. I will file on behalf of her estate so that we can monitor her bank accounts, if there is activity that might prove she is alive then we won't need to file…" she trailed off as Lexi began to quietly sob. Nia got up and grabbed a tissue box and sat down next to the other woman. Before she knew it Lexi was in her arms sobbing her heart out. Nia felt for her, she really did. She could only imagine how she would feel if it had been Justine. She still loved Justine, she was angry with her at the moment but also relieved that her anger had caused the break up. She knew that wasn't the end of it by any means but she knew if she had heard that there was a possibility that Justine was dead how she would feel.

It took a long time for Lexi to cry herself out. Many tissues were in her lap by the time she gathered herself. It was obvious she had been crying. Her face was all puffy and her makeup completely gone. She was still a beautiful woman and Nia could appreciate what Sasha saw in her. "How long?" she finally managed to get out to the attorney.

"It really depends on the authorities. Once they give up the search…" she left off. She already had a copy of the guest list and had compared that to those they had from the hospital and authorities confirming the dead and the hospitalized as well as those like Nia who had already been released. There would of course be people who claimed they had been there or some who were there who would never be identified, *if* they found the bodies.

Lexi sighed deeply. She had needed the cry and a sympathetic shoulder. She had already called her children and they had offered to fly out but she had kept her romantic life from them for so long and although they knew about Sasha, they didn't *know* her. She told them to stay home.

❖ CHAPTER FIFTEEN ❖

Nia filed not only for the estate of Sasha Brenhov but for Alice Weaver too as well as one or two others who had been at the party and asked the firm of Chase-Dunham to represent them in petitioning the court for their assumed dead. Kathy Weaver, Alice's wife was contacted and a memorial service was set. Nia planned to attend and had Colleen make arrangements for them to fly out to Los Angeles. First though she had to file a petition on behalf of her clients that these persons were exposed to imminent peril and had failed to return or their remains found. The court would assume the persons were killed, even though the usual waiting time of seven years to declare someone dead had not elapsed. As the explosion of Sasha's yacht certainly proved that the element of peril accelerated the presumption of death in these client's cases the lawyer was granted her petition that these individuals were indeed dead. Death certificates would be issued so that their estates, in the case of both Alice Weaver and especially Sasha Brenhov vast estates could begin to be settled. Should any of these individuals be found alive later, the lawyers could deal with that at another time; right now the presumption was of death. Sometimes, in the case of a huge estate the court delayed ordering the issuing of a death certificate but as the efforts of the authorities including bringing in of the Coast Guard had brought in no evidence of these people ever being found and it was proven they were at the party, the court granted her petitions.

Nia next began the process and preparation of reading the wills for her client. Lexi wanted to wait until after Nia returned from California. She needed the time and Nia understood. Her other clients too were kind enough to wait until she got back and it allowed her to prepare for the reading of Alice Weaver's will to her wife.

Colleen made the arrangements for their flight. They flew first class on a commercial jet. Nia had always made sure her personal assistant sat next to her so she could go over work with her but had found Colleen was an uneasy traveler and could not read on a moving plane. She herself was worn out from her work these past weeks and found herself deep in thought and dozing on the flight from JFK International to LAX. Colleen had booked them into a suite so they had two bedrooms and could rest comfortably before they would head to the memorial service the next day for Alice Weaver.

Nia found herself thinking about the messy scene she had to witness the previous day with Justine who had begged her to take her back. She had refused, not only because she was tired, but because she felt this overwhelming sense of relief to have broken up with her. She hadn't known how she would do it, she had hoped for a strategic withdrawal but the scene yesterday had only strengthened her resolve. Annie had told her the woman had shown up late in the afternoon and refused to leave. Having met her finally she wasn't impressed with Nia's first choice of a woman lover. She had further not liked her personality and had shamelessly listened from the bedroom above in the loft as they fought in the living room. Justine had pleaded and whined and Nia had retreated into her cold lawyer's stance and refused.

"It's over Justine, I can't do this anymore," she had told her more than once.

"I'm almost divorced, it won't be long and we can be together *all* the time," Justine argued.

Thoroughly repugnant was the word 'all' that she heard from Justine's lips, she didn't want to be with her at all anymore. "It isn't the divorce, it's us, we aren't working anymore," she tried to explain.

"What do you mean, we have been fantastic, I love you," she went on and on in the same vein.

Nia had ended up with her in tears but she refused to bend. She had finally told her, ordered actually, to leave the apartment. It had taken some doing but finally she had gathered her pride and left. She couldn't believe that Nia wouldn't even consider reconciliation.

Nia thought about everything she could have said, she could have done, breaking up was painful and she loved Justine but just not enough to continue.

Colleen watched Nia as she dozed on the way out to Los Angeles. She desperately needed to sleep. She had worked so hard since the accident. Although the authorities felt it wasn't an accident, that's what those in the office were calling the explosion. Some of the stories from those partners who had been there were horrific and greatly exaggerated some felt. Nia was very closed mouthed about her own view and participation in the events.

Colleen had had to beg and plead for Cletus to let her come on this trip. It was important to her to take care of her caring boss. She had seen how hard Nia worked; she had seen how much she cared for her clients and their interests. She needed to do her job to the best of her abilities and she'd be damned if Suzette who made no secret of her desire to someday have Colleen's position would go on any of the trips with Nia.

The service for Alice Weaver was very well attended. Both Nia and Colleen attended and Colleen watched Nia watch the widow. Kathy had

been a surprise; she wasn't nearly as intense as the spooky Alice Weaver who scared Colleen. Nia was sure her grief was genuine, as genuine as Lexi's for Sasha. She wondered if anyone, any *woman* would *ever* love her this much in her lifetime.

"Mrs. Weaver, I can't tell you how sorry I am for the loss of Alice, she was a wonderful person," Nia told her the next day.

Kathy smiled, she had heard versions of this for days as she got all the flowers, the condolence cards, and the service had brought hundreds of people out to express the same sentiments.

"I'm sure you want to get down to business though," Nia continued and Portia, her friend and attorney nodded discretely as they sat in the living room of the beautiful house.

Nia had been most impressed. The descriptions that Alice had given her hadn't done the estate justice and she admired the beautiful home. Someday she might want something like this but for now she loved New York and wanted to be nowhere else. This trip to California had been eye opening in so many ways for her.

Nia began to explain that Alice had come to her in New York because of their long association as first college acquaintances and then as lawyer and client and then as a friend.

Kathy was surprised at this as she had never heard Alice mention her but given what she had learned at the service the previous day perhaps she wasn't as surprised as she might have been. She hadn't known half of what Alice had done for others. She hadn't ever mentioned this woman to her, but then there had been so many people she had never known Alice was involved with or had touched.

"She had sold the condo and the boat and a few other properties and wanted to include them in the trust for you and the children as well as to make a few additions," Nia continued as she explained that Alice had listed quite a few properties that she still owned all over the world that would be put into the trust so that Kathy wouldn't be slapped with inheritance taxes. "She said you had a friend who was an accountant that could help you figure out the financial aspects of some of this?" Nia asked.

Kathy nodded thinking of Andie downstairs with the children playing games.

Portia nodded thinking the same as she eagerly anticipated reading over the reams of paper that constituted Alice Weaver's will. Even she hadn't known what that included and having read the old will she wasn't surprised that someone of Alice's immense wealth had added to it. It was the only responsible thing to do when you were that rich.

Nia explained things in a very precise and concise method knowing that Kathy was dealing with her grief and that she might not understand or retain everything she was saying. She explained that she and Alice had gone over many things that she wanted for Kathy and the children, her concern that their quality of life never be jeopardized by her absence.

Kathy was overwhelmed as Nia explained the extent of Alice's generosity and wealth, all of which came to her and indirectly the children. Although Alice had set up trusts for each of the children and there were vast sums set aside for them, they were not to know of the trusts until they graduated from college so as not to let it corrupt or deter them from that goal. Alice had asked that Kathy 'support' the children in the manner to which they were accustomed but not let them know of the monies that would someday be theirs. She wanted them to be responsible for their own happiness, their own lives before they were thrust into the money that awaited them. She didn't want what she had seen in other children becoming spoiled and entitled. Their children would not be getting the trusts until later in life and only if certain stipulations had been met without their realizing that those stipulations were in place. Kathy understood but even she was boggled at the amounts of money and property that had been left to her and ultimately the children.

"People of wealth like this want to protect that wealth," Nia explained simply. "Alice had enough off shore money's and property to buy a country."

When they had gone through it all Kathy's head was reeling. She had no idea. Alice had taken care of it all for them, so easily, so aptly that she had never wanted to know even when Alice had offered to share some of the information with her. The sale of the condo and boat had been only a small blip on her radar as she concentrated on this home and their family. She hadn't known of the loft that Alice owned in New York or the many properties scattered around the country, around the world. She realized the house in the Valley was now hers to do with as she wished and she wondered at that now. What would she do with it all?

"I would suggest a few of the lesser properties be liquidated," Nia recommended and Portia nodded discretely beside her. "Some of the things Alice kept were for sentimental reasons."

Kathy needed to laugh and she nearly did. The only thing that kept her from doing so was that they would think she was going mad, that the death of Alice had simply sent her over the edge. Her overwhelming grief had put her into a tailspin but the guilt she was heaping on herself did more than the grief over her loss. Only the fact that Alice had depended on her to take care of the children was keeping her going. Hearing Alice called sentimental was a laugh, Alice was never a sentimental person in the normal sense of the word. But then, Alice was never a normal person. If

these women knew or in Portia's case sensed how dangerous Alice had truly been they would be horrified. Kathy accepted it a long time ago and had lived with it. It had been stupid not to keep accepting it and forcing Alice to leave.

"Well, Mrs. Weaver..." Nia continued after many hours of talking.

"Please, after all this," Kathy spread out her hands in her gesture taking in the enormous amount of paperwork they had gone over in her living room. Her head hurt but she was amazed how much she had retained. "Call me Kathy?"

Nia smiled, she too had felt after this much information had been shared that they should be on a first name basis but it was up to the client to allow such familiarity. "Kathy, if you have any questions and I'm sure they will come up in the coming days, weeks, heck in the coming months, please don't hesitate to call and my assistant Colleen," she gestured to the mousy woman who sat taking notes and had pretty much stayed out of their way the entire visit. "Will be happy to get them to me," she finished.

Kathy let out a large sigh that they all felt and they all exchanged small smiles of relief after going through so much together that day. "Wow, she was a complicated and complex woman in life and now I can see why." They all nodded. Their own impressions of Alice Weaver complicating what had been a lengthy and thorough reading of her will and trusts. "I cannot understand it all, but for now, I will agree to this being put forward as you suggest in New York and California for probate."

Nia breathed an internal sigh of relief. Some heirs wanted to complicate things further by disputing the validity of the will or argue about incidentals. Not enough time had gone by that Kathy wouldn't be able to say that the older will and its codicils would and should stand; the new will wasn't very old. That she understood everything was a big plus and she would gladly put this forward for probate. The greedy states would be disappointed at its wording as the inheritance taxes alone would have been phenomenal but Nia and the past lawyers had protected their client and been paid well to keep her fortune intact for her heirs. It would continue to generate money for the estate in perpetuity. Kathy wouldn't be able to spend it all in her own lifetime but she could spend fortunes every month and still not make a dent into what Alice had left her.

Nia and her assistant Colleen left soon afterword's with signatures from Kathy that stated she understood the vast will and trusts and headed back to their luxury hotel.

"Oh my God!" Kathy said in relief when they had left.

Portia was looking over the copy of the will that Nia had handed her. She had smiled as Nia said, "Alice told me if I ever met you that this was your version of her book," she couldn't help but laugh at the little lawyers joke. Alice had been very particular saying she knew Portia would help

Kathy in her hour of need. "She told me to make sure you had your very own copy as well as Kathy," she confided. She understood college friendships such as this. She looked curiously at the attorney, vaguely remembering that she had been Connie or Constance Weaver's college friend and not Alice's. Funny how life brought people back into your life like that as Alice had come back into hers.

"I'd have Andie take a look at the books," Portia commented as she remembered things the New York attorney had said. She was good, she was very good. She had been thorough, never condescending, and genuinely concerned about fulfilling Alice's wishes for her wife and family and explaining the mountain of papers before them so that Kathy understood it all, or at least as much as she was going to retain in the state she was in.

Kathy nodded. She didn't care. She had never cared about the money. That had been Alice's job. She didn't want it. Her friends she would hire and retain to take care of things for her now. She needed to grieve over the loss of her best friend, her lover, her wife. She didn't want the responsibility of taking care of what she had been left. Alice had known this when she had made her will.

Nia collapsed on the couch in the suite at the hotel Colleen had reserved for them. She was exhausted and she knew she was over extending her body's ability to cope with its injuries. She still had bruises and healing cuts but she had known her job and done it well. Alice's will had been of nightmare proportions but she could cheerfully submit it to probate along with the copies of Alice's death certificate she had obtained with her declaration. Now she had to worry about her other clients including Sasha's wills to be read and put forth.

"Are you okay?" Colleen asked as she watched her boss collapse.

"Just tired," she said in a big sigh. She looked at her briefcase on the coffee table before her with disdain; she didn't even want to think of the work that was before her. She had been right about the lawsuits coming in. As representatives of Sasha Brenhov the lawsuits had been filed and sent to their offices. She had warned Kathy that some might be filed against Alice as well but as it was Sasha's party, her estate was more likely to be sued.

"Can I get you anything?" Colleen asked concerned. She too had been there for the reading of the will to take notes that Nia might want for future reference. Nothing too much but reminders for her to follow up on and research, etc. She felt it was also her duty to take care of her bosses well-being and this exhausted woman who herself had been in the accident

wasn't the same boss who normally stormed the courthouse for cases she represented.

"No, I just want to stop thinking. I need a vacation," she grouched and knew that would be a ways off. She had to plan those things out months in advance and right now was not a good time with the enormity of work in her lap.

"Did you want to go out to dinner or should I have it sent up?" Colleen persisted in her self-appointed duty as caretaker of her boss.

"Oh gawd, I forgot to eat today didn't I?" she asked. Kathy had offered them beverages and she remembered some sort of snacks but the paperwork had taken hours to go over. The actual reading of the will had been simple and straight forward.

Colleen laughed at her boss, she was so hard working, she needed a keeper but she respected her and admired her.

"Let's go out," Nia finally said and slipping her shoes back on she treated her assistant to a nice dinner out at a fairly nice restaurant where the lights were down low and the atmosphere very warm. Over dinner and a couple of drinks they chatted and enjoyed each other's company. It was as Colleen was laughing over some of the antics and impressions Nia made of some of her court cases that Nia began to realize that the mousy little woman wasn't so mousy.

It began to bother Nia as she analyzed her feelings for her friend and assistant. She didn't think of her constantly but enough that she realized there was a slight attraction there. She thought of the article she had read that had straight women believing that a lesbian, any lesbian, was after *all* women, *any* women. She wouldn't be like that, she couldn't be like that. Colleen was a good friend, she was an excellent assistant. She really did her job well and Nia wondered if perhaps she just had a small crush on the smaller woman.

"You need to take some time off," Colleen felt brave enough to mention. They were after all on equal footing as friends at the moment. She was still always aware of the fact that Nia was her boss.

"I know but when?" Nia asked as she popped an olive into her mouth. "With everything on my desk, my caseload is insane."

"Schedule a vacation," Colleen answered. That trip to Mexico over a year ago had sounded dreamy. She only wished she could take such trips but with a husband like Cletus, that was just a dream. She too popped an olive in her mouth but it wasn't settling on her stomach right. Nothing had today and she wondered at that. Her period must be coming on as she felt a slight cramping twinge in her stomach. She stopped eating anything more and stuck to soda to help settle her meal.

"Yeah, easier said than done," Nia returned. She enjoyed relaxing like this; she didn't do it enough these days it seemed. It was not that long ago

though that Sasha and Alice had insisted she go out to a few clubs with them and she had partied with them and enjoyed herself enormously. Never could she have predicated in a few short weeks alter that both her clients would be dead and she would have to work through their wills and estates.

Nia thought over the work she would do when she got back to the office. She was taking a day off as it was well deserved and she needed no interruptions to a day of relaxation. As she flew across the country she looked out the plane window and re-analyzed the previous night and the quiet dinner she had enjoyed with Colleen. The lighting, the conversation, all of it had shown that Colleen was an intelligent and pretty woman. She had felt herself attracted to her and it surprised her. She would of course never act on it and she hoped Colleen wouldn't ever be able to read her mind.

Nia had taken a long hot bath, washed her hair, and was lying on the couch in a robe as she mindlessly flicked through the channels on the television. It was no good; the briefcase was calling to her to catch up on the mountain of paperwork waiting for her to read. It wasn't going anywhere and she knew it was within hand reach but she simply didn't want to, she was firmly resisting. It was then that she heard the doorbell and then a frantic pounding on the door. It made her start up in alarm. She glared at the door thinking it was probably Justine who she thought had finally gotten the message when her last words were to her, "Don't make me take out a restraining order on you, how will you explain that to your husband?" The pounding and the ringing doorbell though continued and she got up and walked determinedly to the door.

"What!" she nearly shouted without looking through the peek hole at who was pounding on her door.

Expecting Justine she was shocked to find Colleen on her doorstep. She looked worse for wear too. Her hair was in disarray and she looked like she had been crying. Having Nia shout at her she looked scared, very scared but she looked fearfully over her shoulder and asked in a little girl's voice, "Can I come in?"

Nia nodded still shocked and held the door wider for her to pass. She too looked down the hall where Colleen had looked before she shut the door firmly and locked it sliding the dead bolt. She didn't know why but Colleen had frightened her with her appearance. She turned to look at the woman who had walked into the middle of the large room that was her

living room and just stood there looking lost. "Are you okay?" Nia asked her and Colleen was startled out of her stupor.

Colleen turned to look at her boss and friend. Her clothing was in dishambles and she looked like a street person almost with the tears in it. It was mismatched. She had two different shoes on and her hair looked matted. She had a black eye and what looked like a cut on her lip. She blinked dumbly at the question.

Nia walked toward her gently and putting an arm around her steered her to the couch. "Can I get you something to drink?" she asked quietly and at her nod she left her to go into the kitchen and get her a bottle of water. She thought for a minute and stopped at the bar to pour a shot of whiskey for her guest. Carrying both she returned to the couch. She handed Colleen the whisky first and said, "Drink this," in a commanding voice. Much to her surprise she did. Only then did she hand her the bottle of water which she rapidly opened and sucked down.

Colleen was shocked as the whisky hit her stomach and gasped at the sensation. She quickly sucked down some of the water hoping the whisky wouldn't come back up. Instead she bounded off the couch and barely made it to the sink in the kitchen to throw up what had been in her stomach. She didn't stop until she had dry heaves.

Nia had followed her and held her hair back as she vomited in her sink. She turned on the water reaching past the sick woman to turn the spout away from her retching and so she wouldn't get drenched by the running water. When the woman finally stopped she handed her another bottle of water and said, "Drink slowly, sips would be best."

Colleen was grateful and embarrassed. The whisky had come back up but its shock had woken her up out of her stupor. She splashed some cold water from the sink on her hot face. She felt awful.

Nia backed away and went to the pantry pulling out a box of salt crackers and opening a packet.

Colleen gratefully took one and began to nibble as she turned off the faucet after rinsing out the sink. The thought that she had vomited into her boss's pristine kitchen sink appalled her. She'd sterilize it later, she knew where everything was.

"If you are done here, let's get you back to the couch and you nibble on those," Nia said gently as she encouraged Colleen back to the living room.

Colleen carried the crackers and water and sat down. Nia grabbed a blanket off the back of the couch. She could see the woman was shivering in reaction to whatever had happened to her. Now she could clearly see the bruising around one eye and she would bet that the tears on her clothing had bruises underneath. Nia didn't say anything to her as she covered her up. She figured when Colleen was ready, she would talk.

Meanwhile she watched as she gently ate a cracker and drank some water. She sat back and waited.

Colleen felt a little better with the cracker in her but she only managed half a dozen before she had to stop and put them on the coffee table along with the water. The cold water had felt good going down but it felt cold in her hand and she was freezing, she started to shiver in reaction to the cold water and her own nerves. She glanced at Nia finally to find her waiting and staring at her mantle. She gulped nervously and pulled the blanket around her tighter. Before she knew it though she began to doze off.

Nia glanced over after a while to see Colleen slowly slipping down on the couch as she fell into a sleep. She wondered if Cletus was responsible for the bruises she could see and the split lip. She'd have to wait to find out but if he was, and she was sure he was she wasn't going to let Colleen convince her it was rough love play. She either got help and told the police so it was on record or...she wasn't sure she could cut her friend off. She waited until she was sure Colleen was sound asleep before she pulled her feet from off the floor and put them on the couch. She pulled another blanket off the back of the other couch to cover her completely since the first blanket was wrapped around her torso and pulled the mismatched shoes from her feet.

Colleen slowly woke hours later. It was dark outside from what she could see. She was disoriented at first as she couldn't remember where she was and then she began to recognize the décor of the room and the couch she was sleeping on. She was embarrassed that she had fallen asleep but she had been so worried, so tired, and so upset she hadn't been thinking straight. She looked around but saw no sign of Nia in the large open room. Slowly she sat up and seeing the crackers and water still on the coffee table she gingerly tried to eat more. She still felt a little queasy from before but she had this horrible hollow feeling in the pit of her stomach and needed something to fill it. She finished the whole pack and felt much better for having done so. Carefully she gathered the crumbs that had fallen to the blanket into the palm of her hand and poured them back in the container. She slowly got up; she felt a little unstable, she wondered if that was in reaction to earlier or if something had happened this time. She made her way into the kitchen and threw out the plastic wrapper for the crackers and thinking quickly pulled out the cleaner for the sink and cleaned it. She wondered where Nia was and as she thought that she heard the front door open.

Nia walked in carrying a couple of bags of groceries and dinner. Her eyes went directly to the couch and she glanced around calling, "Colleen?"

"I'm here," she answered relieved. For a moment she had worried who was coming through the door when she heard the key in the lock.

"I brought supper," she called as she headed for the kitchen and nearly collided with Colleen in the dark. "Can you get the lights?" she asked.

"Yeah, got 'em," Colleen turned and flipped the switch.

Nia couldn't help but stare for a moment as she got a good look at the face of her assistant. That looked like it hurt.

Colleen saw where she was staring and looked down at the floor ashamed.

Nia, seeing she had made her uncomfortable covered by saying, "You want to help me put some of this away?" holding up the grocery bags.

Colleen quickly took one and began to unpack it. She could see that Nia had shopped at the gourmet section of the local market as the offerings were a little more upscale than she would have purchased. She also had done enough parties in the loft that she knew the local markets.

They were soon eating Chicken and steamed rice. Nia had thought it might be easier for her guest to eat something like this in case her jaw or lip were bad. She didn't ask anything as she watched her each and they drank some carbonated water she had brought. It was great on Colleen's still queasy stomach. Colleen helped her put away the last of the groceries and the leftover chicken and rice in the fridge. Nia's kitchen was as familiar to her as her own.

"Okay, now you are going to tell me what happened?" Nia demanded when they were done. She hadn't asked before and kept the conversation to a minimum sensing that her guest needed to eat and didn't want to talk about it. They were now sitting in the softly lit living room, the Tiffany lamps giving off a soft glow. It was warm and cheery.

"I guess I owe you an explanation don't I?" she asked almost fearfully.

"No, you don't owe me anything but as your friend, I want to know," Nia told her gently. She felt bad for her, she really didn't look well. She wasn't sure she wasn't going to vomit up the excellent meal they had just eaten.

"Well I took the day off like you told me and I was cleaning..." she began. She looked down at her hands that were clasped together.

Nia waited.

Colleen waited.

Nia fidgeted. She almost wanted to shake it out of Colleen but really was trying to be patient. Her lawyer's patience paid off.

"Cletus wasn't happy I was home today, he had plans you see..." she began again and tried to bite her lip in consternation as she thought of how to word this. It hurt her to bite her lip as she had forgotten the cut. She nearly cried out at the pain. She looked up at Nia and seeing her gentle eyes on her waiting patiently for her to continue she tried to be brave. She

swallowed, almost fearfully before she continued. "He had some sort of deal going down today and I was in the way. He didn't want me to see what he was doing and needed the house. We argued and he started to hit me," she sighed deeply trying to get her courage up and failing, she sobbed a little.

Nia made a gesture as though towards Colleen and Colleen put up her hand to halt her. "He couldn't seem to stop today though. He was probably high again." She stopped talking as she thought about it. He hadn't stopped for a while. "I tried to get away, I tried," she sobbed again as she remembered.

"You have to go to the police this time Colleen. You have to get it on record that he is a danger to you." She thought for a moment. "Do you want to leave him?"

Colleen look up for a moment and then down again. She nodded. "I want to but I don't have anywhere to go. He'd find me at a shelter. He has before."

Nia was surprised that Colleen had ever left him before. "He's done this before then, those bruises I've seen before?" she asked to verify.

The mousy woman nodded but didn't look up. She was wringing her hands together in her agitation.

"Okay then. You'll stay here. I'm going to call the police and they are going to come take pictures and your statement. I want you to tell them. Tell them everything and hold nothing back." She was being stern and she could see that Colleen had begun to shake so she softened her voice again. "You need to do this Colleen. He's going to kill you if you don't," she said gently.

Colleen knew it. She had known it for a while. She didn't know why she was so weak and yet she did. She had been conditioned to it. First with her father and now with her useless husband. She nodded instead of answering. She was so ashamed.

"Can you do that for me? Can you do that for yourself? Will you tell them everything?" Nia asked.

Colleen nodded but she was so lifeless, so downtrodden it was barely perceptible. She listened as Nia got up and she glanced up to see her pick up the wireless phone. She looked down again and listened as Nia dialed.

"Hi, do you have the a listing for a police station in the area of," she gave her address. They must have asked her something as she said, "No, it's not an emergency." Nia listened for a moment and then hung up the phone to punch in the numbers again. Colleen could hear her nails tapping on the buttons. "Hello, I need an officer to come to my home and take a statement. A friend of mine has been badly beaten by her husband and would like to file a complaint." She listened and nodded and asked, "Is it possible she doesn't have to come down, she's badly frightened."

Suddenly she realized why Colleen had looked over her shoulder so fearfully earlier. "She's afraid that he followed her here to finish the job, he tried to kill her," she added softly hoping that Colleen hadn't heard but knowing she had by the way she stiffened up.

Colleen looked over at Nia wondering how she had guessed it and thought perhaps it was her astute lawyer's mind.

"Yes, thank you we will be waiting," Nia spoke into the phone and severed the line with a finger to the button before putting the phone back on its charger. "They will be here soon. Are you going to be able to tell them everything?" she asked again.

Colleen looked back down at her hands. She couldn't look at Nia. She was so ashamed. She was an educated woman, she shouldn't put up with such abuse but she couldn't seem to end it. Cletus was so much stronger than she was. She couldn't remember everything that had happened today though. She didn't hear Nia move towards her until she sat down on the other end of the couch from her and spoke to her.

"You know you have to tell them, tell them everything. It's the only way that this works," she said gently to persuade her. She could see that she was uncomfortable that this was difficult. "I'll support you a hundred and ten percent. I'll see that he can't find you or hurt you okay?" she promised.

Colleen looked up at her boss and friend and tears sprang to her eyes. She had never had a friend like Nia before. Supportive and uplifting, always with a kind word when it was merited. She came across as a tough litigator and she was but she was also generous and kind. "Thank you," she said with her whole heart.

Nia grimaced resignedly hoping that Colleen would tell the police everything and they could begin to put an end to all of this.

When the buzzer rang from downstairs she briefly wondered how Colleen had gotten into the building earlier but if someone was leaving the building as she came in it would be that easy to bypass the door and as she was familiar in the building they wouldn't have stopped her. She went to the door pad and looked through the camera to see two police officers, she buzzed them in. She was waiting by the door when the doorbell rang and opened it promptly.

"Hello, I'm Nia Toyomoto," she introduced herself and opened the door wider to let them in.

"I'm Officer Hamad," the burly dark haired man introduced himself and pointing with his thumb at the female officer he introduced her as, "Officer Adams."

Nia knew they probably sent a female officer because of the nature of the call. She hoped Colleen wouldn't be intimidated by Officer Hamad. "This is my friend Colleen, she needs to talk to you," she said almost

unnecessarily, both officers eyes had been drawn to the figure sitting on the couch.

Colleen looked up at them both almost fearfully as they approached.

"Hi Colleen, I'm Officer Adams, I hope you will talk to me," the woman said gently. "Do you mind if I sit down?" she asked politely.

When Colleen nodded she sat next to her on the couch noting the torn clothes and the hair even more disheveled by her nap. The black eye and the split lip weren't missed either.

"Do you mind if Officer Hamad sits too or would you prefer...?" she asked indicating the other officer.

Nia looked on watching as the younger female officer took control of the situation. She was relieved; the woman was asking Colleen questions that required a response and easing her into what would be an awkward recitation of events.

Colleen nodded and Officer Hamad sat down across from her but out of her direct line of sight. Nia joined them taking a chair almost behind Colleen on her left.

"Do you want to tell me what happened today? These did happen today?" the officer began gently as she pulled out a pad of paper to take notes. Nia noted that the other officer too took out a pad to begin writing, she wondered if they would compare notes to make their report later.

Colleen began to tell them what happened today, how Cletus had been angry that she had the day off but that they had been working so hard lately that she needed it. It came out that Nia was her boss and that they worked in the law offices of Chase-Dunham. The name caused a slight raising of the eyebrows and Nia took mental note of that. Cletus apparently had 'friends' coming over today and he hadn't wanted 'witnesses' around in case these new friends weren't so friendly. Colleen was ashamed to tell them what her husband did but she didn't know how she could get around it. He dealt drugs and had done so for a while. He took her money that she earned from being Nia's secretary as well. It wasn't enough and he wanted to move into the big leagues. The friends today were the path to the big leagues. As he began to yell at her for being home he had begun to hit her. Not an uncommon occurrence in their house. She showed them not only her face but shoved up the sleeves to the torn shirt she was wearing and her arms were a mass of bruises.

"Are your legs like that too?" she was gently asked and she nodded resignedly at the question.

She told of how he had knocked her unconscious and she was certain he had raped her, again while she was out. She thought so because when she woke up her underwear had been ripped from her body and she was leaking semen. She had cleaned herself up as best she could and as quiet as she could, she couldn't tell if he was still in the house or was coming

back. She couldn't find her clothes, she had been confused and she only realized now after several hours of sleep and a good meal the clothes she had on were dirty, mismatched and worn as well as ripped. When she had looked for money and her purse she discovered he was still in the house and apparently he and his new friends were sampling the merchandise because they had been startled by her presence and come after her. The rips were caused by them grabbing at her to subdue her. She had barely gotten away. She had begged bus fare to get out of her neighborhood walking far and begging from complete strangers so she could get out and get away. She only vaguely remembered heading for Manhattan and had thought she was heading for work and ended up here.

"Do you know why you came here Colleen?" the officer asked her as she wrote down the story.

"I guess because Nia has been a good friend to me," she said sadly as though she had lost everything.

Both officers looked at Nia who was gripping the sides of the chair she was in tightly. She was angry, very angry. She had known Colleen for years but she had never realized how bad it was. Colleen had in the course of her telling of today revealed years of abuse and rape from the man who was her husband, a drug dealer.

After they had gotten the information out of Colleen the officer gently asked her what she wanted to do. "We can take you to a shelter, they have excellent programs for women..." she began but Colleen was already shaking her head.

"No, he will find me, he has before. Don't you think I've tried to leave him before?" she asked despondently.

"She can stay here, I have the room and he doesn't know where I live does he Colleen?" Nia asked her quietly.

Colleen looked gratefully at the brunette and shook her head. "No, I never gave him the address. But my things, my clothes, my keys, my purse, everything is at the house," she almost sounded like she was going to cry again.

"Don't worry about that now," Nia told her gently.

"We will have to have another jurisdiction look into this and arrest him. You will have a few hours window to get your things and get out," the officer told her. "But that's all; you have to get what you want, what you need then and stay away. Guys like this." She shook her head. "Guys like this think they own you and everything else. It won't take long for him to make bail either if he has the right connections. They won't keep him either if he hasn't a record to keep him inside."

Colleen nodded.

"You'll let us know when he has been arrested so we can go get her things?" Nia asked.

"Will you be going with her Miss Toto…" she mangled Nia's last name trying to remember how she had introduced her earlier.

"It's Toyomoto and yes I will. I think I will want to take a bodyguard and maybe someone to help us move Colleen's things too," she said and the cop nodded at her intuitiveness. If Cletus got released before they got her things out it would be dangerous.

"Just get her things and get out, we don't want him accusing her of theft. Do you own your house Colleen?" she asked her and she shook her head. "Well then anything that is in your name, your clothes, your car, get it and get out," she advised. "You can't go back and from what you told us he is going to be very angry."

Colleen nodded. She was very frightened by what she had done. She also felt light headed.

"I'm going to ask you to let us take you to the hospital so we can get pictures of these," she indicated the black eye and lip. "We also need a rape kit and to check if he raped you," she informed her.

Colleen was so frightened she wanted to refuse. Only the fact that Nia was sitting right behind her and she knew how disappointed she would be in her kept her from refusing.

"Can we follow you down to the hospital in my car?" Nia gently asked.

Officer Adams nodded with a flick of a look directed at her partner.

"Colleen, let me go grab some clothes for you to change into at the hospital and then we can go," Nia said as she got up. She sensed this interview was at an end.

"We will wait in the hall for you," the young woman informed the intimidating attorney and Nia nodded. She recognized Nia now and had been in court a time or two on duty and seen her in action. She looked a lot different now but she still had that same unapproachable demeanor even if she was being kind to her friend.

Nia hurried upstairs and grabbed some clothes she hoped would fit the much smaller woman settling on sweats that she rarely wore but would fit loosely and be comfortable. She slipped them into an overnight bag and quickly rejoined Colleen who already looked like she was in shock again.

"Gonna be okay?" Nia asked her when she returned down to the living room.

Colleen shook her head. She was scared to go to the hospital.

Nia in an unfamiliar gesture she did something that only being with Justine really enabled her to do. She put her arm around Colleen and forced her up, hugging her close to her taller frame and urging her to her feet. "Come on, I'm not going to leave your side, I'm here for you," she said as she waited for Colleen to slip into her mismatched shoes. "I bet you have a pair just like this at home," she joked.

Colleen froze for a moment, looked down at the shoes and started to laugh. She was laughing as they walked out of the apartment together with Nia's arm around her encouraging her to go. Nia grabbed her purse on the way out.

"What's so funny?" the officer asked wondering if they had somehow been duped and the two women were laughing about it.

"Oh, apparently Colleen is going to start a fashion trend, she has another pair of shoes just like this pair at home," Nia said brightly.

The officer looked down and then up as she realized the joke. She also realized it was Nia's attempt to calm the woman who was looking a bit shell shocked. They all walked to the elevator together and went down. The police car was parked out front and they waited as Nia walked around back to her car.

"Nice car," Officer Hamad commented when the Lexus came around the corner with the two women in it.

Nia followed the police car as they drove to the local hospital and parked directly behind it in the red zone. "Is it okay if I leave my car there?" she asked the officers as they all got out. They assured her it would be okay.

Several hours later Colleen felt almost violated again. The rape kit had made her feel dirty and even the well-meaning medical personnel had pitied her as they took pictures that the police had requested. Then Nia had demanded copies as well as a copy of the report that the officers were going to file, it had gotten awkward but she cited statues and they had to comply. It seemed to take forever before Colleen was dressed in the oversized sweat clothes that buried her. She had to roll the sleeves way back and the legs way up to wear them with her mismatched shoes. The clothes she had been wearing were in an evidence bag.

"I'll go get you an outfit first thing in the morning if you'll remind me of your sizes," Nia offered when they were once more settled in her Lexus. It was late and they were both glad to head back to her apartment.

"I just want to forget the last twenty four hours," Colleen said sadly. She was wrung out and very very tired.

"Do you want the couch or the bed because I don't mind sleeping on the couch?" Nia asked her when they got back.

"I can't take your bed," Colleen protested.

"Well I'd offer to share but that would be awkward," Nia teased but that fell flat. "Would you like to take a bath?"

A bath sounded heavenly to the woman. "I'd love to but I'm just so tired," she nearly whined as she saw the two blankets on the couch and headed for them.

"Okay, well in the morning then. I'm going to take a half day and I'll go out first thing and get you some clothes and stuff," Nia told her.

"You'll feel better after a good night's sleep and then a long hot bath in the morning."

Colleen nodded. They had given her a sleeping pill but she was hesitant to take it with the way she felt. She was just so exhausted already. They had warned her that she might have nightmares even though she didn't remember everything of what he had done. They had offered her brochures for woman's shelters and mental health professionals but Colleen just wanted to get out of there and had refused.

Nia locked up and turned down the lights as Colleen headed for the couch, kicked off her shoes, and just climbed between the two blankets curled up in a ball. She wanted to go to her and comfort her but thought perhaps for now sleep was for the best. It had been a trying day and an equally trying night.

Nia insisted Colleen take a week of sick leave. Not only to give her body a chance to heal but her mind as well. She had never used any of her sick leave before so she had accrued quite a bit and although she objected, argued really, she was no match for her persuasive boss.

"Look, he will be looking for you at your job, if you aren't there, he can't track you here," she told her reasonably.

"I can't impose," she tried.

"You aren't imposing, you more than make up for the space you take up. That breakfast was amazing and you don't have to cook!" she told her guest heatedly.

"But I can't sleep on your couch forever," she argued back.

Nia had to concede she was right but she had an idea about that and by the end of the second day had arranged for a Murphy bed to be delivered and set up in the empty bedroom upstairs. When the inevitable argument came up she pointed out that she needed a good bed for guests and that by having a Murphy bed which came out of a lovely and classic cabinet it could be put away when not in use.

Colleen, who felt guilty by staying with her boss also loved the beautiful piece of furniture. There had been a matching desk that Nia had purchased as well and she purchased two chairs to complete the set. Colleen's clothes fit in the cabinets on either side of the bed and the rich wood of them she rubbed reverently. It really was a lovely piece and she envied Nia's ability to be able to afford the fine pieces of furniture. She was grateful to Nia for so many things. She had been as good as her word the next morning when they knew Cletus had been arrested and was out of the house she had driven them out there and been met by two burly guys that could help move her things as well as act as bodyguards. Nadia, from the group of friends had arranged it for Nia as she needed someone who

wouldn't ask questions. They all quickly gathered Colleens clothes, what there were of them as well as the few sentimental things she treasured and got them out of there. There were pathetically few boxes for her to bring into Nia's apartment and she quickly hung her suits in the closet and put them away.

Most days she lay on the couch and rested until the bruises faded enough that she could go back to work without embarrassing questions. She had learned over the years how to cover most of those that were visible and what clothes to wear to hide others. She went back much sooner than Nia would have had her but really she was needed in the press of work that Nia had in the office. Suzette had been overwhelmed and while she envied Colleen her position she no longer was as cocky and sure about obtaining it someday.

"Look, I can't stay here forever," she told Nia a week later. They were preparing dinner together and Nia was amazed at how effortlessly Colleen made it.

Nia shrugged. "Where are you going to go? Back to your house where Cletus is or a shelter? Do you have first and last for a place and how about furnishings?" she argued reasonably.

"I'll rent one of those hotel rooms but I can't stay here," she tried to explain.

"Why not, no one needs to know. It's none of their business anyway. You stay here for now where it's safe and see how this plays out in the courts," she advised.

Cletus had not only resisted arrest but several kilos of cocaine and other drugs had been found in his possession. Since it was under him on the couch within easy reach the search and seizure warrant had been executed and they had found his stash. Apparently the couch, a pull out couch at one time had a large cavity where the mattress had once gone but was then replaced with shelving to hold up the structure of the couch and provide a nice hiding place for his illegal drugs.

Colleen had been furious to realize he had not only taken her paychecks, leaving her with little to pay the bills but to buy more and more of his crap. The bank accounts they found and were able to trace were all local; he hadn't been too bright in hiding his illegally gotten gains. The public defender was trying to convince him to compromise but he arrogantly assumed he had done nothing wrong and that the government was out to get him. His wife's testimony he discounted as he felt she could not testify against him because of their relationship. He was wrong on several counts and his attorney tried to explain it to him but *he knew* better.

Nia had one of the other associates handling Colleen's divorce and tried to have it expedited. The landlord had already been informed that Colleen was leaving the house and had in fact moved out. Since Cletus had arrogantly assumed all the bills saying he didn't 'need that bitch anyway' they had gotten everything out of her name and into his so she wasn't responsible for them. He did however want to see her and demanded to know where she was. No one was telling him and that infuriated him no end.

Nia had also discretely alerted security at the building and in the firm of what was going on so that Colleen would feel safe at work. She needed her on top of her game, there was a lot of work coming through the office just then and dealing with Sasha as well as Alice's wills were the tip of the iceberg.

❧ CHAPTER SIXTEEN ❧

"What else you got going on?" Stewart snuck into her office to get a cup of her fantastic cappuccino; she still wouldn't give him her source even though he saw the bags he couldn't find out where she was buying them.

Nia had given them all a briefing at the status meeting but she was distracted and only listened with one ear. She had more than enough work for her associates and research assistants. There had been complaints but the work continued to come in and she was on top of most of it. She sat back for a minute at his question as she watched him eagerly consume the strong brew. She wondered if he really wanted to know what she was working on or was after her cappuccino. She smiled as she began to tell him some of what she had on her desk that hadn't made it into the status meeting today.

"Damn, you sure do keep on surprising me. If I had had a daughter Nia, you would have been my choice," he told her affectionately as she caught him up to speed. His advice had almost been unnecessary he realized but she had listened patiently and respectfully and he wondered if she was beyond him already in her strategies.

She puffed with pride, Stewart was a surrogate father in some ways, she'd like to think her own father would have been just as proud. She had affection for the older man but she never forgot he was her boss and treated him with the respect he not only deserved but commanded. "If we have the others go in this direction I am sure we will distract whoever is feeding them the information on this," she indicated another stack on her desk.

"We have to find the breach," he said emphatically. If any clients found out about it they'd lose trust and for them that was paramount.

They discussed a few more things before he asked, "What's going on with…" He pointed with his thumb out the door and she knew he meant Colleen.

"I have one of the associates working on it to make it as smooth and painless as possible."

"I've been asked why we are doing this gratis," he commented.

"She's one of ours but if that's a problem, send me the bill. She is an excellent employee. She doesn't deserve the lot she was served in life," she said passionately, almost too passionately in her friend's defense. It was why she wasn't handling the case herself, she was too close to the issue at hand. She felt horribly guilty that she had ignored the warning signs for so long.

"I don't object to the man hours," he said raising his hand in peace. "But her father actually called to speak to me and try to convince me that my firm shouldn't represent her."

"He did?" Nia said rising slightly out of her seat in consternation. The little she knew of Colleen's father didn't bode well. The nerve though!

"I told him in no uncertain terms where to get off," he answered smugly. It had felt good, the man had lied his way through his own assistant Sally to get to Stewart and that had pissed him off. Hearing the man berate and objectify the woman that was his daughter had shocked him, in this day and age who did that? "I told Donald about it so he was prepared in case the father made anymore waves and so he could discuss it with Colleen." He glanced around and knew that Nia was anxious to get back to work. "How's she doing?" he asked out of genuine concern.

"I think she is doing okay," she said carefully. She was concerned for her, she was too quiet, too diligent at her job, but she seemed depressed too. She hadn't wanted to go to the weekly dinner with her friends. As Nadia had helped get her moved there was a certain amount of gossip among the women and she had quelled what she could.

"Do you know where she is staying?" he asked innocently.

"Yes but we are keeping that a secret for her safeties sake," she answered that carefully too. While she trusted Stewart absolute she didn't want any questions to arise about her involvement in her secretary's private life. She was more than an assistant, she was a friend. Nia was just glad she could help.

Stewart accepted that and let her get back to work as he left her office. He glanced at her two assistants and saw them diligently at work. A law clerk passed him with an armload of paperwork and files for her. He shook his head. That woman would make a great wife someday, she was so efficient and he hadn't seen anyone work as hard as she did.

The work was catching up on Nia. She was tired; she rarely went out now that Colleen was staying with her. She had to make sure the woman didn't do work at the apartment which was so easy to fall into since they were both there. She insisted though on going out with her normal group on Thursday nights, just to get out.

"How's Colleen?" was a familiar phrase as she had been accepted into the group long ago and they were concerned now that she was leaving her husband and divorcing him. They all knew now that he was a wife beater and a drug dealer. That he had remained free on bail was only due to a good public defender and that he hadn't been caught before so had no prior record.

She shared what she could without violating her friendship or confidences with Colleen. They were all used to her vague answers after all she was a lawyer.

When they had a minute alone Eleanor leaned in and asked, "And how are YOU doing?"

"I'm little tired, but why do you ask?" she asked in return as she fiddled with her wine glass looking into the burgundy color.

"The only socializing you do it seems is with us, you never talk about going out, you don't even go antiquing anymore from what I gather. Has the loft lost its appeal?"

"Not at all. I'm just so damned busy these days. You know I'm handling the Brenhov estate and there are others as well as my usual case load. And I bought a Murphy bed not that long go for the spare bedroom as well as matching furniture so I'm ready for guests," she told her, not telling her she had a guest already in the form of her personal assistant. She didn't want to spread that around although Nadia knew from having helped move her out.

"What would you say if I asked you out to the theater, when's the last time you went?" she leaned a little closer as some of the women were returning and she didn't want to be overheard.

When was the last time she went to the theater? Probably with Justine before they began to lie low and go nowhere. She didn't take too long thinking about it either as she sensed the invitation was for her and her alone with Eleanor lowering her voice and leaning in. "It's been a while and yes I'd like that," she answered.

Eleanor gave her a brilliant smile. "Good, I'll call you with the details then."

A few days later she was getting ready to go out and Colleen was again in the bathroom. She seemed to spend a lot of time in there and Nia had noted she was upset frequently at work.

"You have got to stop letting this situation get to you," she advised. She always seemed to be upset about it and talking about it could reduce her to tears. Nia tried not to bring it up unless Colleen did.

"I know, I'm trying," had been the response.

Still Nia worried about her friend, she had her ups and downs but mostly she was afraid of what her husband would do if he found her or where she was staying.

As Colleen came out of the bathroom and Nia came downstairs fastening an earring to her ear she gasped at how nice her boss looked. She was wearing a long dress in black that draped on her elegant frame

with it cinched at the waist and a diamond studded clasp. She wondered if they were real diamonds.

"Could you help me with this necklace? I had my nails done and now I'm afraid of chipping them," Nia asked her.

Because she was so much taller than Colleen she had to sit on the couch for her to fasten the matching necklace, again diamonds in graduated sizes about her neck. At her ears were two dangling diamonds to complete her look. Her hair was swept back but still down and allowed the viewer to see her elegant neck.

"You look fantastic," Colleen said as she sat there on the couch in her sweats feeling dowdy.

"Thank you, we are going to the theater and Eleanor said tonight was ritzy so I wanted to look nice," she said in return as she got up to check her appearance in the mirror she now had hung by the front door. She pulled her wallet from her everyday purse that matched her briefcase and slipped it along with tissue, keys, and her cell into a clutch purse, the combination barely fit in the much smaller purse.

"Eleanor? As in Eleanor James?" Colleen asked wondering miserably if she was going to have to run back to the bathroom to throw up once again. She had really felt awful and the worries over Cletus hadn't helped. Her father had called to berate her once or twice and her mother was strangely quiet.

"Yes, she invited me to the theater," Nia said absentmindedly as she closed her clutch. She walked over to the closet by the door and chose a suitable coat to go with the outfit. She wouldn't need it in this weather but one never knew.

"Are you two dating?" Colleen asked. She knew Eleanor James was a lesbian by the women she had dated and seen her with but she had never suspected Nia was one and it shocked her.

Nia laughed as she turned around from her selection. "Us? Dating?" She chuckled hard. The thought was ludicrous. And then she thought again. "Noooo," she said slowly as the humor died. Was Eleanor asking her out as merely a friend or as a potential date? "I think she just wanted me to get out. After all I've been practically no where other than our Thursday night get together's in a while." In fact the last time she dressed up she had ended up swimming in the ocean, she hoped tonight would be better.

"You do know she is gay don't you?" Colleen asked seeing the expression on Nia's face and to her it looked like shock instead of the deep thought that Nia had fallen into.

"Yes, I surmised that by the women I have seen her with and she has brought to my parties," Nia answered carefully still analyzing Eleanor's motives for asking her out.

"Okay, just thought you should know," she answered and picked up a magazine to read trying to keep her nausea at bay by not thinking about it. It was getting easier not to think about Cletus and she wasn't throwing up as often these days but every now and then something triggered it...

Colleen made herself absent when the doorbell went off. She didn't want to be seen in her sweats by the much more elegant Eleanor James and she didn't want to get in Nia's way. She still felt like she was over staying her welcome but she was so grateful for somewhere to hide and especially so nice a place to stay. She paid it back by creating delicious meals for Nia whenever she could. It was made easy by the beautiful kitchen she so enjoyed.

"Ready?" Eleanor asked as she eyed the elegant gown that Nia was wearing.

"Do I pass?" Nia teased giving a little swirl.

Eleanor grinned and did a swirl of her own. "You do! How about me?" she asked playfully. She was wearing a rather attractive pantsuit that was obviously silk with darker lapels and a matching stripe down the pants leg. It looked good on her frame and she wore a big bow on the matching blouse.

"That's very nice, where did you get that?" Nia asked fingering the silk with her done up nails.

"Oh, there is this store on Fifth," she began and then noting the time she said, "Let's get going, I took a cab and catching one is going to be a beast," she added.

"Do you want me to drive?" Nia offered and once again wondered at the nature of this invitation.

"Would you? That would be great," she replied happily. "There is of course valet parking."

Nia was glad to drive, she loved her Lexus.

The night was filled with excitement as they watched a beautiful rendition of Gypsy. It wasn't on Broadway but the off Broadway cast was very good. They had a marvelous time and Eleanor introduced her to some interesting people. Several of the women were obviously there with their partners and Nia had to wonder again if this was a date as she was eyed speculatively.

They went out for a few drinks and Nia kept hers non-alcoholic. She didn't need a DUI with all the bad boys she dealt with on a weekly basis in her practice. She could mentally read the headlines now and it made her shudder.

"Oh shoot, I think I ripped my hem," Eleanor complained on the ride back to Nia's apartment.

"Uh oh, is it major?" Nia asked naively.

"No idea, can't see a thing," she answered.

"Well I'm sure I have a sewing kit in the kitchen drawer back at my apartment and you can put a safety pin in it so you don't ruin it further," Nia offered.

Eleanor smiled and thanked her, she was satisfied that her plan had worked. Nia had no idea that she had planned this, the date, the drinks, the people she had met. She really had thought it was just two friends going out and while Eleanor was a little insulted by that she also hoped to change Nia's mind with this ploy. It would really be a feather in her cap if she landed the high powered attorney. Being seen with her tonight would spread through her friends with the gossip it had engendered.

"I think it's in here," Nia said as she put her clutch down on the counter and pulled open a drawer where she kept such things. Colleen had organized much of this and Nia wouldn't have thought of having one but it came in handy. As she turned with the small kit in her hand Eleanor captured her face in a kiss with both hands. Nia was so surprised she dropped the kit which scattered all over the hardwood floor. "Ooops," she said as she stepped back and looked down at the mess.

"Here, let me help you with that," Eleanor said. She wasn't sure that it wasn't deliberate; it was something she would pull to get a woman on the floor with her but as Nia was genuinely trying to gather up the rolled spools of thread, the needles, and the little bits and pieces of the kit she had to wonder. Between the two of them they soon had it gathered up.

"I'm going to have to vacuum in here to make sure I got it all," Nia said absentmindedly as she thought over what had just happened. She was a little embarrassed. "Here, this is what I went for," she said as she handed Eleanor a safety pin for her supposed rip. She wasn't as fooled as Eleanor thought as she realized she had been manipulated into inviting the other woman up to her apartment so she could kiss her.

"Thank you," Eleanor said as they both rose up from the floor. She leaned in for another kiss and Nia backed away.

"No Eleanor," she said quietly.

"Not interested?" she asked surprised. Eleanor knew she was an attractive woman and she had hopes here.

"You are my friend, nothing more," Nia said kindly. She didn't want to upset Eleanor or lose her friendship but she was a little annoyed that she hadn't been upfront about what this night was about.

"Okay," Eleanor said ruefully, she was disappointed. "No harm no foul."

"Are we okay?" Nia asked hoping she hadn't made a mess of it or lost a longtime friend.

"I had to try," she answered with a grin.

Nia smiled in response to the grin and said nothing.

"I'd better be going, it's late," Eleanor stated to hasten her exit gracefully.

Nia walked her to the door.

"See you Thursday?" she asked.

"Of course," Nia responded and wondered if that would be awkward. She closed the door firmly and stared at it. Hearing a noise from up in the loft she wondered if Colleen had observed any of that.

Colleen heard Nia walk up the stairs. She hadn't known Nia was with anyone in the kitchen when she heard her come in. She saw the kiss that Eleanor had laid on the much taller Nia and quietly returned to her room. She wondered now if Nia was a lesbian too but she didn't dare ask her. She wasn't sure how she felt about it.

❧ CHAPTER SEVENTEEN ❧

"Where did you get that cup?" one of the other lawyers asked Nia as she sat down at the conference table at their weekly status meeting.

Nia was carrying a mug that read: GOOD LAWYERS Never Lose Their Appeal. She laughed and shrugged. "Oh Colleen gave it to me at Christmas I think."

"That's hilarious," he commented before the meeting got started.

"Nia, I see one of your bad boys is in the news again," Phillip Anders commented as the meeting began.

"Yes, he is in violation of several points of his contract with not only the team but with us. We will be meeting later to discuss it with him and give a news brief afterwards so the press can lie about it," she said cynically. Several of the lawyers muffled laughter at her sarcasm. "I've got a handle on it; it was only a matter of time before he couldn't help himself."

There were several other lawyers who gave status reports on the various cases they were handling and then once again they came back to Nia. "What's going on with the Weaver Estate?"

Nia explained she was working in conjunction with her Los Angeles counterparts as well as the widow Kathy Weaver. Kathy's lawyer Portia was helping to settle everything but it was complicated by the many layers of property and accounts that Alice had owned. Every time they peeled off one layer another few showed up, it was like an onion and crying about it certainly didn't help.

"Is it tied in with the Brenhov Estate?" another lawyer who had been absent from several meetings asked.

"Only in the one deal. The Brenhov Estate is entirely different and is an outright gift to the heir Alexis," she said annoyed. An unprepared lawyer irritated her no end and as he had missed several meetings this had been gone over before. Several of the associates had been handling things with her and he would be aware of that if he had attended or paid attention.

Several other cases were discussed, some Nia was involved with and some that she merely listened to so that she stayed on top of the news within the firm. It was a long meeting, they had a lot of cases pending, in various stages of completion, and a couple that had been settled. It was a large firm and they all had work to get to. Nia was among several who were glad when the meeting ended.

"You have a two o'clock meeting with a new client and another at four," Colleen told her as she went over her afternoon schedule.

"That's like the sixth one this week, what the heck is going on?" Nia asked as she looked up from her lunch that was spread out on the table of her office.

Colleen shrugged and smiled. She knew it was a happy complaint. "You're popular," she teased.

Nia laughed as expected. "Hey do you want me to pick up some more of that wine we finished the last one the other night."

"You finished the last one," Colleen clarified and then looked guiltily over her shoulder out the open office door and lowered her voice. "Stop that, people will realize where I'm staying."

Nia looked at her for a moment and then realized what she had done and nodded.

"I better find a place," Colleen said for the umpteenth time since she had been moved in with her pitiful belongings.

"Stop it, I like having someone there and unless you can't stand living with me it's fine. It's not like the room was in use," Nia argued in return.

Colleen knew that Nia didn't mind her there but after what she saw the other night she wondered a lot more about Nia's personal life than she should. At first she had been a little shocked at the possibility that Nia could be a lesbian but then as she thought about it she realized not only was it none of her business but if it made Nia happy she wasn't going to judge. Strangely as she accepted it more she thought about Nia more and wondered what made her tick…she hadn't been very social beyond her group of friends or when putting on a party for work was necessitated. She looked down at Nia's calendar again and stated, "You have a party at Stewarts next Friday too you asked me to give you warning."

Nia rolled her eyes. That meant she had to find another outfit to wear, after all being seen in the same one twice wasn't allowed. Then she thought of the one she had worn the other night with Eleanor and wondered if she could get away with wearing it again to this party. She hated things like this but they were a necessary evil and with Stewart as the lead partner in the firm it wasn't like she could blow it off. She sighed and made a mental note to go shopping and tonight when she picked up wine for the apartment to look for a nice expensive one for Stewart's party gift or better yet a bag of his favorite cappuccino that she had imported by Tiffany and had told no one.

Colleen was feeling better these days. She didn't get nauseous all the time from thinking about what Cletus could do to her and the lawyer in the firm, Donald was handling the divorce for her and had managed to keep

her out of the negotiations so she didn't have to face him. His lawyer was useless, both Nia and her lawyer had assured her and while they would have to agree to a fairly fifty-fifty split of their 'assets' they were pretty sure they could get out of paying him alimony because of his drug arrest and it's impending conviction. The goal was to get her divorced before he went to court on his drug charges but that wasn't likely as slow as divorce court went. Cletus wanted a face to face meeting and they were all trying to keep that from happening for Colleen's sake but she was starting to feel braver these days as she felt better. Being away from him had done her a world of good and being among friends. Nia had been terrific about letting her stay in the apartment but she now had more money to do with as she wanted without him stealing it all or her having to pay all the bills, she was saving for her first and last months as well as security deposit on a place and when she had enough she was going to start looking.

"Allison Gottfried is on the line from Gottfried Pharmaceuticals," Colleen announced over the phone intercom and Nia asked her to put her through.

A few minutes later Nia came out of her office to address both Colleen and Suzette. "I need you both to cancel all my appointments for the next week and you," she turned to Colleen. "Pack a bag as you will be going with me. Allison needs to meet with me and I need you there to keep notes and the files. Make copies of those that were sent over so that we have them with us for the trip." She turned back to Suzette, "I need you to make first class reservations to Miami for tomorrow and book us a suite at the hotel we used last time I was there so that I have working room. Arrange for a car rental and I'll probably be gone the rest of the week." She watched as both women jumped to it and she turned around to go finish some work she had on her desk that would need to be done before she left. She turned back to tell them both, "Also send a memo to the other lawyers I have working with me about where I will be the rest of the week and ask them to file motions for any cases to be delayed or any meetings we have to cancel," she reminded them knowing the efficient women would have a lot of work to do until she left.

Nia worked late that night and received memos from the other attorneys involved in many of her own cases. It was a team effort a lot of time and keeping each other apprised of things like this took up a lot of time. It was a good thing she had excellent assistants to keep her looking good and on top of things.

"I have my bag packed," she said to Colleen that night as she dropped it by the front door next to her bulging briefcase and purse. The file folders

that were part of Colleen's luggage were sitting there as well disguised as an extra suitcase.

"I'm ready," Colleen said as she brought her own suitcase down the stairs and put it by Nia's. She knew they wouldn't have time in the morning for forgotten things and had packed tonight to be ready for the first flight out. Allison Gottfried and her businesses were more important than some clients so her call must have warranted a 'drop everything and run' which was what this was about. "Do you need me to pack anything else?" she asked as she looked at the small pile.

"No, just relax, that's what I intend to," Nia answered as she headed for the kitchen with Colleen following close behind. "Damn, I never got to shop for that wine. Guess I'll have to make do with another kind."

"None for me, it didn't set well last time," Colleen responded as she reached for an orange juice.

They both reached into the fridge at the same time and laughed as their hands collided. Nia looked at her for a moment longer and pulled back allowing her to get her juice bottle before she reached for the open bottle of wine in the fridge.

"Is Ms. Gottfried really upset or something?" Colleen ventured to ask.

"Oh you know, when someone of that caliber barks we listen. I need to check on some of the things I set up in place when we got the account and have the other attorneys get on some things but she wants to meet with me in person so I want to be well prepared," she glanced at the suitcase of files by the door as she poured herself a glass of wine.

They chatted as they put in dinner to heat it up. It was nice having the two of them there in the apartment, neither was lonely and they didn't talk just about work which was fine for both of them. As Nia felt the effects of the wine she couldn't help but notice that Colleen seemed to be glowing. Being away from Cletus after all this time was really making her blossom into a very pretty woman. She swallowed her libido though. She didn't want to ruin what was a very good friendship; she wasn't going to hit on her friends just because she was horny.

Colleen, although she hadn't drunk any of the wine was having problems of her own. For some reason her thoughts of Nia and the kiss she had seen her exchange with Eleanor seemed to play over and over in her head. She had begun to wonder if Nia might find her attractive and as she had never had a kiss much less a relationship with a woman she wondered if she perhaps was 'turning' gay. She rationally dismissed that thought but couldn't seem to stop thinking about Nia. She knew she admired her, had admired her for years and was grateful for everything she had ever done for her. She couldn't help wondering though what it would be like to kiss her.

"There, you've got something," Nia pointed as they finished up their meal.

"Where, here?" Colleen wiped at her mouth with her napkin.

"No you missed it, there," Nia pointed again and when Colleen wiped and missed it again she took the napkin and dabbed at the spot on the corner of her mouth. She looked into Colleen's eyes for a moment and froze.

"Nia," Colleen breathed suddenly feeling the moment. She swallowed nervously. Her hands twisted in her lap.

"Um, Colleen," Nia said feeling nervous as she tried to pull away with the napkin.

Colleen's hand shot up to hold it to her face as she leaned into it and closed her hand slightly rubbing against it.

"I...I don't think this is a good idea do you?" Nia asked suddenly wanting to lean in and kiss her assistant.

"Probably not," Colleen conceded. She opened her eyes further and looked at Nia. "Do you find me attractive?" she felt brave enough to ask.

Nia nodded, she was mesmerized for the moment in Colleen's gaze. It felt like the most natural thing in the world to lean in and hesitantly kiss her.

Colleen closed her eyes as she felt Nia's lips on her own. She breathed into the kiss, she hadn't known she was holding her breath but it felt right, it felt natural, and she deepened it unconsciously. Hesitantly her tongue darted and licked at Nia's lip.

Nia groaned slightly feeling the tongue and widened the kiss with her lips, her own tongue coming into play with Colleens. Her hand let go of the napkin and cupped into Colleen's hair holding her in place for her onslaught.

Colleen slipped from her chair to stand before Nia and her own hands slipped to Nia's shoulders for balance as she returned the kiss. She was feeling dizzy suddenly and she needed that anchor.

Nia wrapped her own arms around Colleen pulling her closer to her in the chair, her legs widening to pull her between them. She wanted to wrap her legs around the woman but at the same time didn't want to frighten her. She kissed her deeply and held her warm body against her as they both explored.

"Nia," Colleen moaned as she pulled back slightly to catch her breath. Not enough oxygen was coming through her nose to her lungs and she felt the need to pull back.

Nia let her pull back as she caressed her hair and looked warmly into her eyes. "Are you okay?" she asked wondering if she had just blown a good friendship. This was sexual harassment by anyone's book even if Colleen had kissed her first. She was still her boss.

"I'm fine, I'm wonderful actually," Colleen whispered with a hint of a grin as she looked at the darkness of Nia's eyes, they seemed almost black at the moment as she breathed hard. After a moment she asked, "Are *you* okay?"

Nia examined Colleen's face up close and looked her over as she avoided her eyes for the moment trying to gather her thoughts. "I'm fine," she echoed Colleen just as softly and then added, "I'm just surprised."

Colleen tried to pull back further but with Nia's arms wrapped around her she couldn't move far. "I'm sorry, I was out of line," she began to babble as she blushed and looked down. She pulled her hands back from where they were behind Nia's back.

"Wait," Nia smiled encouragingly. She could hear the hesitation and the hurt in Colleen's voice. "It's okay," she soothed. "I kissed you back you know," she added.

Colleen nodded as she looked up again. She knew she was easily led but she had enjoyed Nia's kiss, much more than she could admit at the moment. She looked down again ashamed as though she had done something wrong.

"I want you," Nia said simply trying to keep this from getting out of hand, from losing a cherished friend, from being sued for sexual harassment. Her lawyer's mind began to kick in and she hated it at the moment. "But I want to be sure you want this too," she said quietly.

Colleen's head reared up at the words. Nia wanted her? *Her?* She was *nothing* compared to Nia whom she felt was so smart and sophisticated. She was eager to acquiesces and see where this would go but then she realized that Nia was a woman and she had no idea what that involved or what she would do. What if Nia made love to her and found her lacking, what would she do then?

Nia could see all the doubt in her assistant's eyes and her heart warmed for her once again. She had always felt something for Colleen, she had felt she was the underdog and championed her cause. Even hiring her had surprised many. Seeing the bruises she had been sure there was more there but had believed her excuses of rough sex, having them confirmed to be the brutality of that asshole she had been married to had only angered her on Colleen's behalf. Now she felt nothing but compassion for her, well maybe more than that. She had been in her place before, unsure of herself, she had felt the same emotions that she could see in Colleen's eyes. "I want you," she repeated looking deeply into her eyes. "I just don't want you to do anything you don't want to do; this will change everything between us. Think about it before we go any further," she advised.

Colleen almost immediately said she wanted her too but then common sense stepped in as she nodded to agree. She should think about it.

Nia smiled slightly. As much as she wanted to make love to Colleen, *here*, *now*, she wouldn't pressure her. She still held her in her arms as they spoke but she released her slightly so she could step back but before she could she leaned in to kiss her again. Her arms let her go completely as she kissed her and Colleen responded.

Colleen didn't know what was wrong with her but she was light headed and eager to respond to the kiss that Nia gave her. She wasn't holding her anymore and she could leave at any time but those lips held her in place as she hesitantly explored them. They felt so nice, so warm, so inviting she couldn't help but bring her tongue into play, she wanted more and moved to take Nia into her arms but Nia grabbed her by the shoulders and firmly set her back so she could slide off the chair and stand up next to her.

Nia looked down warmly into Colleen's eyes as she smiled at her in appreciation of the shared kiss. "Think about it," she advised again. Then with a little smile she gathered her dishes and took them to the sink to wash them off.

Colleen thought it might be awkward after what they had just shared but Nia easily changed the subject back to something they had spoken about over dinner. She wanted to cover her still bare walls with artwork and wanted Colleen to go with her to look for pieces that would increase in value over the years and add to the beauty of the apartment. The little each of them knew about art they discussed as they cleaned up their dinner.

The next morning was hurried as they carried their luggage down to the waiting car. Suzette had a Park Avenue limo waiting for them as she knew Nia did not like stretch limos and using a limo verses a cab made more sense. She hadn't even thought anything of it when Colleen said she was to 'meet' Nia at her apartment so they could go to the airport from there. No one knew they were sharing Nia's apartment and for now that was best.

Nia had slept well despite the thoughts on her mind. She could hear Colleen across the hall in her own room as she tossed and turned and she could see the evidence with her own eyes that she hadn't slept well as they got up, got ready, and went to the waiting car.

Colleen had a lot on her mind. If she entered into a relationship with Nia it might destroy the friendship she had with her boss, something she valued and cherished. If she didn't though Nia might not like her anymore, so she felt pressure there. She knew logically Nia wouldn't hold it against her but after having been manipulated for so long by an expert like Cletus she didn't have a lot of confidence in herself. She wanted Nia, she was sure of that. She was very curious about what women did together and would have researched it on the internet if the object of her curiosity wasn't sitting next to her, first in the car, then at the airport, then on the

plane. She was also wondering a million other things and wondered if Nia ever felt uncertain.

Nia was wondering about Colleen. She was strangely silent and she hoped she hadn't hurt their relationship by kissing her. It had been a nice set of kisses and from what she had learned with Justine she knew herself enough to know she wanted to take it further. It was up to Colleen though, she had to make the decision, Nia didn't want her regretting it. She had already thought further and what would have to change if they entered into a relationship. They wouldn't be able to work together if it became intimate, not for long anyway. She knew she had feelings for her but she didn't just feel sorry for her, there was more and always had been and while she wasn't sure it was love, not yet, there was enough affection that she had to wonder if it was turning into love. She didn't mention anything though as she and Colleen got in the car and their cases on the plane. Colleen's was overweight because of the files and Nia paid the extra fee without a blink as she whipped out her credit card. She laughed at Colleen who felt guilty for doing her job and shook her head.

"Don't worry about it, it wasn't your fault our paperwork was so heavy," she teased as they made their way to the walkway towards where their plane would be taking off.

"I know but I'm so used to…" she began but Nia cut her off.

"It's not your fault, we have to work on your self-confidence," she said with a smile.

Colleen smiled in return. Now that she thought about it, Nia had always bolstered her ego. She felt confident at her job; she knew she was an efficient and valuable assistant. She was good at her job and it was thanks to Nia and her ability to make her feel good about it. At that moment the admiration she had felt for her boss blossomed into more, not quite love but if she could have kissed Nia at this moment she would have.

"Do you have your notebook?" Nia asked as they sat to wait for the announcement of their flight.

Colleen was efficient and had it ready as she began to take notes as Nia began dictating them. They moved to a quiet corner when they realized other passengers were taking an interest in their conversation and worked until the loudspeaker announced their flight.

"Would you like the window seat?" Nia offered generously as she put her hand on the small of Colleen's back and 'escorted' her down the small aisle in first class.

Colleen liked the touch and feel of Nia taking care of her, however small the gesture, and accepted the seat graciously. She had often wondered if other executive assistants got the attention Nia had given her, the small gifts, the perks, the genuine appreciation. These little things now that they were taking an interest in each other took on new meaning in her

mind and she was grateful for having Nia in her life. They continued working through the flight and discussed several things Nia wanted done when they landed and when they got back to the office. Colleen was pleased that the flight didn't make her queasy in any way as she was done with throwing up over her situation with Cletus, in fact she didn't want to think about him at all while in Nia's company.

"What do you mean you don't have a reservation for my car?" Nia asked as she blinked at the condescending clerk at the car counter.

Colleen effortlessly pushed Nia out of the way as she pulled out her ever present notebook and read off the numbers and gave the clerk merry hell. How dare they make a mistake over Nia's reservation, something that happened from time to time with the amount of trips she took?

Nia watched amused as Colleen took over. It was a side of her that didn't come out too often but when it did it always was a surprise. She was so confident now. She wondered if she would be this confident in a relationship. Last night she knew it would have been easy to lead her into bed with her but she wanted her willing, she wanted her like this, confident. She didn't want her regretting the impulse or feeling pressured into it.

They were soon on their way and Nia drove down to the hotel where she had stayed with Justine in the past. They gave her a suite with a room for each of the women and a living room between them. There was no mess up this time over the room reservation and Nia was grateful for that as the clerk downstairs she was sure remembered her from last time. She didn't want Colleen to know she had been in the same hotel with another woman.

"Well, I have the meetings in the morning, what do you say we change into shorts and walk along the beach to go get dinner?" Nia offered.

"Sounds wonderful," Colleen returned. She was so thrilled that Nia needed her on these occasional trips. It had been hard to get away in the past with Cletus so suspicious but now she felt free, she felt wonderful and the prospect of a romance in the air was making her feel…different. She hurried to go change.

"Wow, we have to get a tan on those legs," Nia teased her when she got a look of her in shorts. Her own legs were not tanned naturally but they looked nothing like they had been after her trip to Mexico. In comparison to Colleen's skin color though she looked dark.

"I know, I'll have to wear a sun-tan oil, we will have to pick some up," she said as she looked down ruefully at the 'glow in the dark' color of her legs.

Nia chuckled. "We should maybe get a spray on tan for you so the glare doesn't blind anyone and I have to defend you in a lawsuit from them running into something."

"C'mon, they aren't that bright," she answered with a grin and then looked down again and had to concede Nia might be right. "Maybe they are," she said ruefully.

They were laughing and teasing as they made their way along the beach in Deerfield feeling the warmth of the sands on their bare toes as they carried their sandals. When they reached the end by the roadway they returned the sandals to their feet and crossed the road to eat at a beachside restaurant.

"No, I don't want to drink anything alcoholic, my stomach has been upset for so long, I'm babying it to keep from being ill," Colleen told her as they ordered.

Nia understood. Colleen had been so upset for so long that she didn't want to add to the pressure of starting something with her. It certainly hadn't gone unnoticed how often she ran for the bathroom. She wanted her though and seeing her looking relaxed and happy here in Florida made her want to seduce her, she was tempted, *very* tempted to start something and yet she knew it had to be Colleen's decision, she kept telling herself that.

Nia was giving herself away in little ways though as she took 'care' of Colleen. Not used to being 'taken care' of in any way Colleen seemed hyper aware of the little things. The subtle ways that Nia was showing that she cared from pulling out her chair to correcting the waiter when he repeated her order back incorrectly. She made sure Colleen was comfortable and enjoying herself as she steered the conversation well away from work and personal problems and entertained her with stories about her best friend Annie and even a couple of college stories about her friend Alice when she had been younger, vibrant, and alive. Her leg accidentally brushed against Colleens under the small table they shared at the restaurant and the bare skin against bare skin was distracting. Even her hand brushing against her as they were jostled by the dinner and drinking crowd around them seemed to distract her.

Colleen watched Nia avidly for some sign that she still wanted her. She had been friendly, polite, and professional on the way down here and in no way putting pressure on to her. It had taken a while to realize she was leaving the decision up to her and for that she was grateful…and intimidated. It was a lot to think about and she was thinking about it. It seemed though as her body was thinking about it a lot more than her head as she felt she was in a constant state of arousal. It had been a long time that she felt arousal for another person, Cletus had killed that a long time ago and feeling it again and for a woman totally surprised her. She could feel it though, she felt like she was in heat around Nia. She wanted her and while she didn't know exactly what that would involve she wanted to find out.

"Geez, we should head back and avoid all this," Nia said once they had finished and she had paid the bill. The jostling crowd was increasing and twice she had to turn down inebriated vacationers who had hit on her. She found herself curiously angry when it had happened once to Colleen who had blushingly declined his invitation to drink with him.

"Let's go," Colleen said relieved. She hadn't liked it as the crowd got more boisterously drunk and the guy hitting on her made her feel dirty, as dirty as Cletus often had. She felt almost guilty as she turned him down and looked over at an amused Nia who didn't really look amused.

They quietly made their way back on the now dark beach as they walked towards their hotel. The difference from the crowd in the restaurant to the almost empty beach was quite alarming; both of them had ringing ears.

"Whew, what a relief," Colleen said after a while. The tension she felt building in the restaurant was beginning to wane as they walked along.

"What, you don't like drunks and crowds?" Nia asked amused as she looked down at the woman and thought how attractive she looked in the casual attire and how relaxed.

"No thank you, I could do without drunks for the rest of my life," she said in genuine gratitude.

Nia mentally cursed herself as she had unintentionally brought up Cletus and that was not what she wanted to do. She stayed quiet and Colleen glanced over at her wondering at the silence.

"Something wrong?" she finally asked.

"I didn't mean to bring up bad memories," she said uncomfortably.

Colleen was surprised. Nia was always so considerate towards her and for that she was grateful. "You didn't, you can't worry that anything you will say will remind me of him," she said gently.

Nia stopped to look down on her as she wondered if she was just being polite. She could make her out clearly in the street lamps that lined the beach. She looked so earnest, so cute; she wanted to kiss her but stopped herself…barely.

Colleen felt no such compunction and leaned up toward Nia to kiss her. She was so tall though she had to bring her hand up to cup behind Nia's neck and pull her down slightly so their lips could meet.

"Mmm," Nia said encouragingly as their lips began to move against each other. "Are you sure?" she mumbled around their kisses.

"Yes, I'm sure, I want this," Colleen answered.

Nia wasn't going to be a saint here, she had asked and it had been confirmed. She wanted Colleen and was taking her agreement to mean they would take their relationship to the next level. She took her hand and led her toward the hotel. She dropped it to walk through the hotel and only

took it again when they were in the hotel room and out of sight of any possible cameras.

Slowly she advanced on Colleen and leaned into her. She kicked off her sandals that while they hadn't added to her considerable height by much they were enough that she wanted them off. She leaned down to kiss Colleen thoroughly and absolutely. Again she leaned back to ask, "Are you sure?"

Colleen had been confused on the beach as Nia led her across the beach and to the hotel only to release her hand and gently push on her lower back through the hall and to the elevator staring at her intently in the elevator and again gently pushing her towards their suite. She had lost her confusion as they began to kiss again in the suite. "Yesss, I'm sure," she said gently as she worked to get closer to Nia and take her in her arms.

Nia, realizing their height difference was going to a problem at the moment pulled her close and led her to the couch to gently sit her there, sitting herself next to her so she could pull her once more in her arms and begin to kiss her in earnest. Colleen was an enthusiastic partner and more than willing as she wrapped her arms around her to return the kisses. Nia soon found herself straddled and an enthusiastic Colleen in her arms kissing her ardently. Nia tried to slow the pace down but found it nearly impossible as Colleen was like an excited puppy as she kissed and caressed her. Knowing how crushed she would be if she suggested they slow down Nia just tried to keep up and keep it a pleasant experience for her partner as she kissed, caressed, and fondled her lover.

She did manage to get them to her bedroom as she merely suggested, "Let's go to bed," and had Colleen jumping up and pulling her hand towards the room. She was attacked and born backwards on the bed by Colleen who was taking the upper hand as she showed how much she wanted this.

Colleen thought by throwing herself at Nia it would make up for her lack of knowledge but she was also afraid Nia would change her mind and she didn't want her to change it. She wanted to know what it was like to make love to a woman but not just any woman, Nia Toyomoto. The woman she had so admired all these years had said she wanted *her*, Colleen, whom no one wanted before except to use. She wanted to show she was deserving of that, that she could hold her own, and yet she had no idea what to do as she kissed her enthusiastically.

Nia finally realized the problem as they began to undress and Colleen continued her frenzy. Slowly she slowed her movements, showing her what she wanted. Capturing her hand she slowed the frantic caresses to make them more sensual, to make them arousing to them both as she showed her own caresses on Colleens welcoming body.

At first Colleen seemed hesitant to touch more intimate places beyond her shoulders, her back, her arms but at the first touch on Nia's breast she seemed to get bolder, feeling as though she had gone that far she could go further. At Nia's gasp of pleasure she leaned back and seeing Nia's eyes half closed in enjoyment she continued touching her, first through her clothes and then later as she got bolder inside them as they slowly began to melt away from the body she was exploring.

Nia was pleased as Colleen seemed to lose her shyness. She didn't even realize as Nia slowly stripped away her shorts and blouse and she was left with barely-there underwear that Nia had bought for her oh so long ago. She had been right; it looked fantastic on her body. She couldn't wait to take it off and discover what it was hiding beneath its lacelike fabric. Slowly she kissed down Colleen's neck and chest, caressing away her clothes where she could and enjoying the feel of her heated body against her own. She rolled them so she had the upper hand and could remove her own clothes, she desperately craved feeling skin against skin and Colleen seemed content to making love to her through the clothes and only occasionally venturing inside them.

Colleen got the hint and helped Nia to remove first her blouse and then unbutton and wiggle out of the shorts she was wearing. She gasped at how sexy and alluring Nia's underwear looked on her tall frame. She immediately felt inadequate and frumpy but managed to hide it as Nia began making love to her in earnest.

Slowly she removed Colleen's bra and then her panties until she lay there exposed and available to Nia's eager hands as she caressed every inch arousing her to a fevered pitch.

Colleen couldn't remember when making love had brought her so much pleasure; it had been so long since she actually made love that she was tempted to take her pleasure so she could concentrate on Nia and making her enjoy the moment. Masturbation had been strictly forbidden in her relationship with Cletus and to be honest she knew she hadn't wanted pleasure with him after she realized what a selfish bastard he was. She tried hard not to remember him as Nia made love to her so sweetly she wanted to cry. She couldn't help it and thinking about him was ruining the moment for her.

Nia saw the tears and stopped instantly. "What's wrong?" she asked, immediately assuming that she had somehow hurt her or that she regretted where this had gone.

"Nothing," Colleen tried to tell her but was failing as she looked down at her so sweetly.

"It can't be nothing if you are crying," Nia said reasonably. She leaned up on her arm to look down into her lover's face. The tears began to leak from the corners of her beautiful eyes.

"I'm sorry, I can't…" she began to blubber as she tried to hide in Nia's long hair.

Nia took it that she had changed her mind about lovemaking and regretted letting it get this far. "It's okay, really it is…" she tried to placate the upset and naked woman. She gulped feeling like a heel for somehow pressuring her into this situation.

"It's it's…" she tried to explain. Nia was being so sweet and she didn't know how to explain, now was not the time to discuss her soon-to-be ex-husband. She lay there in Nia's arms as she sobbed a little into her hair.

Nia was at a loss. She had learned a lot with Justine but this was way different and now she wondered if she was 'qualified' to initiate another woman into the ways of making love to another woman. Perhaps she had done something wrong. She held her awkwardly as she patted her and let her sob into her shoulder. She felt stupid but didn't know how to extricate herself from the situation.

Slowly Colleen calmed herself and became aware once again of the fact that she was naked and Nia nearly so and they were lying in a bed together on the verge of making love. She also realized she had ruined the moment by thinking of Cletus. Nia must think she was stupid. Slowly she gathered herself and looked up to see Nia looking down on her, waiting for her to say or do something. She swallowed the last lump in her throat. "I'm sorry," she apologized. She had learned long ago to always say that first and she was good at it.

Nia looked at her thoughtfully for a moment and asked, "For what?"

Colleen hadn't thought she would respond like that. She blinked. She then tried to gesture but her hands were wrapped tightly against Nia who had held her and comforted her as she sobbed into her hair. She looked perplexed as she said, "For this, for crying, for ruining the moment," she babbled trying to get out as many excuses as she could as fast as she could so that Nia wouldn't get angry.

Nia smiled down at her and brushed back her hair from her face so she could look down at her clearly. Her own hair she threw back over her shoulder. "It's okay, if you aren't up to this, I understand…" she began placatingly.

"You don't understand," Colleen rushed. She could hear the rejection in Nia's voice, the withdrawal. "It's not this, it's me," she burst out with.

"What do you mean?" Nia asked gently.

"I was enjoying this, I want this, and then I realized how wonderful it was and that no one has ever made me feel like this before," she answered and then glanced down as a blush tinged her cheeks.

"So why the tears then?" Nia asked puzzled.

"Because it was so beautiful, you made it feel so nice, and then I thought of Cletus and compared the two and..." she buried her head again in Nia's hair to hide her mortification. "I ruined it."

Nia smiled and lifted Colleen's chin. "You didn't ruin anything. You are still here. I am still here. You needed a moment," she said softly trying to bolster the woman's courage. "We don't have to do anything you don't want to do."

Colleen looked up surprised. Rarely in her life had anyone not berated her when she did something wrong but not this woman. Even in the office when she had screwed something up Nia had gently corrected her or explained how things should be done. Never had she let her down and Colleen had always been confident in her job. Why not now when she was where she wanted to be, with Nia, in her arms, in her bed? Cletus was far away and hopefully would never bother her again. She leaned up to kiss Nia in gratitude.

Nia let her, she seemed to need it. She didn't return the kiss but she didn't reject it either. She let Colleen set the pace of it and when she deepened it she responded in kind once again letting the passion rise.

Colleen was so grateful and quickly excited by Nia that her earlier enthusiasm returned and she rapidly got brave enough to reach inside Nia's bra and caress her breast and nipple. Nia's sigh of delight pleased her to hear it and she kissed her way down her chest to gently take the left nipple in her mouth, caressing and tweaking the right one with her hand. Nia arched into her mouth and hand showing her pleasure at the gestures. This emboldened Colleen and delighted her, she reached around with her free hand to hold Nia closer her to her and to reach down and caress her long back and tease at the edge of her panties.

Nia wasn't going to allow Colleen to keep the upper hand this time, she didn't want to stop, she didn't want to be left hanging. Her disappointment had been well hidden but she didn't want to scare Colleen with the passion she wanted to unleash, not this soon, not this time and she gently but firmly rolled Colleen to her back and began to kiss her passionately and firmly as she made love to her with her hands, her body slightly grinding against her naked form. Colleen reached around and unhooked the expensive lingerie and those breasts fell willingly into Colleen's face as she whisked the bra from her body. Slowly she felt emboldened enough to hook her fingers in Nia's panties and peel them down off of her buttocks. Nia wriggled against her to shimmy out of them and flick them to the floor with her foot.

Colleen couldn't imagine how wonderful Nia's body would feel against her own naked one. She hadn't realized how two women would make love and how good it would feel. She held Nia close to her as she nuzzled at her breasts, first taking one and then the other into her mouth to lick at

them and pleasure Nia. She was certain she was doing it right too as Nia gasped in pleasure.

Colleen's head though had to fall back as Nia caressed and nibbled and licked her way to Colleen's own breasts. Never would she have thought that the tiny scrap of a bra Colleen had used to enclose these would hold them. They seemed overly large as Nia fondled and caressed them. Colleen couldn't believe how the gentleness aroused her and the breasts hardened under Nia administrations. Slowly, so as not to alarm her Nia began to caress lower. She avoided the V between Colleen's legs and caressed her hips, her thighs, and as far down as she could reach on her lover's legs, getting her used to the feel of her, touching her everywhere. Colleen jumped a little when Nia touched her buttocks and squeezed gently, pulling her against Nia's form.

Colleen was anxious, she couldn't wait to have Nia touch between her legs and yet she couldn't seem to make her needs known. She arched into Nia's hands, against her body, unconsciously writhing and squirming against Nia's already aroused body, further enticing her with her responses.

Nia appreciated it and finally she began to caress her way inward. The curls under her fingers made her smile at their silky softness but it was the wetness she was looking for and she was pleased to find Colleen wet, very wet. In fact the gushing she felt beneath her fingers was more than she could remember ever feeling with Justine and then feeling bad to be comparing the two she suppressed those thoughts and concentrated on Colleen. She could sense how tense and nervous Colleen was and she kissed her deeply as her fingers played with the wetness, feeling the folds, her hands slick from the moisture. She ran her fingers up one side of her clit and down the other teasing her as she touched her intimately.

"Gawdddd," Colleen moaned into her mouth at the touch. Never had it been so gentle, never had she felt this wet before. She unconsciously raised her hips towards Nia's touch, inviting her in as she spread her legs for Nia to settle between them.

Nia wanted to fling Colleen's legs over her hips and thrust her fingers inside deeply but she didn't want to frighten her, she wanted this time, this first time to be special for her lover. She leaned up on her one hand and gently inserted one finger to test her and see how tight she really was. She wasn't surprised when she found she could thrust in a second one. She reached up and in and bent her fingers slightly to caress along the tissue inside. Colleen went perfectly still beneath her. At first Nia thought she had hurt her and then she realized Colleen's eyes were rolling in her head at the incredible pleasure she had just given her. She grinned slightly as she kissed her way down her neck and towards her ample chest, thrusting,

caressing and then for an added bonus, she rubbed Colleen's clit with her thumb.

Colleen was so horny, she just wanted the thrusting, the time this was taking was driving her to distraction. She had never felt inside of herself and didn't know about her own G spot so when Nia caressed it softly her body went still in surprise and the most delicious feeling went through her body. As Nia continued Colleen tried not to think, getting lost in the feelings of what was being done to her body. The thrusting, the caressing inside, and the rub though were driving her out of her mind. Her breath was coming in pants as her hands fell to either side along her head in supplication.

Nia grinned into her skin realizing how she was letting go and getting excited at what she was doing to the woman. She licked and sucked at the engorged and erect nipple, hardened even more by the excitement surrounding Colleen's body.

Colleen felt an odd little tingling beginning in her nether regions and heading down her legs. Her mind followed it and she couldn't believe as it grew and exploded. Her body felt outside of her head. She didn't understand it as continued and her body began to jerk and her breath came hard and fast. "Ohhhhh," she moaned and she ground and writhed beneath Nia.

Nia smiled as she made Colleen cum. She had felt it begin inside her as she tightened around her fingers. Seeing and hearing her though only added to her own excitement. She was hard between her own legs and needed release. She wanted to pull out and put herself over Colleen's mouth but instead she ground against the back of her hand in time with Colleen's thrusts against her and satisfied herself with a micro-orgasm. Slowly she slowed her fingers inside of Colleen and let her come down. Her own orgasm, while satisfying wasn't quite what she had wanted but really it hadn't been about her, it had been about her lover and she could see by the stunned look on Colleen's face that she had enjoyed it. "Are you okay?" she asked.

"Oh God, yes," Colleen breathed not willing to open her eyes from the incredible pulses that were thumping through her body right now.

Nia smiled, she could hear the passion filled voice of her lover and removed her hand to bring it up and taste her.

Colleen squinted open her eyes to see Nia licking carefully at her fingers and wasn't sure if she was grossed out or aroused by the sight. She decided it was sensuous and Nia seemed to enjoy the taste. She wondered what she tasted like and found out after Nia was done as she leaned down to kiss her gently. The taste on her tongue and lips was like nothing she had ever tasted before and she began to wonder what Nia tasted like.

Nia kept her body from lying full on Colleen and gently began to scoot over to lie beside her. She was sweaty from her efforts and snuggled close for the warmth her lover's body gave her.

"That was something," Colleen finally sighed.

Nia propped her head up on her arm to look down into Colleen's wondering face. Her leg began to unconsciously rub against Colleens in a sensuous way. "Haven't you ever cum that way before?" she asked curious.

"I've never cum," Colleen admitted.

Nia looked at her surprised. She realized in that moment they had a lot in common, she too had never had an orgasm from a guy. For a second she resented that hers with Justine had taken so much longer to achieve and Colleen's seemed so easy. She squashed that resentment immediately as she took in how vulnerable Colleen seemed at that moment. "Well, here's to the first of many," she tried to joke.

Colleen smiled up at Nia, grateful to her in so many ways, not the least of which was making love to her and making her cum. She also felt exposed and buried her head in Nia's long hair, breathing in the scent of it. She felt incredibly relaxed and tired suddenly and was soon falling asleep in Nia's arms.

At some point Nia had to move and she gently eased Colleen off of her. She pulled the top sheet and blanket from under her and tucked her in, getting in beside her and lying close. She wasn't surprised to find her wrapped around her in the morning, Colleen was a cuddle buddy.

Slowly Colleen woke up. She realized immediately she was in a strange bed in a strange hotel room and it took her a moment to realize she wasn't alone. Slowly she turned her head as the sound of someone else's breathing became obvious to her. She looked in surprise to see Nia Toyomoto lying next to her, quite naked. In a flash the previous night came back to her and she was shocked to realize it wasn't a dream; she hadn't let her over active imagination get away from her. She looked at the Eurasian beauty and couldn't believe what had happened to her. She was naked, in bed, with Nia Toyomoto! It wasn't so long ago that she would have argued to anyone that Nia was straight and here she was in bed with her. Remembering the previous night she obviously knew what she was doing in making love to a woman. Now she wondered if Eleanor James had ever been her lover and she felt a twinge of jealousy. She also wondered who else in Nia's life had been her lover and as she knew the friends from Thursday nights she couldn't help but begin to assess all of them including Annie whom she had met a time or two.

"Why are you frowning?" Nia's sleep filled and eminently sexy voice came through the silence.

Colleen started in surprise as she glanced down at the amazing brown eyes that she had fancied were black the previous night. "Just lost in thought," she hedged.

"Must not be good thoughts then," Nia said as she snaked her hands around Colleen's naked body and gave her a good morning hug. Naked against each other it wasn't surprising that both of them felt an immediate arousal. Glancing at the clock and realizing they both needed showers and to get ready though Nia reluctantly halted her lovemaking. "Not that I don't want this to continue but we have to get up," she said sadly.

"Oh," Colleen said clearly disappointed. She had thought for a moment she had done something wrong.

Nia's eyes sparkled as she looked down at her lover. "You don't regret last night do you?" she asked to be sure.

Colleen then thought about the implications of their relationship and the worry danced across her eyes. "No, I don't regret it..." she began. Remember how wonderful it had felt she couldn't regret it. "I enjoyed it, really I did," she tried to reassure her lover...and boss.

"I just don't want you to change your mind later," Nia said with a hint of humor in eyes. They were laying there naked and she could tell if she had continued that Colleen would not have objected.

Colleen saw the humor and smiled, she relaxed a little. Nia wasn't worried so why should she? "I enjoyed it," she repeated in a slightly different tone.

"You cannot corrupt the willing," Nia said succinctly with an eyebrow raised.

"Is that what it was, you corrupted me?" Colleen asked feeling the desire for this woman begin again inside her. She felt horny again and wondered if perhaps lesbian women felt like this more often than heterosexual women.

"Well only if you want to be corrupted," Nia said with a grin and kissing her lover with a peck on the lips, she made to get up. When Colleen would have held her there she grinned down and said, "If we don't shower we won't get a decent breakfast before this meeting...I thought we'd shower together, you know...to save time?"

Colleen's eyes widened as she realized what Nia was implying. Showering with her sounded so decadent and yet...she released Nia to follow her into the unbelievable bathroom the hotel had supplied them with. As the suite had two bedrooms they had two equally beautiful bathrooms. They both had tubs and showers and Nia led her to the shower and turned on the hot water.

"C'mon," she encouraged her as she led her into the glass enclosed shower that quickly steamed up around them.

The hot water felt good on her skin and the added bonus of the massaging pellets against muscles that had unfamiliar twinges in them from her activities the previous night. Plus Nia began to caress the luffa sponge against her after squirting some liquid soap into it. The hotel soap smelled delicious and the feel of having Nia's soft hands against her was heavenly. "Wow, that's incredible," she murmured as she felt the caresses of both the sponge and Nia against her.

Nia smiled as she watched Colleen enjoy being pampered. She had to admit it was pretty sensual to bathe the other woman and she was enjoying herself. Ever mindful of the time she also washed Colleen's hair using the little soaps that the hotel supplied and because it was a classier hotel they were a little more on the chicer side of products. They smelled wonderful and Colleen's hair looked silky soft as Nia used it on her own tresses.

Colleen wasn't confident enough to return the favor but she enjoyed the view immensely. Seeing Nia wash herself, her hands that had given Colleen so much pleasure wiping the soap all over her body was positively sensual, Colleen wanted her so bad right now but knew they were on a limited time table as she stood in the downpour of the large showerhead. She couldn't help admiring the long body, the firmness of it, the high uptilted breasts, and she was amazed at how different it looked from the business suits she was used to Nia wearing. She looked up to avoid letting Nia see her staring at her beautiful body.

Nia was well aware of her scrutiny, her peripheral vision was excellent and she had taken full advantage of washing Colleen's body to rub her own against her under the guise of washing her. If they only had more time she would enjoy going down on her in this steamy shower stall but again she wasn't sure how much Colleen was prepared to do or take and they simply didn't have enough time. She had to get her head in place for the work they had to do.

Stepping out of the shower Nia handed her a bath sheet which she wrapped around her completely and Colleen felt it's luxurious feel against her naked skin. Nia would have rubbed her down but trying to keep her mind on work she took her own bath sheet and wrapped herself grabbing another towel to rub her long hair.

"My stuff is in the other room," Colleen began awkwardly.

Nia smiled and leaned down to kiss her gently. "Okay, go get dressed; I'll meet you shortly in the living room so we can go to breakfast." She patted her on the rear encouraging her to leave.

Colleen was relieved, she wasn't sure how to take her leave and she really wished she could have learned more about Nia's body. She realized now that Nia had done everything and while she had enjoyed that she

wondered if Nia had cum when she had. She felt a tad bid selfish as she thought it over and hoped that Nia wasn't angry with her over it but she realized she was just being silly as Nia didn't seem angry at all.

Nia got ready in record time using the hotel hair dryer to dry her underarms so she could roll on antiperspirant and then dry it with the same dryer as she brushed out her hair and dried that as well. She put on her underwear while the bathroom aired out and the steam dissipated. She laid out her suit for the day and went to put on her makeup and jewelry. By the time she was dressed fully at least a half hour had gone by and she was in the living room making sure her notes and briefcase were in order. Colleen showed up a few minutes later.

"Is there anything I can get you for the meeting?" she indicated the suitcase they had brought along with all the copies.

"Not right now, let's get some breakfast and then we will see how long it takes us to get to the meeting," Nia said sounding distracted.

Colleen wasn't sure how to act around Nia right now but as she was behaving like she always did she took her cue from her boss and tried to ignore the fact that she had seen her naked, been made love to by this admirable woman, and that she felt herself falling in love with her.

The meetings were long and boring and Nia argued her points with finesse. She wouldn't allow her client to panic any more than she had on the phone the other day. She assured her by producing paperwork that she was on top of the various lawsuits and other work that she had been given and in a matter of one day instead of the week she had anticipated she calmed the client enough that they soon wrapped up their business.

"God Nia, why can't you live here in Miami so you could come by more often," Allison Gottfried complained good naturedly. "None of these idiots get it," her arm took in the hastily leaving team that Nia had for her client and who answered to her.

"For one, it's too damned hot down here," Nia said in joking manner and Allison grinned. "For another, I live in Manhattan and I love it. I just decorated my apartment and I'm not moving. For you or any other client."

"I could make it worth your while you know," Allison mock threatened as she got to her feet with Nia who was closing up her briefcase.

"I know, but don't. I like the variety of what I do in Manhattan and I like my freedom," Nia told her honestly.

Allison nodded and eyed Nia speculatively for a moment. She glanced at the little mouse that was her secretary and saw her efficiently closing up the notes she had taken in her notebook. She must be a good secretary to work with someone like Nia. She glanced again at Nia. "We should go out and celebrate while you are down here," she offered.

"I'd like that but we will have to do it another time, I do have work to do," Nia told her with genuine regret. "I have a few more meetings with

the gang," she indicated the retreating lawyers that were on staff for Allison. "And then I must get back to my other work."

"All work and no play makes Nia a dull girl," Allison said playfully echoing something Stewart had said to Nia once.

"Ah but the early bird gets the worm," Nia countered and smiled.

Allison held out her hand and shook Nia's and smiled. "Thank you for straightening out that little crisis for me; I wasn't sure where these idiots were going with it all."

"No problem, that's what I'm here for Allison, you know you can count on me and my staff," Nia assured her as she gathered her case and Allison began to walk with her to the door, Colleen followed behind her respectfully.

The meetings with the other lawyers were fruitful and Colleen filled a second notebook with notes and transcripts of the meetings. While they were recorded and would be transcribed that way the combination assured the accuracy of what was said and what Nia dictated to the staff for Gottfried Pharmaceuticals. While they worked on site, Nia still held the reigns of the legal coordination and flew all over the country for the client to be sure that the pharmaceutical company which was sued on a regular basis received the best representation from her firm and the people they worked with all over. Nia earned her paycheck.

"Gawd, I thought they would never shut up," Nia complained as she sprawled on the couch in the living room after the second day of meetings. She had been too tired the previous night to make love to Colleen and had apologized for the lapse but held Colleen close all night.

Colleen had been disappointed that they hadn't made love the previous night too but she understood, Nia had been incredible to watch as she exerted her authority over the men who felt since they were on the site that they knew more than she did. She was amazingly well informed, knowledgeable, and quickly put them in their place. One of the lawyers had received his walking papers when he could not or would not see that she was the ultimate authority where the legal matters pertained and she had fired him. Nia knew her job, very well, but it had been exhausting to play the mind games and she had needed her sleep.

Tonight though she looked at Colleen thoughtfully and gestured to her to come closer and sit on the couch. "I'm sorry, I feel like I neglected you the past two days," she said as Colleen sat down next to her. She sat up to give Colleen a kiss now that they were alone together.

"No, it was awesome to see you in action," Colleen excused her. She knew that Nia's work was important; she of all people understood that. She was articulate, firm, and kicked ass when necessary.

"Well you know that work will always have to come first but I didn't want you think that it was a one night stand kind of thing," Nia answered as she leaned in for another kiss.

Colleen hadn't thought that and until Nia mentioned she hadn't felt insecure. She knew the work was important, that millions of dollars were at stake, that Nia and the firm received a percentage of the litigation, but suddenly she felt a little used…that was until Nia kissed her. Suddenly the world felt right and Colleen felt special, as though the sun rose and set and all because Nia Toyomoto wanted her.

Nia was able to multi-task in that amazing brain of hers. While she had been working with the other attorneys and the client she had thought about her relationship with Colleen. She knew that eventually Colleen couldn't work for her if this relationship continued and for that she was sad but she wasn't ready to end it or to talk to Colleen about it. Right now she wanted to explore this relationship more with her. Kissing her was only the first part and she eagerly pulled her closer as she started to recline on the couch and pull Colleen with her to the cushion. Feeling Colleen's body on top of her own felt oh so right….

Colleen, heavier and rounder than Nia worried that she was crushing the much thinner woman but feeling her under her, full length she couldn't help the arousal that immediately started within her. She loved the feel of the body pressed up under her. Nia arched into her and lifting her tight skirt to free her thigh she wrapped a leg around her. Colleen felt bold enough to caress up her leg feeling the nylons against her leg that looked so sexy when she crossed them in the board room.

"Gawd, what is this power you have over me?" Nia murmured as she kissed along Colleen's jawline. Her mousy hair had lightened in just the past couple of days and already Nia could see some blonde streaks. She nuzzled into her ear and gently mouthed along her ear. Hearing the intake of breath from the caress of her lips pleased her enormously. Her hands began to play with Colleen's hair messing it up.

Colleen desperately wanted to see Nia naked again, it surprised her as she had never wanted to see another woman naked before but kissing her, having made love with her, she wanted more of what she had gotten. She leaned down to kiss her again but before she could Nia nuzzled into her ear. The wonderful feelings assailed her senses as the tickling erotic sensation of Nia's lips on her ear began to penetrate her psyche. She could feel the goose bumps that formed on her arms. She squeezed her legs together and bore down on her kegel muscle to clench them together, a shudder ripped through her body as the kegel muscles caused a corresponding sensation throughout.

"Are you cold?" Nia asked as she felt the shudder.

"No, just horny," Colleen whispered as she wondered how to hurry this along.

Nia pulled back wondering what that shudder and her being horny had to do with each other but seeing the desire in Colleen's eyes she shrugged it off as she swooped in to kiss her deeply and was pleased to find Colleen's tongue ready to tango with hers.

Just then a knock sounded at the door. Colleen shot up as though they had been caught. Nia looked up dazed for a moment before sitting up and looking at Colleen amused. She nearly ran across the room to get away from the couch and what they had been doing. Nia got up slowly and checked herself in the mirror before answering the door.

"Allison?!?" she said surprised at seeing the head of Gottfried Pharmaceuticals standing at her door.

"Hello, I was hoping to catch you before you went for dinner and perhaps we could eat together?" she asked quickly as she stood there at the door.

"Um," Nia glanced back at Colleen for a moment and said, "No, we haven't eaten yet."

"We?" Allison asked confused. She glanced beyond Nia to see the secretary standing across the living room looking decidedly uncomfortable.

"Yes, we just got back from your offices," Nia explained. "Would you like to come in?" she offered politely.

Allison walked in and took in the hotel room. It was nice, not penthouse nice, but nice all the same and she wondered at the relationship between her attorney and her secretary. It looked innocent but as she was here to ask Nia out she had to wonder. "Would you like to go out to dinner?" she asked and glanced at the secretary to include her in the offer and sincerely hoped she would decline.

Colleen took in the look and understood it immediately. Swallowing nervously she said, "You should go Nia, I'm so tired from today and yesterday I'm going to order room service."

Nia knew Colleen wasn't that tired and she understood the by-play very well. She was too astute to not see what had transpired here but at the same time Allison Gottfried was too important a client to turn down if she was asking her out to dinner. Still, for forms sake she asked Colleen, "Are you sure?"

Colleen waved her hand dismissively. "Yeah, go ahead. I'm looking forward to pajamas and room service, maybe some bad cable TV."

Actually, that sounded good to Nia too but with Allison looking on expectantly that wasn't going to happen. She smiled though and nodded as she picked up her purse by the door. "Shall we go?" she said to Allison and shot Colleen a look that promised conversation later.

Allison had dismissed Colleen much sooner and gladly took the lead out the door with Nia following. One last glance at Colleen with an apologetic look that Allison could not see and Nia closed the door.

Colleen hunched her shoulders at the situation. She knew she wasn't in Allison Gottfried's class and even in Nia Toyomoto's class. Hell, what was she thinking? She couldn't compete with these women. They were mover's and shaker's and she was just simply a personal assistant. What was she thinking getting involved with her boss?

Nia had a nice time with Allison. She was smart, she was witty, she was everything Nia might have looked for in a dinner companion but something was missing and she realized it early on. She wasn't Colleen and while she enjoyed the meal and the conversation, she turned down the obvious ploy to get her into bed. While Allison was disappointed she valued her attorney too much to make a big deal of it. She graciously accepted Nia's rejection and let it go.

Nia got back to the room late and went to her room to change out of the suit she had worn all day. She was disappointed not to find Colleen there but she understood. Changing into a nice sexy nightgown she went to seek out Colleen finding her in her own room asleep with her hand tucked under her chin. She looked like she had been crying and Nia wondered at that as she watched her sleep. She was restless and obviously not sleeping deeply. Nia wondered if she should wake her or leave her alone. It wasn't as though she had wanted to go to dinner with Allison Gottfried, it was business, nothing more and she hoped Colleen would understand. The tears though, they bothered her more than she would admit. She quietly turned out the lights that had been left on and slipped into Colleen's bed. She lay there a while wondering if she should take her in her arms or curl around her. She wanted to make love to her but only if Colleen wanted it. Everything about this had to be Colleen's decision. She debated over it but when the restless woman turned over and feeling or sensing Nia there in her bed, she wrapped herself around her that decided it for both of them. Nia sighed happily and holding Colleen she soon drifted off. Colleen slept soundly after that.

Slowly Colleen woke up the next morning. At some point in the night she had woken up and realized Nia was there with her. At first she was resentful but then so grateful to find her there that she snuggled back in and went back to sleep. She had wondered briefly if Nia were using her when she could have someone like Allison Gottfried instead of just a nobody like Colleen. She didn't care at the moment though as she woke

and found Nia had managed to get her pajama bottoms and panties off and was at the moment going down on her. The feeling of that warm tongue on her clit had Colleen arching into the mouth that so lovingly was creating pleasure for her. She gasped in delight as two fingers entered her and pushing up and in at the same time caressed the one spot that had her going instantly still with the pleasure it engendered. Looking down at Nia's dark head between her legs she couldn't coherently think, she couldn't resent it, and she loved the feeling that she was causing inside of her.

Nia had been pleased that despite the late night that she woke up before Colleen. She was further pleased when she managed to remove her pajama bottoms along with the panties that seriously needed an update in the wardrobe department. She had wanted to go down on Colleen from the first time they made love and not had the opportunity. She wasn't going to ask this time, she was going to take and from the first swipe of her tongue she knew Colleen's body was not in synch with her mind as it began to respond to her ministrations. It wasn't long before she could sense Colleen waking up, slowly and surely and then with a gasp and an arch into her mouth she was smiling into her clit as she brought her fingers into play. The answering wetness told its own tale. It didn't take long to bring Colleen's mind up to speed that her body was already there. In no time at all she was gasping and grinding against Nia's agile mouth and was soon crying out in ecstasy.

Colleen had thought of this position since they first made love but didn't know how to initiate it herself and certainly felt inadequate to ask Nia to do this. It was what lesbians did wasn't it? She had fantasized about it that first day after...and then Nia had been too tired to make love to her. This though, *this* was more than she had fantasized. She couldn't have imagined the feelings and sensations that would be coursing through her body. She briefly thought it was taking unfair advantage of her unconscious state but really, the reality of it had her gasping for more and grinding into Nia's face. The added feel of her fingers inside her and the petting of her G spot had her squirming, she couldn't wait for more and her body was way ahead of her on that score as she began to buck and writhe in ecstasy. She cried out Nia's name in her passion and delight.

Slowly Nia brought her down and then began to kiss her way up Colleen's body, wiping the passion from her face on the pajamas. She lifted Colleen's shirt so she could get at her breasts and kiss them both good morning. Each erect nipple got some attention as Colleen nearly came off the bed at the sensations as she grasped Nia's head to her chest. She came out from under the shirt to grin delightedly at Colleen who kissed her passionately in reverent gratitude for her wakeup call. Rolling

slightly she was on top of Nia in a flash grinding down, kissing her passionately, loving her back.

"Good Morning," Nia said around the kisses as she enjoyed the rolling around on the bed.

"Good Morning," Colleen responded as she sighed into the delightful kisses.

It became a wrestling match of sorts, Colleen on top as she began to remove the beautiful nightgown Nia had worn to bed, the satin feeling soft and expensive beneath her fingers. Nia finally managed to remove the pajama top that Colleen was wearing to expose the skin to her touch.

Colleen wasn't sure of the protocol, if she should ask but after what Nia had just done to her she wanted to try it, she had tasted herself again on Nia's lips and she wanted to taste Nia the same way. Asking though sounded stupid in her mind so she made an effort to kiss her way south across Nia's long body. Her legs came up and wrapped around Colleen effectively trapping her as she kissed and played and fondled Nia's breasts. Nia smiled as she played with Colleen's lightening hair and then released her as she indicated she wanted to move. She was thrilled as Colleen began kissing her way across her stomach and towards the V between her legs.

The first taste on Nia's clit with her agile little tongue was a surprise to Colleen. She wasn't sure what it would taste like. She had thought musky like her own taste from Nia's tongue. But instead it tasted...almost...sweet. This surprised her but also made her want to taste more. She indulged. She was soon positioning herself, settling comfortably with Nia's legs on either side of her shoulders, in fact she gently nudged them onto her shoulders as her face plunged between them and she licked to her heart's content.

The visual much less the visceral feeling of what she was doing excited Nia beyond measure. She didn't want to let go of her passions but it was a near thing. Colleen's nails needed trimming but that was a minor inconvenience as she began to feel Nia up. The response of her body though told her that she was doing well if the gasps, whimpers, and slight moans couldn't tell her.

Colleen was proud of herself, she could tell she was doing well and although she had never done this before she was thrilled to be giving Nia the same pleasures she herself had experienced. As Nia came in her mouth she was surprised at the additional liquid, it was different from the thicker fluids she had been licking and almost the consistency of water. Surely Nia hadn't peed on her? Seeing the taller woman arched back in surrender to her orgasm she couldn't ask her and merely kept on with what had caused this reaction.

"Fuck me," Nia said bluntly as she came down from her clitoral orgasm.

Colleen was at first shocked at the blunt words but realizing what Nia needed she gladly began to plunge her fingers in and out. She began to kiss her way up Nia's body as her hand and arm pistioned back and forth.

Nia arched into Colleen's hand providing her access by spreading her legs wide and as Colleen began kissing up her body she thrust her nipple into her mouth grabbing her head to hold her there.

Colleen smiled realizing the immaculate and always controlled Nia was losing her vaunted control in the moment of her passion. She loved it and while she had been surprised as Nia grabbed her hair she enjoyed causing the woman to lose control from what she was causing in her. She thrust harder and faster, her arm becoming tired but she kept going until Nia exploded underneath her.

Nia turned Colleens head at the last minute so her lips were available to her as she kissed her deeply and hard. She cried out into her open mouth as her body burst in orgasmic bliss.

Startled, having never seen another human being so vulnerable before, Colleen wasn't sure how to act but her arm was tired and she began to slow as Nia wrapped her legs around her body to hold her there. It was exciting to know she had caused this in Nia and as she calmed she was pleased with herself. Slowly Nia's legs fell away to the bed as her body went limp. Her head fell back among the mussed sheets. Her fingers released Colleen's hair and she caressed the back of her head from where she had held her in place.

Colleen just lay panting on top of Nia having witnessed something she felt honored to have shared with the woman. She wondered if she would ever be that passionate and then wondered what she looked like when Nia made her cum.

Nia lay there in a haze enjoying the pulses throughout her heated body. She had let go and enjoyed every moment of it. As she became aware of her surroundings again she focused in on Colleen and wondered if she had hurt her. She pulled her head up from where it had been laid back against the bed and looked at Colleen for any tell-tale signs that she had lost control. Other than the dazed but delighted expression on her assistants face she only saw a beauty that was uniquely Colleens. "Are you okay?" she asked, a familiar refrain.

Colleen nodded as she eased her body to the side and smiled up at Nia. "That was incredible," she said understatedly.

Nia smiled. She was glad she hadn't hurt Colleen. Justine had backed off from such passion and while it had bothered Nia at the time she realized not everyone had the same passion levels. She wondered if

Colleen would surprise her that way someday. She eagerly looked forward to finding out.

After a long shower together where Nia once again went down on Colleen, washing her thoroughly…*with her tongue*, they got ready for their day in casual clothes.

"I'm done, and if they need me we will be here through Sunday," Nia explained. She hadn't needed the whole week but since she was here she was taking some personal time on the company's dollar.

"What shall we do?" Colleen asked eagerly. The thought of taking a vacation, even a mini one with Nia was heavenly.

Nia had plans. They rented two motor scooters and cruised up and down the roads that lined the beaches and then along houses for the inter-coastal waterway, the canal that allowed boats up and down in front and in back of houses that were built all along the coast. A kind of water highway. The next day she rented wave runners and they cruised up and down the inter-coastal becoming hopelessly lost but having a wonderful time. They both got sun burnt and enjoyed themselves enormously as they relaxed, got to know each other better, and made love over and over again. By the end of the weekend they both felt in love.

"How could this happen, I've known you for years, I never knew you had feelings for me?" Colleen asked.

"I didn't, not that way. It surprised me too but I just realized one day that you were more than an employee, more than a friend, and I admired so much about you," Nia told her honestly.

"You? You admire *me*?" she asked incredulously.

Nia nodded. "I don't think you realize what an asset you are, what a help. You have so much knowledge about things I never even thought of."

"That's nothing, you're the one with the Harvard education, you're the partner in a Manhattan law firm."

"That's book smarts, you have smarts I can never hope to understand," Nia countered.

"I think we are going to have to agree to disagree on that one," Colleen laughed. Imagine, Nia Toyomoto saying she admired her!

"You underestimate yourself, haven't you ever had dreams?" Nia asked. They were sitting on the beach in the sand, having dug down and reclined against the warm grains. It was a glorious afternoon and their burns were turning to tans. The rain that came almost daily had come and gone and they watched the clouds in case it came through again.

"I had them, once," she confessed. She didn't want to think about her early dreams, her ambitions, or her husband Cletus. She didn't want to confess that he had killed all of them, one by one. She didn't want to think

about him at all and ruin the only good time she could remember having in her entire life.

"You can have them again," Nia said quietly as she sensed Colleen's thoughts. "You're whole life is ahead of you now."

Colleen thought about that. Nia was right. She would be divorced in about two months according to the lawyer Nia had hired for her from the firm. She didn't like him too much, he was too condescending but he was good and Cletus wasn't taking her to the cleaners. She was fortunate that none of his drug convictions affected her in anyway and they could use the arrest against him. "Well for now I'm just happy being your assistant," she asserted stoutly.

"Well that may not be possible after a while," Nia told her gently trying to ease into this uncomfortable conversation.

"Why not?" Colleen asked wondering if she had missed something, was she being fired?

"Easy," Nia said hearing the panic in her voice. "I just meant as this," she gestured at the two of them. "Develops, working with me may not be an option anymore."

"You mean I'd have to transfer to work with someone else?" Colleen asked. Her heart was beating hard. She loved working for Nia, *with* her.

"I was actually thinking you might want to move up," Nia said trying to calm her, she could hear the anxiety in her voice and it was escalating.

"What if I don't want to move up?" she asked feeling trapped. She had made love with this woman, she loved this woman, and now she was being told she couldn't work with her? How fair was that?

"It's nothing to worry about," Nia placated her. "I just thought, eventually, you might want to move up."

"I don't want to work with anyone else," she asserted.

"I didn't say that, I said move up," Nia reminded her gently. Colleen's voice was raising in her anxiety and she wanted to calm her down.

"Move up? To where?" she asked confused. Her emotions were creating havoc with her mind in this conversation.

Nia shrugged and then told her, "I always thought you were as good a researcher as some of the Legal Assistants, you'd make a great Paralegal."

Colleen relaxed a little. She wasn't in danger of losing her job from what she could tell. Nia was just discussing her options. She could at least listen without getting upset.

Nia went on to explain what would be involved in her getting an associate's degree so she could become a Paralegal and then she mentioned the starting wage and Colleen was definitely interested.

"When would I have the time for that?" she mused as she considered what Nia had just told her.

"Well nights but really if you could afford to go back to school full time you could have it in no time, I'm sure you would qualify for student aid."

"But then I'd lose my job as your assistant. Are you trying to get rid of me?"

Nia looked out at the ocean where it met the sands they were sitting in. "Someday you may want to leave me," she said quietly. "I just thought I'd help you."

"Nia," she said just as quietly and waited for the dark haired beauty to look at her. "I don't think I ever want to leave you."

Nia smiled and teared up a little. She wanted Colleen to stick around too but someday it might become an issue since she worked for Nia. As a partner in the firm, she had to look out for things like this and having an affair with her secretary, much less her female secretary, would be strictly a no-no and frowned upon. By having Colleen moving over to the Legal Assistants pool she would not only work for others but still be in the firm or better yet, moving up to becoming a paralegal, she would be invaluable for many of the partners and associates. "I hope you always feel that way," she said a little choked up. She wanted to reach out and touch her but not knowing who may be watching she stopped herself. Her look though said volumes. "Why don't we continue this conversation upstairs in the suite?" she asked her with a grin.

Colleen grinned in return. Knowing that Nia wanted her was the best feeling. Loving her in return she couldn't wait to show her. She got up and headed inside with Nia close behind her, brushing against her 'accidentally' as they headed upstairs in the elevator to their suite.

The passion they shared between them surprised and pleased them both. Colleen learned so much and Nia was pleased that there were no restrictions. There were no pre-determined things that they would or would not do together as there had been with Justine. Although Colleen was technically still married, Justine had been married and it wasn't until the end of their relationship that she even started her divorce. Nia had worried that somehow she would be dragged into that mess. With Cletus nearly out the door and Colleen already living with her she hoped this time her relationship would go smoothly.

It was with a sad heart that they got on the plane back to New York on Sunday. Both were relaxed and tanned from the extra days in Miami. Their client was pleased with the work Nia had done with and for her and the team in place could handle things as Nia supervised from afar. Although Nia hadn't slept with Allison they were still on good terms and looked forward to working together in the future. The two lovebirds though were sad that their idyll had come to an end.

"I love you Nia," Colleen was the first to say it. She didn't regret being the first but the look on Nia's face made it all worth it as it lit up with joy.

"I've loved you for a while Colleen, I was afraid to say it though," Nia confessed as she held her. They had just gotten home and Colleen was standing on a step leading up to the loft so she was even with the much taller Nia.

"I can't imagine you afraid of anything," Colleen said as her hands pulled Nia closer, since she could.

"Oh, I've been afraid, many times," she admitted. "Making the first move on you, what if you had rejected me. Where would our friendship have gone from that mess   ?"

"Were you really in doubt that I'd reject you?"

"Colleen, you aren't a lesbian or rather you weren't," she pointed out reasonably.

"Well, I don't know that I am one now but for you I will be," she declared as she grinned.

"I don't care if you are or aren't as long as you are mine," Nia said with a lowering of her voice.

"Yours, that sounds heavenly," Colleen declared as she leaned in to kiss Nia, because she could.

The two of them went back to work the next day and worked hard to make sure no one would suspect their relationship. People stared enviously at their tans that they had acquired while 'hard at work' in Miami. Stewart was pleased with the work Nia had done for Gottfried Pharmaceutical and keeping such clients happy was one of her many talents. If she got the work done early and enjoyed the beach, he was happy for her. He was surprised to see the blond streaks in Colleen's hair that she had acquired by being out in the sun so much and the tan she too had developed, he guessed he hadn't thought of an assistant as having time for the beach when they worked for the partners as they did.

"I think I'm going to have my hair professionally streaked in the future. I've gotten more compliments on it since we've been back," Colleen told Nia a few days later when they were immersed in work again.

Nia, looking up from the stack of work waiting for her and the things she had to delay because of the trip smiled at her absentmindedly. Getting up from her couch she went over to the door and locked it behind her before heading for her assistant.

Nia came up behind Colleen and wrapped her arms around her nuzzling into her neck she whisperedly commanded, "Don't move," as her hands began to feel her up. Colleen couldn't help the little shudder of anticipation as Nia's left hand began to raise her blouse and her right slipped into the band of her slacks quickly going past the scrap of lingerie and finding her already moist clit. Rapidly and with expertise Nia rubbed

the little nubbin of flesh and Colleen felt herself melting in Nia's arms which held her firmly and tightly as she kissed along her neck biting a little for variety. Nia's left hand fondled her breasts as her arms held her up.

Suddenly and without warning Colleen felt the orgasm wash over her, it felt violent and she bucked and cried out as her body convulsed. She tried to keep it quiet but the feelings were so overwhelming and Nia so good at making her feel good that she couldn't. Nia did not let up though as her fingers went further south and entered the wet channel that further drove Colleen wild, she bit her lips to keep from making any noise but the whimpers and groans in her throat told the taller woman what she was doing to her over-heated body as if the convulsing did not. The sounds of the fingers plunging in and out made a squishy sound as the wetness tried to cling to Nia's fingers and she plunged harder and harder causing the orgasm to become not only clitoral but vaginal and making Colleen's body sag as it overwhelmed her and she gave up to the sensations.

Gently Nia held her as the orgasms waned from her body and she kissed along her neck and shoulder murmuring in her ear, nonsense that no one would believe that the impeccable Nia Toyomoto would utter but making the experience that Colleen had just felt all the better. Slowly Colleen's senses returned to some semblance of normalcy. She knew she would have to use the private bathroom to clean herself up but as she stood back on her own two feet and turned she nearly lost her balance as she saw Nia lick her own fingers clean from what she had done to Colleen. The twinkle in the Eurasian woman's eyes made Colleen feel incredibly special as she smiled up at the woman.

"We can't do that here," she gasped in surprise as Nia finally let her go.

"We just did," Nia said feeling proud of herself and her audacity. She had never felt so playful, so alive.

"You will get us caught," Colleen told her as she headed into the bathroom to clean herself up.

Nia had to concede it hadn't been wise but she was proud of herself and the spontaneity of her actions. She grinned as she walked in to wash her hands too and leaned down to place a firm kiss on her assistant's lips. "It was worth it," she whispered with a smile.

Colleen shook her head and realized that while she loved Nia she could see how secretaries got caught in these things with their bosses. She also realized the sense of Nia's conversation on the beach about becoming a Paralegal now. They might not always be able to work together.

❖ CHAPTER EIGHTEEN ❖

Colleen didn't know what had come over her but she couldn't wait to get home with Nia every day. Most days they drove in together and no one had really noticed as Nia's windows on the Lexus were tinted and they went into the covered parking garage together. Originally it had been to hide from Cletus but Colleen no longer felt he was a threat as she regained her confidence under the glow of her love for Nia. She caught herself daydreaming about her constantly and stopped herself from gazing at her with her love. She couldn't wait to make love to her daily, sometimes twice daily and working with her was becoming difficult.

Colleen went to see Priscilla in human resources to inquire if the firm had some sort of program in place for her to go back to school and become a paralegal.

"I thought you loved working for Nia Toyomoto?" Priscilla asked as she got the forms for financial aid.

"I do, I do, but someday I should advance. I mean, I can't be an assistant the rest of my life you know," she answered honestly. It even sounded reasonable and Priscilla bought it.

"Do you want to start right away?" she asked as she helped her fill in the forms.

"Well I was thinking the sooner the better. My divorce is almost final and I'd like to help train my replacement. I wouldn't want to leave Nia in the lurch."

That sounded plausible and believable and Priscilla thought about who from the secretarial pool was deserving of such a promotion. Working for a partner was rather prestigious. But who would be able to work with Nia Toyomoto, she was an exacting boss and Colleen had put up with her for years and managed to survive. "What about Suzette?" she asked about the second assistant that was already in place. It would be natural that she would move up.

"She already said she couldn't handle it but would be happy to assist whomever Nia approved," Colleen told her.

Priscilla had forgotten that Nia would have to approve whoever was put in place. So much for giving perks to any friends, especially any who couldn't work with such a boss. She vaguely remembered that they had burned through several secretaries before Colleen managed to last; no one had expected this mousy woman to be able to stand up to the pressure. It had almost been a joke to send her to interview with Nia. Not only had she gotten the job and survived but for many years.

Colleen filled out the paperwork and sent it in and waited. She still got her mail at the house she had shared with Cletus but it had been forwarded to Nia's apartment. She had told no one that she lived there and she hoped no one would find out. She was happy for the first time in her life and didn't want to ruin it. As far as anyone knew, they were just roommates. But since their return from Miami she shared Nia's bed every night.

"What's this?" she asked Nia as they got ready for bed. She had opened the side table and inside were a couple of sexual toys.

Nia glanced over where she was neatly laying out her clothes for the morning. She felt laughter bubbling up but refrained when she saw Colleen's shocked expression. "Well, those are toys," she stated the obvious.

"Yes but why?" Colleen asked confused. In the weeks since they had begun their love affair Nia had never mentioned anything like this and it puzzled her now. These were things that people bought off of those awful websites that popped up occasionally when you went on the internet.

Nia shrugged unapologetically at them as she finished. She turned to get into bed with Colleen who was already dressed in a nightgown that Nia liked on her, not those awful pajamas or the housecoats that Cletus had approved of. "I used to need those to have an orgasm, it was the only way when I was alone," she explained.

Colleen felt uncomfortable by the toys in the drawer. She hadn't meant to snoop but had been looking for a tissue and opened the drawer. She glanced back at the variety of toys in the drawer and her eyes were drawn to the dildo like apparatus inside. One of them looked like a gummy worm, only larger, had a penis-like head at each end. Her eyes nearly bugged out at the site of them. She gulped feeling strange about finding these.

"I don't need those now although we might someday like to introduce them to our love play," Nia said looking over her shoulder.

Colleen looked at her disbelievingly and appalled at the idea.

"That one, I've never used but I'd like to try it out," she said pointing to the blue double headed dildo that Colleen had thought was like an overly large gummy worm. "See, it's still in the plastic."

Colleen wasn't sure she liked the idea of using things that were so unnatural.

"The others though I'd want to replace if you wanted to use them," Nia continued. "I don't think it's proper to share toys and they should be new if we decide to try them out."

Colleen answered to that statement, "You mean you've used these on other women besides yourself?" She was surprised to finally feel brave enough to ask Nia about her past lovers. She had been very careful not to, feeling it was none of her business and yet she had been curious.

"Yes, a couple of those I shared with my girlfriend but that's a while ago and I wouldn't use them on you." She wrinkled her nose at the thought. She then could see in the reflection of the dresser mirror that Colleen seemed a little upset. "You know I have had someone before you don't you?" she asked. She didn't have to name names and she didn't want her to know how few lovers she really had had for some reason. She wanted Colleen to be comfortable though with her past, she had one if limited.

"I figured," Colleen sounded a little hurt.

"You've had other lovers too," Nia pointed out trying to dismiss the feeling that she was justifying the toys in her drawer.

She had to admit Nia was right. Although Cletus was her only lover she felt a bit proprietary about Nia now and the toys had shocked her. It gave her something to think about and she was surprised that by the next day Nia had disposed of the other toys except for the one still sealed in its wrapper. It began to make her think and as horny as she had been lately she began to think a lot about the double-headed dildo and wonder how they would use it. When she finally got brave enough to ask Nia about it, Nia had her period and wasn't about to show her. Nia did however insist on 'taking care' of Colleen, period or no and didn't want it reciprocated while she bled.

Nia was amused at the questions that Colleen asked her about the toy and how it was used. Admitting she had never used one or tried one made it an adventure between just the two of them and she looked forward to trying it out. She could see the genuine interest on her assistants face when she asked about it. The conversations were necessarily brief as Colleen was embarrassed and Nia didn't know a lot about it but the interest was there and when she felt better they intended to try it out.

Their opportunity came about a week later and after a nice candlelit dinner with steak and potatoes, a Long Island red wine, and great conversation that did not include one bit of work; they spent the night learning to dance together. That led to a kiss or two, caresses, and eventually they ended up in bed together making love.

"I want to try this," Colleen asserted as she pulled the plastic wrapped twelve inch double headed blue dildo from the drawer.

"Oh you do, do you?" Nia asked amused but she was aroused, she was willing and she wanted to please her lover who was fascinated now by a toy she had previously been appalled at.

Unwrapping the obviously new and unused toy Colleen suddenly looked up and asked, "How does it work?"

"Well, I'm not sure but I think we can figure it out," Nia admitted.

Their first attempt was laughable and they ended up in giggles over the attempt to face each other and insert it into each of them at the same time.

Their knees touching they realized the twelve inches wasn't long enough for that position. Then they tried one leg over the other and while that brought their V's closer they still couldn't get a rhythm that didn't have it falling out continually. It wasn't until Nia lay back and inserted it and it stuck up rather grotesquely that Colleen got the idea to ride it, to ride Nia and between them they were able to establish a rhythm that they both not only enjoyed but excited them to the point that they could orgasm.

When Nia realized that her strong kegel muscles enabled her to thrust with the toy like a strap on she got very excited at mounting her girlfriend and pleasuring her like that as it kept her hands free to touch, caress, tease, and tweak. Knowing she was giving her such pleasure only enhanced her own as Colleen couldn't do it in return.

Instead Colleen learned to thrust with it seeing Nia arch into it and receive its abbreviated length. It was exciting to see the tall litigator lose control as she cried out from the pleasure Colleen learned to give her and invented.

They both felt though that together, the rhythm they learned together using such a toy was the best when they felt the need for the added bonus of a toy. It only enhanced their lovemaking, adding an element of surprise now and then and they didn't depend on it as they learned each other.

"I think it will take a lifetime to learn everything that pleases you," Nia said with a smile as she looked down and kissed Colleen. She was leaning over her in the bed and was pleased with herself and how much love they shared between them already in so short a time.

"I'd like that," Colleen admitted shyly. She was still so surprised that Nia loved her, that she wanted her around all the time. They were still learning boundaries in their relationship and really finding out how compatible they were on so many levels beyond the friendship they had already forged.

"I'm serious, I think I want you to stay around for always," she said meaningfully and leaned down to kiss her once again, because she could.

Colleen kissed her in return and rolled so she was on top of her girlfriend and looked down with love filled eyes and gratitude for the love she had found after so many horrible years. Maybe Nia was her reward for having put up with so much for so long.

❖ CHAPTER NINETEEN ❖

Colleen wasn't feeling well. Cletus had said he wouldn't sign the final papers unless she agreed to meet with him. Although New York had a no fault in its divorce cases, meaning either could divorce without laying blame and they could go their separate ways, no signature would be required to obtain the divorce if one party wanted out, she knew it would go faster, smoother even if she cooperated this once. It had been months since she had to worry about him. Being with Nia had given her confidence and she was looking forward to going back to school so she could become the paralegal as Nia had suggested. She was dressing better; her paychecks no longer squandered and not having to pay rent by living with Nia had enabled her to splurge a little on herself. The thought of this meeting though was making her ill, she was sure of it. The thoughts of Cletus always made her ill. It had taken her weeks to get her stomach under control and stop throwing up at the thought of him catching her again. To have to meet with him, even this one time, really upset her and Nia had offered to attend the meeting even though her attorney would be there for her.

"He will wonder why you are there?" Colleen said worriedly. She was certain she might throw up again.

"He can't read your mind, he doesn't know we are lovers," Nia said reasonably as they drove into the building to park in her assigned spot. The other expensive cars parked around them gave testament to the success of the firm and its partners.

"What if he finds out?" she asked but knew it didn't matter now. In a matter of weeks she would be free of him and his 'power.' Her father did not approve and wouldn't let her mother even talk to her. Having Nia had been a godsend and she was grateful for her love and support.

"So what if he does?" Nia blew it off. Their only concern was if their co-workers found out and with Colleen going to college soon for her degree and them looking for her replacement that would negate the problem that would have arisen. She fully intended to tell Stewart once Colleen was training her new assistant. She would miss having her there to depend on but really it was the only way she could see for them to continue their relationship.

"You don't know what he's capable of," Colleen warned as they got of the car together. Few if any other employees of Chase-Dunham were around to see them and Nia had long ago explained that she picked up Colleen for her safety. No one needed to know they also lived together.

"I'm very well aware of what he's capable of," Nia said instantly angry as she remembered the bruises she had seen on Colleens body much less the knowledge that he had raped her more than once. That would never happen again if she had anything to say about it.

Colleen glanced over at her boss's tone. She knew Nia could be protective, she loved that about her, she felt the same but she was frightened of Cletus, genuinely frightened of what he could do to her. That he hadn't found where she was living was due to her matching her hours perfectly to Nia's so that she could ride to and from work with her. He couldn't see when she came or went to her job. Now, this meeting meant he would know exactly where she was even if just for this meeting.

Nia had made sure her schedule was clear for the meeting between Colleen and her soon-to-be-ex-husband. She didn't want Cletus upsetting Colleen any more than she already was. Knowing how ill he had made her, sending her frequently to the bathroom to throw up over those many weeks as he made her life hell for filing for divorce meant that Colleen was constantly upset, her nerves shattered. This pissed Nia off as it gave him some sort of power over the woman she loved and she wasn't happy about it. She had made some discrete inquires with the district attorney's office about his drug case and it would take a while to meander through the court system because they were so backed up on cases and this was his first offense.

Colleen was dressed in a smart suit that bespoke her status as the personal assistant of one of the firm's partners. Nia was dressed in a suit that cost thousands of dollars and looked it as it fit her perfectly. This was deliberate. It was intended to intimidate the slovenly Cletus whom they both knew owned one suit and this one stained from his carelessness in wearing it.

From the moment Colleen entered the conference room with her lawyer Cletus glared at her. 'Look at how uppity that bitch is. I just need five minutes alone with her to teach her who is boss. Working in this place,' he thought but he was intimidated by the Manhattan offices of Chase-Dunham which 'had turned her head.'

Colleen wouldn't look at him. Instead she looked down at her shoes, a luxury she couldn't have afforded if Nia hadn't insisted she get the shoes to match her suit. Normally she had worn only two pair that she owned, sensible black, that matched every outfit she wore for work. Even having two pair had been a luxury when she lived with Cletus and only the fact that they were nearly identical kept him from realizing she was 'squandering' money on herself like that.

"Now, this meeting is at the request of my client," began Cletus' attorney. Nia knew who he was. He was a sleezball who had probably bribed someone to pass the state bar. He was dressed in a polyester suit

that looked like upholstery and was already sweating in the air-conditioned offices. His comb over hid the fact that his sparse head of hair was missing patches on top. He oozed slime from his pores and represented clients like Cletus because they paid him in cash. He didn't care where the money came from as long as it was in cash.

"Yes we are all aware of that," interrupted Donald, the associate attorney that was handling the divorce for Colleen. He was very aware of the partner Nia Toyomoto in this meeting sitting back to 'observe.' He knew she held her assistant in great esteem and wanted the best for her.

For about five minutes Cletus' attorney attempted to finagle more out of the arrangement but their divorce was fairly simple and while a fifty-fifty state Colleen had earned the lion's share of the legitimate monies earned in the relationship. When alimony had come up they had wiped that off the table with Cletus' drug bust and as those monies could not be tabulated they had to be a little sneaky in how they avoided paying him.

Finally after listening to the arguing attorney's for so long Cletus interrupted with, "Honey, I want you back. I can forgive you for this," he spread his hands pleadingly.

Colleen glanced up briefly. Her heart was beating hard in her chest with him so close. Despite having the other attorney's there. Nia was there. Even a guard disguised as a clerk was there. She was afraid he would lunge across the wide table at her and she was sweating from her fear. Her glance took in the familiar grease stained hands, the dirt of years of working on engines imbedded forever in the skin, his ill-fitting and old fashioned dirty suit, she could see the sleeves didn't quite meet the ends of his arms and he apparently hadn't washed any further than his wrists at the dirt that was revealed between the end of the suit arm and his wrist. She swallowed nervously as she didn't answer and merely shook her head.

"Don't you understand? I'm willing to forgive you," he pleaded and he meant it. She just didn't understand. She was just a woman, how could she understand the superior mentality of a man. He glanced at her boss sitting in back and 'observing.' He despised women like that. The hoity-toity bitch. He knew women like that were dangerous. They thought they were too good for men like him. They gave easily-led women like his wife, *his* wife, and gave them ideas above their station. It was working here that had led to this divorce. He didn't think about all the money she had earned by her own merits and he had spent so frivolously. He blamed her for his drug bust. He blamed her for the fact that he didn't have as much money to play around with. He blamed her for the eviction notice he had gotten for not paying his rent. He blamed her because there was no food in the house when he wanted it, the cable had been turned off, and the electric. He blamed her because *that* woman, *her boss*, had given her ideas.

"Sir, I would appreciate it if you would address your comments to me, my client has no wish to speak with you," Donald said glancing at the white pallor of his client. He glanced back at Nia knowing she was itching to take this over but her specialty was not family law, she only handled divorces for high powered clients backed up by associates such as himself. He wanted to work with her again and knew he better not screw this one up.

"She's my wife!" Cletus snarled.

"No sir, she will shortly be divorced from you. That order of protection means you stay away from her," Donald said firmly and with a warning glance at Cletus' lawyer.

Cletus and his attorney huddled and spoke soto-voice so that no one would hear them. By the glances they were sure everyone could hear them.

Donald wrapped up this meeting as soon as he was able to. It was just a matter of time before New York granted the divorce anyway. They had hoped to appease Cletus and his attorney by this meeting but really it was a waste of time for everyone involved. Cletus was uncooperative and seemed to have an inflated sense of what 'justice' was owed to him. "Sir I might remind you that this meeting was staged for your benefit. You agreed to sign the papers to speed up the divorce if my client agreed to the meeting. We've listened to you now long enough. Sign the papers and be done with it."

Cletus and his attorney refused but it was really a moot point. The state would allow the divorce and with drug and other charges pending Colleen was well off without him. Nia escorted Colleen out another side of the building back to their offices where she wouldn't have to see Cletus leave. The guard had made sure he left with his attorney and Nia took Colleen into her office where upon locking the door she took the shaking woman in her arms.

"Shhh shh, it's okay, it's over now," she caressed Colleen's hair back and held her close.

"He's so angry," Colleen blubbered.

"It was just a way to get to you, don't let him," Nia advised. It didn't matter what walk of life her clients were from, rich or poor, they all wanted a touch of revenge. Cletus had just wanted to intimidate her one last time. She hoped the state threw the book at him and that he went away to prison. Then she would finally be free of him.

"He just scares me so. He's always scared me. My father though loves him more than me," Colleen answered feeling sorry for herself.

"I love you though, you don't need people like that in your life," Nia told her gently as she kissed her tear soaked face.

Colleen sagged against Nia feeling relief that it was over. In a couple of months she would finally be divorced from the bastard. The initial filing of her divorce had included a stay away order that stated he could not come any closer than three hundred feet of her and while she knew Cletus didn't give a rats-ass about the paperwork, only the fact that he didn't know where she was staying protected her from him. She let go of Nia abruptly to run to the bathroom to throw up. When she returned Nia didn't say a word as she handed her a white soda to help with her upset stomach. She also had some Pepto-bismol if she had wanted it but the idea of the chalky tablet didn't appeal and the soda helped somewhat.

It took a good hour for Colleen to calm down enough to return to work. They worked through their lunch including Suzette so the three of them could coordinate the mountain of work that came through Nia's office.

"This goes to," she named off lawyers as she put post-it notes on each stack so that the assistants could get them to right offices. "And this to the paralegals, make sure they read my notes this time," Nia said angrily. She didn't like being caught unaware and had almost lost a case because someone had dropped the ball. "These need to be filed in the following time frame," she said through her cashew chicken as they continued to eat and work. It was another hour before the three of them parted with the paperwork and files that Nia had gone over with them.

"Hey, I'm done unless you have something else?" Suzette said as she turned off the light on her desk across from Colleens. She enjoyed the work but was very grateful she didn't have the work load or the responsibilities that Colleen had. Nia Toyomoto hadn't been as bad a boss as everyone had warned her before she accepted this position. She wasn't going to go for Colleen's and hoped that whoever replaced her was equally as helpful and kind as Colleen had been.

"No, I'm good, you have a good evening," Colleen answered as she absentmindedly said her good-byes. She never even looked up to acknowledge her as she had her own stack of work to finish before she left.

A while later Colleen stuck her head into Nia's office and asked, "You about ready?" She hated doing that but Nia would stay at the office all night if she didn't remind her of the passage of time.

Nia looked up from her own work and smiled at the woman. She really enjoyed working with her and loving her was an added bonus. She glanced out her windows to realize how late it really was. She sighed and rubbed her face being careful not to rub her eyes and mess up her makeup. "Okay, let me pack this up, I'll meet you at the car?" she said with a smile.

"Okay, not too long though okay? I put a roast in the crock pot on slow cook and it should be done by now," she looked at her watch.

Nia laughed at her assistant. She really looked forward to eating dinner with her over a nice wine and roast sounded heavenly. The leftovers alone would be worth it for meals. "Okay okay, I'll hurry," she answered with a grin as she rose from her desk and began gathering what she would need to work at home, not too much only a few 'catch up' things as Colleen had made it clear that she couldn't work at the dinner table. It would all be here in the morning anyway.

Colleen straightened up the reception area making sure nothing of consequence was visible and put away the files she had been working on locking up the cabinet with her key. No one, not the cleaning crew, not the other people in the office, no one but Colleen, Nia, and now Suzette had keys to the files and she was very careful about leaving anything out for anyone to see. She had heard of sloppier assistants who had been fired over such things and she wasn't going to get caught that way. She got her jacket from the closet and her purse and feeling dizzy for a moment she breathed deeply to get her equilibrium back. It had been a full day and she was looking forward to a nice quiet evening alone with Nia. She relished the time where Nia was all hers and had come to cherish living with her and loving her. She had shown her what love really was.

Pushing the button to the parking level Nia mentally checked what she had in her briefcase and then shrugged off that nagging feeling that she was forgetting something. The work would still be there in the morning and while she had a lot of it, it would get done when it got done. She was looking forward to the promised roast and if she knew Colleen, and she did know her, there would be potatoes and carrots thrown in for good measure. Her mouth was watering at the thought. As the elevator doors opened she headed for her parking spot and noted there were few cars left from her partners as she made her way to Lexus. She frowned not seeing Colleen standing next to it, she hadn't been that long in packing up and she looked around for her, maybe she took the stairs for some reason? Swiveling her head around she walked past her car and then she saw her, lying down next to the car.

"Did you lose something?" she asked. It looked like she was looking under the car for something. As she walked closer she saw it, blood. Shocked she knelt down next to Colleen and shook her. "Colleen? COLLEEN?" She could see a small pool of blood from where her head had connected with the concrete. "Colleen?" she asked again and reached for the pulse in her neck to see if she was dead. She was grateful to find a faint pulse as she dropped her briefcase and her purse to reach for her cell phone.

"Hello, this is Nia Toyomoto, I need the police and an ambulance at," she gave the name and address of the building. "My," she hesitated at the label for a moment. "Assistant, Colleen Hodsworth has been attacked and

is unconscious in the parking garage on the partner's level which is the fifth level," she was trying to stay calm and speak clearly into the phone to the operator. "She is bleeding from her head, I get a faint pulse, but please hurry," she said with feeling, her voice was about to break.

The operator asked her to repeat the information which she did efficiently and without emotion, she was drawing on her expertise in the courtroom where no emotions were necessary or invited. "Do you know who attacked her?" the operator asked.

Nia knew, in her gut she knew but she could only give her opinion, no facts as she hadn't seen it happen. "She is going through a divorce from her husband Cletus. He was here today in the offices and it didn't go well. I didn't however see anything but I'm certain security would have something on the tapes." She thought for a moment and looked around uneasily. "This had to of just happened, she just left the office and I came down not even five minutes later. He could still be here! I need to call security," she said and hung up the phone. They had the address, they had the location, she needed to make sure she was safe so she could take care of Colleen. She glanced down at her as she dialed the number to the building and asked to be transferred to security. Colleen hadn't moved in the time she had been with her. Her breathing was shallow, very shallow.

The call was answered. "This is Nia Toyomoto, I am a partner in Chase-Dunham. I am in the parking structure on the partner's level by my car. There has been an attack of my personal assistant; the police are on the way. I will need a copy of the security cameras for this level," she ordered. "I want a couple of officers down here immediately to protect me and the building searched for anyone who doesn't belong here. Specifically a tall blonde man in a cheap fitting suit," she described Cletus as she remembered him from the meeting earlier that day. She gave them further instructions emphasizing the importance of what she was requesting and what the police would expect. By the time she got off the phone she heard sirens and saw two security officers coming at a run from the stairwell.

"Don't move her," she cautioned as one of them knelt to check for a pulse. At his look to her where she stood there she explained, "I don't know if her neck is hurt."

It seemed a long time at the moment but in a relatively short time both police and paramedics were there and assessing Colleen. Nia had to give a statement but they wouldn't let her go with Colleen who was still unconscious when they loaded her into the ambulance.

"So you think it's this Cletus Hodsworth who is her husband?" the officer asked her for the third time.

Nia, getting impatient went to brush by him to see them load her in on the gurney. They had determined that she had been beaten and knocked

out, the blood on the floor was from her injuries and not from her fall, but that was all they would tell her.

"I need your statement," the officer tried to grab her arm to detain her.

Nia looked down from her height, the officer was only an inch or so below her own height and she said in a menacing voice, "I've given you the same statement three times. I'm done; if you want further information from me contact my office."

Something about her demeanor, not the tone, but her presence made him remove his hand instantly. He had admired her at first at how well she kept herself together and answered their questions concisely. When it was revealed she was a partner in the firm upstairs and he had even heard of them, he hadn't believed her at first but another partner had come along and verified who she was. He realized she was a force to be reckoned with and she had given them the statement they needed, they had only had her repeat it to see if there was some discrepancies. He let her go without another word.

As she watched the ambulance pull away she went to get in her car and realized with the police there and now several people watching she couldn't get out of her stall. Having just pissed off the officer in charge she got in the car anyway and started it up and began inching it until people moved. It seemed to take forever and really angered her as she wanted to follow the ambulance which was now out of sight.

When Nia arrived at the emergency room and identified herself as Colleen's friend and boss it didn't work, they wouldn't let her see the still unconscious woman. They wouldn't tell her anything either which further annoyed the woman. She waited in the waiting room to hear something, anything and they kept her waiting there. Her attempts to finagle or cajole the nurse into telling her something, anything were met with a stoic, "I'm sorry but unless you are a relative I cannot release any information regarding our patient." When the same annoying nurse approached her later for information on Colleen, in particular she wanted her 'husbands' phone number to contact him regarding the patient's 'accident' it so infuriated Nia that she had to take a walk. It was a good thing too as she was ready to explode and it gave her perspective to walk away. When she returned the annoying nurse was gone and her replacement was willing to listen.

"Look, my partner Colleen Hodsworth was brought in earlier, she was attacked," Nia said carefully cringing at the partial lie. She technically was 'just' a friend and while they were lover's they hadn't identified themselves as anything more. The world didn't know about them and Nia hadn't even told her closest friends including Annie.

"Just a moment, I'll check," the perky nurse told her as Nia smiled in gratitude. A few minutes with the woman out of sight and Nia was

ushered through the doors to the emergency room and through the bullet proof glass that protected the ER from the waiting room. "This way," she was told and taken to a small examination room where Colleen was hooked up to an I.V. and looked the worse for wear.

Nia was relieved to see her but still concerned at her apparent unconscious state. What was going on?

The nurse must have sensed her upset as she said, "The doctor will be with you shortly," and left her there with Colleen.

She looked at her with sympathy in her eyes. Her right eye was black and purple and looked like it had gotten a direct hit. Her cheekbone had a large bandage on it. Her hair was a mess, the mousy brown color making it look limp and unkempt and with the blonde streaks making it look almost greasy. Her lip was cut in several spots and was very swollen. Her nose looked swollen as well and with the tubes running up each nostril it didn't bode well. Her neck had fingermarks around it bruising exactly where the hands had been, her arms were full of bruises, some looked like they had just appeared, others, deeper and just waiting to appear showing promise. Nia wanted to take her in her arms and tell her everything was going to be okay but she didn't know it would be.

"Ma'am?" a voice said behind her and Nia turned to see a man in a white coat. "You are Mrs. Hodsworth's," he hesitated over the next word, "partner?"

Nia nodded instead of saying anything and at her nod he gestured her out of the room. With one last glance back at the sad looking Colleen she followed him out of the room.

"Mrs. Hodsworth has sustained a lot of injuries. She's been badly beaten and has several fractures, nothing completely broken," he quickly said as Nia looked thunderous at the news. "It's going to take a while for them to heal of course," he told her and then as an afterthought he cheerfully added, "and the baby is okay, we've checked."

Nia froze. Baby? She stared at the doctor shell shocked. Colleen had lived with her for months and never mentioned she was pregnant. She blinked thinking about that little tidbit of information. Had Colleen known? Her lawyer's mind contemplated all the repercussions of that information as well as how it would affect her and her relationship with Colleen. She realized the doctor was waiting for some sort of answer and she nodded and said, "That's good."

"Yes we weren't sure for a while there but Obstetrics assures us that the baby should be fine, most of the blows were to her head and arms. Whoever did this didn't kick her but knocked her down by the bruises we read on her legs. If they had kicked her though…" he left off talking as he realized that this 'partner' of his patient was probably the other parent to the unborn child and didn't need the details or speculations of what could

have happened. "It looks like she protected the little nipper and he should be fine."

"It's a boy?" Nia asked surprised.

He shook his head and answered, "We didn't look for the sex however if you and she would like to know…?" he asked with a questioning look.

"We'll let you know," she told him dismissively. Then she thought to ask, "Has she woken up?"

He shook his head. "No, the blows she got to her head and the one that must have been to the concrete have kept her unconscious. It might be a blessing in disguise as she will be in a lot of pain when she does wake up and we have to be careful what we give her because of the baby."

Nia nodded understandingly and looked back at the room thoughtfully. "How long will she be here?"

"We aren't sure yet, let's see how she does and when she wakes up we will reassess her. She took a helluva beating but should be fine; the concussion isn't as severe as it could have been."

She was annoyed by his explanations but she was also relieved. He didn't really have answers to her questions which made her have another couple of questions but she was just happy to know that Colleen would survive and eventually wake up. A baby though? What the hell were they going to do with that?

Colleen woke up to the worst headache of her life and squinted out of the one eye she could see out of. She tried to lift her hand to wipe at the one she couldn't see out of and found her hand full of tape and she followed it up to an I.V. She was in the hospital? She glanced around and the sterile atmosphere of the room made her realize she had to be. She wondered why she was here. Just then Nia came in the room carrying a coffee cup and stopped when she saw the one eye glancing around.

"You're awake," she said unnecessarily.

Colleen went to speak but for some reason her throat hurt. She nodded to acknowledge what Nia had said and then a puzzled look came over her one good eye. She frowned and raised her eyebrow hoping to speak without words.

"You are in the hospital," Nia told her in unconscious response to her actions. "You got pretty beat up. Do you remember what happened?"

She shook her head and wondered when that had happened. Then remembering Cletus and that she had left him she wondered if that was the beating that Nia was referring to. Suddenly the time didn't make sense. Had everything that had happened between her and Nia only been a dream? Something in her imagination? She looked worried and upset

and Nia reached over to take her free hand into her own and give it a squeeze.

"Relax, no one can get you here. I've arranged for a guard at the door and they are looking for whoever did this to you," she told her being careful not to plant who she *thought* had done it in Colleen's head. When she could speak, it would be up to her to tell the police her version of what had happened. She hadn't seen the tapes yet but expected to tomorrow at the office. Glancing at the clock it was after midnight and she wondered if she would get any sleep tonight. She sipped the coffee to keep herself awake.

Colleen wanted to laugh at the grimace over the taste of the coffee as Nia took a drink. She knew she was particular about which brands she drank and had gotten spoiled over having her own cappuccino maker in the office. Her look of amusement caught Nia's eyes.

"Oh you want some of this?" she teased and grinned down at her lover.

Colleen shook her head slightly but it hurt to move and her headache was legendary. At her grimace of pain Nia was instantly contrite. She let go of Colleens hand to reach for the call button. At the answering call she said, "Colleen is awake."

The nurse and doctor who responded had a lot of questions for Colleen who nodded or shook her head and when she tried to speak the doctor warned her against it. "You are lucky that your trachea wasn't crushed but it's going to hurt for a few days while you heal."

The police weren't as understanding about her inability to talk but her right hand wasn't taped up so she could answer their questions with written words on the pad they provided for her. By then her head had cleared enough that she remembered the incident and was able to write down details that Nia noted and the police were happy with. Cletus had been waiting in the parking garage and had attacked her.

Nia realized he had used the meeting as an opportunity to get not only into the building but the parking garage and must have been waiting to see if Colleen would show up. As there were many levels there would have been a lot of time for him to have to remain hidden and she wondered how he had managed that. She would call the building security and ask them to view all their tapes from the past day and put them together for her and the police, not just the attack.

Nia stayed with Colleen until she dozed off again and while she wanted to go home too she slept in a chair they had there that reclined back and allowed her to sleep next to her friend and lover. It was a restless night for both of them. Colleen, unable to be sedated because of the baby she didn't even know about was fidgeting and Nia woke frequently to reassure her by holding her hand and squeezing. She wanted to take her in her arms now

and tell her it would be okay but seeing how bruised up she was, Nia decided to wait.

"Go to work," Colleen rasped out the next morning seeing how Nia looked from spending the night in the chair by her bed. She had woken often enough in pain that she knew she had been there all night.

"Yes, I'll do that after the doctor comes by," Nia said to her fondly. She felt terrible but after seeing Colleen in the light of day knew she was better off than the brunette.

The doctor came by early enough that Nia was able to go home and shower and change her clothes and to turn off the now dried out roast. There were blood splatters on the side of her car she noted and shuddered as she realized they were from Colleen. It disturbed her more than she realized as she wondered what work would be like today.

Suzette tried to fill in for Colleen but she wasn't up to the standards that the personal assistant had set. Another gal came from the secretarial pool but was only able to follow basic instructions and Nia was constantly interrupted by the two asking questions and she had to unlock the desks and filing cabinets for them to find things, if they could.

"Nia?" Stewart Dunham and Grayson Morse another senior partner entered her office. She had left her door open for her secretaries who seemed to be in and out as they adjusted to the workload and the many questions they had for Nia today. They were jittery too as the police questioned various people from the firm. The gossip was running wild and Nia could only imagine as she tried to get some work done. She looked up at the familiar voice of the senior partner.

"Stewart!" she smiled in welcome. "Hello Gray," she stood up to welcome them both.

"Got a minute?" he asked rhetorically.

Nia nodded immediately and then saw he had turned to close the door and she got a glance of a startled Suzette before the door closed. "Can I offer you some cappuccino?" she asked graciously.

Stewart smiled with genuine pleasure. "Yes, yes, of course. You have to tell me where you get this stuff," he teased. She had given him a box of the delicious brew for Christmas but wouldn't tell her source. "Gray, you have got to try this," he said as she expertly brewed the concoction for her guests.

Once the cups were placed before the men who were now seated at her coffee table she sat down to join them and waited for one of them to begin.

Gray cleared his throat and began, "As Colleen was hurt in our parking garage and is a part of the firm we want to be kept apprised of everything regarding her," he told her.

Nia raised her eyebrow but didn't lose her 'court' face which she had slipped her mask on for this meeting. She had of course expected it but not this soon.

"Yes, we are concerned for her welfare," Stewart added.

Nia was much more astute than that. "You are afraid she will sue the firm aren't you?" she asked.

The men exchanged a look before Gray asked, "Do you think she will?"

Nia shook her head. As a lawyer she knew the angles but she also knew that Colleen wasn't the type. "No I don't believe she will. She will have to heal for a long time and we will show the utmost consideration for her." She didn't mention that Colleen was pregnant; she hadn't even discussed that with her lover.

They discussed the various repercussions of the incident from the day before as well as Nia filling them in on what she knew from the police. At this time they were looking for Cletus and as he was out on bail for his drug arrest and other charge he would be taken into custody immediately when they found him.

After they left, Nia called down to the security office to ask where the tapes she had requested, demanded really, were. She was informed they had been delivered that morning, copies to her assistant. Getting up angrily she went to the outer office and asked Suzette only to find out the temp had them and had gone on break. "Tell her I want to see those immediately upon her return," Nia said angrily as she returned to her office after looking for them herself and not finding them, she couldn't help comparing the two to Colleen and realized she was biased towards her lover, she sighed. Colleen would have to get well and train the replacement but it didn't mean either of them had to like it.

"How are you?" Nia asked with a smile around the giant bouquet of flowers she had brought Colleen.

"I'm okay," Colleen said quietly not entirely convincing the taller woman.

Nia put the flowers down on a table as she looked down at the beaten and battered woman, she hoped the police had taken more pictures, she looked worse today. "What's wrong?"

Colleen looked at Nia like she was nuts. "Um, everything?" she said sarcastically and then immediately regretted taking her bad mood on her boss, lover, and friend.

Nia sat down and reached for Colleen's hand squeezing it gently she asked in a soft voice, "What is it honey?"

Colleen looked at Nia and shook her head, the headache had subsided somewhat so she was able to do that without too much pain. Tears began to form in both her eyes but the swollen one was too swollen to release them. They started to roll down her one good eye down her cheek and across the cut that was there into the bandages.

"Is there something else?" she asked and then indicating the many bandages she continued with, "Is there something more?" She hoped they had told Colleen she was pregnant and she wanted Colleen to be the one to tell her.

Colleen shook her head as she began to sob.

Nia, despite the many bandages on her lover leaned over her and cupping her hand to the side of Colleen's head she tucked her own head in her neck. "Shhh baby, shhh, its okay," she said comfortingly.

"You don't know that, you don't know…." Colleen hiccupped.

Nia pulled back far enough that she could look deeply into the one good eye. Hoping this was the opening they needed to discuss things she asked gently. "What don't I know?" she said carefully.

Hiccupping a bit more but comforted by Nia's presence she swallowed, coughing a little, she began, "I'm pregnant…."

Nia waited. She wanted to know if Colleen had decided anything. She didn't realize by her silence, her patience that Colleen would worry.

"I should get rid of it but they tell me it's too late," she looked worriedly into Nia's amazing eyes. She saw compassion there, love, and something more that she couldn't identify.

"Too late?" Nia asked afraid to really ask what that meant.

"I'm too far along apparently for them to end it," she said sadly.

Nia wasn't sure if she had the right to have an opinion on this. She had always believed in a woman's right to her own decisions regarding her body but this was her lover, her friend, and she wasn't sure how over the line she might be if she expressed herself in this. Biting her lip thoughtfully she asked, "Do you really want to get rid of it?"

Colleen looked at her horrified not even realizing Nia was caressing the side of her face gently and sweetly, pulling her hair back from her face. "You can't think I want a baby as the result of rape can you?"

Nia had had more time to absorb the news and realize what it could mean to her lover. She sat on the edge of the bed and took her hand away from Colleen's face and her hand into hers again petting it absentmindedly as she thought about what she had to say. "You didn't suspect you were pregnant?" she asked wondering about all the clues that now seemed transparent and obvious.

She shook her head in anguish wondering how Nia felt, for the first time she began to think of someone other than herself since the doctor had come in and told her the news, thinking to cheer her up with the news that

the attack hadn't affected the baby and that she was going to be 'fine.' Her shock at the news hadn't registered with him as he continued cheerfully outlining her recovery.

"Well, you can give it up for adoption if you really want to get rid of it," Nia continued carefully. She swallowed and wondered what she would decide. It would affect them both, she wondered if Colleen realized that.

It was at that exact moment that Colleen had a thought. Glancing at Nia's kind and concerned face she realized they were talking as a couple and it felt strange to realize that. While they had been living and loving together now for weeks, months really, she had always felt like a guest in Nia's home. "What do you want me to do?" she asked quietly. Her voice was still a little hoarse from the choking. She had seen what she looked like when they took her to the bathroom and the police had taken pictures, many many pictures.

Nia wasn't sure she should let her own feelings on the matter sway the decision but she had asked. "You know I'll support any decision you make?" she began

"I know you will but what do you want?" Colleen rasped.

"I want whatever you want," she evaded and glanced down.

"What if I want to keep it?" she ventured wondering what Nia really wanted.

Nia glanced back up to see if she was serious. "Then I guess we buy nursery furniture," she said tentatively waiting to see if Colleen really meant it.

It couldn't be that simple. "But do you want a baby around?" she asked wishing Nia would just tell her.

Nia was careful in her answers. This couldn't be her decision. The relationship was so new and she herself wasn't sure what she wanted from it. "I'll do whatever you want to do. If you decide to keep it we will work on that, if you want to give it up I'll help you find other parents."

It wasn't the answer Colleen wanted or needed right now but she did have a lot to think about since it was Cletus' child too.

"Oh, I didn't know you had a visitor," a nurse came in right then. Nia turned to look at her, she was a new one but there were a few she hadn't met.

"Oh, this is my…" Colleen faltered glancing up at Nia and wondering how to introduce her. "Boss," she finished feeling kind of lame.

Nia was amused but she understood the hesitation.

"Well your husband called and we assured him that you and the baby were okay," the nurse told them in a chirpy little voice that irritated more than her words.

"Wait a minute, her *husband* called and you gave him information on her condition?" Nia sounded ominous.

The nurse blinked and nodded. "Well of course," she said as though it were obvious.

"What about privacy laws?" Nia continued angrily. "You think the cop on guard at the door is there for the fun of it? Her *husband* did this to her!" she raged at her.

The nurse realized the error and her eyes widened in shocked dismay. "I didn't know," she said backing away and shaking her head, she put her hands up as if to ward off Nia who was advancing on her.

"Get me the doctor and get him *now*," Nia ordered her in a tone that brooked no interference.

The nurse practically sprinted from the room and Nia turned to look at the alarmed and scared woman in the bed.

"If he knows where I am," she began and then glanced down at her twining hands. "He knows I'm pregnant too now," she said dispiritedly.

"It's okay, we will keep you safe," Nia tried to assure her hoping she was right but the cops hadn't found him and it was confirmed from the tapes that it was him that had beaten Colleen in the parking garage. Why security hadn't acted on it earlier was under investigation but several of the partners had expressed their dissatisfaction in the building's security after this incident and some heads would roll from it.

"I have to get out of here," Colleen said and threw off the blanket to try to get out of bed. She swung her legs over the side.

Nia rushed to the bed to hold her there. "You can't, you have to heal, you can't leave but we can move you until you are well enough to go home."

"Home? Your place? He will find me there," she said frantically. She was obviously panicking and it was transferring to Nia who felt the need to protect her.

"It's worked this far, we can keep him away," she said practically trying to stay calm. Her own heart had dropped into her stomach at the nurse's pronouncement though. She wondered if he had called other hospitals too.

"I'm not safe, he found me at the office," she said as she weakly pushed against the must taller Nia.

"He knew you were there that day, he waited for you. The tapes caught glimpses of him," she told her.

"How do you know that?" she looked up with her one good eye trying to peek out of the swollen one.

"I've seen them, I ordered them before you were even in the ambulance so that a copy was sent to me before the police even got it," she told her trying to think of what would reassure the panicked woman.

"He was waiting for me…" Colleen said musingly as she looked down.

"You need to get back into bed," Nia said calmly and soothingly, hoping to convince Colleen that they could and would keep her safe.

"What's going on in here?" an authoritative voice asked from the door.

Nia whirled having not heard him come in but was relieved to see the doctor. "I'll tell you what is going on. My friend who was beaten by her *husband* has just been told that her husband called and one of *your* nurses told him not only that she was *here* but that *she is pregnant* which he did not know until that moment," her tone brooked no argument, it was what she used in court to cow the defenses witnesses.

He gulped realizing the enormity of what had just occurred as he looked at her horrified.

"I need to get out of here," Colleen rasped.

"That's out of the question. You have several fractures that need to be looked after," he began becoming all business.

"Then you better move her to another floor with better security than you have," Nia told him and he nodded and left. She followed him to the door and told the officer on duty what had happened. He nodded and pulled out his cell to call his superior and inform him. She turned back to see Colleen trying once again to get out of bed. She rushed to her just as she collapsed onto the floor, her legs giving out from under her. "Nope, no, you have to stay here. I'll take care of everything," she assured her as she lifted the smaller woman by her armpits not wanting to touch her bruised and bandaged arms and worried she might break something.

"I have to get out of here," Colleen insisted looking up pleadingly at Nia.

"You have to get well and take care of that baby," Nia countered and looked sternly down at her lover. "Please, be reasonable. We will take care of it for you. Trust me," she pleaded softly.

Colleen looked up and seeing those amazingly feline like eyes looking at her so tenderly she nodded once and allowed Nia to help her back into the hospital bed.

Nia helped tuck her in and was straightening things when the doctor returned with two orderlies and another nurse.

"I've got her into another ward," he told her as they began preparing to move her, bed and all. "I am sorry for this and the nurse in question will be retrained," he informed them.

"You do that," Nia said shortly with a nod but her tone was menacing.

Nia didn't know it but the doctor knew who she was. She had defended another doctor a couple of years ago and her name meant something, he was now worried that the hospital would be hit with a suit and was doing everything he could to avoid it, already the administration was informed of this breech. They moved Colleen up a floor and down to the other end of

the hospital into the maternity ward. Nia wondered at the location but she hoped it would help hide her as the police officer stationed himself outside the door of her private room.

"I can't stay here," Colleen hissed.

Nia grinned. "Of course you can, think of it as a trial by fire," she quipped trying to lighten the mood.

Colleen glared at her from her one good eye. "I haven't said if I'll keep it or what," she answered pouting.

"No, this isn't about the baby although you are right, you haven't said." Nia didn't allow her own feelings regarding the situation enter into her tone before she continued, "But no one will think of looking for you here."

Colleen was still worried that Cletus was looking for her. He'd identified himself as her husband to get the information on her and knew what hospital she was in. Now he knew she was pregnant and she knew he would want the baby even if he couldn't provide for it. It would be a matter of pride with him, that he sired a child. She had wanted to wait until they were better off financially but that was never to be with his habits.

Nia stayed until Colleen was served a late dinner before she headed home. Colleen was much calmer by then and they had chatted easily for hours.

✤ CHAPTER TWENTY ✤

The next week they released Colleen to Nia's care and she arranged for a nurse to visit daily to bathe Colleen and take care of her but evenings she was there and actually enjoyed taking care of her for a change. It was then she realized how much Colleen did for her both at work and at home and felt the inequality of it. She enjoyed evening things up for a change even if Colleen was impatient to return to work. Nia let her hear the cases she was working on but she refused to bring much work home with her because she had started taking the files to organize them, sure that her 'replacement' wasn't doing things right in the office. Nia assured her that no one could replace her and she eagerly looked forward to her going back to the office to find and train someone.

"You don't want me back?" Colleen asked unreasonably.

"You are going to start school soon and you also told everyone you would train the replacement," Nia said just as reasonably trying to point out the obvious. With the news she would be pregnant other adjustments would have to be made.

Nia rubbed her forehead in vexation, this week had been hell. "Mr. McCormick I'm sure you realized that 'Attorney Assets' is a fictionalized version of what really happens in the courtroom. You can't commit a crime and expect everything to be cleared up including court time in a matter of days or an hour of television time," she tried to tell him patiently.

"Well I saw…" he began earnestly.

"Its television, it's not real. That is NOT a true representation of what happens. This is going to take months," she interrupted equally as earnestly.

"I tried to tell you," his manager said to him.

"But I tell you I saw…" he began again.

"It's a television show!" Nia repeated getting a little angry at the waste of her time. "That's why you hired me, to separate out the fact from the fiction. You need to tell me the truth, not portions of it or what you think I need to know but *all* of it!"

He subsided but looked at her skeptically still not sure she was right after what he had seen on the television show.

Nia sighed and began again outlining their defense and case as she repeated herself for the umpteenth time to her hard headed client. She was tired, very tired, having to take care of Colleen when she got home and

worrying about her otherwise was wearing on her and with her case load she was feeling the fatigue.

"Colleen?" she called as she came into the apartment and dropped her keys on the table by the door along with her briefcase.

"No but will I do?" Annie asked with a grin as she came out of the kitchen eating something that looked yummy.

"Hey you, what are you doing here?" Nia asked delighted as she walked across the room with her arms open for a hug.

"Thought I should check up on you as I never hear from you these days. You've been busy," she said irreverently as she inclined her head upstairs and returned the hug.

Nia glanced upstairs and saw the nurse come out of the bedroom and head down the stairs. Ignoring Annie for a moment she turned to the other woman to ask, "How is she today?"

"Ornery," the woman said testily and sighed. "I think she is getting cabin fever," she said with a wry little grin.

Nia grinned sympathetically. "Thank you so much for what you do for her," she said reverently.

The woman shrugged and then asked, "Do you have someone coming over the weekend?"

Nia hadn't thought of anyone for the weekend. "No, I guess it's just me then," she answered.

"Good luck," she said as she reached for her coat and bag.

Nia saw her out before turning back to Annie. "Who let you in?" she asked.

"The nurse but only after Colleen told her I was okay, what's going on that I can't use my key?" she asked concerned.

"It's a long story," Nia said and glanced upstairs wondering if she should check in.

"I'm here for the weekend and apparently there is a room all ready for me," she said with a tongue in cheek look.

Nia wrinkled her nose at her best friend before heading for the stairs. She would explain more but she felt the need to check on Colleen. She found her trying to get into a bathrobe dressed in the pajamas she had been wearing almost every day since she got home. Fortunately the washer and dryer in the apartment were handy and she had several pair to change into daily but they were ugly and Nia hated them.

"Hi, how are you?" she asked unnecessarily as she walked into the master bedroom. Glancing at the other bedroom that Colleen used to live in she wondered at Annie's flippant comment.

"I'm okay although that witch wants me to do physical therapy," Colleen informed her.

"Will it help?"

Colleen shrugged wincing at the pain that caused her. She had bruises that she hadn't known were there and they seemed to be taking forever to heal. Now that they knew she was pregnant they had given her all the pre-natal vitamins too so she should be healing sooner, or so the doctor told her.

Nia watched her fumble with the robe and went to help her. "Are you going somewhere?" she asked amused as she started to change out of her business suit.

Colleen watched her realizing how much she wanted to physically be with Nia again once she healed but Nia was careful around her, she held her at night but nothing more and she missed the more.

Nia changed quickly pulling on slacks and a nice blouse and as Colleen made her way painfully to the door she caught up with her saying, "Here, let me help you."

Annie watched the two of them come down the loft steps. Just the fact that Colleen had come out of the master bedroom and had offered her the bed in the spare bedroom told her a lot about their relationship and she wondered when that had changed. Nia hadn't told her anything and she certainly couldn't ask Colleen.

"What do you say I order dinner?" Nia asked once she had Colleen settled on one of the couches.

Annie, who had hoped to have dinner with Nia alone, frowned at the suggestion but Colleen answered with, "I could make us something," and tried to get up but Nia put her hand on her shoulder and held her down.

"You are supposed to be resting," she told her in no uncertain terms.

Colleen sighed and settled back as Nia took her hand off her shoulder, rubbing it affectionately before she walked towards the bar and the phone on it.

Annie mouthed words, "What's going on?" and Nia shook her head.

As they ate Italian Annie regaled them with tales of her latest paramour who apparently was keeping her busy and lasting longer than most.

Colleen watched enviously at the easy camaraderie that was between Annie and Nia that came from longtime friends and laughed at Annie's stories. She was soon tired out though and Nia helped her upstairs after dinner and to wash up for bed.

"Have fun," Colleen said as Nia lovingly tucked her into their bed and then left the bedroom, closing the door behind her.

"What is going on?" Annie asked suspiciously as Nia handed her a wine glass.

LAWYERED

They were sitting on Nia's little used balcony and enjoying the summer night's air. Partly to enjoy the sounds of the city and partly for privacy so they couldn't be overheard. Nia knew Colleen could be left alone for a while and she needed to talk to Annie, she had missed her. She looked around at the homey touches Colleen had instigated even here on the balcony with long draping type plants that were in boxes over the edge of the rail and climbing in and out of the railings. One of them was flowering and the scent was heady.

"Well, as you can see Colleen is staying here with me," she began.

"Duh," Annie said with a sneer.

Nia chuckled and lifted her own wine glass to take a sip. "Well," she shrugged. "What can I say?" she hedged.

"Ummmm, you could start at the beginning. How long has she been staying with you? Does she sleep in your bed alone?" Annie rolled her eyes at her best friend for effect.

Nia smiled at her and began to tell her about the relationship. She had finished her second glass of wine before she finished the story.

"Holy shit, she's pregnant?" Annie asked unnecessarily. "How do you feel about that?"

Nia shrugged still not sure *how* she felt. "I love her so it's really up to her what she wants to do about it."

"Wow! You with a woman, permanently?" Annie questioned the world, not directly to Nia.

Nia took up the question though. "I love her, I think I have for a while but it took me some time to admit it and realize it, much less act on it."

"Who'd a thunk it?" she answered shaking her head at the way things came about.

"What? She's a terrific woman and she loves me too."

"I get that but really who wouldn't love you, you have this terrific home, a fantastic job, and you aren't bad looking either," Annie countered.

"She has a heart of gold, she's going back to school to get a better job in the firm, and I like her looks," her lawyer's arguments began to arise.

"You could do better."

"Could I? I don't think so."

Annie was surprised. While she was all for experimentation and dated men and women over the years she hadn't thought Nia was that inventive. But first with Justine and now with Colleen, she couldn't believe she had jumped the fence and was staying over on that side. "Does your work know yet?"

She shook her head. "They don't need to know, not now, not yet. She has to heal first and then there is the baby. A lot could change."

"I can't see you with a baby, do you want a baby?"

Nia hesitated in answering. She had been very careful about answering that with Colleen. This however was Annie, her best friend forever. "I don't know. I want it to be her decision, not mine."

"I can't see you changing diapers though," she said with a grin at the picture in her head of her elegant and sophisticated friend doing parental duties.

"You never know."

"C'mon, did you ever think you'd have a child?"

Nia had thought about that very thing many times since she had found out Colleen's condition. She remembered back to her own childhood and while her parents had been loving and good parents, she had been an only child. She had never been around babies. She hadn't thought about having one of her own. "I don't know," she answered honestly. "It's not mine," she pointed out.

"If you and Colleen are together, isn't it yours?"

"We've never had that talk."

"Maybe you should," she said quietly and finished the wine.

Nia thought about the conversation the next day at work. It was Friday night and Colleen had called to tell her that she felt well enough to go out to dinner and that Annie and she had a surprise. She wondered what her two best friends had been up to while she had been at work. She couldn't worry about it but it brought a grin to her face in anticipation of what was awaiting her when she got home. She had a lot of work to get done though before she could leave and not the least of which was a new case.

Nia listened to the new client and her husband as they outlined what had happened to them. Frequently the woman was interrupted by her husband and this alone annoyed Nia who had agreed to listen to the woman and wasn't expecting the husband. She wasn't taking new cases due to her workload but had agreed as a favor to one of the partners to listen and give her expertise on it.

"So don't you think the restaurant should pay us for the incident," the husband Robert, Bob he said to call him, kept interjecting. Nia could see he was in this for the money.

The wife, who had tried to tell her story from her viewpoint repeatedly, had instantly gone silent each time Bob voiced his opinion as to his version of the story.

After he had done this for the umpteenth time Nia finally answered his question with, "No, I don't think they should have to pay for this." She said it quietly and without anger although she was fed up with his greed.

"But that one company paid that old woman millions for coffee spilt on her!" he spat angrily.

"You are talking McDonalds paying that woman in New Mexico for the coffee spilt on her lap?" she clarified.

"Yah, she got millions, we should get something for this!" he said with so much enthusiasm Nia thought he was going to come off her couch at her.

"That case was unique and she didn't get millions. The jury awarded her millions but on appeal McDonalds and I think the lady's name was Linebeck or something but she got about half a million. All she had ever wanted was her medical expenses."

"But it was a frivolous lawsuit! All the papers said so..."

No," she interrupted. "It was about negligence. She wasn't even driving. They had stopped to pick up the coffee, her nephew or grandson or someone parked so she could sugar and cream it. She put it between her legs and opened the lid to remove it and accidentally spilled it all over herself. Since she was wearing sweat pants or something it absorbed the overly hot liquid and gave her third degree burns. She had only about twenty thousand in bills," Nia remembered the case from law school.

"But she got a couple of million for fifty cent cup of coffee!" he interrupted again.

"No, she got her medical and lawyer expenses paid for. McDonalds appealed and settled," she repeated. "It was not a frivolous lawsuit at all and the jury got them for negligence for over-heating their coffee."

"But the media said..." he began again and Nia raised her hand.

"Look, her injuries," she said indicating his wife. "Are minor, you are believing media accounts and I have the facts. You can't win this other than making it a nuisance lawsuit. I'm in it to win and I tell you this is not winnable. I'm sorry but I will not take this case," she said firmly with a sorry look to the wife who really did look like she was in pain.

"You're wrong. We can win this with the right attorney!"

"Then I'm sorry, I'm not that attorney and I'm not going to waste anymore of your time," Nia said as she rose from the couch and waited for them to do the same.

"Good attorney my ass, I'm going to speak to Walter about referring us to you!" he threatened.

"You do that, I will be sure to tell him my side of the story as well," Nia answered without batting an eye.

"Goodbye, thank you for your time," the wife said in a small kind voice and the hurried up to catch up with her husband who had already left the office.

Nia shook her head and headed for her phone to call the lawyer who had referred them to her. She wanted it on record what had happened and why she wouldn't take the case.

She didn't take any work home with her this weekend. She wanted some time off from the pressures of work and with Annie as well as Colleen there she wasn't planning on doing anything but relaxing.

"Where are we going?" she asked Annie as they got into a taxi. Colleen and Annie had been waiting and they were impatient as she dressed for an evening out.

"I'm not allowed to tell," Annie said as the taxi took off with the handwritten address Colleen had given him.

Nia rolled her eyes and looked at what they were all wearing. She had dressed up in a nice casual dress that showed off her long legs, was midnight blue in color and held in with a sash at her waist. Colleen was wearing a burgundy dress she hadn't seen her wear before but it looked nice on her and she was wearing flats as she still felt a little uneasy on her feet occasionally. Most of her bruises had faded and were not visible any longer but the it would take time for the cuts and abrasions and the ones on her face she had hidden with makeup. Her black eye was only a faded yellow now. Annie was wearing a sleek pantsuit with a pinstripe down the side that ran from her armpit to the wide lapels on the pants. It looked chic and expensive and Nia was certain she had just bought it recently as she knew she had never seen it before.

As they walked into the little Greek restaurant Nia wondered why they were coming here, she had never been here before and then in front of them there were cries of 'Surprise!' and she could see people from all over that she knew coming forward to hug and kiss her on the cheek. All the women from her Thursday night get-together that she had missed so often with Colleen ill including Tiffany, Eleanor, Nadia, Millie, Gail, and Lila. Then there were people from work, she spotted Priscilla and Betty from human resources, Stewart, his assistant Sally and her assistant Bette, Grayson Morse, Donald and many others from the firm. She smiled as both Suzette and the temp came up to wish her a 'Happy Birthday' and to hug her.

"Were you surprised?" Colleen asked her as she took it all in. It had taken some serious planning and several of the Thursday night girls had helped out as well as Annie when she had called her.

"Very," Nia answered but didn't have the heart to tell her or anyone that it wasn't her birthday. How they had gotten this date she didn't know but she wasn't going to ruin anyone's time by correcting them.

They had a blast as the restaurant served authentic Greek food, smashed dishes, and taught them all traditional dances. Nia was surprised to find herself on the floor in a line, arm in arm with several associates from the firm and kicking her legs out as they danced to traditional Greek dances. Frequent shout outs of "Upa," were heard as they toasted drinking some pretty intense alcoholic beverages. The licorice taste of one such

concoction was delicious but potent. Nia stopped drinking anything but water at one point as she see saw her friends becoming soused.

"Everything okay?" Stewart asked her at one point as he indicated Colleen who sat chatting with others from the secretarial pool and drinking ice water.

"Everything is fine," Nia assured him as she smiled at her girlfriend and then averted her eyes almost guiltily.

"We hope she will be back at work shortly," he told her gesturing with his drink.

"Yes, she told me she would be coming back next week," she informed him. With all the work that had gone into this party Nia was sure others had helped but she was glad Colleen would be back to work soon.

The night was a success and several people helped pack up the many gifts Nia had received and would open at home being careful that the cards were attached to them.

"I've got this batch," Eleanor assured her as she put one more box in the back of her car to take them to Nia's for her.

"You three want a ride?" Millie asked as she finished packing the rest in her car.

"Um, I've got one," Annie told them as she left with one of the associates for an after-party party.

Nia laughed at her fun-loving friend and got in Millie's car with Colleen. They all chatted at the hijinks they had observed at the party and then the three of them got the presents up to Nia's before Eleanor even arrived with the second car.

"Can I interest you ladies in a glass of wine before you go?" Nia offered politely.

Eleanor had noticed how at ease Colleen seemed in Nia's apartment but she had wondered about the assistant a time or two. The two had been friendly at the party but nothing that raised her antennae.

"Oh no, I had some of that Uzo at the party and no more for me tonight," Millie answered shaking her head and putting up a hand in surrender. "But you be sure to host another Thursday night soon okay?" she asked as she left the apartment.

Nia assured her friend that she would and Eleanor who had followed Millie's lead leaned in and asked, "You do like the apartment still?"

"Oh I love it," Nia assured her as she waved them to the elevator and went back in.

Colleen was arranging the presents on the dining room table. "Doesn't this look nice," she gushed over one of the gaily wrapped packages.

"It does," Nia agreed as she locked the front door and turned to her girlfriend whose delight was apparent on her face.

Colleen looked up and smiled at her and asked, "Did you have a good time?"

"I did," she nodded and didn't have the heart to tell her the truth about the date.

"Even though it wasn't your birthday?" Colleen asked with a knowing grin.

"What?" Nia asked surprised. "You knew?"

Colleen walked over to take Nia in her arms, her hands coming around her to hold her body close. She had wanted to do that all night long but couldn't with all the guests around them. "Of course I knew. I know everything about you. Don't you think an efficient personal assistant would know such things?"

"Then why...?" Nia began puzzled.

"Because if we had it when your birthday really is, you wouldn't be surprised," she answered with perfect logic.

Nia started to laugh and then seeing the equally amused look on Colleen's face she leaned down to kiss her. "Thank you," she murmured against her lips.

"You're welcome," Colleen tried to answer back but her lips and then her tongue were busy answering Nia's.

The passion between them flared and as it had been several weeks since they made love it was mutual, very mutual. Nia hadn't wanted to unintentionally hurt Colleen and Colleen had noticed how careful Nia was towards and around her. Not so now, she held her firmly in her arms as she kissed her deeply, passionately, and very very deliberately to arouse her.

"God I've missed this," Nia breathed as she nibbled at her lips.

"I've missed you," Colleen said fervently as she cupped Nia's ass and ground against her suggestively.

Nia groaned into her mouth as she raised a leg to wrap it around the smaller woman, the dress helped facilitate that and she ground back against her. "Let's take this upstairs," she murmured imagining them doing this naked.

They barely made it into the bedroom before they were pulling each other's clothes off. The party had allowed them both to dress up, look exceptionally attractive, but with a hands off approach it had wetted both of their appetites.

Colleen was easily able to pull Nia's dress from her tall body; the slip she was wearing beneath it revealed that she was only wearing the slip...and nothing else. Colleen groaned as she realized how naked Nia had been all night and only yards away from her. The thought made her extra wet as she realized she would get to possess her momentarily.

Nia grinned mischievously at what was revealed. She had felt like being a little naughty tonight and thought no one would know. She certainly hadn't expected a party in her honor with her business partners, her friends, and everyone delaying her getting home from what she thought was dinner out with two friends. It had worried her for a while and she didn't sit down the entire night just in case her disarray would be revealed but now that it was over she was laughing at herself over it and seeing Colleen's reaction delighted her.

"Oh gawd, what you do to me," Colleen breathed as she buried her face between Nia's breasts. Being shorter than Nia was making her the perfect height to nuzzle in like this. Never could she have imagined falling in love with her boss or a woman for that matter. But love her she did and touching her was such a great thrill. Nia seemed to enjoy touching her as well and the pleasure she gave to her showed how much she loved her on so many levels.

Nia quickly removed Colleen's clothes and not that she hadn't seen her body in the weeks since the attack, but she had averted her eyes from the many bruises and abrasions. With the pajamas that Colleen had chosen to wear it hadn't been too appealing but now, now she wanted to touch every inch of her, to taste her, to make her gasp in delight. Once the clothes were gone Nia pulled Colleen's naked body against her own satin slip, the coolness of the material against Colleen's skin making her nipples harden. Nia had to taste. Colleen's head fell back from the sensation as her lips make contact with her neck. Slowly she kissed her way down Colleen's neck to her chest and towards the already erect nipples aching for attention. Her mouth wrapped around the hard little nub and she glanced up to see Colleen arch into the sensations that her lips were causing at her center. Her hand massaged the other white orb.

"It's been so long," Colleen whined a little as she enjoyed what Nia was doing to her and let her.

"Too long," Nia agreed as she pushed her back onto the bed and kissed her way down across her belly. Was it her imagination or did Colleen actually have a rounded little belly now? She wondered if it was all in her mind but ever since she had learned of her condition she had looked for some signs that she was pregnant. She had even read a little up on it on the internet hoping to understand what would be happening to her and her body soon and not having had an interest in it for her own body...ever. She found herself fascinated by the changes she was already seeing in Colleen's body and she was still not certain what Colleen had decided about the baby but she was certain her breasts were already fuller.

Colleen was feeling a whirlwind of emotions. She could tell she was horny beyond anything she had felt before. The doctor had explained the changes in her body was due to the baby growing inside of it and she had

denied it as long as she could, already her jeans were a tad bit tighter and her breasts hurt. Nia's touching them though triggered a release that she hadn't expected and caused her to clutch the woman to her harder than she intended and pull her up for a kiss but she *wanted, needed* her so incredibly much at the moment. "I want you so much," she whispered as she nuzzled into Nia's neck under her hair and along her long neck under her ear.

Nia leaned back down to where she was slowly but surely making her way down to the juncture between Colleen's legs. She could smell the distinctly musky odor that told her how aroused her lover was and she couldn't wait to play with it. When Colleen pulled her up for her kisses she was grateful but she wanted to taste her lower lips now, *right* now and hear her excitement from what she was doing to her. She nudged her legs apart with her leg and then insinuated the second one between them spreading her as her hips eased between them spreading them further for her body. She had Colleen's legs over the edge and as she shimmied down her body caressing and kissing her way south she took first one and then the other and placed them over her shoulders so she could nuzzle between them, spreading the wet lips that presented themselves to her so enticingly. Eagerly she leaned in for a lick, smiling to herself as Colleen arched to present herself more, her legs unconsciously clenching at the sensations. She was gratified to know that she could cause such reactions in her lover.

Colleen knew how lucky she was to find out that Nia loved her much less that she could cause her to lose control of her body. Never had Cletus caused her arousal to such fever pitch and while she was young enough that she knew her body could become aroused, he hadn't cared enough beyond his own needs to take care of her in that way. Nia engendered fantasies she hadn't known she could have. She had found herself thinking deliciously naughty thoughts about her ever since they had become lovers and she was grateful for the turn of events that had brought them together. Her only worry was that it would end now that she was pregnant with Cletus' baby. Nia hadn't really spoken to her about it and she hadn't brought it up because of her fear of rejection. Meanwhile, she was going to enjoy any and all affection that Nia bestowed upon her.

As Nia played, first with her breasts this triggered a corresponding tug and wetness between her legs and then when she went down to lick and suck on the hard nub that rose up and demanded attention, Colleen just laid back and enjoyed the sensations that Nia engendered inside of her. She seemed to know what Colleen needed and wanted. Colleen didn't care what Nia did to her as long as she loved her but it was a bonus to feel so incredibly good from her lovemaking.

Nia enjoyed the feel of Colleen's body under her as her fingers played along with her tongue. The angle was perfect and she knelt willingly

between her girlfriends legs as she thrust her tongue and then later her fingers inside of her. Her tongue laved attention on the erect little clit and she gently sucked and tongued it taking absolute delight in the reactions of Colleen beneath her.

Colleen reached down to twine her fingers in Nia's hair and hold her head there as she ground down against her lips, tongue, and fingers. "I want. I need," she babbled incoherently as the sensations threatened to overwhelm her. Her other hand lay there at her shoulder clenching and unclenching unconsciously in supplication.

Nia smiled into Colleen's clit as she sensed her extreme arousal, hell she could taste it as Colleen gushed into her mouth in her enthusiasm. Her body was clenched tightly around her fingers.

"I need more," Colleen managed to gasp out as her body writhed trying to orgasm against Nia.

"What do you need babe?"

"The double-headed," she rasped out as her body responded to yet another thrust by Nia's agile fingers.

"Oh no, not while you are pregnant," Nia refused her and then while Colleen considered begging she added another finger to her thrusting. This difference was all it took as Colleen was sent over the edge at the fullness inside of her. Her body bucked and writhed as it orgasmed under Nia's ministrations.

Nia grinned at what she had caused in Colleen. It was so fulfilling to know she could make her lose control. She felt bad denying her the dildo she had requested but felt it would be better if they no longer used the toys that they both enjoyed while Colleen was pregnant. She had a mental image of thrusting it inside her lover and hitting the kid in its head. Slowly, ever so slowly she stopped her thrusting and pulling her fingers out one by one she licked them as Colleen gazed with lust filled eyes.

"C'mere," she rasped as she tried to pull Nia up her now sweaty body.

Nia smiled as she rubbed her body against her lover, the heat from it warming her and inflaming her aroused body. She hoped Colleen wasn't too tired to take care of her but if she was it was going to have to be a self-service moment as she needed fulfilment and soon.

"I love you," Colleen told her emotionally as she kissed her on the lips, tasting her own musky flavor on them.

"I love you too," Nia repeated almost automatically as she leaned her hips into Colleens suggestively.

Colleen gasped at the sensation, she always did. Once she had her orgasm, any additional pleasure always surprised her. Nia seemed to want to extend her pleasure for as long as she could and Colleen loved her for that generosity. She could only return the favor as she rolled so that she was on top of Nia and pressing down.

Nia smiled as she wrapped her legs around her lover's body feeling a fulfilment she had never felt with others. She knew and could appreciate the difference after being disappointed for so long. She felt almost complete with Colleen and yet something was missing, something she couldn't put her finger on yet but was niggling in the back of her brain. She wasn't going to analyze it now though as feeling Colleen against her was arousing her and she needed to have that outlet, that ultimate feeling of fulfillment that only Colleen could give her.

Colleen returned the smile as she leaned down to kiss her lover in gratitude taking her lips firmly as she plunged her tongue inside and dueled with Nia's agile tongue as they enjoyed each other. Her hands firmly caressed down Nia's long body removing the slip that was between them and the sensation of the satin and skin between them pleased them both. For Nia it was the warmth of Colleen's body on her own, the caresses helping arouse her. "Can I use a toy on you?" Colleen asked, almost in permission but more to ascertain what Nia wanted. At Nia's nod she reached up and over to the bedside table and opened the drawer where the toys were kept. Nia leaned back a little to let Colleen reach but her eyes took on a decided gleam as she came up with the rabbit and turned it on to make sure the batteries worked. Without looking she reached down between Nia's legs as her lips began to dance along Nia's jaw and neck and down to her breasts. With how wet Nia had become it was effortless to thrust the toy inside of her and she gasped in delight at the sensation. Letting go of control was a hard issue with Nia but with Colleen it was easy and she lost herself in the sensations caused by her lover as she thrust inside of her for a while rousing her to a fever pitch before turning on the ears of the rabbit and grinding them against her overly-sensitized clit.

"Oh oh ohhhhh," she groaned out as her body immediately went into convulsions. She grasped onto Colleen to hold her to her body as she arched up and the thrusts and rabbit ears continued to play havoc with her body. Her grasp became almost painful and the veins stood out on her neck as she almost fought the sensations and yet her body clenched against the toy. "Oh my god, oh my god," she cried out as she came so hard that she lost her sight for a moment as it swam before her. "Shit, shit, shit," she cried as it seemed to go on for an inordinate amount of time before beginning to calm. As Colleen stopped the thrust and turned down the ears she slowly relaxed her body and enjoyed the coming down.

Colleen smiled knowing that sometimes wild and hard was what she needed and while she was disappointed that they hadn't tried out the double headed which she had come to really enjoy she loved what she had just done to the normally reserved Nia. When she let go like she just had she was actually quite incredible to see and she appreciated that it was because of what she did to the woman. Smiling she gently brought her

lover down from the incredible high she had achieved before turning everything off and pulling the toy from her body and dropping it to the side. "Are you okay?" she asked the familiar refrain that was between them.

"Mmmhmmm," Nia drawled out from the intensity of the orgasm. She didn't want it to end but at the same time knew she needed to come down from it. It was really fantastic after the couple of weeks they hadn't made love that had built up almost a residual effect to her body. As Colleen attempted to roll off her and lay next to her, Nia's hands came up to capture her naked body to her own. She reached down to hold her naked cheeks in the palms of her hands squeezing them slightly as she held her lover in place against her.

"Ohhhh," Colleen gasped at the sensation. She loved lying against Nia but being the heavier of the two was more conscious of her weight and now with being pregnant she wasn't sure she wasn't too heavy on the much thinner and taller woman.

"That feels nice," Nia murmured against her hair.

"Oh yes," she answered dreamily her head tucked into Nia's neck as her nose took in the scent of sex in the air and the personal odor of Nia that was so arousing to her senses.

"I think you could lay here forever and I wouldn't mind," Nia said with a smile.

Colleen could tell Nia was smiling as she felt the muscles of her face against her head and she smiled in return. Nia rarely spoke non-sensical things but when they made love the closeness was so special. Slowly though they both became aware that they were outside the blankets and Colleen had worked up a sweat in their lovemaking. She began to squirm uncomfortably.

"Are you okay?" Nia asked her sleepily. She could have slept with Colleen on her body clasped to her body by her hands on her buttocks.

"I'm getting cold," she complained good-naturedly and then hearing a noise from downstairs remembered that they had a guest in the apartment that was due home anytime.

Nia released her so she could roll to the side. She too had remembered that Annie was staying the weekend with them and she got up to pull the top blanket down for her lover to scoot in under the blankets and between the sheets. She headed to the bedroom door to close and lock it so Annie wouldn't interrupt them as she returned to the bed to slip in beside Colleen. "Sleepy?" she asked unnecessarily as her lover cuddled in next to her and put an arm across her rib cage.

"Mmm," Colleen answered and in moments was snoring lightly next to Nia.

Nia laid there a while before she too succumbed to sleep; it had been a full day.

LAWYERED

❧ CHAPTER TWENTY ONE ❧

"Welcome back Colleen," and "Welcome back," greeted her left and right as she made her way towards Nia's office. Nia had been stopped by one of Stewart's assistants at the elevator for a meeting with the partner's and had veered away towards the conference room.

"Hi Colleen, I have your paperwork for you," Priscilla from human resources was waiting at her desk for her with another woman.

"Paperwork?" Colleen asked confused.

"For the classes you are taking to become a paralegal?" Priscilla frowned as she wondered if Colleen should still be out on leave from the attack or if she had changed her mind about the classes.

"Oh yes, I had almost forgotten that," Colleen laughed. She hadn't been expecting that first thing on her return.

"And this is Lynda," Priscilla introduced a woman Colleen vaguely knew from the secretarial pool.

"Hello Lynda," Colleen nodded.

"Colleen, nice to see you back," Lynda returned.

"Thank you."

"Lynda is interested in the position you will be vacating and as you said you would train your replacement…" Priscilla explained.

For a second Colleen felt as though she were dizzy and was going to be sick. It felt as though she was going to be fired. She must have paled a bit as Priscilla looked alarmed.

"Are you all right?" she asked in a worried voice.

"Oh yes," she returned brightly. She had said she would train her replacement but as she glanced at her desk, the desk Nia had let her pick out and the outer office she had decorated she felt a sense of loss. No one had let her have such freedom to do something like that before. She didn't want to leave but she understood Nia wanted more for her. Nia had said that if anyone ever found out they were a couple it could cause a scandal.

"Well Linda is going to shadow you for a few days and if Nia doesn't scare her off," Priscilla offered a grin to show she was kidding but everyone there including Suzette who was listening avidly knew she wasn't. "She will learn your job from you before you leave to go work and shadow someone in the paralegal pool," she said practically.

Colleen had known it would work like that and now that she realized the date she knew she would be starting classes shortly but with the attack and her time off and everything else on her plate it had gone so fast she wasn't prepared. She smiled gamely though at Lynda and Priscilla and nodded. "Of course," she agreed. Colleen pulled up a chair to her desk for

Lynda to sit on once Priscilla left and began explaining the procedures that she had put in place to help Nia's office run smoothly and effortlessly from paperwork to the cappuccino machine.

"Good luck with that," Suzette gripped, she had never mastered that complicated little machine and it annoyed her no end.

Colleen ignored Suzette as she put a real effort into training Lynda who seemed to pick up things a lot quicker than she had. She resented her to a degree but didn't let it show. Lynda seemed nice enough and wanted to learn but it was obvious she was intimidated by Nia when she returned.

"And who is this?" Nia asked as she walked into the outer office where they all were.

"This is Lynda, Priscilla brought her up," Colleen explained feeling a little hurt that she hadn't been consulted and Nia had picked her replacement without her.

"For?" Nia asked distractedly as she began to go through some of the mail that sitting on the edge of the desk for her.

"My replacement?" Colleen asked dryly trying to remind Nia.

"Your replacement?" Nia asked looking up but seeing the warning in Colleen's eyes she nodded and looked warmly at Lynda. "I hope you will be very happy here," she said not meaning a word of it but causing resentment in Suzette who hadn't been welcomed like this when she came on board.

"I'm sure I will be, Colleen has been showing me around and so far it seems very straight forward," Lynda said respectfully. Nia Toyomoto had a reputation for chewing up assistants and didn't suffer fools gladly; there was already a betting pool of how long Lynda would last. The fact that Colleen had lasted years under her dictatorship had garnered a few people's respect.

Nia nodded in reply and taking her mail went into her office closing the door.

Nia drove Colleen to work as she always did. There was a notice on her vehicle warning her not to park in the space behind the building where she lived anymore. She had forgotten she had gotten notice that they were going to be building a parking structure where the current parking lot was located and would start construction shortly. That meant she would have to park on the street, a precarious prospect at any time on the busy city streets. It was going to really suck if she had to run in to the apartment from down the street or further. The paperwork on the construction had said they would have it built in time for winter but knowing how often that didn't happen she wasn't optimistic.

"This is going to be fun," she said sarcastically as she and Colleen got in the Lexus.

"Think of it as a challenge," Colleen grinned as she teased her.

"Uh huh," Nia answered as she negotiated the already heavy early morning traffic.

As they parked in Nia's parking spot at the office she wondered if she would have a 'spot' in the parking structure. When they rode up in the elevator together she waited until a few people got off before she asked Colleen to look into the paperwork for the new parking structure and if she would have to 'buy' one of the parking spots for her car to park it next to her building. They were discussing it when they got off the elevator on the partner's level.

"Ms. Toyomoto?" a hesitant voice stopped Nia as she headed towards her offices with Colleen.

"Yes?" Nia asked irritably. She didn't like the weak voice of Stewart's second assistant. Bette was a timid little thing and for some reason it irked her.

"A meeting has been called for all partner's first thing," she answered visibly intimidated by Nia and swallowing nervously.

"Do I have time to get my cappuccino?" she asked with a grin directed at Colleen. Not many of the associates or assistants knew Nia even had a sense of humor and this startled Bette.

"They have coffee, donuts, and fruit all set up in the conference room," she was told.

Nia sighed, this was a mandatory meeting then and she nodded and headed off in a different direction away from her offices and Colleen went on to them.

"Ah Nia, good morning," Grayson said when he spotted her.

"What's going on, I got shanghaied at the elevator?" Nia asked.

"Security meeting," he said briefly before greeting someone behind her.

Nia looked around and saw most but not all the partners were present. It wasn't necessary to have everyone around the large table and she wondered what this was about. Then spotting Stewart she began to make her way towards him across the large room but he turned and with a gavel got the meeting in order.

"Places people places, everyone take a seat," he commanded.

Nia grabbed an empty seat and put her briefcase next to her on the floor as she looked up to listen.

"As everyone knows we had one of our own attacked a couple of weeks back," he began. Nia squirmed mentally realizing he was talking about Colleen, *her* Colleen.

"Since then," he continued. "We've looked into private security for the firm, it's a good idea and with the size and scope of our clientele a necessary evil in this day and age."

"I've been interviewing firms for the past couple of weeks and we have narrowed it down to this firm," he gestured and with that several people walked in.

Nia nearly gasped as she recognized Simone, Alice Weaver's ex-roommate from college. They had still been friends when Alice died. In fact Simone had been living in Alice's loft when Alice's wife Kathy had come to claim the property. She had since heard that she had moved out to her own place. She had never expected to see Simone again. She watched as the blonde followed two men up to the front of the meeting to be introduced. She didn't hear the introductions as she stared at the blonde hard.

Stewart explained that they would be putting in wireless camera's at certain locations in the firm on all the floors to supplement the buildings own security measures. "We will be hiring guards that work exclusively for Chase-Dunham and will keep us all safer."

Nia knew the moment that Simone recognized her as she was looking at each and every one of the partners present in the meeting. It was hardly more than a cursory glance but lasted longer than the others. Later as the partners asked their questions she caught Simone looking at her more than once. The little mix and mingle before partners started going back to their own office allowed her to approach the blonde. A slight shake of the head warned her not to acknowledge that they knew one another as Stewart introduced her to one of the 'owners' of the security firm they had just hired.

Nia was puzzled as she hadn't known that Simone worked for a security firm much less owned one. In fact she hadn't known that Simone even really worked. When they had partied with Alice and her friends she got the impression that Simone didn't do a lot of anything and any inquires had produced vague answers so figuring it was none of her business she had let the subject drop. She herself had work to do so with one last glance at the security specialists they had hired she headed back to her offices as she had a meeting for later that morning to prepare for and this meeting had put her behind a little.

"Nia, got a minute?" Stewart stopped her on her way to the elevator.

Nia looked up from the paperwork she was reading as she walked along and smiled at the senior partner. "If you'd care to ride with me I do," she answered as she gestured towards the elevator.

"I do," he said with a disarming smile as the door opened and a couple of employees got off. The box was empty as they got in and Nia pushed the fifth floor where her car was parked.

"You withdrew from the Mancini case?" Stewart began as soon the doors closed.

Nia stuffed the papers in her case to face him and talk to him directly realizing what this was about. She nodded. "Yes, I did," she answered without elaborating which she knew would annoy most people but as a lawyer he used the same tactics to people.

"Would you care to tell me why?" he asked and inwardly smiled. This was a game that lawyers played, with other people, with other lawyers, with judges. Nia was one of the best.

She smiled. "If I said 'no' you'd still want to know though wouldn't you?"

He chuckled and nodded waiting patiently.

"Henri was cooking the books," she said simply. "My investigations showed that and I refused to represent him."

"But Nia, not all our cases are winnable and the Mancini case means a lot of prestige. He also requested you specifically," he answered exasperated.

"It wasn't a matter of winning the case and I could have but I didn't like the way I would have had to do it. I do have a conscience," she said with a raised eyebrow. She knew that having a conscience as a lawyer was a tricky thing.

"So he skimmed a few bucks. You know if we only represent the innocent we will go out of business. Is that any reason to withdraw?"

She nodded. "That and the fact that he nearly assaulted me when I refused to date him," she answered and then put up a hand at Stewarts angry look of concern. "Verbally, not physically," she qualified.

He nodded realizing it was an integrity issue, not just a moral one. He understood that and while the repercussions would hurt their firm when he went elsewhere, they could put a spin on it that made people wonder why they had released the client.

Nia could see the wheels spin in Stewarts perfectly coiffured head. She respected him. He had been her mentor for a long time and championed her becoming a partner. She also knew him to be a lethal lawyer when necessary and while he didn't mind bending the rules, he wouldn't break them and for that she respected him.

"Well then of course you were justified in refusing to represent him," he said as though that settled the matter.

Nia knew it might not. Even though she was a partner, other partners felt they had the right to question each other's decisions and authority and as one of the youngest and newest partners they still wanted to treat her as

an associate occasionally. Only the fact that she was good, *very* good at her job kept her on top of things and out of their crosshairs.

"Have a nice day," Stewart said to her absentmindedly as he put his facile mind to the problem at hand and let her off on the fifth floor.

Nia got out of the elevator just as thoughtfully and smiled at her boss as she made her way to her car. It still unnerved her occasionally that Colleen's husband Cletus had managed to evade arrest and had been on this very floor next to the spot where her car was parked and hurt Colleen. If she looked very hard she thought she could still see the blood stain on the concrete that had been washed down. She got into her Lexus and started it up. She didn't know if she was imagining it but she thought she saw someone watching her. She blew it off as her over active imagination and a lot on her mind.

Parking on the street was just as difficult as Nia had thought it would be. She let Colleen off in front of the building and proceeded to drive around and around until she found a spot only to get cut off and have it stolen from her. The joy of living with other New Yorkers. She finally found a spot but it was a block and a half from the apartment and she wasn't happy with the arrangement. As she walked towards her apartment building she saw they had already ripped up the parking lot next to it in anticipation of building the parking structure.

"Here it is," Colleen showed her the paperwork she had received as an owner of an apartment in the building. It explained exactly what was involved in the building of the parking structure, who would get first choice in the parking lottery that would be used to choose spaces. Spaces could be then 'traded' to other tenants in not only their building but the one next door as they shared the structure that they assured all tenants would only take a few months to build. Nia looked it over, filled out the paperwork to send it in the next day and enclosed a check for her deposit for the lottery.

"This is really screwed up, on top of my mortgage I'll have to pay annual fees for parking!" she said shaking her head at how people nickel and dimed others to death in the city. "I should move out to the country and commute," she threatened.

"Oh, come move by me!" Annie enthused.

Nia looked over at her friend and asked, "And what are you still doing here?"

"Well, I didn't have to be back at work until Wednesday..." she began with a grin knowing she annoyed Nia now and then.

"And we are the cheapest hotel in town?" Nia finished for her with an answering grin as she watched her help herself to some food.

"And Colleen cooks better than any hotel," Annie finished for herself.

Colleen looked up in gratitude from the dinner she was creating for the three of them. She didn't mind, she liked cooking and Nia's kitchen was a dream to work in. Some nights Nia insisted they order out but they rarely *went* out anymore.

The three of them enjoyed a nice dinner together, Colleen effortlessly included in their friendly banter and friendship. Annie was genuinely surprised that Nia and Colleen were an undeclared couple but hearing about the new secretary that Colleen was training she thought she understood why. "So if you two work together it's a problem but once Colleen becomes a paralegal you can date?" she asked.

"Something like that," Nia answered as she blushed slightly.

Colleen squirmed a little but nodded.

Later when they were in bed Nia asked her out right, "Are you okay with the new position?"

Colleen smiled at her concern. "Yes, it's exciting to start school tomorrow but I'll miss working with you and taking care of you," she admitted.

Nia smiled as she leaned in to tenderly kiss her. "I'll miss you too but we will have this," she reminded her.

"Then you want me to stay?" Colleen asked surprised.

"What do you mean do I want you stay?" she asked alarmed as she frowned at her.

"Well I thought with this," she gestured at her stomach. "That things might have changed." She looked down ashamed and eagerly anticipated what Nia would say. They hadn't really talked about it and she didn't want to force the issue.

"Anything you want and decide I'm okay with," Nia told her truthfully and fully believed it.

Colleen decided to be brave as she looked up into Nia's beautiful brown eyes and asked, "But what do you want?"

"Whatever you want..." Nia started to say the party line but was interrupted by Colleen.

"But what do YOU want?" she asked forcefully.

Nia grinned ruefully. She had been hedging. She had watched Colleen and wondered what she was going to do about the baby. They certainly couldn't ignore it and now that they were both aware of it, she had seen Colleen on more than one occasion cupping her belly as though she was feeling for the tiny infant inside of her. She had wondered what Colleen would decide. "I really do want whatever you want," she began and held up her hand when she was about to be interrupted. "For me though, I kind of like the idea of having a little one around. I don't think I will ever have a child of my own," she confessed as she looked earnestly into Colleen's

worried and troubled eyes. "If you want to keep the baby, I will help you in any way I can. I don't know how much help I will be as I've never been around children, but if I can help you, I will."

Colleen was surprised. She had thought Nia would encourage her to give it up. Ever since she was a child she had wanted a child of her own. Married to Cletus though she hadn't thought that dream would ever come true. "What about Cletus though?" she asked worried about that.

"Well, after his attack on you, when they find him, *if* they find him…he's going to jail as it violates his being out on bail and I'm pretty certain he isn't going to beat the drug rap much less his original assault on you," she answered matter of factly. Seeing the relief on Colleen's face she added, "This will be your baby, not his. Maybe ours," she said gently.

Colleen couldn't believe the relief she felt at hearing this from Nia. She hadn't expected it. The sweetness of it though made her wrap her arms around her and pull her close. "I thought you would want to give it up," she sobbed into her neck.

"Only if that's what you wanted," Nia countered as she hugged her back just as hard and patted her. She tried to pull back to look at the crying woman but Colleen had her in a choke hold.

"I thought you wouldn't want the bother, babies take up a lot of room," she sobbed and hiccupped.

Nia chuckled. "They don't take up that much room; they actually take up very little. It's when they become teenagers that you want a room between you and them and we can worry about that then," she told her amused.

Colleen pulled back to look at Nia and to make sure she was serious. "You think we will last that long?" she asked earnestly.

Nia's look was one of puzzlement as she asked, "You don't?"

Colleen smiled through her tears in delight. "I wasn't sure. I hoped. But I didn't want to presume," she started to cry again.

Nia smiled and shook her head. "I think we need to communicate more," she said understating the obvious. "I want you to stay, indefinitely. I love you Colleen."

"I love you too," she cried as she began a new round of sobbing in happiness and tried to hide it in Nia's neck.

"Now, enough of that," Nia stated uncomfortably. She knew Colleen was happy but this was getting ridiculous…and uncomfortable.

Colleen wasn't finished with her though as she asked, "But what are we going to do about Cletus, it's his child too and now that he knows…"

Nia knew that too. "I'm not a family lawyer but maybe we should look into getting his parental rights terminated since he did attack you and he is such a fine, upstanding member of the community," she finished sarcastically.

Colleen chuckled but the worry didn't go away. She might not be a lawyer but even she knew they didn't arbitrarily eliminate a parents rights. Although she let the conversation drop she couldn't stop her thoughts. Slowly she relaxed and fell asleep next to Nia who took a lot longer to fall to sleep as she wondered at what would come next between them.

Lynda learned so fast and was so competent that Colleen felt grossly inadequate next to her. The day that she found Nia and Lynda laughing over something she felt the knife of jealousy twisting in her chest. She knew the two weeks that human resources had set for her training period wouldn't be necessary so she went to Priscilla to see if she could start her new position earlier.

"Lynda is really quite good, she doesn't need to shadow me or have me hovering over her anymore," she praised the replacement while all the while she was hoping she would somehow screw up. Not really as it would affect Nia and she didn't wish that on her at all.

Priscilla was pleased as so far they hadn't heard any complaints about Lynda or from Lynda with working with the difficult Nia Toyomoto. She had worried about out maneuvering Nia over interviewing Lynda but it had all worked out it seemed. She took Colleen's advisement under consideration and arranged to have her start her research in legal. Although she couldn't do what a paralegal did she could assist them and learn the job until she was qualified to take on the title.

"You're leaving me?" Nia asked surprised and a little hurt to be losing her early.

"You don't need me and Lynda is fantastic," she said forcing herself to be bright and cheery.

Nia had to admit Lynda was a good assistant, much better than Suzette who crumbled every time they had to work together on anything. She wasn't however Colleen, and Nia would miss seeing her a bunch of times a day. She sighed and nodded and rose to give Colleen a hug. "I'll miss seeing you all day," she said and remembering the time she had seduced her in the office she was tempted to repeat that.

Colleen was remembering the seduction as well and knew that glimmer in Nia's eye. It made her feel good to know that this powerful and brilliant woman desired her. *Her.* Little ole Colleen. She was proud to be Nia's girlfriend and wanted to shout it from the tallest building but discretion was best for both of them at this point and she and Nia both knew it. Her leaving Nia's office meant that there would be no impropriety and anyone who mentioned it after the fact wouldn't have a leg to stand on, there was no proof that they started seeing each other before her move within the firm. "I'll see you every night," she promised.

"After your courses and then you will have homework," Nia bitched good-naturedly. She was so proud of Colleen and how far she had come. The little mouse was blooming in more ways than one and she was happy that she had contributed a little to it. Seeing her build self-confidence slowly but surely was impressive. She had seen the potential but had never thought that it was her love that would bring the woman out of her shell. She thought of it as totally Colleen's own doing.

"Oh no, does that mean you will have to cook?" Colleen teased and then gasped for affect.

They both grinned knowing that cooking was not Nia's forte at all. "We are going to starve," Nia said dryly as she smiled down into Colleen's face.

Their lives seemed to calm down for a while. Colleen had school several nights a week so their time together was limited. She was also becoming tired more often as the pregnancy continued. Nia didn't know really what to do with her but tried to make things easier whenever she could even to buying a great second hand Mercedes for her to get to and from school in. It was safe, it was luxurious, and it was convenient for the now obviously pregnant woman.

"I don't need that," Colleen had protested.

"I want to know you aren't out there so late without your own vehicle," Nia countered.

"I can take a cab." With not having to share her money with Cletus she actually was able to save a good bit of the money she earned. Nia wouldn't take 'rent' but she didn't object to her stocking the kitchen with delicious food that neither really had the time to prepare.

"No, I'd rather you use the Lexus but there are some nights I need it," she worried as she thought about the meetings where she had to leave work early and meet with a client or other lawyers at their home or at a dinner and a cab wasn't always convenient. So she went out without Colleen's help or advice and bought her the Mercedes.

"It's just such a hassle to find parking," Colleen complained good-naturedly. It wasn't really that much of a problem but she already felt like she was ballooning up and walking for any length of time made her ankles swell.

Nia had taken her in her arms and said in a no-nonsense way, "I want to know you are safe and a cab that late at night isn't the answer."

Colleen preened at the caring tone in Nia's voice. She had surprised her in so many ways even going to child birth classes with her. They were one of many same-sex couples and it really was enlightening for both of them.

"You don't expect me to cut the cord or anything do you?" Nia had asked with distaste.

Laughing at the taller woman she had hugged her and said, "No, I just want you to be there." Colleen was thrilled that Nia was going to be there for her through all of it. She had dreams of them raising the child together.

"Do you know the sex?" Nadia asked at one of the Thursday night get-togethers that Colleen was able to make with her now infinitely busier schedule.

"No I don't, I want it to be a surprise," she answered truthfully even though she knew Nia wanted to know so that they could turn the spare bedroom into blue or pink...she had chosen yellow which was neutral enough for either. Nia was having fun finding things for the decoration of their nursery when she had the time to shop. She glanced at Nia and quickly looked away, they still hadn't told anyone they were a couple and she didn't want to blow their 'cover.' Even driving to the get together in separate cars protected them to a degree.

"So where are you living these days?" Eleanor asked. She had seen the older Mercedes that Colleen driven and wondered how much they paid their legal assistants over at Chase-Dunham.

"With a friend," Colleen answered airily, deliberately keeping it vague as all these women knew Nia much better than they did her and she didn't want to cause any waves in their friendships. She glanced towards each of the women and saw Nia was in earnest conversation with Tiffany who imported things from all over the world which had gotten her in hot water a few times.

"Are you ready to buy your own place?" Eleanor persisted, ever the consummate saleswoman.

"No, not yet," she said blushingly. She always felt a little over-whelmed by women like Eleanor, a little too pushy for her liking.

Eleanor looked at the younger woman knowingly as though she had a secret that they alone knew but she glanced at Nia as well wondering about their relationship since Colleen's promotion.

"Do you have any names picked out?" Nadia persisted hoping to trip Colleen up so she would reveal the sex of the baby. She had seen something at the baby department in Sacks that she really wanted to buy and since Colleen was the only pregnant woman she knew she wanted it to be for the right sex.

"No, since I don't know the sex I haven't really decided on one," she shook her head as she answered.

The women had been really supportive since they found about her 'accident' as everyone called it. The attack and her subsequent pregnancy had really given them food to gossip about between them when their own news wasn't much to share. Nia had already arranged for a baby shower

for the following Thursday with help from Annie, Sally from the firm, and a few others. It was going to be a blast and she was looking forward to it if she could just get Colleen to go.

"Oh I don't know, I'm so tired. You go without me," she complained the night of the shower. Nia had been trying to persuade her to go out to meet with the women for the usual Thursday night get together.

"You know soon enough that you are going to be stuck in the apartment recovering. You should get out while you can," Nia tried.

Colleen wasn't looking forward to that. She had arranged with the school to do a lot of home studies for the weeks she would be out but without work she wasn't sure how she was going to fill her days. Her teacher at the child-birthing courses had been amused when she heard that one. The baby should fill her days quite nicely.

"I'm just so tired. They can miss me one night."

"You only went last week, you hadn't been in weeks. Come on, I'm not taking no for an answer. I'll drive you if you are too tired," she offered.

Colleen had no clue and was totally surprised as they walked in to the multitude of people and their yells of, "Surprise!" She was shocked to see the turnout including people from work and the normal group of women they met with on Thursdays. Nia had included some of the men she now worked with as well. Colleen would hear later how frightened the men had been when Nia personally showed up in their work area to invite them. When asked later Nia said she had been told it was the 'to do' thing in this day and age and that men weren't excluded from such parties anymore.

Nia had refused to include the stupid baby games that some people insisted on but a few of the women did it anyway but enough women and men didn't participate and merely watched and had a good time as the pregnant woman was showered with gifts and really felt extra special for one of the few times in her life. When her mother walked in near the end of the party she couldn't stop crying over it.

"You came? You came?" she couldn't get over that her mother had been brave enough to come despite what her father must have said or dictated.

"Well someone named Nia insisted and she even sent a car for me," her mother said as she took in how pregnant her daughter really was. While she didn't approve of her divorcing Cletus she knew she didn't have the full story and her husband wouldn't allow her to participate otherwise. She had had to lie to come to this and the whole drive had been fearful of the repercussions but seeing Colleen like this she was so grateful she had come.

"You have to meet Nia, she was the best boss," Colleen told her joyfully.

"Was? You don't work there anymore? How are you going to afford this baby?" she began worriedly. If Colleen moved home there would be hell to pay.

"Relax Mom. I just transferred within the firm. I'm back in school so I can become a paralegal. Who knows, maybe someday I'll be a lawyer," she teased. She looked at her mother raptly having not seen her in so long because of Cletus and her father. She looks so tired and worn out...so old before her time, she thought. "Nia though helped arrange the shower and my friends," her arm encompassed those who had come and she considered friends, "They all came," she said proudly. She was urging her mother over to where Nia was standing drinking a martini with Eleanor and Millie, the trio looking very powerful and intimidating in their power suits.

"Nia," Colleen started to get her attention from the others. "I'd like you to meet my mother Jolene Picket." She turned to her mother and said, "Mom, I'd like you to meet my old boss, Nia Toyomoto."

"Old?" Nia murmured in amusement as Eleanor and Millie hid their own amusement. "How do you do Mrs. Picket, I hope the ride wasn't too strenuous?" she asked courteously seeing how tired out the woman appeared.

"Oh no, that was a right nice car you sent for me to see my baby, thank you so much for everything," she said sincerely.

"I'm so glad you could make it. I can see Colleen is really happy to have you here," Nia said graciously.

"You're not at all what I expected from Colleen's descriptions," she said ingeniously. "You don't look Oriental at all," she said turning her head sideways as though to get another view.

Nia wasn't sure how to respond to that and glanced at Colleen who was laughing at her mother and shaking her head as she rolled her eyes. "Mom, let's get you something to drink," she said to get her away from the women who were about to burst a seam from what she could see from those that had overheard.

"Well I don't want nothing that's too strong. You know how I feel about such," she said as she glanced at the drink Colleen was holding.

"It's lemon water Mom, nothing stronger," Colleen assured her as she put her arm around her to lead her off.

"Old eh Nia?" Millie teased as soon as the older frumpy woman was out of earshot.

"I'll give you old," Nia turned with a glare and then ruined it by laughing. She was feeling good tonight and the party had been a smashing success. She could see how happy it had made Colleen and she was glad the girls had suggested it. It had taken a lot to coordinate and normally she would have her assistants take care of such for her but it had been a

challenge to do a lot of it herself. She had secretly loved the look of fear on the paralegals faces when she personally invited them, handing them their invitations and telling them to keep it a secret from her former personal assistant. Her reputation as a litigator much less a hard task master had preceded her. No one had ever thought of her as the type who would give a woman a baby shower. She was pleased for Colleen's sake.

"We are going to have to pack these in your car too," Nia told her as they filled her trunk and backseat with the many gifts. It reminded her of her birthday.

"Where are you taking them?" Eleanor asked astutely.

"To Colleen's," Nia told her adroitly, she knew Eleanor was fishing and she wasn't taking the bait.

"I don't know why I can't ride with you?" Jolene was asking Colleen. "How can you afford such an expensive car?"

Eleanor tried to overhear that conversation but missed whatever it was that Colleen told her mother. She was interested in the answer as well. She did hear Colleen say, "Well Mom your car will take you to your hotel for the night and we will have the morning before I have to be at work to visit and then the night before you have to leave." She already knew her mother had only managed one night away from her father and she hoped to have time to spend with her.

"Well you should stay with me or I should stay with you so we have more time together," her mother asserted.

They soon had everything in the two cars and Jolene in the hired car to take her to the hotel that Nia had arranged. Nia had given specific instructions to the driver as Jolene was not very sophisticated and probably had never been in a hotel by herself. He was to make sure she got inside, checked in properly, and taken up to her room. She even tipped him and asked that he tip the bell boy for Jolene as she was certain the woman had no extra cash for such.

"I'll follow you," Nia said as they got in the cars. That sounded plausible to anyone listening and she knew Eleanor wasn't finished in trying to find out where Colleen lived. Annie got in her car with her.

"So, we are going to 'Colleens'?" she asked making quotations marks as she laughed in amusement.

"Yeah, we are. You saw how Eleanor was fishing."

"She was. She isn't going to give up either you know," Annie said astutely.

"No she is a Rottweiler like that," Nia said resignedly.

They got the doorman to help them take up all the many packages to the loft. It took several trips since they weren't the only ones using the elevator. They never noticed the man who had followed their cars or

managed to slip by the doorman into the building and taking the stairs he then followed them to the loft.

"What is all this?" Nia asked Annie as they brought in a couple of bags for her alone.

"Oh, I'm involved in a charity event and I'm giving the kids my old stuff I don't use anymore," she told her as she hefted the sports bag.

"Since when did you play basketball?" Nia asked raising an eyebrow in amusement.

"That's why I'm donating the stuff, I don't use it anymore. But I'll tell you, you meet more women on a basketball court than you do in a gay bar, I swear," she held up her hand solemnly.

Nia shook her head in amusement as they brought up the last of the gifts, the door had been held ajar as they emptied out the elevator.

"Oh my, look at all this," Colleen said tearfully. "I don't know where we will put it all!"

"I take it my bedroom is turned into a nursery?" Annie said dryly as she looked at the mound of presents the expectant mother-to-be had received.

Nia chuckled. "The Murphy bed is still in there, it's too heavy to move anyway," she informed her.

"If it hadn't been too heavy though it would be where?" Colleen smiled in amusement.

"Probably in the office," Nia grinned. She had meant to hire someone to move that heavy piece of furniture.

"Tell me you didn't paint it pink though?" Annie asked in mock dismay.

"No, yellow," Colleen entered the teasing.

The three women laughed as they began to take the presents to the dining room table to spread them out.

"You are going to have to return some of these," Nia commented as she pointed out the things she had already purchased for the baby.

"I feel bad about that, they were gifts!" Colleen said regretfully.

"Well use the money for things for the baby. They cost a mint!" Annie chimed in as she placed another box on the table. Something caught her eye in the shadows of the kitchen and she glanced that way.

"How do you know?" Nia teased Annie.

"How do I know what?" Colleen murmured back, she was clearly distracted.

Nia looked to where Annie was looking into the dark and her heart leapt into her throat as she made out a man in their kitchen clearly holding a knife.

"What's wrong?" Colleen asked seeing the two women freeze.

Nia pretended she hadn't seen the man and glancing around she spied the suitcase and sports bags they had hauled up of Annie's. She saw a

zipper in the end of one of them and crossed her fingers. "What else are you donating?" she said to distract Annie as she went to the bag to open it. She felt for a baseball bat and was relieved when she felt something wooden and solid. She slowly pulled it out of the bag using her body to block the line of sight from the kitchen

Annie didn't answer as she saw the outline come out of the shadows and become a man standing there with a knife.

Colleen glanced from Annie and frowned at Nia. It wasn't like her to go through someone else's bag and she wondered what was going on. Her back was to the kitchen and seeing Annie's face she followed where she was looking. The sight that greeted her made her gasp.

"Cletus!" she said in fear remembering the beating he had given her in the garage at the office all those months ago.

"You think you can get away from me Colleen? You think you can take my baby?" he sneered as he came forward. "Look at you," he gestured with the knife to make his point. "Sucking up to these rich bitches to get all this. You think my house isn't good enough? You think I can't provide for my child?"

"I think you should go Cletus," Nia said to distract him from approaching any closer to the clearly terrified Colleen.

"You think I should go," he mocked her as he sneered some more looking at the tall and sophisticated lawyer. He didn't like women who were taller than he and she wasn't afraid of him. "I'm not going anywhere without my wife!" he stated indignantly.

"She's divorcing you. Shortly she won't be your wife," Nia pointed out reasonably as she held her hands behind her back and walked forward slowly to put herself between the enraged man and her girlfriend.

"And whose idea was that?" he spat out. "Your's?" he gestured with the knife again. "It's you, you turned her against me! Working in your high falutin' firm. She got ideas above her station!"

"No, I think it was you being arrested for dealing drugs, raping her, and then beating her that decided it for her," Nia said to antagonize him and keep him focused on her.

"Nia," Colleen breathed fearfully. What was she doing? He had a knife.

"Who is this?" Annie asked as she glanced between Nia and the man holding a knife.

"My soon to be ex-husband," Colleen said bravely.

"Not if I have anything to say about it," he answered nearly shouting.

"I don't love you Cletus. You are a bad man. You treat people bad. I won't stay married to a drug dealer and abusive son of a bitch like you," she nearly shouted back. She felt braver with Nia there than she had if she

had dealt with him alone. Seeing him with a knife didn't scare her as much as it once had.

"Yeah, and who got those thoughts when she got that raise and promotion eh?" He sneered at her as he berated her. "You're nothing but a white trash girl married to a white trash guy, you're nothing!" He walked closer. "You think by hanging out with these high powered women that you are one of them?" he asked her. His eyes were wild and he badly needed a shave. His hair didn't look like it had been cut or combed in weeks. There was a distinct odor permeating the apartment from his body.

Colleen shook her head dismissing his questions and statements. "No Cletus. These women treat me like a normal human being. There is no difference between them and I. They don't treat me like dirt beneath their feet. I love being with them." She lifted her chin in defiance and knew that annoyed him more than her words.

"So what, you become a woman lover now?" he said derisively. "You one of them *h o m o s e x u a l s*?" he drawled out deliberately making it sound insulting and disgusting.

Colleen didn't answer but Nia took another step forward putting herself within arm's reach of the man. "I think you should leave," she repeated to bring his attention back to her.

"Oh you do, do you?" he said flashing the knife at her. When she didn't appear afraid it enraged him. "What, you hide my wife from me for months. You think you won't pay for that lawyer woman?" he said as spittle began to build at the corners of his mouth causing a froth. It only served to make him look more like a rabid dog.

"I think you better leave my apartment before you get hurt," Nia said ominously. Both of the other women looked at her in dismay and then Annie noticed the bat held behind her back and glanced up at Nia's determined face. Colleen recognized her court face, she was a no-nonsense type of lawyer and she wasn't going to back down from Cletus despite the knife.

"No Nia," Colleen gasped as she saw Cletus taking a firmer hold on the knife and flashing it before himself. "I'll go with him if he leaves peacefully," she volunteered so that Nia wouldn't get hurt.

"No Colleen. We both know if you go with him he will hurt you. I can't allow that ever again," Nia said without taking her eyes off the man. Analyzing him up close like this made her realize how much he had to of hurt Colleen over and over again. He was a beefy guy despite the fat and those muscles had to of given her the bruises she had sported with little effort. She couldn't imagine how those bruises and cuts and scrapes had hurt her much less the rapes she had endured.

"I won't hurt my wife. She's *mine!*" he spat out as he lunged at Nia who leaned back and he missed as it unbalanced him. She didn't miss though as she brought the bat up to hit him across his shoulder as it went by. He dropped the knife as his arm went numb from the blow. "What the hell?" he said as he tried to grab at her. Nia was too quick though and she quickly struck again, this time at his head causing an abrasion and blood. "You bitch!" he yelled as he lunged at her again.

Nia's longer reach is what helped her avoid him and she deliberately turned so was not going anywhere nearer Colleen. "Call 911," she yelled as she struck at him again. Annie reached for her cell phone as Colleen stood there shocked at the violence being directed at Cletus for a change and by Nia of all people.

"I'll fucking kill you lawyer bitch!" he yelled as he tried to lunge again.

Nia swung again catching the ribs under his outstretched arm and causing him to lose balance. Vaguely she could hear Annie in the background on the phone as the blood rushed in her ears and she raised the bat again to hit him. He got lucky though and his body slammed into hers causing her to fall backwards over a chair and sending her sailing. She didn't lose her grip on the bat though and as he came running at her intent on mayhem she used it like a pole and his body weight slammed into the end of the bat right at his midriff and the air was knocked out of him and he went down. Nia quickly got to her feet and kicked off her heels to move better but he was down. "I'd advise you to stay down," she told him as she gestured at him with the bat.

Colleen came to stand beside Nia to look down on the battered and bruised Cletus. "I didn't know you had that in you," she said in awe.

Nia chuckled as she put her arm around Colleen in a sideways hug. "I didn't want the bastard to touch you," she told her and glanced down at her. That was her mistake as Cletus lunged up and tackled Colleen. The three of them went down and Nia lost her grip on the bat.

"You bitch!" he said as he tried to attack Nia but she used her nails to scratch down his face and he backed off in surprise. She kicked out at him looking around for the bat. "I'll fucking kill you!" he repeated his earlier threat.

They were both surprised when the pregnant and ungainly Colleen used the bat to hit him over the back of the head and knock him to the ground. He wasn't out but he was stunned.

Nia got up quickly and started to help Colleen who stared at Cletus and the bat in horrified amazement at her own daring. "Come on, let's get away from him for now," she said as she gathered Colleen close to her and led her back to the dining area leaving Cletus on the living room floor.

"The police are on the way," Annie informed them as she pulled out a dining room chair for Colleen to sit in. Nia nodded as she sat Colleen down.

"Are you okay?" she asked the familiar refrain to the now crying Colleen as she took the bat from her hand.

Nodding Colleen started to cry harder in reaction to the events of the last few minutes raising her hands to cover her face. "I thought, I thought…" she stuttered. "I thought he was going to hurt you!" she sobbed.

"And I thought he was going to hurt you," Nia repeated back to her as she held her to her midriff. With Nia standing and Colleen sitting it was the perfect spot to hold her to her as she cried and clutched at Nia.

"I didn't know you had that in you?" Annie said in awe, unknowingly repeating Colleen's exact words.

"Me either," Nia said in return and looked at her best friend over her lover's head as she rubbed her shoulder and held her close.

Annie grinned. "Maybe you should help with the baseball game. You've got a helluva swing there," she complemented her and was pleased to see the normally unruffled Nia start to blush.

"Yeah right," Nia grinned at her irreverence. She knew it was Annie's way of distracting her. She felt like shaking but was keeping it together for Colleen's sake. She rocked the sobbing Colleen relieved she wasn't hurt and didn't realize the passage of time until she looked down at her.

"I should let the police in," Annie said as she saw Nia glance down at Colleen.

Nia pulled back from Colleen to ask, "Are you going to be able to talk to the police?"

She nodded and sniffed as Nia reached over to the bar for a towel for her to cry into. She glanced at the floor in the living room and was horrified to see the man was gone. She quickly looked around wondering where he had gone. "Where's Cletus?" she asked the room at large as she scanned the living room, the dining area, the front area and then peered into the kitchen and flipped a switch to light it up. There was no sign of him. "Where the hell did he go?" she asked the other two looking around wildly.

Just then there was a knock on the door. "Police!" the call came through the door.

Annie unlocked the door rapidly as Nia continued to look around wildly. Two New York police officers were standing there and she welcomed them in. "He's gone!" she told them as Nia continued to look around.

"Who's gone?" one of them asked stupidly.

"Cletus Hodsworth was here in my apartment," Nia began to explain from across the apartment and quickly explained the rest of what had occurred and the other two chimed in. She found it interesting to hear the other two women's perspective of what they had seen. It gave her a new insight to how witnesses observed things so differently.

The two officers searched the downstairs and found where he had gone out on her balcony and dropped to the one below them. They quickly left to contact the tenant below Nia and check out the apartment.

"What the hell?" Nia asked and wondered if Cletus had really left or was waiting for the cops to leave.

"They didn't sound impressed," Annie said dryly as she remembered their derision over Nia's explanation about the bat. They had made it sound by their questions that Nia had hit the guy, not in self-defense but rather in retaliation. Nia had merely tried to inform them that Cletus was wanted for assault, rape, and was in violation of a conditional release for drugs until his trial.

"No, I would say they weren't," Nia answered angrily.

Over the next couple of hours a series of cops came and went and Nia had to repeat her story several times not only to uniformed officers but to detectives and even one who was familiar with Cletus' arrest for drugs. Each of the women were interviewed together and separately and as their stories were similar they were at least partially believed by the cynical cops. They had taken in the upscale apartment and location versus where Cletus had lived with Colleen and made judgments.

"Mrs. Hodsworth, you are lucky we aren't charging you on these drug charges that your husband is up on!" the detective threatened ominously.

Nia raised her head like she had whiplash. "How dare you?" she asked rising angrily. Colleen tried to stop her but her arm fell weakly to her side. "How dare you speak to her that way?" she rose to her full height towering over the officer. "It was already shown that she had nothing to do with his drug business and she has been staying here for months so there is no proof she was involved with him!" she contested hotly.

"Proof is that," he said pointing to Colleen's belly.

"The result of rape and if you did your job correctly you would know that instead of picking and choosing what you decide to bring up. You're incompetent, get the hell out of my apartment!" she told him angrily. She was getting madder by the moment.

"I'm investigating this!" he tried to intimidate the taller woman. He didn't like looking up at her and he adjusted his belt pulling it up on his hips, emphasizing that he wore a gun and a badge.

Nia wasn't impressed. "Then get your supervisor down here because you are incompetent!" she repeated.

"I'll have you know…" he began but Nia interrupted him holding up her hand.

"And I'll have your badge, get the hell out of my apartment and don't come back!" she told him.

"I can arrest you for interfering in a police investigation," he told her hotly. He'd seen her around the court system and was certain she *could* have his badge; he wouldn't go down without a fight though.

Nia leaned in causing him to bend backwards slightly to get away. "You do that, you arrest me and we will see if you will ever have a career in law enforcement again. I might add a few things to the charges that will be leveled at you!"

"I've done nothing wrong but ask questions," he countered weakly but her threats were working.

"Get out of here, that's your last warning," Nia dismissed him and turned back to Colleen who was looking pale from their ordeal.

With a snort of indignation he turned and left, slamming the front door for effect.

"Ma'am, he won't let that be the end of it," one of the other officers told Nia respectfully. He was impressed, no one spoke to Macready that way, he usually bullied his way into situations and when caught bullied his way back out.

"Who is his supervisor?" Nia asked. She was soon on the phone with the police station leaving messages for a Lieutenant Aarons and when he wasn't available she went up the chain of command to a Captain Leon. Both were left messages regarding the situation and the behavior of the officer they were both ultimately responsible for. Nia was very careful how she worded the messages but left no doubt that he was not only unprofessional but lacked in many ways and she wasn't going to tolerate it.

"We will be right outside ma'am," the respectful officer told her as he went to stand at his post with the other officer assigned to protect them. No one thought Cletus would come back, the entire apartment and building had been searched, blood found on both balconies but they hadn't found him, and they weren't taking chances.

"Are you okay?" Nia asked the familiar refrain of Colleen.

"I'm okay as long as you are here," Colleen said caressing her arm. She had seen Nia in many situations over the years but her defending her lover hadn't been one of them.

"Do either of you want anything to eat or drink?" Annie asked from where she sat at the bar. She too had seen Nia in many situations and had still been impressed. That cop had been out of line on so many levels. His homophobia palpable, his questions nasty and insinuating.

"I'm good, would you like something?" Nia looked back down at Colleen lovingly. She was worried; this couldn't be good for the baby.

"I'm fine, I'm awfully tired," Colleen said and then yawned for effect.

"Do you want me to help you up to bed?" she asked concernedly.

"I'm fine," she assured her lover and smiled up at her. After seeing her in action she knew she was taken care of and that comforted her beyond measure.

Nia and Annie watched as the hugely pregnant woman levered herself off the couch and waddled towards the stairs and up them. Nia began folding the blanket to put it on the back of the couch.

"That was fun....*not*," Annie said unnecessarily and poured herself a generous helping of scotch.

"You are going to have trouble sleeping," Nia teased.

"Um, I don't think this," she gestured towards the drink she had just taken a healthy pull of; her voice was a little breathless from it. "Is what would keep me awake," she finished unnecessarily.

Nia grinned at the by-play but she was worried. Where the hell had Cletus gone?

❧ CHAPTER TWENTY TWO ❧

"Nia? Got a minute?" Stewart Dunham poked his head into her office. Nia looked up from the pile of law books she was going through.

"Old school?" he teased her pleased to see she didn't rely on her clerks and other staff but looked up things for herself, it meant that she was better prepared than those who did or just looked up the books on line.

She smiled as she stood up to welcome him into her office. She saw the startled look of Suzette in the outer office before he closed the door. "Well, what do I owe the honor of this visit?" she said cordially but she knew, deep down she had been waiting for someone from the upper echelon of partners to come and talk to her today.

"May I?" he asked and proceeded to pour himself a small cup of cappuccino from her maker on the shelf.

Nia wondered briefly how startled he would be if she had said no. She laughed inwardly knowing this conversation was going to be a cat and mouse if she allowed it.

"Please sit down," he said as he joined her sitting down across the coffee table from her and sipping at the excellent brew. "Ah that's good, that's real good," he said as he glanced out at the view her corner office afforded her. He wondered how often she daydreamed into the view but knowing Nia Toyomoto, probably not much. Her back was to the excellent view and he wondered if she looked out at it or noticed it at all.

"So what do I owe the honor of this visit?" she smiled as she repeated herself and she shoved aside one of the books she had been studying, a thick volume of law that took up a lot of space on the coffee table.

"You were in late today?" he commented and asked at the same time as he took another sip watching her intently.

"Yes, I had some personal business," she replied willing to play the game.

"I heard about the party last night, very successful," he commented in the same controlled voice.

Nia wondered when this would get to the point but she played along. "Yes, it was a total surprise for Colleen. Everyone had a nice time." She looked him directly in the eye waiting to challenge him when he attacked.

"Yes the office likes Colleen," he admitted wryly. By office he meant the entire firm who well knew that Colleen was the victim of abuse and was pregnant by her husband's rape. Many considered her long suffering for having worked for Nia Toyomoto for these many years. It didn't make the conversation that was coming up any more comfortable though. "Do

you care to share what personal business kept you from coming in on time this morning?" he asked as though to throw her off.

Nia wasn't buying it as she shook her head. "No I don't," she answered shortly as she viewed him through unimpressed eyes. Her personal life was hers; she had to put a limit on it after the firm had her alter things in her life. She wasn't willing to share any more than she had to.

"Colleen is living with you?" he began again, trying to throw her.

Nia bristled but it didn't show on her face. "Yes she is," she answered keeping it short and sweet. The less information she gave out the better it was for everyone involved.

"Do you think that is wise?"

"May I ask where you got this information?" she countered.

He smiled seeing her go slightly on the attack. Taking a sip he made her wait. "Manhattan law is a small town of its own. The police being involved makes it even smaller," he added knowing she got the full implications of what he was saying.

She nodded. She had known the secret was out as soon as the officers took their names and began questioning the situation last night.

"Don't you think you should have informed me?" he tried the fatherly approach as he finished the small cup of cappuccino.

"No, I don't. I handled it," she replied feeling like a chastised child and not allowing him to know.

"She did work for you," he began to point out but she interrupted.

"She doesn't any longer," she answered and there was a defensive note in her voice. She had known they would be found out, someday. She had several conversations in her mind about the impropriety of getting involved with her personal assistant but they didn't need to know the date it started. All they needed to know was that they no longer worked together.

"She didn't come in today?" he asked trying yet another approach hoping she would open up.

Nia shook her head. "No, last night was rather...upsetting," she finished almost lamely. She hadn't gotten much sleep and it was affecting her.

"Are you okay?" he asked triggering her familiar question and she almost smiled at it.

"I don't know. I don't understand why they can't find that bastard. He assaulted me and now I know a little how she felt," she added giving him a little of the information he was seeking.

"Were you hurt?" He eyed her long sleeved blouse as though to see any bruises.

Nia wasn't going to give him a blow by blow. He had probably already read the police report so why a first-hand accounting? "Just my pride mostly but yes it was a shock to the system. I'm amazed what one is capable of when they need to be. It makes me appreciate what some of my clients come up against better." She smiled at the thought of how many people she had defended against assault charges.

"One never knows what one needs to do until one has to do it," he agreed. Then, hoping to disarm her he asked, "Are you a lesbian?"

Nia looked him straight in the eye for a moment until the quiet in the room got uncomfortable. When she saw that he was a little off she asked, "Is my employment here contingent on the answer to that question?" She didn't bat an eyelash. She had been prepared for this. She was also prepared to sue the pants off of every partner in the firm if judgment was being made.

"Not at all," he assured her knowing what her agile mind had probably already contemplated. "Are we going to be sued for sexual harassment?"

"By whom?" she asked frostily.

"By your former secretary!" he was feeling uncomfortable and it angered him that it had come to this. Nia Toyomoto was one of the most respected female attorneys they had ever brought into the firm and their reputation as well as hers would take a hit from this news.

Nia chuckled as she shook her head. "No, Colleen won't be suing the firm."

"You realize some of the firm's clients aren't going to like this?" he asked making reference to what they were indirectly talking about without asking it specifically.

"Then they are free to go elsewhere. My reputation as an attorney is well earned from the cases I have won. Even the ones I have lost were fantastic PR for the firm," she pointed out.

"In this economy we can't afford to lose clients," he pointed out the bottom line.

"You aren't looking at this from every angle then Stewart," she started in a new line to get him off balance. "This will bring in many more clients that realize that Chase-Dunham is a *liberal* firm that not only promotes women from within but is hip with the times and has talent in its upper echelon of partners."

He hadn't thought of it that way. He was thinking that it could become a nightmare. As it sunk in he also realized whether she was a lesbian or not wasn't the issue. She was and had always been a top lawyer in her field. She had brought in one of the richest women in the world as a client and since that client's death her partner had brought more and more business to their firm. He was in negotiations with offices in Los Angeles, London, and Paris to handle some of their international clients thanks to

this woman. He nodded thoughtfully. "You're right of course." He smiled relieved. He had thought this conversation would result in her possibly leaving the firm, them getting hit with a lawsuit, or worse. He should have known she didn't do things that didn't benefit them...eventually. She always knew the options and angles she needed to win her cases, they didn't always work but she was clever that way. She must have thought it out before she pursued this 'relationship.' While he personally didn't approve of that lifestyle, if she was one, or if people thought she was one it would bring in more clientele for that very reason. He got to his feet leaving his cup on the coffee table. "If there is anything I can do..." he said vaguely but hoping that she wouldn't ask.

"Of course Stewart, I'm glad we had this little chat," she mouthed the words not meaning a word of it but she was an expert at saying one thing and meaning another. She escorted him to the door.

As Stewart left her office Lynda was just about to knock. "Oh Nia, a Simone with the security firm is here to see you? You called and asked for her specifically?" She seemed a little put out that she hadn't handled that phone call for Nia.

Stewart glanced at the woman from the security firm the firm had hired many months ago after Colleen's attack and nodded absentmindedly at her as he acknowledged her and then he walked away musingly. He was curious as to why Nia would need to see her but he wouldn't ask. He had a slight headache from the short meeting he had had with the woman just now. He realized Nia could talk circles around anyone if she wished.

"Ah Nia, it's nice to see you again," Simone said as she walked forward in a tailored suit looking very professional and her hair perfectly coiffured. Her blonde good looks gave her an androgynous look but she was still feminine in her own way with a bit of makeup.

"Nice to see you Simone, please come on in?" Nia asked as she stepped aside to usher her into her office.

Simone looked around curiously. She had been in every office of the firm's along with other employees of the security firm that she worked for. She hadn't realized this was Nia's office though as there were no personal pictures to tag it and she hadn't noticed the name plate on the wall next to the door.

"Would you like a cup of cappuccino?" Nia asked as she shut the door behind Simone and nearly in Lynda's face. Normally her assistants served clients and guests but she wanted this meeting and had called for it so she would handle it, alone.

"Cappuccino?" Simone asked surprised and then glanced at the bookshelf where the maker stood waiting to brew it.

"Yes, would you like a cup?" Nia asked again as she made her way towards the machine.

"Yes I would," Simone asked as she made her way to the windows that lined the office walls and looked out at the view. It was a misty day and she couldn't see far but the view was still incredible and she could only imagine what it looked like on a sunny day.

Nia efficiently handled the complicated machine blessing the day Colleen had taught her so it made her look proficient. She quickly had two small cups of the powerful brew ready and brought Simone's to her as she looked out at the view. "Nice view eh?" she commented as she took a sip of the drink.

"Mmm, this smells heavenly," Simone commented as she sipped it and looked out beyond the cup to the view. Taking her sip she smiled, it was equally as delicious as it was fragrant. "And yes, it's a nice view," she grinned.

"Would you like to take a seat?" Nia indicated the couches in her office on each side of the coffee table.

When they were both seated and sipping at the delicious cappuccino they played a momentary waiting game. Simone, because she was curious as to why Nia had phoned her company and specifically asked for her presence here in her office. Nia, because she was good at it as a lawyer to create anticipation and drama.

"I suppose you are wondering why I asked you to come in?" Nia began quietly. She had often wondered about Simone. She was quite frequently on the 'outside' of friendships and always a little odd, but being a friend of Alice Weaver's that didn't mean anything as Alice was one of the most odd women Nia had ever known.

"Yes I am," Simone admitted with a smile. She briefly wondered if Nia could read minds. That would be an excellent feat in a lawyers cross examination but a dangerous one for someone employed in the occupations that Simone chose.

"I need your *expertise*," she said cryptically and with a knowing little smile.

Both of them wondered which expertise she meant. Simone was a good player though as her many faces in her chosen careers necessitated. "Which part of my expertise do you need...*exactly*?" she asked as she sipped at the brew.

Nia almost laughed aloud and wondered how much of what she surmised was true or was it merely speculation based on some cryptic comments Alice had dropped over the years? "I have a problem with security at my apartment and I'm hoping you and your firm could take care of that?" she explained.

Simone listened as Nia explained what had happened the previous night, her concerns on where Cletus had disappeared to, and a very vague reference to her relationship with her former assistant and now 'friend.'

Simone was very astute and filled in the gaps as she remembered being out with Nia when Alice was around both last year and in college and what little she knew of the high powered attorney. As their meeting came to a close she rose and shook Nia's hand. "I'll have someone there tonight and we can map out what you need and discuss it with you and your 'roommate,'" she finished in order to keep Nia from squirming over the terminology she was being so careful to hide behind.

That night as they installed some basic security cameras in the form of fiber optic lenses that no one would notice Simone explained how it would work. As she cased Nia's apartment she realized she couldn't exactly do anything to this particular apartment since she considered Nia a friend. It was too bad though as she had some really nice stuff. That dragon on the mantel alone was worth a mint.

"See, this will allow you to switch to any camera you want both inside and out," she said showing Nia and Colleen the monitor and the simple computer they had hooked up for their safety. There were cameras on the balcony, in the hallway outside their apartment and in the actual apartment. Since it was all digital it didn't take up much space and they left it on a shelf below the bar out of sight and behind a sliding door. It could record up to twenty cameras at a time but they didn't have nearly that many hooked up.

"Amazing," Nia said as she watched Simone and a technician drill discrete unnoticeable holes into her apartment at various intervals. The heads of the fiber optic lenses gave them an enormous view of the apartment but were so small and discrete no one would see them.

"Now we can hook this up to our offices if you wish monitoring," Simone offered but as Nia raised her hand and started to mouth an objection she continued, "but this is closed circuit here for now so no worries about someone getting your signal or a view of the apartment."

Nia relaxed a little at that. She wanted them safe but she didn't want anyone else monitoring them. As she saw Simone out she murmured, "You'll send me a bill?"

Simone smiled and saluted her as she and the tech left the apartment.

"Do we really need all this?" Colleen asked slightly frightened.

Nia shrugged dismissively but said, "I'd sooner have it and not need it than need it and not have it." She took Colleen into her arms and held her close. They were both still shook up from last night and Annie hadn't left to go out until Nia came home so that Colleen wouldn't be alone.

"Are they going to fire me on Monday?" Colleen wondered aloud as they discussed Nia's day and what had occurred at the office.

"You have nothing to worry about, you have deniability," Nia explained. Over the weekend she coached Colleen as she would any of her clients. They hadn't done anything wrong, that anyone really knew. They would fudge a little on the dates of what occurred but other than that, what they did in their personal lives was no one's business but their own.

LAWYERED

❈ CHAPTER TWENTY THREE ❈

"Whether Nia Toyomoto is a lesbian or not it is not an issue," Stewart contested hotly. He wished this conversation wasn't taking place but a few of the older senior partners were concerned. Not everyone had been privy to the police report Stewart had read and the gossip was running rampant, not only in the firm, but on the streets.

"It is when it affects our bottom line!" Grayson contested just as hotly. "This is a disgrace to the firm. How dare she make us look bad!"

"I haven't made you look bad Gray, I have merely defended my home from an intruder," Nia interrupted as she came into the meeting uninvited. She had known when she saw the older members of the firm head for the conference room what was up. She had unashamedly listened at the door and she appreciated Stewart defending her but the horror in the voices of the other old crones had pissed her off. "Anyone nowadays is subject to a home invasion," she said practically. "It doesn't mean I'm a lesbian," she pointed out.

"You weren't invited to this meeting," another one of the partners pointed out.

"Really Edward?" she said turning to him. "I thought I was a partner in this firm. We believe in transparency between partners here at Chase-Dunham. Meetings between several senior partners to discuss another partner is not very transparent. You've judged me without giving me a chance to defend myself and you are assuming things without the facts," she pointed out.

"Yes, Nia deserves a chance to defend herself," Lawrence Allred pointed out.

"Not if it's regarding my personal life I don't," Nia pointed out. "My personal life is off limits to this firm. I might point out though if I were a lesbian I'd be honored to be called one. God knows I've been called worse. I might also point out the clients I've brought into this firm such as Alice Weaver, Sasha Brenhov, and Allison Gottfried among many others are out lesbians and would take a very dim view of your firing me if that is your intent."

"Alice Weaver and Sasha Brenhov are both dead," Edward pointed out.

"But their spouses," she saw him cringe at the word and idea. "Aren't, and they have both brought us more business," she pointed out.

"We can't have you diddling a secretary for God's sake," Grayson said as though appalled by the very idea.

"But it's okay if you were diddling a secretary or perhaps a *law clerk*?" she asked with enough insinuation that he backed off. She glanced around

at the senior members of the firm. "If I or Colleen Hodsworth choose to live together or even *fuck* together," she nearly laughed at them flinching at the crudity of her chose words. "It is none of *your* business."

"Now Nia, there is no need to get this upset," Stewart began but Nia interrupted him.

"If you plan to have meetings such as these," her hands encompassed the senior partners. "And it's regarding me and my personal life, *again*," she added with enough insinuation to make a few of them squirm. "I think there is a need for me to be upset. I suggest you all drop it and let the dust settle. If you keep talking about it the other members of the firm will wonder at these kind of meetings and word will get out somehow. We don't need this kind of publicity and our clients only need to know if they ask that I defended myself when attacked in my own home."

They were all taken aback by her words. Not only the crudity of a few of them but her logic. They hadn't been thinking of it from that angle. Many realized she had valid points and her mentioning of three very wealthy clients whose business had brought in others really struck home to a few of the others. They also realized that some clients, if Nia ever chose to leave, would leave with her.

"I don't think we need to discuss this any further. Nia is right, this is her personal business and our involvement only centers around this office," Randolph Jacobs interjected to try to quiet the others murmurs he was hearing. A couple wanted to fire Nia for cause, what cause would that be? It would be a nightmare waiting to happen.

Nia looked around at the old fuddy duddy's that compromised the senior members of the firm. She looked at each one of them knowing a few of them would feel decidedly uncomfortable and she watched them squirm. She nodded at Stewart and she walked out of the meeting closing the door firmly behind her.

"We can't have that..." Grayson began almost sputtering in his indignation.

"This is over Gray!" Stewart said firmly. He among several others realized not only that Nia had a point but her naming specific clients the implication was there; she could, and would, let them know if this wasn't dropped. If she left, they would go with her. Her multi-million dollars in billables yearly were a little too much to be thrown away like that.

The few partners who muttered were soon silenced as they broke up this ill-advised meeting of the senior members of the firm. They didn't like it but really, there was nothing they could do about it.

"Are you okay?" Nia asked as she came up behind Colleen. She had waited until she saw her alone at her desk.

K'ANNE MEINEL

Colleen whipped around. She was shocked to see Nia. She looked around to see if anyone was listening.

"It's okay, I waited until they left," Nia assured her. She wanted to take her in her arms and comfort her but not here, never here.

"They are treating me coldly but a few obviously don't care," Colleen reported to her. She was feeling ostracized but she had known that was a possibility. What she feared the most was being called into personnel or one of the other partners offices for 'a talk.'

"They shouldn't care, it isn't as though you did anything wrong. You are the victim here; no one has the right to judge you." Nia could see that Colleen was tired and as pregnant as she was, it didn't look good on her.

"They seem to think they have the right to judge me," she complained.

"Then you need to ignore them but if you are called in, refuse to answer any personal questions," Nia advised her quietly. She could hear some of the others returning and she needed to go. "Call me if you need me," she finished before squeezing Colleen's hand and disappearing out another door before several others returned. They looked at Colleen curiously before averting their eyes and returning to their own work.

Another week went by and Nia and Colleen were both on edge both at work and at home. Colleen was having a few early labor pains but the doctor assured her that was normal and that she needed to relax as her blood pressure was getting dangerously high.

Colleen didn't know how to relax at this point. She was afraid to get out of her car in case Cletus was waiting for her. Parking was a nightmare near the apartment and a couple of times she left the car at the office and took a taxi to class and then to the apartment. Nia was doing the same as construction around their building continued. The huge hole that was dug next to the building and the work that was underway on the parking garage was a mess for everyone living in the building. The noise was horrendous as long as it was light and sometimes they continued on with huge lights, dust settled over everything and they couldn't open their windows. Cars were frequently full of the dust around their block and people were complaining.

Nia was getting a bit nervous too. Why the hell couldn't the cops find him? Wherever Cletus had gone to hide, it was good but in a city of several million people she supposed there were a lot of hiding places.

❧ CHAPTER TWENTY FOUR ❧

Colleen went into labor late one night a few weeks later. Nia managed to hold up and keep her cool and help her with the labor from the classes they had taken together. Colleen was astounded as the sophisticated and professional Nia Toyomoto treated her with tender loving care, not that she hadn't seen her tender and loving but this was different, vastly different. She mopped her brow, she comforted her as the pains took away her ability to breathe, she reminded her to breathe in the calculated way that helped clear her mind from the pains.

"I can't do this anymore," Colleen cried as the pains came quicker.

"Yes you can, you want this. It's almost over," Nia told her trying to reassure her.

"How do you know it's almost over?" Colleen challenged.

Nia shrugged her elegant shoulder and laughed. "I heard them," she indicated the doctor and nurses attending Colleen.

Colleen laughed a little but it was smothered almost immediately by more pain.

"Come on, PUSH," they shouted at her.

It took about five hours but they assured her that was relatively short before her son was born. Nia found herself crying with Colleen as they viewed the bloody and wet baby who cried heartily at being expelled from his mother's warm and comfortable body. He looked a lot better after they cut the cord and cleaned him up a bit. The grey mucus like tissue over his body was gone and he looked pink and healthy.

His cries ceased once they handed him to Nia. She looked down wonderingly at the small baby. She had never been around a baby before and at first nervous she found he felt right in her arms as she held him.

Colleen looked at Nia holding her son. It looked so...right. She had never thought Nia Toyomoto and a baby would look right together but strangely it did. The look on her face was something Colleen would never forget. It was so tender, fragile, and...loving...words alone couldn't describe it and she felt so loved when Nia gently put her son into her arms and put her arms around both of them holding them close as she looked down on the little boy. None of the resentment she felt towards Cletus entered her mind at that moment. For all intents and purposes this was her son...and Nia's if she let her.

Nia called a few of the girls from their Thursday night group who then spread the word and Colleen soon was having visitors. Some from work

came as well and the little tyke soon had stuffed bears and balloons, and other gifts in abundance. The large bouquet of red roses no one was sure where they came from but they were beautiful and commented on. Colleen didn't tell anyone it was from Nia but they both knew it was.

"What are you going to name him?" Colleen was asked time and time again. She didn't tell anyone the name she had decided on.

"I don't know," she kept saying. Nia had informed her as she was the only one on the birth certificate unless she wanted to name Cletus; she could also choose to give the little guy his name, including a different last name. It gave her a lot to think about.

She decided to name him Nathaniel Jacob and since she was taking her maiden name back she gave it to him. Nathaniel Jacob Picket was a mouthful and she soon heard Nia shorten it to Nate which everyone who visited seemed to pick up on.

"So, are you two going to admit to being a couple, yet?" Eleanor asked as she held the baby, quite expertly it appeared. She looked at the two of them over his head.

"She's just my roommate Eleanor," Nia repeated the party line. "It was a two bedroom apartment you sold me remember? Three if we count the office."

"Uh huh," Eleanor said in disbelief. She wasn't the only one though. None of the Thursday night girls believed they were 'just roommates.'

"Do you think we should make an announcement someday?" Colleen asked tentatively when they were alone.

Nia shook her head immediately from where she was watching Nathaniel sleep. She looked up to see the hurt on Colleen's face. "I denied it, you've denied it. Why can't two women in this day and age live together without being involved?" she asked practically.

"Because we *are* involved?" Colleen asked confused.

"Let's just let it ride for now. I don't need the pressure at work. There is enough speculation and really, it's none of anyone's business but our own," she tried to reassure her but the hurt bothered her for a while as she thought about it.

"Careful now, careful," Nia worried as she brought Colleen home and they went through the front door. Colleen was holding the baby but she was more than able to walk without Nia's concerned assistance.

"Let's get you on the couch, comfortable," Nia insisted as she then proceeded to help her as though she was an invalid.

Colleen shook her head as Nia not only helped her to sit and made sure she and the baby were okay but then kept hovering and asking her if she

needed anything. "I think I just need to sleep," Colleen told her and made to get up.

"Why don't you sleep on the couch so you don't have to risk the stairs," Nia said practically. She then quickly made a 'bed' for Colleen on the couch with the baby in a carry all car seat next to her on the floor. Nia kept looking down on the baby fondly.

Over the next few weeks Colleen watched in awe as Nia took care of her and the baby. Whenever she wasn't at work, and she had stopped bringing work home to spend more time with the two of them, she was with them both. Helping Colleen cope with being a new parent, changing the baby, even washing little Nate. She also called several times a day to check on Colleen and the baby, to ask if she needed anything, and if she was going to work late to keep Colleen informed. Colleen felt very loved and couldn't imagine a better second parent for her baby.

❧ CHAPTER TWENTY FIVE ❧

"Nia, got a second?" Donald poked his head in Nia's open office.

Nia looked up from the brief she was reading and smiled at the associate who had represented Colleen in her divorce. Putting down the paperwork on the coffee table she answered, "Sure Donald, what did you need?"

He walked in and closed the door, she could see beyond him to Lynda and Suzette working on something at Suzette's desk before the door closed. "We have a problem," he said as he approached her to sit on the couch facing her. "You aren't going to believe this."

"What would that be?" she asked him since they didn't work on too many cases together.

"Cletus' attorney has contacted me regarding Colleen," he told her.

Nia froze for a micro-second. "Shouldn't you be telling Colleen this?" she asked as she put on her game face.

He nodded and then, "Normally I would but I know you two are friends." Nothing in his tone indicated a second meaning in his words. "I want you with me when I tell her as this is going to upset her."

"What did he want?" she asked curious. She knew she shouldn't be the one he came to with this news but she appreciated the courtesy.

"Cletus wants rights to his son," he told her.

Nia looked on incredulously at him. "Isn't he wanted by the police for many things including assault on me?" she asked.

He nodded. "His attorney said he didn't know where Cletus was but he had phoned him and asked him to handle this for him. He wants rights to his son."

"Does he realize he can't see the boy without coming out of hiding? That he would be arrested on sight?"

Donald shrugged. "I don't know if he knows that or not, but he does have rights by being the biological father of the child," he pointed out.

Nia was furious but you wouldn't have been able to tell it by her face. Her heart was beating, hard. She had made a happy family with Colleen and she had almost forgotten Cletus' part in the biological aspect of Nate's life.

"She's still out on maternity leave isn't she?" he asked cautiously.

Nia nodded. "She's got several more weeks before she has to return."

"Well, if he files for paternity rights he does have a case," he pointed out.

Nia knew that but she also knew that Cletus was just making trouble. Legal trouble that he wouldn't win. If this went to court he would be

arrested, she'd make sure of that. Maybe they could get him arrested before any of this escalated. Her facile mind began to think. Family law was not her forte but she'd worked enough cases with her contemporaries that she knew a few tricks. "Can you call the slimeball of an attorney back and tell him that Colleen is demanding a paternity test?"

Donald looked up surprised. "I thought he raped her?" he asked confused.

Nia nodded. "He did, but if he has to prove he is the father it will buy her time and maybe we can get him caught. He is up on a lot of charges not the least of which he never showed up for his drug hearing. I want him arrested for assaulting me and I'm sure the D.A. has a few other charges to add to the list."

He nodded and smiled at her cunning. "I'm sure I can make that call."

"I'll call the D.A. and see how long the list is on him and we can see about laying a trap for one Cletus Hodsworth!" she said conspiratorially. She wasn't going to allow that bastard anywhere near her beloved Nate and she wanted to avoid getting Colleen upset if she could.

"Do you want me to tell Colleen, I could call her…?" Donald asked as he rose from the comfortable couch.

"No, let's see if he calls our bluff and what we can find out before we inform her." She looked at him innocently. "If all goes well he will be arrested and in jail before she has to know."

He nodded but frowned at the idea of not informing their 'client' but she was a partner and he a mere associate. He would follow her lead.

Nia was distracted that evening as she ate a late dinner with Colleen.

"Hello?" Colleen said as she waved her hands in Nia's face from across the table. Nate had gone down for the evening and she probably wouldn't feed him again until two a.m. She was enjoying a meal with Nia but her distracted look meant her mind was on work and not on the meal she was slowly eating and was going cold on her plate.

"I'm sorry, work," Nia mumbled as she contemplated the plan the D.A. and she had contrived. She was fortunate that the D.A. and she got along, usually they were on opposite sides of the fence with clients but this one, Emily Barnes was fairly new to the D.A. staff and as an Assistant District Attorney wanted to make a name for herself. She also detested drug dealers and wanted Cletus to go down not only for the drugs but the rape. Add the charges from his attack on Nia she was livid to catch this guy and all ears about how to do it. If he showed up for a paternity test a few undercover police officers would be waiting for him.

"You need a weekend away," Colleen laughed. She was hoping to resume their close relationship soon. The doctor had cleared her health

wise but she wasn't so sure about making love post baby with Nia. Nia held her at night, every night. She kissed her, but she had made no advances on Colleen since well before the baby had been born and now Colleen burned for her touch. She wanted her but didn't feel attractive enough to make the first move. She had gained weight with her pregnancy and didn't have the confidence to make a pass at Nia.

"Isn't Annie coming into town this weekend?" Nia asked bemusedly as she tried to remember her schedule and focus on home life instead of her own little world.

"That's right, she did send us emails to remind us," Colleen confirmed.

"That's us, Hotel Central," she laughed as she shook her head. She didn't mind. Annie was great fun and her teasing had changed since the baby and Colleen had become a regular part of her life. She had changed but she hadn't realized it yet.

"She's always welcome," Colleen said as she rose to remove the used plates.

"That she is," Nia agreed. "That she is." She too rose and began to help with the dirty dishes.

"So she's like making all these gagging noises and I'm about asphyxiated by her so that was our first and last date," Annie was telling an outrageous story that had them both in tears.

"But you did sleep with her?" Nia confirmed through the laughter.

"Of course, I'm not going to let something like that pass, but after that, hell no!" Annie choked out.

Colleen felt like she was going to wet her pants from the laughter. Annie was always a good time and she enjoyed her visits. She had become a good friend to Colleen and like the Thursday night girls, all through Nia.

Just then Nate woke up from his nap and Nia, hearing the baby, got up to get him and bring him downstairs so Colleen could feed him.

"Wow, I'd have never thought it?" Annie murmured watching her friend walk up the stairs to the crying baby.

"Thought what?" Colleen asked as she sipped the beer they were all drinking. The doctor had told her that the hops were good for her, even nursing, and that it wouldn't affect the baby. It was relaxing besides and she enjoyed a nice beer now and then, it was a break from the usual wine that Nia drank. She hadn't objected to switching to beer for a while for the sake of milk production either.

"That I'd see the day when Nia Toyomoto was playing mom," Annie took a swig of the beer she was drinking and eyed it suspiciously. Nia had seldom drunk anything but nice wines in the time she had known her.

Even when she wasn't a partner, she had drunk only a glass here and there but it was always a quality wine.

"She's good at it," Colleen felt the need to defend her.

"And that is the biggest surprise of all," Annie agreed. In the time she had been here she had seen Nia change a diaper, give the baby a bath, burp him, and if she could have she was certain she would have fed him too. She had seen the look on Nia's face as she watched Colleen feed the little guy and it was actually a look that formed a lump in Annie's throat to see how happy Nia really was.

"So why are you in town this weekend?" Nia asked as she brought Nate down the stairs. She didn't like Colleen to do it and it made her nervous to see the mom carrying the little baby on the steps. She had begun to think she should look for a bigger flat, all on one floor without any steps but when she tried to bring it up with Colleen she had sworn she loved the apartment with its loft and didn't want to move, not now, not yet.

"Well, for one, I have a date," Annie blushed and before she could continue Nia pounced on that information.

"A date eh, what's new about that?" she teased. She'd seen the blush and Annie didn't blush often.

"Well this one is kind of important," she murmured embarrassed.

"Really?" Nia asked surprised and then decided not to upset her friend, if it was important, she would tell her when she was ready.

The three of them had a marvelous time together when Annie was there but even without their vivacious friend they took walks in the parks and on the city streets. Nia had given up worrying about Cletus behind every tree and felt his attack on her and her defense might have scared him off. Little did she know Colleen didn't feel the same way and felt jumpy when they went out. She in fact didn't go to anything but the occasional class when she didn't take them on line. She didn't take the baby out without Nia or someone else with her at all. She just didn't feel comfortable as he knew where she was and at any moment could show up again. Her divorce was final and Nate was hers but she still felt until he was caught and behind bars that he could hurt them.

"Well thank you both for having me, I'll be back next weekend if it's okay with you?" Annie asked hoping she wasn't over staying her welcome.

"We will get the Murphy bed taken down to the office so you don't have to share with Nate anymore," Nia informed her as she hugged her friend goodbye.

"You don't have to go to so much trouble…" Annie began but she hoped Nia would do just that. The bed, while comfortable, was too close

to a baby who insisted on meal times in the middle of the night and day and while Annie wasn't there most nights, she needed her sleep when she was.

"Not at all, Nate needs the whole room to himself," Colleen laughed for a tiny baby to take up so much space. "Besides it will look better in the office with the furniture in there," she smiled as she hugged Annie.

"Thank you guys, see you," Annie answered as she waved goodbye and walked out the door.

Nia walked over to the bar and watched as Annie got on the elevator. No one knew of the little micro-fiber camera that they had in the hallway for their convenience. It at least told them if someone was coming down the hall. She didn't know that Colleen frequently looked at it in paranoia when she was home alone with the baby.

"Would you like to eat out tonight?" she asked courteously to Colleen as she slid the door closed to hide the monitor that showed all the cameras and could easily be touched to show one in particular on the whole screen.

"I have the last of that roast I made the other night, we should finish up the leftovers," the always efficient Colleen reminded her. Nothing went to waste here anymore with her at the helm of their kitchen.

Nia smiled. She could never have imagined having a 'wife' take care of her but when she thought about it, Colleen was the perfect 'wife.' As she walked past her though her arm snaked out to prevent her from walking into the kitchen. Colleen looked up questioningly as Nia leaned down to plant a kiss on her mouth. "I just want you to know how much I love you," Nia told her softly as she looked down with all the love and affection she could put into her warm eyes.

Colleen smiled the biggest smile she had as she returned the kiss wholeheartedly. Nia was one of the kindest women she had ever known. She knew that her reputation was of being a bitch but Colleen was lucky enough to know this side of her and loved her for it. She had admired her from afar for years and never imagined a relationship such as this with her but she was glad they had pursued it. Nia loved her; she made her feel safe and cared for. She appreciated everything she did for her. It was a far cry from her marriage to Cletus and while a lot of people wouldn't approve of such a relationship she realized she didn't care, she loved Nia more than she could have ever imagined. She slipped her hand into Nia's suit, and gently caressed her breast suggestively; Nia's gasp of delight thrilled her, knowing she could affect her this way.

Nia walked through the kitchen to the balcony that stretched the length of the apartment and looked out at the construction site. Colleen had complained with all the noise they made it was hard to keep Nate asleep during the day. The large hole they had dug looked foreboding with all the water that had accumulated from the rains and held up construction. It

looked like one large mud pile and not much 'work' had been accomplished. She wondered how long it would take them to pour the cement and how long until she could park her car in the structure where she had already purchased a 'space.' She reminded herself once again to purchase a second space for Colleen's car and if they got lucky they would be next to each other. It looked like they were going to have a large parking structure next to the apartment but it wouldn't reach up this far, she hoped.

Later, as they got ready for bed Colleen approached Nia. "The doctor told me something the other day that might interest you."

"Everything okay?" Nia turned from removing her blouse standing there in slacks and a bra and beginning to look worried.

"Everything is fine," Colleen assured her as she took her in her arms because she could. Nia had given her this confidence she had never experienced before in her life and she was reveling in it. A couple of people had commented on the change in her and thought it was from having a baby but she knew it was because someone believed in her wholeheartedly and supported her and her decisions. She hadn't known that she needed that in her life. Nia gave her so much love and support that she couldn't help but grow from it. She smiled up at the taller woman and it turned provocative. "She said that I could 'resume marital relations' if I wanted," she laughed at the wording but the doctor hadn't known how else to tell her she could have sex once again, her body could handle it if she wanted.

"Oh really?" Nia grinned at the words. She had followed the doctor's orders to the letter in the past and although it had been difficult, she wanted Colleen so much sometimes, she had tamped down her desires in order that Colleen get well and feel good about herself. The months of forced abstinence had been difficult, she had been distracted by turns as she watched the changes in Colleen and patiently waited for her.

"Which means…" Colleen continued as she began to caress Nia's long back and gently cupped her buttocks through the slacks. "We can have sex," she finished mischievously.

"We can, can we?" Nia pretended to consider as her heart leapt from the touch that had turned decidedly arousing.

Colleen nodded as she grinned. "Yes, we can…that is…if you *want* to?" she teased.

"Hmmm," Nia pretended to consider musingly. "Can I get back to you on that?"

"Why you!" Colleen swatted her behind and Nia started to laugh as she looked down on her and leaned in for a kiss to silence her mock outrage.

The kisses they had shared in the last couple of months, while loving, weren't nearly as passionate as this one. They poured all their need, all their want into it. Months of pent up longing and frustration went into it. Both knew this would be quick, it would be heated, but they both wanted each other badly after not being able to express themselves sexually for so long.

Colleen reached for the button holding Nia's slacks to her slender body and released it. Sliding the slacks over her narrow hips she smiled at the matching panties to the delicate little bra that was holding up Nia's gorgeous breasts. Slipping down with the slacks to her knees she gently began to peel away the satin and lace, first with her teeth and then when she scented Nia she used her hands to pull them down to Nia's knees, effectively hobbling her.

Nia looked down at the head between her legs and put her hand on the back of it to encourage her. She hadn't expected this tonight but would accept it in any way she could get it at this point. The forced abstinence could have been relieved by her partner any time but Nia hadn't wanted to make Colleen feel bad because of what they couldn't do and she figured if she couldn't give Colleen everything in full then she would wait until they could. She had thought of taking care of her orally and had even offered only to be rejected from time to time with the stress Colleen was going through and the pregnancy she had lost her drive for a time. Seeing her initiate this, taking it on like this, the first touch of her tongue on Nia's waiting clit was magical and she gasped and threw her head back looking up at the ceiling and relishing the feelings that coursed through her eager body.

Colleen smiled into Nia's clit as she sensed what she was doing to the woman. This power, this absolute control was heady stuff. She glanced up to see the woman arched back in her pleasure. She could sense her immediate arousal at her actions and brought her fingers into play, spreading the folds to access the slick heat within. Nia gasped again as she ground down. Colleen thrust immediately, there was no time to just play and she licked fervently at the clit standing at attention waiting for her ministrations.

"God, oh God, yes baby, that's it," Nia gasped out, the need was too great and too pent up and she came almost immediately...hard. Her bucking and grinding into Colleen caused her to clasp her head with her hand almost pulling the hairs and roots from her head. "God yessssss!" she hissed as she came.

Colleen was almost shocked but oh so gratified to hear Nia. Knowing what she could do to her was an aphrodisiac and she was creaming in her own panties. Gently she removed her fingers and licked them clean while looking up at Nia once she released her head. Smiling mischievously she

rose up, feeling a little ungainly over her additional weight from the pregnancy.

Nia grasped her arms though and holding her close kissed her deeply and began to undress her. "Wait," Colleen gasped as she reached for her breasts and Colleen removed her clothes including a nursing bra and pads. "I need to expel this," she said as she indicated her milk full breasts.

"How long?" Nia groaned wanting her, wanting all of her....NOW!

"A few minutes, please be patient," she begged wanting Nia just as much now that they had started this dance.

Nia watched Colleen hook up the pump to both her breasts at the same time. It hadn't grossed her out as she thought it would when she considered it similar to milking a cow. Instead it surprised her how attractive Colleen looked doing it. Even with her little Buddha belly, a remainder of her pregnancy, she looked beautiful. No longer the little mouse, but a beautiful woman who had struggled through and brought a life into this world Nia found herself wanting her more and more. Mischievously she began to tug at Colleen's pants.

"What...?" Colleen asked as she adjusted the pump and looked down at a near naked Nia removing her clothes for her.

"I'm not going to waste time later," Nia grinned mischievously as she removed Colleen's socks and shoes along with her pants. Then she reached for the panties.

"Wait..."Colleen protested but there was no stopping the determined woman.

Nia stripped her bare from the waist down and spread her legs reaching up and in to pull her to the edge of the chair where she was pumping. Seeing that she was already wet, scenting it, she was anxious to taste...she didn't wait. She leaned in for her first taste in months.

"Ohh, God. Nia," Colleen leaned back in the chair unable to do anything as she pumped. She watched as Nia looked up mischievously again, her eyes sparkling, turning black in her desire.

The taste was different from what she remembered. She wondered if the pregnancy had changed anything else about Colleen but she didn't care as she began to lave attention on her clit and the surrounding lips. It was awash with moisture from Colleen's arousal. She gently began to play with it with her fingertips and watching Colleen's reactions she inserted one finger delicately.

"Moreeeeee...." Colleen groaned from her position. Her hands were full with the pump and she couldn't do anything but take it...it felt so good.

Nia inserted a second finger into the slick wetness and bending them she pressed on the spot she knew so well. Colleen's body went still at the pressure and emotions that went with that sensation.

"Oh my gawd," she whimpered having forgotten how good that actually felt as Nia expertly played her body.

"You taste so good," Nia murmured enjoying herself and the affect it was having on her.

The milk sloshed in their containers as Colleen writhed. She wanted more but Nia's delicate touch was so magical. "More," she commanded and was gratified to feel Nia start to thrust in and out of her, occasionally petting her G spot and causing more sensations to rock her inflamed body. She glanced down at the milk containers wondering how soon she would be finished with this and if she would cum first or finish expelling the milk from her breast's first. She didn't care as Nia took her body and didn't stop.

Tentative at first from hurting her where the baby had come out of her body and its subsequent healing for so many weeks, she now began to rub and twist and thrust with increasing speed as she licked and sucked and tasted to her hearts content. She could have stayed there all day long she felt as she enjoyed herself but she could feel how the muscles tightened inside of Colleen and she continued to build it up for a moment only to let her have her release almost as quickly as she had had her own.

"Oh my god, oh my god, oh my god," Colleen nearly shouted but mindful that the baby was across the hall and sleeping she bit her lip as the orgasm overtook her body. Still holding the milk bottles and pump in her arms she had no control over her lower extremities as she came...and came...and came.

Nia was fascinated. Never before in their lovemaking had Colleen responded so quickly or so violently. Abstinence obviously affected them both and she gushed over the edge of the chair before Nia caught it in her mouth drinking at the buffet before her until she felt it lessen and pulled away. Looking up she rubbed her chin on her arm and grinned satisfied that she had given Colleen a fantastic set of orgasms.

"That was unfair," Colleen admonished her with a grin in return.

"How was that unfair?" Nia asked almost innocently but she knew, she knew very well she had taken full advantage of Colleen's position as she pumped.

"Paybacks are a bitch you know?" Colleen stated ominously as the first breast was properly deflated and she removed the pump from that side.

"Promise?" Nia grinned harder as she looked eagerly up at her lover.

Colleen laughed as expected and removed the second suction cover from her other nipple and put a cap on the milk. "I need to um...clean up...would you put these in the refrigerator?" she asked handing Nia the two milk bottles.

Nia laughed delighted as she anticipated the rest of the evening between them as they rediscovered themselves and each other.

❧ CHAPTER TWENTY SIX ☙

A few days later they were sharing 'family' time with Nate between them as Nia attempted to get some work done when the buzzer went off downstairs. Looking up at the unexpected noise she went to the intercom. "Yes?" she called into it and tried to look at the fuzzy picture. It showed two dark blobs and she shook her head wondering if Simone could get them a better intercom camera, the ones around the apartment were crystal clear.

"Nia Toyomoto?" they botched the pronunciation of her name garbling it horribly into the intercom.

Nia shrugged, few people got it right the first time and she'd accepted that long ago. It wasn't worth getting upset about. Graciously she answered, "Yes?"

"Police," they said and a badge was held up to the intercom camera, for once it showed very clearly.

Nia blinked wondering what they wanted. Colleen looked up questioningly, a slightly frightened look on her face.

"May we come up and talk to you?" the voice asked respectfully but determinately.

Wondering what they wanted Nia pushed the access button without answering which would allow them to get to the elevator.

"What do you think they want?" Colleen asked nervously as she held Nate close to her, almost to protect him from what she did not know.

Nia shrugged. Who knew with all the clients she had what this might be about but she didn't like them bothering her at home about work. She walked over to the camera monitor and watched for them to get off the elevator. Two plain clothed police officers got off. She saw by the way they walked when one of their coats parted that there was a badge attached to his belt and then she glanced and saw a gun. Walking determinedly across the apartment she was at the door when they rang the doorbell. Opening it she kept her foot behind it by habit to block it and asked, "How may I help you?"

"May we come in, we have something to discuss with you?" one of the officers asked eyeing her.

"May I ask what this is regarding?" Nia asked just as respectfully but taking a 'no-nonsense' approach that she frequently used in the courtroom.

"A body was found this morning at the constructions site next door to your building," one of the officers began and the other held up his hand to quiet him as they both stared at her intently.

"And why are you on my doorstep?" Nia asked suspiciously. They had to be here for a reason.

"The body has been tentatively identified as Cletus Hodsworth," the first officer said watching her for her reaction.

They all heard the gasp from Colleen across the room on the couch. Nia turned to look at her effectively unblocking the door and both officers entered, uninvited. Nia looked at them in annoyance but they both made a beeline for Colleen on the couch as they looked around the open apartment at its nice furnishings. Nia closed the door and walked behind them with her arms crossed and wondered what this was about. Surely they didn't suspect Colleen's involvement?

"Are you Colleen Hodsworth?" one of the officers asked Colleen watching her with the baby held protectively close, almost as a shield.

"I was Colleen Hodsworth; I took my maiden name back after the divorce. I'm Colleen Picket again," she told them with a little raising of her stubborn chin, almost defensively.

"May we sit down, we have a few questions we would like to ask the two of you?" the second officer asked.

Since they were already in the apartment Nia figured she should hear them out but she exchanged a look with Colleen who looked frightened. She hoped Colleen would stay silent and let her handle this.

"Please be seated," Colleen offered generously.

Nia barely restrained herself from rolling her eyes at the offer. She didn't want these two plain clothes police officers getting comfortable! She did however want some answers. "You said that Cletus's body was found in the construction site next door?" she asked taking on the tone she used to cross examine witnesses in the courtroom. She came to sit next to Colleen, touching her but not making it obvious. The baby began to fuss at the tension he sensed in his mother.

The officer ignored Nia's question and focused on Colleen. "The baby is yours and his?" he asked instead.

"No, the baby is mine," Colleen said defensively holding him tighter which caused him to squirm. Nia saw what was happening and gently took the baby from her.

"Here, I'll take him," she said gently in the voice the baby recognized. He smiled up to her as she cuddled him close and rocked a little on the couch with him in her arms hoping he would go to sleep. Colleen had just breast fed him so he was full. She looked up to see both officers looking at her surprised.

"I meant, is he the father of your baby?" the officer tried again.

Colleen raised her chin defensively as she replied, "He's no father!"

"Easy Colleen," Nia said quietly and then turned to the officer to answer his question. "He is genetically the father but I'm sure you know

of the pending rape charges against Cletus regarding that," she told him with a glimmer beginning in her eye.

"And you intend to raise him alone?" the first officer asked writing notes in a notebook.

"I'm not alone," she answered, still defensive.

The officers exchanged looks between Nia and Colleen. Nia looked them right in the eye daring them to say one word about their relationship.

"Um, you two…are a couple?" he asked.

There was the word, Nia almost said something but Colleen beat her to it. "We are. Do you have a problem with that?" Nia could hear the same feisty Colleen that had drawn her attention so long ago when she was defending Nia or protecting her at work.

"Look, what is this about? Yes, we live here together. Yes this is Cletus Hodsworth's biological child. No, he isn't going to be father of the year regarding this child that was conceived through rape. What else do you need to know?" Nia asked sarcastically but in a tone that brooked no nonsense and yet never rose above a certain level. The baby thought she was almost crooning to it as he began to close his eyes.

"We believe Mr. Hodsworth may have fallen from your balcony," the second officer said for effect.

Nia's eyes nearly bugged out of her head and she glanced at Colleen who looked horrified.

"Do you know how he may have gotten there?" Nia asked hoping they had some evidence to back up their conclusion.

"No, we are hoping you can help us with that. We know you two were divorcing…" he began but Colleen interrupted.

"We *are* divorced!" she said angrily. She didn't like where this going. She wasn't glad Cletus was dead but she wasn't unhappy about it either. She could rest easier knowing he was gone and wouldn't interfere with Nate. She and Nia could raise him alone, together, and no one would come between them.

"Yes ma'am, you've said that," he said kindly to her. "We do have to investigate every avenue. His body was found in the pit they have dug for the garage next door and it indicated he fell from a height and your balcony is above it," he pointed out.

"So on that assumption we pushed him?" Colleen asked hotly.

"Colleen," Nia warned. Even a sarcastic comment could and would be used against them if the two cops got pissed off. "Why don't you take Nate up to bed," she said handing her the sleepy infant. Getting her out of the room wouldn't be a bad idea.

"Did you push him?" one of the officers quickly asked.

Nia glared at him but Colleen looked at him dismissively and shook her head at their stupidity. "Of course I didn't, you know very well I was being flippant!"

Colleen knew Nia was getting her out of the room but she took Nate anyway and flounced away up the stairs to his room. Both officers had risen with her out of respect and watched as she climbed the stairs. They sat down in unison as well much to Nia's amusement. She sat back waiting for their questions.

"When was the last time you saw Mr. Hodsworth?" the questions continued.

"You have that in your reports as well," Nia pointed out knowing giving any more information than they had was a bad idea, she wanted information from them. "He attacked me in my own apartment and I'm sure you will find all that out if you don't know it already. What was he doing here again? How would he have gotten on our balcony? And why haven't the cops been able to find him all this time since he attacked Colleen and then myself? He is wanted on drug charges, rape, and assault and you couldn't find him?" she attacked with lightening swiftness to keep them unbalanced.

The two officers exchanged a look between them. One of them began defensively, "Well, we don't know about all that, all we have is a body in the site next door and your balcony. You have a history with him..." he was cut off by Nia.

"We have a *history* because of his attacks on our person. There are also other balconies on this building," she pointed out the flimsy 'evidence' they were giving her. "You obviously know of our 'history' because of the past cases. Furthermore there is a garden on the roof and he could have accessed that."

They exchanged a look again and the other officer asked Nia, "Do you know why he would have been coming after you again?"

Nia stared at him like he were stupid and didn't answer. Of course she knew why he would have come after them again. His 'wife' had left him. She was succeeding without him. She had fallen in love with another person, a woman. She'd had a baby that he felt he owned just as much as he owned his wife. She knew why he would come back. It also meant the feeling that someone was watching them was correct, he had been. She wasn't however going to do their jobs for them. They had come here for a reason, a fishing expedition and she wasn't going to take the bait. She had gotten Colleen out of the room to prevent her justifiable anger over Cletus from causing her to give them something. "Who knows, he was disturbed I believe. He felt he owned his ex-wife," she told them, nothing that wasn't in other reports if they chose to read them.

"So are you thinking he may have been coming for her?" one of them asked.

It was then that Nia realized they hadn't introduced themselves or shown their badges and she began to get suspicious. She went into lawyer mode. "Excuse me, but may I see your identification?" she asked surprising them both.

One of them immediately reached into his overcoat and retrieved a wallet from his jacket pocket, as he pulled it out she spied the badge on his belt she must have seen in the camera, she also saw a shoulder holster holding a gun. The other eyed her suspiciously. "Why are you asking now?"

Nia countered with, "Why aren't you more forthcoming with the information?" her head nodded to his partner who was pulling out the wallet. He glanced over and resigned reached for his own.

Nia was satisfied when she had Detective Sal Paris and Detective Martin Lenowski in her memory for future information. She looked closely at both I.D's to be sure they were authentic and then realized if they were fake, she would have no idea anyway. She handed them back to both officers and Colleen came back down the stairs to join them.

"Are you done?" Nia asked into the silence of the last few minutes as she had examined their identification.

"No, we have just started," began one of the officers.

Nia looked at him and then at the other officer only to ask, "Then you get two more questions, that's it, I'm done with this."

"Look, you don't seem to understand, this is a murder investigation!" the other officer, Detective Paris interjected.

"And you don't seem to understand. We have cooperated with this farce long enough. You cops couldn't find him after he jumped for the drug and rape charges. He attacks me in my home and now you come here with questions because he is dead next door? I have heard nothing that really implicates either of us." She exchanged a look with an anxious Colleen before turning back to the detectives. "You said it's because of our history with him and the fact that our balcony overlooks the site where you found him?" She sneered at the lack of evidence. "I could make up better than that. I suggest you both leave now and if you have any further questions, get a warrant and serve me at my office, anytime," she finished sarcastically rising to her feet and after a moment Colleen followed and stood up as well.

"What about our two questions?" Detective Lenowski asked almost petulantly as though they had been found out.

Nia's eyes narrowed at his tone. "Unless you have more than suspicions, I suggest you get the hell outta my apartment. I have and I will take it farther up the food chain in your precinct. To be honest, I don't

have a lot of faith in the cops around here to find a needle in a haystack much less solve a case. For months you couldn't find this guy and now you say he's turned up dead next to our apartment?" She let out air in exasperation giving her opinion of their work efforts. "Make your questions official in the future because I'm done, I'm so done," she said as she walked towards the door to open it for them.

"We're not done with this," Detective Paris said forcefully, almost bullyingly.

"We are for now," Nia returned almost tauntingly.

"We will be back," Lenowski promised.

"Make it official," Nia told him as she shut the door.

"I thought you said to say nothing?" Colleen asked as she stared at Nia. She hadn't seen this side of her in a while and she found it rather attractive and exciting.

Nia was angry for losing a little bit of control but she was angrier at their nerve. "They were on a fishing expedition. They don't have jack and they both know it. They were hoping we would give them something to pin it on, perhaps us." She walked determinedly across the apartment to the bar and slid open the cabinet door to look at the camera's. Pressing the screen for the camera that took in the balcony she tried to pull up the last hours on it. "Do you know how this thing works?" she asked exasperatedly.

"What are you looking for?" Colleen kneeled down next to her trying to see what she was doing.

"I want to get the footage for the camera on the balcony, we should probably go back at least twenty four hours or more," Nia told her as she pushed buttons but nothing happened.

"Well, that's not going to work, the disc is missing out of the recorder," Colleen told her pushing a button as the machine shot out the tray for the disc.

"What the hell, I know there was one in there; I changed it just last week!" Nia said exasperated. "Did you take it out?" She looked at Colleen wondering why she would remove it.

But Colleen shook her head. "I watch the monitor but I never touch this stuff," she indicated the simple digital video recorder that could put weeks of video activity onto one small disc since it only recorded when there was motion. Nia had taken it upon herself to change it periodically and Colleen didn't do anything else with it.

"But you didn't take the disc?" she asked to be sure hoping there was a reason for it to be missing.

Colleen shook her head again as she got up. "No, I didn't touch it," she assured her.

"Damn," Nia swore aloud. "Did I forget to put one in last week?" she asked more to herself as she got up too.

"You told me last week that we needed to pick up some new ones, that first pack was almost empty but I saw you put one in the recorder," Colleen reminded her.

"Then what the hell happened to the one that was in there?" Nia asked as suddenly looked around wondering if their 'security' wasn't all that secure. Colleen was here most days but she had just started back to work recently and the place was empty for those hours. The fact that she had been alone here though with the baby concerned Nia the most. Nia reached for her cell phone which was charging on the bar.

"Who are you calling?" Colleen asked curious.

"Simone, she's the one that installed these camera's. Maybe there is a backup we don't know about but we need that disc. Those yahoo's that were just here are looking to pin a murder rap on someone and I don't want either of us to be the target. I also want to know who the hell has been..." she left off as she got the recording for the security company.

'Hello, you have reached Stalwart Security, if this is an emergency call," it droned on and Nia listened until a directory came on and she pushed the appropriate buttons to get Simone's extension and left a message for her to call.

"Now what?" Colleen asked.

"I don't know," Nia answered and then looked through the kitchen to the balcony. "You know, those cops were acting odd. They didn't even ask to see the balcony or take fingerprints or anything," she mused as she thought aloud.

"Can you get someone to come and take them?" Colleen asked concerned.

Nia nodded and called back the number for Simone's security firm and to leave a second message for her.

Nia was not happy. The police had followed up with an 'official' questioning of both Colleen and Nia and they seemed to think one of them was involved in the 'murder' of Cletus Hodsworth, or at least that was subtly implied. With the partners already grumbling over her relationship with Colleen, having the police show up on 'official' business was not making her popular at the firm. Nia could feel the pressure mounting. To top it off, she couldn't get a hold of Simone and this bothered her more than she would admit. She had warned Colleen to say nothing to the police about her suspicions or the balcony or the cameras even. As a result her interview came across as stilted and the cops were now suspicious of

the 'ex-wife.' It created a tension between the two of them that they didn't need right now.

Nate seemed to pick up on the tension and was acting up, crying a lot and being fussy. It could also be that he was in daycare for part of the day now that Colleen was back at work. But between work and school, the baby made her frazzled and Colleen seriously thought about dropping school and going back to being a legal secretary. She didn't want to fail Nia though and if she dropped out she knew how disappointed Nia would be for her.

"Look, Ms. Toyomoto, you have to give us something to go on," pleaded Detective Paris in exasperation. He had looked into her background and found her to be a top litigator. Her tight lipped responses to their questions though had given them nothing.

"I have nothing further to say to you gentlemen, that is all," Nia told them in response, a standard response that had frustrated them. She really had nothing to give them and she wouldn't be confessing to anything any time soon.

"Nia, you need to settle this, these officers coming around does not look good for the firm," Stewart told her one day.

"I know Stewart, I've told them everything I could but they are looking for something that is simply not there and they won't drop it," she explained patiently trying to hold her temper. Although Stewart had been her biggest supporter for years, this 'outing' as it were, although unconfirmed by Nia, had strained their relationship and she felt, lost his respect.

"Why do they keep questioning you here, at work?" he asked as he looked around.

"I asked them to," she told him.

"Why here?"

"Because they were trying to be intimidating at my apartment and were purely guessing there. Here they had to make it official and I had the home court advantage," she tried to make light of it.

He laughed as she hoped he would. "Well this is the third time they've been here. Finish it up would you?"

"I will try," Nia answered and nodded as she turned to go to her office. Her assistants looked at her curiously and she ignored them. This was when she missed having Colleen as her assistant. She was supportive, non-judgmental, and she felt loyal. Neither of these two generated loyalty. She had taken Suzette on one trip with her a few months back for a client and it was a disaster. Lynda had been super-efficient when she took her but she felt like the woman was trying to second guess her all the time. She missed the convenience of having Colleen around and had gotten used

to her. Who was she kidding, she just flat out missed Colleen when they weren't together.

❧ CHAPTER TWENTY SEVEN ❧

"I'm sorry, I was out of the country on business," Simone said for at least the third time as Nia raved at her in anger.

"I wasn't aware your security firm did international security," Nia countered having looked more into the contract between Chase-Dunham and Stalwart Security and learning what exactly they offered in terms of service. The firm was well taken care of and she had felt confident hiring Simone for her home but there was still…something about her.

"This wasn't for work, this was personal," Simone said looking around the apartment but not elaborating on what was so personal that she was unavailable to clients for weeks on end.

Nia explained what the cops had told them, she also told of her suspicions regarding their 'investigation.' "I'd like you to fingerprint the apartment and balcony, tell me who has been in here recently and out on the balcony particularly."

"Can you see from the video?" Simone asked as she looked and assessed the value of some of the items in the apartment and wondered how much one could get for a jade dragon in this day and age.

Nia explained about the disc. "And that's another thing, we both saw me put a new one in the recorder, so what happened to it? Did he have one on him, I've asked what was found on the body and gotten blank stares. They don't like having questions asked of them, they only like asking the questions," she complained about the cops.

"Yeah, they are like that," Simone said as she looked around some more peeking her head in and out of things. "I'm going to need your and Colleen's fingerprints to rule them out and I'll have to run a few through a database or two," she told Nia and waited for the inevitable questions.

"Is it legal?" Nia asked realizing what Simone was saying without saying it.

"It will be if you need it for defense," she was assured.

Nia and Colleen watched as Simone and a couple of other people she called came in and dusted for fingerprints. It was a messy, dirty job but they were efficient and got quite a few off the balcony.

"No there is no backup," Simone assured Nia when she was asked. "Have you been recording since then?" she asked to change the subject; she could see Nia didn't quite believe her. She grinned to herself realizing that Nia was too astute and rethought her assessment of her and the apartment. She reminded herself that Nia was a 'friend' and would practice a hands off policy regarding her apartment, but it was tempting, oh so tempting.

Nia told her everything the cops had told them and Colleen contributed the questions she had been asked. Some of it even surprised Simone who was angry that they were attempting to pin it on someone, anyone, but most particularly the ex-wife.

"Do you have contacts, can you find out some more about this?" she practically pleaded with Simone.

"There are a few things I can find out for you," she promised and wondered if she couldn't get them by legal means how far Nia would really want her to go?

"I just want this to be over with, we need to move on with our lives and the stress isn't welcome," she answered.

Simone just nodded in agreement as they packed up their things. "Sorry about the mess but fingerprinting dust does that," she said with a little shrug.

"Yeah, that's okay," Nia assured her but she was appalled at the mess and not willing to clean it up herself or have Coleen do it she would have a crew in later that day if she had to pay extra for their services.

Simone got back to her a few days later. "You were right, the cops are trying to pin it on you or Colleen," she told her.

"But why? Pinning it on me makes no sense and Colleen divorced the slime ball!" she said as they sat in her office. Colleen was on her lunch break, the only way they could conduct this conversation without someone getting in a snit over favoritism or something like that. Nia was beginning to think that some of the hassles of a large firm were a little over rated. She was sick of the nit picking.

"Yes but as a drug dealer the slime ball had friends in all the right places, why do you think they couldn't 'find' him when they went looking?" Simone alluded.

"You mean the cops are involved?" Nia asked angrily.

Simone nodded and continued, "He had an apartment set up right across the street from your own, they've known about that for over a week now and gathered evidence that he has been trying to watch you. Your blinds though stymied him from what I could see."

"You've been there?" Nia asked aghast.

Simone nodded but then added, "Not technically if anyone asks. But he was pretty frustrated that you kept those closed except during the day and when no one was there he couldn't see anything. It's obvious he had anger issues by the temper tantrums he took out on the walls over there. I think that's why after Colleen had the baby he decided to see what he could see for himself and climbed down from the roof of your building from the roof next door. I think he may have slipped and fallen from that

and although I found his fingerprints on your balcony, I don't think they are recent."

"But the cops keep hammering at us for information like we know something!" Nia said angrily.

"And they will keep that up as long as someone in power has something to hide. The disc taken from your recorder for instance, that wasn't a coincidence," she sat back taking a sip of the excellent cappuccino that Nia had offered her.

"How do you know for sure someone took it?" Nia asked suspiciously.

"They didn't take the time to wear gloves when they took it from the recorder," she said dryly. She didn't add the information she had that she could not or would not disclose to Nia at this time.

"So you got a fingerprint?" Nia said excitedly and glanced at Colleen who looked frightened that someone had been in the apartment.

Simone nodded and then said, "Yes but it was a cop so we have to tread carefully, I'm not sure how high up this goes and I don't want to get caught in the crossfire. I have my own business and reputation to protect. It's a good thing you have a clean reputation as a litigator, that is going to go a long way when the shit hits the fan."

"Look, I don't care who they are at this point. I want the harassment to stop. The stress isn't doing any of us any good," she glanced at Colleen who looked worried to her. She knew Colleen hadn't been sleeping well and Nate was fussy as a result.

"You might if a judge or two are involved," Simone informed her.

"What?"

Simone nodded. "Drugs are big business; there is a lot of money involved. Cletus was small potatoes and if he hadn't gotten himself killed they probably would have taken him out if he had survived to go to prison."

Colleen put her hand to her mouth in horror at how nonchalantly Simone was talking about her ex-husband. She had hated him but not to the point of wanting him dead, not like this.

"I have a few more bits of evidence to collect and I'll let you know before I turn it over to the 'right' people but I'll send you and a couple of other people copies just in case the one that I'm sending it to isn't as clean as I think he is."

"Who is it?" Nia asked wondering how deep this went and what evidence Simone had other than what she had revealed.

Simone told her and both Nia and Colleen's eyes rounded. "How can he do anything?" Nia asked astounded that Simone had that kind of pull.

"Let's just say he owes me, big time. I collect favors from time to time and this time I'm asking for one." She got up to leave after finishing her cappuccino.

Nia saw her out and turned to Colleen. "What the hell did we get ourselves into?" she asked her not expecting a reply.

Colleen got up too and went crying into Nia's welcome arms. "I'm sorry, I'm so sorry," she sobbed.

"What? What for?" Nia asked trying to hold her away from the expensive silk blouse which would be destroyed with tears. She wanted to comfort her and had held her for a moment until she realized she was crying.

"For getting you into this mess, for Cletus," she sniffed and Nia handed her the box of tissues.

"You didn't get me into anything. Cletus was a shit." She sat Colleen down putting her arm around her as she reasoned with her. "You can't forget how far you've come since you left him. What he was into was of his own free will. You didn't know what he was up to. Let it go. Concentrate on Nate and us and let's move on from there. This will all blow over and there will be something new for people to gossip about," she told her. She also knew it hadn't been easy for Colleen since she came back, people whispered behind her back and with the police showing up to interview her they hadn't been happy with her over that either.

Nia comforted Colleen but they were interrupted by Grayson Morse who barged into her office with Lynda saying in the background, "You can't go in there, she's in conference!"

Seeing Nia with her arm around Colleen he looked at them accusingly as they looked up surprised.

"Can't you do that on your own time?" he asked scathingly pointing a finger at the two of them.

Nia stood up angry. She could see both Suzette and Lynda staring in horror outside the door at Gray. Lynda's face was flushed and she could only imagine it was from trying to stop the senior partner. "How dare you come into my office unannounced!" she attacked.

"It's the middle of the day, can't you two wait until you get home?" he nearly spat.

Knowing what he was accusing her of and knowing she had to play the part Nia made a great show of looking down at Colleen and back up at him. She narrowed her eyes slightly before she replied. "How dare you imply that? I'm comforting my friend on her lunch hour regarding the situation she finds herself in and in no way is that anything of which you are implying! Was there something in particular you wanted Gray or was this surprise visit planned to make accusations?" she attacked again.

"You can't behave like that in here," he said accusingly as he shook a finger at her.

Nia realized what an old crone looked like as she looked at the older man and how apoplectic he looked in his outrage. She shook her head.

"And you took it upon yourself to enforce the rules? You are way off base here Gray!" she shot back.

Nia was surprised when Colleen got up and wiping her nose said, "Mr. Grayson, you are a dirty old man. Nia has been nothing but warm and generous to me and what you are implying is wrong. I don't think you'd want your dirty laundry aired like this and I'm sure slamming into offices like this for effect isn't going to keep that dirty laundry quiet."

Nia stared at her in absolute astonishment. Colleen wasn't the bravest of women but coming to Nia's defense always seemed to make her spit like a kitten. Her barbs though had worked as Grayson deflated at her words. His 'dirty laundry' he certainly didn't want aired. Nia realized Colleen's quiet words had gone into the outer office and both Lynda and Suzette had heard her quite clearly. She realized Colleen had had a devastating effect on all their gossip and innuendo and since they hadn't made an announcement, hadn't confessed or defended themselves, hadn't said anything about their relationship and living arrangements the gossip had been pretty intense.

"I suggest unless you have some business for the firm to discuss with me Gray that you leave my office at once," Nia ordered.

Slightly hunched over he looked at her for a moment. She thought she saw a spark of resentment in those old eyes but then he turned about face and marched out of the office. Suzette and Lynda looked busy at Suzette's desk when he walked by but looked up as soon as he left. Nia made a come here gesture to the two women inviting them into her office.

"Please close the door," she told them when they were both inside. She stayed standing as did they. Colleen at her back she addressed them both. "I think you both know I've been very supportive of Colleen as a friend but I want you both to know that the gossip in this firm has got to stop. Behavior such as Grayson's will not be tolerated and I expect my own staff to back me up one hundred and ten percent. If neither of you can do that, tell me now and you will be replaced." She waited a moment for either of them to make a motion but they stood there frozen like statues. "I think you both know I'm not easy to work for but I'm fair and if push comes to shove I'll win," she veiled her threat softly. "Colleen has done nothing wrong here and the word on the street stops there, do I make myself clear?" They both nodded. "Thank you, we won't speak of this again," she told them dismissively. She watched as they both turned and closed the door behind them after they left.

"You didn't have to do that," Colleen sniffed.

"Yes I did. It's getting impossible to work here. I love my job but I'd leave in a heartbeat if they threatened you and you know that don't you?" Nia asked pulling her into her arms again. She didn't care about the silk blouse now.

Colleen held her tight knowing how much Nia loved her and grateful for it. "I just don't want you to lose your job," she whispered in a frightened voice.

"They can't fire me, they have to buy me out now and as I didn't do anything wrong they'd have a fight on their hands," Nia told her astutely. "They also don't want to lose the millions in billables that I have under my belt and they would go with me if I opened my own firm. I don't want to have to do that. I don't have it in me to run my own firm but I will if they force me to."

"Can I work for you if you open your own firm?" Colleen teased. She knew how much working at Chase-Dunham meant to Nia. How hard she had worked for this partnership. She had observed some of it and was only grateful that she had been privileged to work for her because it meant that the relationship they had developed had started here.

"Of course, you can go back not only to being my legal secretary but with what you are learning at school you can be my paralegal too!" she teased in return.

"God, what time is it? I'm going to have to run and feed Nate if I'm to be at my desk on time," she suddenly remembered her schedule. "Don't forget to pick him up tonight after work from daycare," she reminded her as she leaned up for an expected kiss.

Nia obliged and then laughed at her. They had given nothing away but friendship and while there was speculation rampant around the office, for all anyone knew they were just friends raising a baby together. She wasn't naïve enough to think that they didn't know but they had neither confirmed nor denied the accusations. She watched as her efficient little girlfriend hurried to get to 'their' son on time.

❧ CHAPTER TWENTY EIGHT ❧

"Nia, this is a side of you I never thought I would see," Eleanor commented as Nia maneuvered the baby car seat that carried Nate onto a chair next to her at the Thursday night gathering.

"Well, Colleen had a class and he isn't up to being on his own," she joked.

They too had speculated and word out on the street that they were living together had of course reached all their ears. A few had openly asked if they were a couple and Nia and Colleen would neither confirm nor deny their questions. "We are *friends*," was the party line that both used. A couple of times Nia had snapped, "Does it matter?" and they had backed off.

"But you seem to know what you are doing," Tiffany commented as she watched Nia effortlessly pick him up and hold him up so he could see all the people and the lights and things. It would entertain him for a while.

"I'm sorry but no one under eighteen is allowed in the bar area," a new waiter tried to tell Nia.

Nia looked at him as though he had lost his mind. The other women all hid their laughter behind their hands as they watched the drama unfold before them. "I'll be sure not to slip him a beer okay?" Nia asked sarcastically.

"Ma'am you can't have a baby in a bar," he said condescendingly wondering if she was going to be trouble.

Suddenly remembering that she knew the owner from all the years she had been coming here with her group she smiled at an odd little coincidence. The waiter wondered why she was smiling but the women around her eagerly anticipated what she would say next. "Ask Nate if he really wants to kick out his namesake here from my table."

"Um, you know Nate?" the waiter asked suddenly nervous.

Nia nodded and waited. "Go ask him, see what he says." She watched as he walked away and several of the women began to laugh at how calm Nia had remained.

"Did Colleen name him after Nate?" Nadia asked behind her laughter.

Nia shook her head. "It's a common name after all but hey, I'll use what I can get."

They didn't see that waiter again that evening but Nate, the owner did come over. "What's this I hear that you named your baby after me?" he said in his big blustery way.

"Well not my baby but Colleen's," Nia informed him as she handed the baby across to Colleen who had just joined them as well. She also adroitly

avoided his question and her eyes twinkled at Colleen as though they had some shared joke.

"Well, any baby of yours is welcome here, just don't go getting me in trouble hey?" he asked and then pointing at Nia he added, "Or you will have to get me outta it okay?"

"Okay Nate, it's a deal," Nia promised laughing at his exuberance. He bought them a round of drinks on the house and the whole 'issue' died down among laughter and shared friendship.

It was one of the last times they laughed in a while. Nia explained how she had gotten around the rude waiter who didn't know they had been long time customers and Colleen had laughed at the coincidence. She hadn't known the owner's name was Nate but thought it clever of Nia to use it.

The next week all hell broke loose. Nia had expected it after a package from Simone was delivered to her and while she didn't appreciate some of the evidence that Simone provided her with, especially copies of the missing disc showing Cletus indeed trying to get into her apartment from the balcony one day and another one of the day his body hurtled by the camera's to his death in the parking construction.

In another one there was a mystery man in their apartment reaching for the disc that was included in the video portion of the packet and he would later be identified as a police officer.

"How far do you want me to research this?" Simone had asked her but she didn't expect the results when she had innocently asked for everything.

Apparently Cletus had been thrown from the rooftop garden above their apartment and not accidentally as he tried to access the apartment. Nia would have handled it differently.

Simone had also gone to all the television stations in the New York City area and even down to Washington D.C. with the information she had showing corruption in NYPD and several captains, lieutenants, and other police officers were arrested as the evidence also ended up on Internal Affairs and the FBI's desks. There was no way they could keep it quiet that drugs and money, prostitution, and surveillance as well as intimidation, illegal search and seizure and many other activities had been going on. Simone had been thorough and she knew the people to contact to get the evidence. Each packet had been customized to the recipient and the news broadcasts were full of what they had.

"How did you get all this?" Nia asked in consternation as they met several weeks later in her office. Even the law firm's investigators weren't this thorough or had such access. It was obvious that Simone had been in the police department at some point or been given information and video that would compromise them.

"Do you really want to know?" Simone asked with an eyebrow raised.

Nia looked up at her sometimes friend and considered. Sighing she realized that perhaps it was better that she didn't know. The damage was incredible and she had a lot of cops angry at her and their firm. Swallowing she nodded.

"Are you sure?" Simone asked with a tilt of her head.

Nia stared her down.

Simone nodded in agreement. "In my lines of work and we both know that I don't just do 'security work,'" she said using quotation marks with her fingers.

Nia nodded in agreement encouraging Simone to continue.

"In my line of work," she paraphrased. "I have to have friends in all lines of work and 'expertise,'" she again made the marks.

Nia was feeling uncomfortable. She dealt with criminals in all sorts of things in the law but she had never had anyone basically admit it. She realized Simone was being very careful in how she admitted it. Nothing she had said could really be used against her.

"When you asked me to look into this I began to follow a few of the officers involved. There was a lot of excitement in the apartment building that is being remodeled across the way and I followed up on it."

"Did you go into it legally?" Nia couldn't help herself from asking.

Simone waited for her to realize she wasn't going to confirm or deny it.

"After following the cops in question and finding what I did in that apartment I began to piece together the scenario. When the drugs came into play," she began but Nia put up her hand.

"That's enough, I don't want to know anymore," she stopped Simone from continuing. "I thank you for all the leaks and the evidence but I don't want to know how you got it. Please send me your bill," she said as she stood up from the couch and waited for Simone.

Simone grinned. Funny how people didn't want to know the truth, the full truth. Nia was one of the good people in this world but she could be a little naïve about the harsh realities of what was out there. "I will," she said as she shook Nia's hand.

"I may have some work I could send your way from the firm if you are interested in this," she thought about the proper word to use. "Extra-curricular type of work?" she phrased.

Simone grinned and nodded. "Anytime."

Nia wasn't surprised when Stewart asked her to come into his offices.

"Nia, I'm going to retire. Drama like this is the kind of thing I've avoided my entire career. I'm going to recommend to the board that they issue an apology for what they have thought about you and what they

intended to do to you," Stewart said to her one day as they met in his office. "I'm sorry you went through all that. Your life and your relationships with your friends is none of our business and I can see you always had the firm's best interests at heart. Especially when you had Colleen go into the other department. What you and she have is no one's business, especially this firms. I don't pretend to understand such a friendship but if you are happy, if she is happy, then it's none of this old man's business either. I wish you well."

Nia absorbed the words he had just told her. Her father figure, her mentor, was *retiring*? "How long?" she asked, neither confirming nor denying the rest of what he had just said.

"I figure six months will be long enough for the partners to squabble over my office and place," he joked.

"You will be missed," she told him wondering how long she would stay after he was gone. The thought of opening her own firm was sounding better and better. Grayson wasn't the only old foggie that didn't like the idea of a homosexual in their firm although she personally knew of several that they didn't realize were gay that worked there.

"I hope you will stay," he said knowingly, almost as though he had read her mind.

She smiled giving nothing away. "Who says I'm going anywhere?"

He smiled in return realizing she was good at her job and they would be fools to antagonize her any further with their gossip and innuendo. "My grandson Chase is in law school now, I'm hoping in a few years you could mentor him," he said with a hopeful look in his eye and a note of almost desperation in his voice.

"Ah, the heir apparent," Nia said knowingly. This changed a few things. Having a member of the Dunham family in the firm would mean its continuation and she could help form its future. She remembered meeting Chase at a few firm picnics. He was a bright young man even years ago before he went to college. He had ignored his father who wanted him to become an accountant like him but instead decided to become a lawyer like his two grandfathers who had founded Chase-Dunham and for whom he was named.

"There is still a place for you here Nia. You can bring these old farts into the twenty first century. It's about time they got their heads out of their rears and realized that the old family values are still there and this new generation just handles them differently. I know you have never said but if you stay I'd like to see where you'd help take this firm. You are one of the good ones and I know even I'd be surprised eventually. You've always held a place in my heart that my own son didn't," he told her.

Nia was thrilled. She felt the same. She decided to test him though, "So if I say I wanted to openly support LGBT causes with the firm's

backing, you'd see that Grayson and the others stayed off my back so I could work?"

"What does LGBT stand for?" he asked unsure of what she was asking and hopeful that she would stay with him retiring. He wanted Chase to have a chance to mature and get his feet more than wet, someday this place would be his. He'd stay if it meant grooming the young man but he wasn't that young anymore and Nia seemed to have her pulse on the newer generation.

"Lesbian, Gay, Bi-Sexual, and Transsexual," Nia informed him nearly laughing as the last two words caused him to raise his eyebrows.

Swallowing at what that just might imply and unsure of himself he nodded and said, "You might have to pull us into that twenty first century after all, myself included but bear with us and we will adjust. We have enough of the old types of clients to keep them happy but if the newer generation wants us to accept this we will have to adjust our way of thinking or step aside." He looked around musingly before continuing. "Maybe I'm not the one who should retire, maybe Grayson and a few others should..." he left off as he looked back at a now visibly amused Nia.

She was trying not to laugh. Stewart was older than most of the senior partners and he was willing to accept anything she did and defend her against those who would object.

"Don't you one day want to marry?" he asked changing the uncomfortable subject. He pierced her with his still sharp eyes.

She tried to turn the laughter into the new subject. "Who would I marry? I'm married to my job."

"You can't bullshit an old bull shitter Nia, I've seen how you soften around her and defend her to your last breath. Someday you might want to make an honest woman of her." He held up his hand as she went to interrupt and deny. "I know, I know, you never said but I've got eyes in my head don't I? I used to be pretty good at this game and you've never let your personal life interfere with the work at hand so I know you can handle the bullshit that will come your way. I've decided," he slapped his hand down on the desk. "I'm gonna stick around a while and see the fight and you know it will be a fight," he fixed an eye on her but there was a twinkle there. "I want to see you win it too!"

She smiled as she took that as a dismissal. "I'm glad you aren't going anywhere," she murmured and touched the back of his hand with a small caress of her own. She felt suddenly weepy and counting the days thought perhaps she was hormonal. She realized the gift Stewart had given her though as she returned back to her office. She must have been distracted as she didn't notice anyone watching her and many watched Nia

Toyomoto, out of fear, out of envy, out of the gossip they had heard. She saw none of them as she returned and daydreamed her afternoon away.

Picking up Nate, Nia took him home and found a great parking spot in front of the building where their apartment was. Building on the parking structure had resumed and it almost looked as though they were hurrying it along. She hoped so as she now had two parking places side by side and nowhere to park at the moment.

By the time Colleen came home from school, exhausted from a full day of work and school on top of it, Nia had the dining room table set, the candles lit, and the dinner delivered and in attractive dishes on the table for them.

"Oh babe, that looks so romantic," Colleen exclaimed seeing the effort Nia had made on their behalf. She put down her book bag by the door and looked it over.

"I happen to think you are worth it," Nia told her leaning down for a kiss.

"But what's the occasion?" Colleen asked trying to remember if she had forgotten the date or something.

"No special occasion, just why not?" Nia returned as she indicated a chair Colleen should seat herself in.

"I've got to feed Nate," Colleen complained and made to go towards the stairs since the baby was obviously not in the playpen in the living room.

"He's already bathed and asleep, I used the milk you pumped so if you want to pump before dinner, we can enjoy this when you are ready," Nia informed her.

Colleen was so grateful she wanted to cry. Just when she was ready to give up, Nia did something sweet or thoughtful and made it all worthwhile. School tonight had been informative and interesting and she had enjoyed that as well. Coming home to this and having Nate already asleep, icing on the cake. She quickly sat down in a comfortable chair in the living room and pumped both her breasts to fill bottles for Nate when she couldn't manage to breast feed him. Her breasts felt infinitely better after draining them. Nia was ready and waiting at the dinner table when she was done and had washed her hands and stored the bottles in their refrigerator.

"This looks delicious," she said as Nia seated her.

"I ordered it myself," Nia bragged teasingly.

"Even ordered, presentation is everything," Colleen complimented.

They chatted about their day, keeping work related things to a minimum. Colleen told her about class and what had interested her and

Nia could talk knowingly and informatively to her on any of the subjects she was taking. It had actually given her insight that her fellow students didn't have. Her research papers had all earned top marks because she had a living, breathing, encyclopedia of law living with her.

After dinner and desert they continued their conversation until Colleen slowly wound down. Nia had wanted Colleen relaxed and had drawn out her entire day from her before she got to the point of their romantic evening.

"I had an interesting conversation with Stewart this afternoon," she brought up work, something she had been careful to avoid through most of the dinner but as they worked at the same place even small incidents always involved work.

"Oh really?" Colleen asked nervously wondering if the drama going on behind the scenes had caught up with all of them. She knew the firm wasn't happy with the information that one of their own had helped take down several dirty cops and a drug ring. Nia denied her involvement but since Cletus was involved, that brought Colleen into it a bit and even Nia. It actually had been all Simone's doing but no one was telling that side of it as the packets of information had all been 'anonymous.' Nia had been annoyed by the footage of her apartment that Simone had but Simone had assured her she would turn it off and showed her how to keep others from picking up the signals of her cameras so it was now a closed circuit to her apartment only.

"Yes apparently he wants to retire," Nia told her as she took a sip of the wine she had served with dinner.

"What does that mean for you?" she wondered.

"Well, he wants me to take his grandson Chase under my wing when he graduates from law school in a couple of years. He thinks my ideas and kind of clients are the future of the firm and that we should get into the twenty first century. By the time we finished our chat he had decided to stick around and see what I could get them into," she laughed as she remembered the meeting and her day dreaming all afternoon long.

"Kind of clients?" she echoed wondering what that meant.

"I asked him if he wanted me to take on more LGBT clients," she laughed.

Colleen, who had just taken a sip of her own wine nearly choked on that. Nia hadn't actually taken on any LGBT clients, a few were openly gay or lesbian but she hadn't sought out that kind of client. "Are you going to do it?" she asked.

Nia shook her head. "I won't turn them down if they come to me but I won't be seeking them out either. What he meant was that he would support me in any form or avenue I choose to take. I asked him that as a test and he rose to the occasion."

"A test? A test for what?" Colleen was confused.

"Of where the firm will go and how much they want me as a lawyer. Apparently he sensed my unease at the firm and he wants me to stay. To the point of backing me whatever I decide. That's why I took the afternoon to think this over and really it didn't take that long to decide..." she hesitated long enough for Colleen to interrupt.

"Decide what?" she looked at her, she was certain she was missing part of this conversation.

"I decided to ask you a question." With that she slid off the dining room chair and got to one knee taking Colleen's hand in her own. "I decided to ask you to marry me?"

"You want to marry me?" Colleen squeaked out her eyes going round.

Nia nodded and then she asked. "Colleen, would you marry me?"

Colleen though was thinking of all the repercussions and how they had hidden it. "But what about..." she began.

"None of that matters," Nia interrupted holding up her hand dismissing it. "If they know I love you, that is all that does matter. We've denied it long enough and if you will have me, I'll marry you in any manner you want. We can tell everyone or no one. It's really no one's business after all. If you don't want to get married we can live like this indefinitely," she finished giving her an out but her heart was pounding and she wondered what Colleen would say.

Colleen was shocked. She had thought they would live together forever but married? She had never even dared daydream about it. She had been content to have Nia in whatever capacity she could have her. She was so honored that someone like Nia would want her and would make such a public declaration, after all marriage certificates were a matter of public information. She realized she didn't care if anyone knew or not, she loved Nia for more than simple gratitude, Nia had loved her before she realized her potential. Realizing Nia was waiting for an answer she started to tear up as she nodded and said, "Yes Nia, I will marry you."

The End

LAWYERED

* The character of Alice Weaver is from my MALICE series and Simone, Sasha, and Alexis make an appearance in some of those books as well.

** The character of Simone is from my CHARMING THIEF series and Alice makes an appearance in those books as well.

*** The characters of Sasha and her partner Alexis are from the short story book KEPT that I released years ago and intend to continue into a full length book, of course the experiences here and in the next book will appear in there.

**** The landlord and Nia's building are in a potential book tentatively titled Lost in New York City.

If you have enjoyed *LAWYERED* you'll look forward to a sample of K'Anne Meinel's splendid and unforgettable novel:

REPRESENTED

In print and E-book and available at fine retailers.

Coming out is hard. Coming out in the public eye is even harder. People think they own a piece of you, your work, and your life, they feel they have the right to judge you. You lose not only friends but fans and ultimately, possibly, your career...or your life.

Cassie Summers is a Southern Rock Star; she came out so that she could feel true to herself. Her family including her band and those important to her support her but there are others that feel she betrayed them, they have revenge on their minds...

REPRESENTED

Karin Myers is a Rock Star in her own right; she is one of those new super promoters: Manager, go-to gal, agent, public relations expert, and hand-holder all in one. Her name is synonymous with getting someone recognized, promoted, and making money. She only handles particular clients though; she's choosy...for some very specific reasons.

Meeting Cassie at a party there is a definite attraction. She does not however wish to represent her despite her excellent reputation. She fights it tooth and nail until she is contractually required to do so. In nearly costs them more than either of them anticipated....their lives.

"Holy Crap!" Molly pulled her feet up before they wiped her out as they rolled by her on the couch. She watched in alarm as they body slammed each other. The cat's ears were totally back and the dog's expression was gleeful as they attacked each other time and again wrapping their paws around each other in a bear hug.

Miranda finished her cigarette and came to the door of the patio and asked Karin who was enjoying the show, "Don't they ever get hurt?"

Karin shook her head. "They'll stop if one of them yelps in pain but they both enjoy these little work outs. Later they will groom each other and go to sleep for hours on end. They are the best of friends."

Just then the best of friends were trying to kill each other as they kicked and struggled to get on top of each other.

"This is why I don't have any plants in here, they'd knock them over," Karin said as they both got on their back paws and boxed.

After a long mock battle they were both panting and called it a draw. It had given Jana enough time to finish her breakfast and she went to get ready.

"Where are we going?" Miranda asked as they went down in the elevator and hailed a taxi.

"A friend of mine owns a sight-seeing tour company and I called him this morning. He's meeting us and showing us New York City and Manhattan," Karin answered.

They got into the taxi and Karin said, "56th street helipad please," as the taxi took off she glanced at Miranda but she was talking with her girls in the backseat and hadn't heard her.

As they pulled up though Miranda looked at Karin in alarm. "We're going up in a helicopter?"

Karin nodded as she paid the taxi. "Are you game?"

The girls were immediately enthusiastic but Karin could see Miranda wasn't too thrilled. She let them pull her along though as they entered the

building. Karin grinned and followed. She went to the counter and said, "I'm Karin Myers and I believe..." but was interrupted by the clerk.

"Of course Ms. Myers, Chuck is waiting in the helicopter. I'll have someone escort you and your party," she signaled to someone behind them and they all turned to see a guy in a jumpsuit and helmet nod to them and indicate the doors at the far end of the building. They followed him out onto the helipad where a helicopter was warming up. He opened the back door and they all clambered in.

"Hi Karin!" the pilot shouted over the noise which wasn't that bad once the door was closed.

Karin smiled and gave him the thumbs up as they all got into their seat belts. There was plenty of room for the four of them. Chuck indicated the headsets that were hanging on hooks above their heads and they all put them on. The noise was even more drowned out by the muffling of the headsets. "All set?" the pilot asked, his voice sounding tin like through the headsets and Karin nodded and smiled as she looked to see her friends were all belted in.

"I'm Chuck," he looked at Miranda and the girls.

Karin talked into the mike in front of her face and said, "This is my friend Miranda Green and her girls Molly and Jana from Wisconsin."

He nodded and they took off. Karin heard Molly distinctly go, "Holy Crap," as they took off. Both girls had window seats on the passenger side of the helicopter facing each other. Karin and Miranda faced each other and Karin laughed at the glare Miranda was giving her. Chuck took them up and down the river and all over the city. Karin knew he was giving them an extra special tour and over and above the usual 'view of Manhattan' that he and his pilots sold. She appreciated it as it was a view people didn't normally get of New York unless they watched a lot of movies and even then it wasn't the same. The girls seemed to enjoy it and they asked a lot of questions once they got used to the stifling the headset gave them and how odd their voices were through its mechanism. Karin watched Miranda go green, white, and flush by turns. She was breathing deeply and sometimes actually seemed to enjoy herself despite the airsickness Karin knew she was fighting. It was over an hour plus later that Chuck returned them to the helipad and the girls were talking non-stop. Miranda joined in but Karin suspected that was to ignore the thought of throwing up and it distracted her admiredly. Chuck turned off the helicopter completely and the silence was deafening after having got used to the headphones and all. He personally escorted them into the building as a crew ran to take care of the helicopter. It would need refueling and Karin knew they probably had a checklist before it would be taken out again.

"I want to thank you for that excellent tour," Karin began when they got back in the building and could talk normally.

"Ah, and now you owe me," Chuck smiled as he took off his helmet. The girls and Miranda could see he was an attractive sandy haired man with a mustache. He looked down at Karin and smiled.

Karin smiled as she sidled up to him. He seemed a little alarmed as she took up his challenging words. She leaned in close and said huskily, "Oh? And how would you like me to repay that debt?"

His eyes had nearly bugged out of his head as he stuttered, "Din din dinner?"

Karin smiled as she leaned up on her tip toes to kiss him on the mouth, "Done, call me?"

He grinned as his arm snaked around her and he held her close for a moment before saying, "I will!" enthusiastically.

She returned his smile, her eyes sparkling into his before he released her. She turned to her friends and asked, "Ready for lunch?"

Chuck watched her the whole length of the building as they left. The girls giggled about it the during the taxi ride uptown.

"You had him eating out of the palm of your hand," Molly noted as they ate at a sidewalk cafe.

"Well of course, have to keep them in line dontcha know?" Karin grinned at Molly as she sipped a root beer. She turned to Miranda who was carefully eating a light salad, "Are you feeling better?"

Miranda shook her head as she reached for her white soda, "I don't know if I will ever forgive you for that!" she complained but she was grinning. It had been a fantastic morning and she had enjoyed herself despite her queasy stomach.

They discussed what they had seen and the beautiful views and angles they had seen. The Statue of Liberty always looked smaller than the movies made it or so it seemed to Karin and she compared how the girls saw things to her own perceptions. It was interesting to hear their take on things. It had given them a few ideas of things they would like to do with their Uncle Bradley now that they had seen so much. Karin knew she had just made Bradley's life a bit hellish but then she really didn't care.

"There is a man by the name of Brad here to pick up the Greens," the voice through the intercom came through loud and clear. Karin had just answered the buzzer.

"Tell him we'll be right down," Miranda said as they gathered their things for their afternoon and evening with him. They had been ready for over a half an hour waiting for him.

Karin handed Miranda a key chain with two keys on it that both read 'do not duplicate' as she left. "One is for the elevator and one is for the front door," she indicated and then added, "Have a nice time!"

Karin spent her afternoon on her computers and phone. She got a lot accomplished and checked on her various teams throughout the country. She stayed on top of her game that way and they didn't find her interfering. She frequently emailed or texted them too with information they needed to complete their jobs. She expected a higher standard than the other team leaders in the office and anyone lucky enough to work for her understood that. There was always a few that didn't understood or didn't play on a team and these rogues soon learned they didn't play for Karin Myers very long if they didn't listen to her or contribute to her team ideas. She ran her show and she did it very well, don't mess with success.

"Hey, how did your day go?" Karin asked as Miranda came out on the balcony to have a smoke before bed.

"Oh it was nice but Brad was *sick* of hearing about the helicopter ride by the end of the night," she said with a hint of humor in her voice.

Karin couldn't see her face but she knew she was probably laughing, knowing what Karin had pulled. It hadn't been intentional to ruin Brad's plans but he certainly couldn't compete with a helicopter ride.

"We're going to see a Broadway play tomorrow," Miranda informed her.

"Do you need help getting tickets?" Karin asked kindly but knew that her help would be unwelcome where Brad was concerned.

"No, I think he already bought them," she said.

Miranda sat down and lit up. Karin leaned back in her chair and listened to the night sounds.

Karin was getting dressed for the day when she heard the buzzer. Molly beat her to it and let the person up before she could answer. It annoyed her but then they were her guests. The only person though that it could be would be their Uncle Brad and she wasn't looking forward to seeing him again even after all these years. He was an arrogant ass and he blamed Karin for all the evils of the world or so it seemed. They just flat out didn't get along. Karin had met Miranda at a time in her life when her first marriage had crumbled and helped her through it. Brad blamed Karin for Miranda's mid-life crisis. She just thought him an arrogant asshole whose opinion of himself needed adjusting. She never took the bait when he tried to argue with her. It infuriated him no end.

"Hello Brad," she pretended to greet him as she poured herself a glass of orange juice.

Brad didn't answer but then she knew he wouldn't as the girls enthused over the apartment. He looked around. She could tell he was impressed but then compared to his postage sized apartment this was splendor. D.O.G. took an instant dislike to him and wouldn't come near him despite the girls coaxing and for this Karin was secretly glad. C.A.T. made an appearance and Brad nearly peed his pants. C.A.T. sat on the couch and looked every bit the wild cheetah. Karin knew he probably did it deliberately and secretly applauded him. Miranda caught up to them and said, "I'm ready, let's go," as she waved at Karin.

Karin went into her office that morning and cranked out a few reports that were redundantly necessary to her work. It was an essential evil but every time she thought of giving up doing them she thought about the morning and it cheered her immeasurably. It was funny and she had enjoyed it, from annoying Brad with her apartment to the pets. Pets were such amazing things; they sensed when someone was no good. It kept her going and she was ahead of the game which put her in an even better mood for the rest of the day.

Miranda and the girls got home late that evening but Karin didn't mind since they had key's to get in.

"Did you have a good time?" she greeted them as she sat at her kitchen counter eating a cracker with butter on it. It was a type of cracker she always picked up at Trader Joe's and knew they wouldn't like so she didn't offer it to her guests. It was called Kavli bread and it was something she enjoyed from time to time along with the red wine she was consuming. The bread had the consistency of cardboard but she loved the flavor with the butter.

"Yes it was a blast!" Jana enthused as she headed down the hallway to her room.

"I don't know, I think it wasn't as good as it should have been," Molly disagreed as she followed down the hallway.

Miranda grinned. They wouldn't be sisters if they didn't argue regularly.

"Did you eat?" Karin asked as she indicated the refrigerator and then the wine. Miranda rummaged through her cabinets and found a wine glass and helped herself.

"I'm just tired. Dealing with those two any length of time tires me out!" she laughed.

Karin smiled. "I have some news if you're interested...."

Miranda looked up wondering what Karin had cooked up.

"I have to go out to the coast on business and as I wasn't sure how long you three would be here I wondered if you'd like to go along?" she asked

innocently. There was a twinkle in her eye though. She knew the girls could hear her clearly and she wasn't disappointed.

"The coast? As in California?" Jana was the first head out of the bedrooms.

Karin leaned over nearly spilling her wine as she looked down the hallway and smiled. Jana came clumping out of the bedroom like a shot with Molly soon on her heels.

"Yes, I have a client I need to see and hold hands with as well as meet a couple. It's necessary for me to go out to the coast and as I'm taking the company jet there is room for you to go if you're interested..." she left that hanging as though they would say no.

Miranda looked at her incredulously shaking her head.

"Mom can we go?" Molly asked for both of them. They both looked at her expectantly.

"I don't know if we can afford..." Miranda began but Karin interrupted her.

"Afford what? The plane ride is free. I have to have a big room for meetings, you can make yourself scarce then, food is on me as my guests, you might want to buy some souvenirs..." she left off knowing she had her.

Miranda looked at her and her eyes were sparkling. She knew she couldn't say no, not when the girls were standing there looking so expectant. She would do anything for her girls. "When would we have to go?" she asked instead. The girls started jumping up and down in their excitement.

"Well, I don't want you to miss time visiting with your brother, I'm sure he took off work for you especially. Say Friday?" she asked knowing the next two days would be hard on Brad and not caring in the least.

Miranda knew that too and could almost read Karin's mind. She knew she couldn't resist and she wasn't anxious to drive back to Wisconsin, not yet. She had taken a couple of Jeff's calls and wasn't too thrilled with the outcome of them. She needed more time away.

Karin advised them to take less to California but they insisted on bringing their huge bags. She assured them they wouldn't need it all but she was ignored. She wondered if there was a weight limit on the plane and shook her head at their packing everything to bring along. She herself packed two bags, a carry on and a garment bag for her suits so they wouldn't wrinkle. Her ever present briefcase was on her shoulder as she asked, "Ready to go?"

As the elevator took them down Jana asked, "What about your pets?"

"I have a dog walker that will come in once a day and I called her yesterday," Karin informed her as she winked at Carl in the reflection of the elevator. He knew she was gone frequently and knew the routine.

REPRESENTED

A Park Avenue limousine was waiting at the curb and Karin handed her two bags to him as the other three struggled with their huge bags. He too seemed to grunt as they wrestled them into the trunk of the car. Karin sat in the back seat with Miranda next to her both of the girls took the other seat facing them as they tried to act like this happened to them all the time. They were impressed though and couldn't help but grin at their mother as the car drove them through afternoon traffic. Karin was busy on her phone texting someone or checking her email, they couldn't be sure which. The car drove through a special gate at the airport and pulled up on the tarmac near a plane.

"We're going in a private plane?" Molly asked incredulously as she looked out.

The driver opened the door and Karin pushed Miranda lightly on the shoulder to encourage her to get out as she answered, "Jet actually," and then got out herself followed by the two awestruck teenagers. Karin walked over to the jet and mounted the steps as though she did this every day. The other three followed a little more slowly.

"Ms. Myers?" a man in captain's uniform inquired as they all came on board.

Karin nodded and he introduced himself. "I'm Captain O'Reilly, there is a phone call for you," he indicated one of the phones near the plush chairs spaced out in the cabin. Karin saw a red button on it and picked it up.

"Hello?" she watched as a steward began helping Miranda and her girls to their seats. She listened for a while and said, "Of course, not a problem, we will wait," and hung up the phone. She looked around and said, "Captain O'Reilly if you don't mind waiting we have an additional passenger." He nodded and giving her a half salute he left the cabin.

"Would you like something to drink before we take off?" the steward inquired solicitously as he eyed her.

Karin smiled and said, "Perhaps after we take off, nothing for me now."

Karin went to sit next to Miranda and she asked, "Who are we waiting for?"

Karin pulled out her cell phone and turned it off and waving it at the other three indicating they should do the same with theirs, "Oh someone who missed their connecting flight to LA, we're giving them a lift." She heard their luggage being tucked in underneath the plane and then she glanced out the far windows and saw another car pull up and someone get out of it. One of their stewards hurried over to help with their luggage. A woman came up the stairs and Karin rose from where she had been sitting.

"Ms. Myers?" the woman inquired politely.

"Karin, please," she answered.

"Call me Celina," the beautiful blonde smiled. Karin would have recognized her anywhere even if she hadn't known who they were waiting for.

"Let me introduce my friends," she introduced the three of them and could see that their guest was recognized. As one of Hollywood's most beautiful woman she was very recognizable. She had won an Academy Award a few years ago and while South African from birth she had risen to be an international favorite.

The beautiful blonde turned back to Karin after politely shaking the hands of the three of them. "We have friends in common."

"Yes, I know, Elliott called me to arrange your ride," Karin answered.

"No, although he was a dear to call you before you took off, I was talking about Em Phillips?"

Karin's face tightened a little and she said, "Yes, I know Em, how is she?"

Celina smiled knowingly, "She's better, you did a terrific job and she's forever grateful."

Karin shrugged, "Well, it was a while ago, I hope she *is* doing well."

Celina nodded. She knew a lot about it but now wasn't the time to speak of it. "Won't you join me?" she raised an eyebrow and indicated the two side by side chairs further into the cabin from where Miranda and her girls had chosen to sit. Karin never batted an eyelash as she said, "Of course," and followed her. Miranda looked at her strangely but acknowledged this might be work related.

The stairs were pulled up and in the plane sealing it as the stewards checked that their passengers were all buckled in. Karin realized the stewardess checking hers seemed to take an inordinate amount of time and brushed against her breasts unnecessarily. Her startled look was returned with an amused one by the pretty redhead. Karin glanced away momentarily only to catch the knowing look of Celina who seemed just as amused.

They were soon taxiing down the runway and just as quickly in the air and on their way. Celina talked to Karin for a while about mundane things but soon got down to business. She wanted Karin to represent her and wasn't willing to take no for an answer.

"After what Em told me you did for her I want someone I know can help my career," she insisted as she drank the champagne the redheaded stewardess had offered. Karin had refused on more than one level.

"Celina, I appreciate the vote of confidence, I really do. I don't however handle entertainment clients anymore. Elliott knows this and Em especially knows this. I can refer you to any number of people who..."

But Celina was shaking her head and saying, "Look, it was a horrible situation. You handled it with discretion and honor. You shouldn't let it sour you to the whole business though."

Karin smiled, she loved knowing her reputation was such that people wanted her work but she wasn't willing to take the chance. Some people knew about Em but only one other person knew about Phil, she wouldn't go back into entertainment representation if she could help it. It was her choice. She deflected Celina's arguments adroitly and they still managed to enjoy their flight together. It got cozy enough that despite her refusal to work for her Celina managed to make a pass at her. Karin was surprised and then a little embarrassed when she realized that despite the cabin pressure that her guests could hear everything. She caught Miranda's eye and rolling her own she sighed mightily. She pretended to get some work out and went to sit in a solitary chair. Celina pretended to doze as she watched Karin through slit eyes.

They landed late for New York time but still early for Los Angeles time. A car met Celina first and before she left she made sure to give Karin her personal card and lingeringly shake her hand. Karin had to admit she was interested in Celina on a personal level but she also realized that would be a mistake all the way around. Miranda was amused as Karin watched her get off the plane and get into her car. Their own car pulled up shortly thereafter and the stewards quickly loaded their luggage as they got in. Miranda noted that the redheaded stewardess watched Karin closely as she closed the door.

"Popular aren't you?" Molly asked with a grin. Not much got by that kid.

Karin looked at her surprised and not amused. She wanted to pretend ignorance but knew she couldn't get away with it and instead ignored the comment.

"Ms. Myers?" the limo driver called from in front.

Karin looked up inquiringly, "Yes?" she called back.

"Is there anywhere you wish to stop before we go to the hotel?"

She shook her head and sat back in her chair closing her eyes. It had been a long flight.

"Nice digs!" Molly enthused they looked around.

Karin tipped the porter who had brought all their luggage up, on a cart instead of carrying the heavy load and getting a hernia. She thanked him as he wheeled the cart out of the hotel room.

"Your room is over there," she indicated the two doors.

"We have to share?" Jana asked.

Karin nodded as she headed for the basket that was on the bar. Pulling the card she read: Welcome to LA, Elliott. Inside was a fruit basket

surrounding a bottle of champagne. She pulled the bottle out and uncorked it. She showed it to Miranda and asked, "Feel like celebrating?"

Miranda smiled and nodded. It was a nice room. The girls were already fighting over which bed they got in their room. They checked the other room too and found a pair of double beds in there as well. The living room they were standing in was a fair size with two couches facing each other and a desk as well as the bar. The girls converged on the bar and Miranda said sternly, "Don't touch a thing!" Mini bars were notoriously expensive. Karin appreciated it, she didn't want to have to be the one to tell them no.

"I'm hungry!" Jana whined.

"Me too!" Karin said and asked, "Care to order a pizza?"

"Pizza?" Jana asked astonished but then thinking again she reached for the menus that were scattered by a phone.

"What did she really want?" Miranda asked her as they both lay in their beds that night.

Karin turned to face her friend from across the small aisle between the two queen sized beds, "She wanted me to represent her."

"And you won't?" but Miranda had heard the conversation, she also knew why Karin wouldn't.

Karin nodded sadly. She didn't like thinking about what had happened back when.

"She wanted you though," Miranda smirked. It was funny after all these years to see Karin hit on all the time. Yes she had the confidence that had been lacking years ago but there was something more, something almost intangible. It made her desirable. Apparently Miranda wasn't the only one who saw it though. They kept trying to get up her skirt. First the star and then the stewardess, even that woman back in New York at the restaurant, and numerous men including Chuck the owner of the helicopter service, it was amazing to watch.

Karin laughed. She knew that too. She had carefully filed away the business card that had been so subtly given her. You never knew when you might need it...

The next morning Karin was gone before the others even got out of bed. A note was left on the counter for them. It read:

"I'm in business meetings all day, there is a car waiting to take you to Anaheim whenever you're ready," and Karin had left five $100 bills attached to the note with a P.S. reading, "For dinner and other things you might need."

Miranda and the girls got a limo ride to Disneyland and had a blast. The girls wanted to go to the California adventure but Miranda thought

they shouldn't take advantage of Karin's generosity. When Karin heard it though she insisted they go. The car was comped anyway she explained, they just had to pay their way inside and this cost a lot too Miranda found. She wasn't sure this was such a great idea. When Karin realized that she was low on funds though she came up with free tickets to Universal Studios, Knotts Berry Farm, and then suggested they go sight-seeing. By the fifth day though Karin was able to join them and she borrowed a car from her Los Angeles office to sight see with them. They went through Hollywood and saw the famous sign; they drove around Beverly Hills and marveled at the houses they could see. The four of them had a blast before Karin had to return back to New York. The return trip on the plane wasn't as eventful and they all slept across the country.

"I'm going to head back home," Miranda announced on their return the following morning.

"Work everything out?" Karin asked as she ate a croissant.

"No, I'm going to start divorce proceedings. He doesn't get it and he showed up here while we were in California. Fortunately for Bradley he really didn't know where we were."

Karin smirked, she was glad she could help. "I'm sorry," she really was. Her friend had lost out on marriage twice.

Miranda looked at her sharply to see if she was sincere or being sarcastic. When she saw she was sincere she relaxed. It had been a good try. She had been happy for a time but not as happy as she had been when she and Karin had been together. Karin was right, they had given it a shot but Miranda had wanted a heterosexual relationship so bad she had convinced herself that Jeff was the answer. Using Karin again hadn't been a good idea but she was glad they were friends again. Seeing her now she really wished she had been wiser. She was a good person, a good friend. Someone she wished she could be with but had missed her chance. She now wished her happiness. Seeing how much other's wanted her and how she handled it made her wish for more but she settled for a good friendship.

As Miranda packed up her little Saturn she was surprised at its cleanliness. Karin smirked when she spoke on it and then Miranda realized that Karin had arranged for it to be detailed. It was spic and span and any of their 'valuables' that they had questioned whether it was garbage or not was in a box in the back seat. Karin hugged each of the three of her guests as she watched them drive out of the parking garage. She was relieved she would have her spot back; it had been expensive to leave her SUV uptown but for her friend she was glad she could help.

"Karin, I'd like to introduce you to some people," Elliott smiled as he led her to a group of patiently waiting people. She couldn't believe she

was back in Los Angles a week after leaving it but then that was the nature of the business sometimes. Karin recognized one of them faintly but she met people all the time and didn't necessarily put faces with names right away. "Hey you guys, this is Karin Myers, Karin this is Cassie Summers," she realized who Cassie was immediately as she held out her hand to shake Cassie's own. "This is Travis Collins, her manager," Karin smiled at him and he was immediately charmed, her beauty alone had caught his eye. "And this is our host, Michael Turner," she turned her smile on him and only fractionally froze at the incredibly ugly man she was addressing.

"It's a pleasure to be in your home Mr. Turner," she said politely to him having not addressed the other two other than a polite nod in recognition of the introduction.

"I'm so glad Elliott brought you. I've been looking forward to meeting you for some time. You have an incredible touch," he grinned, referring to her talent, "The last novel set them on its ear. And please call me Michael."

She smiled giving him her best smile that she reserved for meeting the public. Not too many people saw the real 'Karin'; instead she kept a few facial contractions just for the 'public' since it was her job.

"I really enjoyed the first book you promoted," Cassie contributed to the conversation and to draw Karin's attention back to her.

Karin turned to her in surprise, certain someone of Cassie's stature wouldn't have known who she was or that she was a promoter, mainly of books. Her eyebrow cocked as she prepared to put Ms. Summers subtly in her place. As she looked her in the eye though she froze. The gray blue eyes held hers and at that moment there was a sizzling sensation in Karin's brain. Her own jade green eyes widened slightly at the sensation. She felt her body stiffen slightly but at the same time she felt curiously weak as her knees nearly buckled. She felt a shortness of breath. Her body instinctively knew though what was happening and rose magnificently to the occasion. This all happened in a micro-second as she came back to her senses in time to ask, "Really? That one was so sophomoric, I think several of my other novelists were much better," she was pleased that her voice sounded normal, at least to her own ears.

"It was the one though that caught my interest in your work; it made me want to read other of your novelists. I think I've read all of them at this point. Maybe I should have had you promote mine?" She grinned.

Karin was studying the dishwater blonde before her. She was a little taller than Karin's own 5'7" and wearing slight heels. Her hair reached halfway down her back and the curls were so country but they looked just right on the slender figure before her. She was an attractive woman by anyone's definition. "Have you read 'Ominous'?" she asked with a slight dimple showing in her right cheek.

Cassie shook her head and Karin was mesmerized by the cascade of curls that she could see with her peripheral vision, her own eyes never left Cassie's as she tried to fathom why she was having such a strong reaction to this woman as she looked up into those gray blue ones.

"You should come to my book signing then," Karin grinned. "Or rather Nina Lall's book signing," she corrected.

"Yes," Elliott put his arm around Karin's waist to break into their conversation, "That's why we are in town. You should come, all of you," he included generously.

Cassie noted that Karin didn't like the casual embrace but you had to really look to see the slight tightening around her eyes. She broke eye contact with Karin to address Elliott, "Maybe we will."

"How about you, what are you doing in LA?" Elliott asked enthusiastically.

Karin looked at him through slightly narrowed eyes. He was always hustling, always looking out for new clients. He had been so thrilled when she agreed to work with his firm but it was a long time in coming and she had made him jump through a lot of hoops before she let him work with her. By then she was neck deep in work and her other managers had been overwhelmed. If Elliott wasn't so good at what he did, she wouldn't have hired on with him. He made her life relatively stress free, provided her with the means, and it gave her a lot more time to do what she loved, promote.

"We're laying down the tracks on a new single," Cassie answered him.

"Is it similar to the ballads you've been releasing or have you gone back to Southern Rock?" Karin put in astutely.

Cassie looked at her in surprise. She had been almost certain someone like Karin Myers wouldn't know who Cassie Summers was much less listen to country or Southern Rock. "Actually, this one is more like Southern Rock."

"Oh that's good; I remember when you came out with Harlot. I fell in love with that video on CMT. I didn't realize then that was even you until years later," Karin admired her.

Cassie looked at her again and captured her with her eyes again. She was genuinely surprised to find that Karin was a fan of hers when she herself was a fan of Karin's and the work she had done. "Did you like any other of my songs?" she asked as the men watching these two faded to the background momentarily for these two women.

"Oh, I liked quite a few of them, I certainly don't remember all the titles but I actually followed more of your career last year after you came out. I read your book 'Inspired.' That was really brave of you and I sympathized." Karin went on to tell her of the music she had enjoyed and

why. She was well informed for someone from the literary community and spoke knowingly about Cassie's first love, music.

Cassie was really flattered that someone of Karin Myers stature had read her book much less that she knew her music. She did know her music too and this was a surprise, she was well informed and very astute. It made her feel warm for some reason. She too had experienced a sensation when their eyes met and she was surprised that someone like this was as knowledgeable as she was. She found her interesting and fascinating and could have spoken to her all night.

"Well, this is all very interesting but I promised a few people I'd introduce Karin to them if I got her here and I see Cedric McCormick over there. It was nice to see you," Elliott nodded to the others effectively taking their leave.

The other's murmured polite good-bye's but Karin held out her hand to Cassie and said, "I've enjoyed meeting you, I hope we run into each other again sometime," she smiled a genuine smile this time as she looked deeply into Cassie's eyes.

Cassie returned the smile as she nodded and shook Karin's hand. She was pleased when Karin gave it an extra squeeze or she thought she did with a glimmer in her eye as she left.

"An amazing woman," Michael commented. "She's handled the career of many people and done incredibly well even with some real duds, she's cold though, very cold."

"I didn't think so," Cassie said quietly as she watched the brunette across the room.

"I've heard people say that she's one of the coolest women they have ever met but then I don't think they met her in a social setting," Michael answered and then changed the subject. Cassie watched her as she was paraded and introduced to several other people in the room. She found her watching Karin throughout the evening as she herself did the same with Michael and Travis. She was pleased to see Karin look up and look for her several times as she quickly looked away. For some reason she found herself blushing at the thought of someone like Karin looking at her and yet she couldn't help herself from looking back.

~End Sample~

❧ About the Author ❧

K'Anne Meinel is the BEST SELLING author of REPRESENTED and SAPPHIC SURFER as well as several other books including her first SHIPS which was written in 2003 over the course of two weeks. She then played with it for several years before publishing it as an e-book and then was approached to publish it in book form. After that it was published on other sites as an e-book. In the meantime she published some 50 short stories, novellas, and novels of various genres. Originally from Wisconsin many of her stories have taken on locations from and around the state. A gypsy at heart she has lived in many locations and plans to continue doing that. Videos of several of her books are available on You Tube outlining some of the locations of her books and telling a little bit more...giving the readers insight into her mind as she created these wonderful stories.

~ Because a publisher should stand behind their authors~

Among the majestic shoreline of the Central Coast of California lies a secret...Leah Van Heusen finds a hidden staircase....

The ancient house she finds among the overgrown foliage is amazing...and eerie, most wouldn't even step a foot closer but she is intrigued and feels drawn to the old mansion....

Leah finds more than she bargains for after seeking out the owner and purchasing the entire estate for a dollar. As she starts to restore it, she finds out who her real friends are, she also finds out who her family really is...What's a few ghosts between friends?

Between repairs, upgrades, and finding out the houses secrets, Leah has her hands full. Finding out her sexuality and dating is the least of her worries. As her beloved dream of an Inn becomes reality she finds it suddenly in jeopardy, who will kill for it or the immense fortune that she has found?

~ Because a publisher should stand behind their authors~

What do you do when you meet someone who changes everything you know about love and passion?

Paige Harlow is a good girl. She's always known where she was going in life: top grades, an ivy league school, a medical degree, regular church attendance, and a happy marriage to a man. So falling in love with her gorgeous roommate and best friend Alyssa Torres is no small crisis. Alyssa is chasing demons of her own, a medical condition that makes her an outcast and a family dysfunctional to the point of disintegration make her a questionable choice for any stable relationship. But Paige's heart is no longer her own. She must now battle the prejudices of her family, friends, and church and come to peace with her new sexuality before she can hope to win the affections of the woman of her dreams. But will love be enough?

~ Because a publisher should stand behind their authors~

As I watch the wormhole start to close, I make one last desperate plea ...
"Please? Please don't make me do this?" I whisper.
"You're almost out of time, Lily. Please, just let go?"
I look down at the control panel. I know what I have to do.

Lilith Madison is captain of the Phoenix, a spaceship filled with an elite crew and travelling through the Delta Gamma Quadrant. Their mission is mankind's last hope for survival.

But there is a killer on board. One who kills without leaving a trace and seems intent on making sure their mission fails. With the ship falling apart and her crew being ruthlessly picked off one by one, Lilith must choose who to trust while tracking down the killer before it's too late.

"A suspenseful...exciting...thrilling whodunit adventure in space...discover the shocking truth about what's really happening on the Phoenix" (Clarion)

~ Because a publisher should stand behind their authors~

When Delaney Delacroix is called to locate a missing girl, she never plans on getting caught up with a human trafficking investigation or with the local witch. Meeting with Raelin Montrose changes her life in so many ways that Delaney isn't sure that this isn't destiny.

Raelin Montrose is a practicing Wiccan, and when the ley lines that run under her home tell her that someone is coming, she can't imagine that she was going to solve a mystery and find the love of her life at the same time.

www.shadoepublishing.com

~ *Because a publisher should stand behind their authors~*

Melanie Walker, a young woman, in good health, clever, quick-witted, unbending and ready to take on the world. She was the type of girl to never back down from anything; instead she pushed forth to stand up against injustice. Growing up, she always felt a connection with Wonder Woman, as if she was indestructible, though entirely receptive to the fact that she was not invincible and with one wrong turn, her life could end at any moment. A lesson a young girl should never have learned.

Samantha Petrino had it all, charm, confidence, a beautiful girlfriend, a heroic career in the advertising world and many love partners on the side. But, when paramedics arrived at a disastrous two-car collision to find an intoxicated Samantha Petrino at the scene, and the passenger of the car dead, a single mistake strips a once proud woman of the life she had built, her career, and freedom were now at stake.

Two women influenced by different cultures find friendship and develop a bond stronger than family or friendship. But, the invisible chains that link the pair, threaten to break as sex, death and betrayal, forge a code that threatens to end their friendship,

~ Because a publisher should stand behind their authors~

Sadie is in love for the first time with Sparrow when a tragedy tears them apart...will revenge finally reunite the pair and will they be together forever?

An E-Book first by Wolfie Stone

If you have enjoyed this book and the others listed here Shadoe Publishing is always looking for first, second, or third time authors. Please check out our website @
www.shadoepublishing.com
For information or to contact us @
shadoepublishing@gmail.com.

We may be able to help you make your dreams of becoming a published author come true.

7061244R00196

Printed in Great Britain
by Amazon.co.uk, Ltd.,
Marston Gate.